The Roots of the Federal Reserve

The Roots of the Federal Reserve:

Tracing the Nephilim from Noah to the US Dollar

Laura Sanger, Ph.D.

Relentlessly Creative Books LLC
2020

The Roots of the Federal Reserve:

Tracing the Nephilim from Noah to the US Dollar

by
Laura Sanger, Ph.D.

©2020, all right reserved

ISBN: 978-1-942790-19-8

Published by Relentlessly Creative Books LLC
http://relentlesslycreativebooks.com/
books@relentlesslycreative.com
Dallas, Texas, USA
303 317 2200

Table of Contents

Acknowledgements

I would like to express my deepest gratitude for my family, the bedrock of my success. I dedicate this endeavor to the love of my life, my husband, Tom. He is my best friend and the wind beneath my wings. I am grateful for the support of my three amazing children, Kailey, Bryson, and Zachariah. They are my biggest cheerleaders. And of course, where would I be today without the enduring encouragement of my parents, Dennis and Phyllis, and my "parents-in-love," Wayne and Laraine. I am overwhelmed by the unique ways you each supported me. I would also like to say a special thanks to my dearest friend, Jennifer, who not only was a sounding board for me through the writing process, but spent countless hours helping me edit.

Thank you to you all for consistently exhorting me to press after this God given assignment. You never stopped believing in me and for that I am forever grateful.

Introduction

"Symbolism will be their downfall."
~ Q

We are about to embark on a unique investigative journey, one that will take us back in time and to lands far away. This journey will require us to consider realms beyond our four dimensions. It's an investigation that will not be limited to the examination of physical evidence alone but will also incorporate the spiritual forces at work in our nation's monetary system.

For me, this journey began in 2008. As the economy was collapsing, I was facing my own collapse. Our youngest son, who was 10 months old at the time, was diagnosed with kidney failure and failure to thrive. He came too close to death for my liking, but Zachariah is a fighter and refused to let the kidney issues and other complications rob him of life. The prayers and support of many friends and family sustained us through those uncertain times. It took me several years to recover from the trauma of his illness, but once I did, I realized that the economy had fallen apart and I had no idea what happened. We were feeling the effects of it on many fronts. My husband, Tom, had received a decrease in his salary, my income was reduced, and we had a mountain of medical debt. Our personal finances were tighter than ever before. I woke up from my slumber, and realized it was time to take the blinders off and start learning what happened to our economy. I read numerous books, watched documentaries and listened to investment webinars. It highlighted the fact that, as an American citizen, I understood very little about the Federal Reserve and its control of our economy. I grew increasingly uncomfortable with my lack of understanding. My gut was telling me that while I am busy living my life filled with its own ups and downs, the Federal Reserve is making decisions that not only affect my family, but our future generations. It was time for me to get serious with our personal finances and our investments. Up until that point in our lives, my husband and I had put our good faith in financial planners to grow our investments. Now don't get me wrong, there are some fantastic financial planners out there, but I've learned that there is a fine line between good faith and naivete.

A friend recommended I watch *Inside Job*, a documentary on how the banking industry caused the financial crisis. I was literally nauseated to learn of the corruption, greed and hunger for power demonstrated by investment managers and the top executives of the "Too-Big-To-Fail Banks." It was hard to fathom that financial planners, who are supposed to have their client's best interest in mind, were telling clients the opposite of what they themselves were doing. They would advise their clients to sell stocks while they were buying those same stocks. As someone who believes the best about others until there is evidence proving otherwise, *Inside Job* was an abrupt wake up call for me. As the curtains were being pulled back on the deceptive practices of the derivatives market and the subprime lending market, there was mounting evidence that the financial world is filled with people that are out for *numero uno*: themselves. I asked myself, "Now what? Do I remain nauseated, bury my head in the sand, and pray that we come out of it okay?" That seemed like the cowardly approach. Instead, I was inspired by Benjamin Franklin's statement, "an investment in knowledge pays the best interest." This was my strategy: to invest in knowledge. It was imperative to understand how to navigate through the unchartered waters of the Quantitative Easing (QE) strategy the Federal Reserve had unleashed. How would this impact our personal investments? More importantly, how would the nation's economy respond to this attempt at solving the banking problems? Whose interests did the Federal Reserve have in mind when they decided to provide massive bailouts?

Before we begin on an investigative journey into the roots of the Federal Reserve, let me share a little bit about myself, how I am wired, and why I felt compelled to write this book. I am a researcher. It's what I love to do. I have been conducting some level of research since 1989 when I embarked on an honors thesis on behavior modification during my undergraduate years. That same year, I was working at the Veterans Administration Hospital in La Jolla, California in the Department of Psychiatry conducting research on the extra-pyramidal side effects of neuroleptic medication (involuntary movements of the hands and tongue caused by psychiatric meds). I went on to graduate school to complete a Ph.D. in Clinical Psychology. I specialized in research and clinical treatments for schizophrenia. I discovered along the way it doesn't matter what the topic of research is, it's the act of formulating research questions, developing hypotheses and discovering evidence to prove or disprove a hypothesis that makes my blood flow at an invigorating pace.

I have had the privilege of being a part of various research teams over the years. By far, the most fulfilling research I have participated in is spiritual mapping. The term, *spiritual mapping*, was coined in 1991 by George Otis Jr. from the research agency called The Sentinel Group. Spiritual mapping is a tool to inform intercession as people pray for the land, people groups, communities, cities, regions and nations. It consists of gathering research on the physical, social and spiritual pulse of a society. It involves digging through history to uncover the ancient roots of defilement for the purpose of cleansing the land, asking the Lord for forgiveness through identificational repentance, breaking curses, and releasing blessings. The ultimate goal of spiritual mapping is to see people, societies and nations transformed for the glory of the Lord.

II Chronicles 7:14 (NIV) *"If my people, who are called by my name, will humble themselves and pray and seek my face and turn from their wicked ways, then I will hear from heaven, and I will forgive their sin and will heal their land."*

When I began researching the Federal Reserve in 2011, I had no idea where this research would lead me. I thought the scope of the project was just to write a spiritual mapping prayer brief (5 pages in length) regarding the nature of the Federal Reserve. In 2014, I distributed the prayer brief to a few intercessors, and we gathered to enter into battle for our nation by targeting our prayers on the issues identified in the prayer brief. For the next several years, I kept sensing the project was incomplete. It wasn't until 2017 that I realized investigating the roots of the Federal Reserve was an assignment the Lord had given me, an assignment to write a book.

In the early stages of my research, I found G. Edward Griffin's book, *The Creature from Jekyll Island,* to be an eye-opening experience. Griffin uncovers the history of geopolitical issues as they relate to the formation of the Federal Reserve. He debunks the myths surrounding the Federal Reserve and reveals the truth of how our monetary system works. Reading this book left me intrigued to dig further. What you will find in the pages ahead is a result of more than a decade of digging. I have been on an investigative journey with the Holy Spirit, following the clues He has led me to. These clues expose defilement, deception, corruption and idolatry that have been shrouded for thousands of years.

If you are an intercessor, this book will fuel and inform your intercession for our nation. If you are a learner, you will find this book educational in that it reveals things that many in the general public have no concept of. If you have a thirst for conspiracy theories, your curiosity and wonder will be quenched, but only if you apply the true meaning of the word. Conspiracy as defined by Webster's New World Dictionary is "a planning and acting together secretly, especially for an unlawful OR harmful purpose."[1] The evidence revealed in the following pages will demonstrate that the Federal Reserve meets this definition.

It is a common coping mechanism for people to label something a "conspiracy theory" as a way to negate its reality. As hard as it may be to accept the truth of how the Federal Reserve was formed and the purpose it was created for, I encourage you to hold your judgment until you have completed reading this book. As you read, be wary of the temptation to label something as a "conspiracy theory" when the harsh reality becomes too hard to swallow. I am looking for those who will read this book with an open mind, holding loosely their paradigms that have been formed regarding the Federal Reserve.

My hope is that the truths we uncover together will help you emerge from the fog of misinformation and conditioned responses. What do I mean by this? Let me provide some context.

As I mentioned earlier, in my undergraduate studies, I conducted research in the area of behavior modification. It stemmed from my participation in a behavioral psychology class in which we applied operant conditioning to pigeons in a lab. The goal was to train a pigeon, through behavior modification, to peck a light to receive food from the hopper. We were applying the classic behavioral learning principles of B.F. Skinner, arguably one of the most influential American psychologists of all time. In order to successfully train the pigeon to do what I wanted it to do, I had to reward successive behaviors until the end goal was reached. In essence, I was controlling the behavior of the pigeon in the "Skinner box" through conditioned responses. During the initial stages of training, if the pigeon slightly turned its head more clearly in the direction of the light, the hopper was released. The next day, the pigeon had to turn its head more clearly in the direction of the light for the hopper to be released. The positive reinforcement linked with successive behaviors toward pecking the light was powerful enough to successfully train the pigeon to consistently peck the light every time it was placed in the "Skinner box."

Little did I know, these same behavioral modification principles were being used to shape the psyche of the American population through "social engineering." Social engineering applies these techniques by using positive and negative reinforcement to gradually sway the masses to behave according to a predetermined outcome. We have been lulled to sleep regarding the larger issues at stake for our nation. The majority of us are working so hard to make ends meet, shuttling our kids from one activity to the next, while battling chronic health issues, that we don't have time to adequately educate ourselves on national issues. We have been socially engineered to exist in the "rat race." The most we have time for is to be spoon fed by the news media what we should think. Have you ever noticed that all the major news stations have essentially the same talking points? If you haven't noticed this, conduct a simple experiment. Turn on your television during a peak news hour and surf the major news stations. Listen for at least 5 minutes to each station. You will quickly discover what I am talking about, the lack of creativity and freedom of speech is eye-opening. It's no coincidence, it's by design, the social engineering programmers are shaping the American psyche. We have been negatively conditioned over the years to let go of critical thinking so that we don't challenge the "party line" or else we face scorn, mockery, and derision administered by the educational system, the entertainment industry, the news media, social media, and protest groups.

One of the narratives we have been Fed (pun intended) since 1913 is that a central bank is necessary for the stability of our economy. This is hogwash, in fact, the opposite is true. I will venture to say, that on some level, you felt the pain of the Great Recession (2008-2010). If you were fortunate enough to come out unscathed by the economic downturn, you probably know someone who either lost their job or their home during that time. Well…we have the Federal Reserve to thank for the INSTABILITY in our economy; they created the Great Recession, just like they created the Great Depression! It's what they do. The evidence of this will be revealed in the pages of this book.

As of 1971, when Nixon officially took us off the gold standard, the US dollar has been a fiat currency backed by nothing. History proves that nations or empires that debase their currencies, collapse! Fiat currencies have failed 100% of the time; they buckle under the weight of debt. Gold always wins! In recent history, approximately every 40 years there is a change in the monetary system.[2] We are now 49 years into a fiat currency system; our economy is on the precipice of implosion. A major structural shift away from a central banking system is critical for the prosperity of our nation. Without this kind of change, it will not be pretty.

Therefore, it's imperative that we resist the mind control of false narratives and instead, rise up with resolve to engage in the battle for our FREEDOM! We have been entangled in the web of debt enslavement courtesy of the Federal Reserve. How do we break free? It starts by thinking outside the "Skinner box." We must first break free from the shackles of presupposition. Consider these quotes as a foundation for our mindset moving forward:

> *"A truth's initial commotion is directly proportional to how deeply the lie was believed. It wasn't the world being round that agitated people, but that the world wasn't flat. When a well-packaged web of lies has been sold gradually to the masses over generations, the truth will seem utterly preposterous and its speaker a raving lunatic."[3]*
> ~ Dresden James

> *"There is a principle which is a bar against all information, which is proof against all argument, and which cannot fail to keep man in everlasting ignorance. That principle is condemnation before investigation."[4]*
> ~ Edmund Spencer

> *"He who answers before he hears [the facts] – It is folly and shame to him."*
> ~ King Solomon

In the pursuit of understanding the system that holds billions of people captive, we must take a closer look at the Federal Reserve—this enigma that seems to control the direction of our nation and subsequently other nations. How did such an entity gain so much power? Today, as I begin writing, Janet Yellen just announced the ending of the Fed's latest Quantitative Easing Program (QE3). Economists are holding their breath to see which way the markets roll. Why do bankers, economists, politicians and market makers hang on every word spoken from the mouth of the Federal Reserve Chair? As with any good mystery, we need to investigate behind the scenes and ask the Holy Spirit to bring to light those things hidden in darkness.

Luke 8:17 (NIV) *"For there is nothing hidden that will not be disclosed, and nothing concealed that will not be known or brought out into the open."*

In this book, we will explore questions such as:

- Were the seeds of the Federal Reserve planted in the soil of Jekyll Island long before the birth of our nation?

- What are the ancient roots of defilement and deception buried deep in the land that nourished the incubation of the Federal Reserve?
- Are there ancient pagan/occult symbols that shed light on the root system of the Federal Reserve?
- Is the hidden agenda of the central banking system intertwined with the Nephilim agenda?
- Who were the architects of the Federal Reserve Act?
- What was the original intent of the Federal Reserve?
- Who are the masterminds that control the course of our nation?
- What has been the impact on our nation's economy and the psyche of the American people with the advent of the Federal Reserve?
- What principality do the masterminds of the Federal Reserve serve?
- Is there hope to chart a different course from the debt cycle the Federal Reserve has created?

These questions form the parameters of our investigation. Pack your bags, grab your passport and get ready for an adventure of global proportions through time and territory.

Section I

Ancient Roots

As we begin our adventure together, we'll start by examining some pertinent facts about the clandestine meeting that took place at Jekyll Island in November 1910. This covert gathering of powerful men, undoubtedly, raises numerous questions. The answers to our investigative questions require gathering behind-the-scenes information. It necessitates extensive digging into history and thorough research through the web of time. In the process, answers to age-old questions will be revealed. There may be moments along the way when you wonder why is this necessary. In those moments, hang in there with me. I can assure you that our investigation, as with most mysteries, will take twists and turns that you cannot anticipate. Our quest for understanding begins thousands of years ago in ancient history.

In this first section, we will explore the megalithic civilizations of ancient Egypt, Great Britain, and the Levant. We will uncover the mysteries of the stone circles, dolmens, pyramids, and temples these cultures constructed. We will look for clues that are buried beneath the surface at these sites. These clues will help us construct a hypothesis as to the purpose these monolithic structures served in ancient civilizations and whether there is a connection to the Federal Reserve.

We will consider questions such as: Is there significance to the location of these various ancient sites? Is there a spiritual component to the design and architecture of these megalithic monuments? I encourage you to make notes in the margins of this book. You are not just along for the ride. This is about you and me, together, discovering what is in the root system of the Federal Reserve. My hope is that by encouraging you along the way, I can actually propel you further than I have gone in this investigation. Buckle up!

Chapter 1

Secrets of a Little-Known Island

*A symbol… points to something unknown and mysterious,
and is often the precursor to a transformation.*
~ Steve Myers

The Clandestine Caper

Our investigative journey begins on a small, Atlantic sea island off the coast of Georgia. Jekyll Island is 7 miles long and 1.5 miles wide (see Figure 1). It's accessible by car via a causeway extending from the mainland.

Figure 1. Jekyll Island aerial view by rod photography. Adobe Stock Photo #259815875

Many details of the escapade that took place more than a century ago have long been washed out to sea with the tide. Only a handful of facts remain. Here is what can be confirmed…

On November 22, 1910, under the cover of night, six men boarded the private rail car of Senator Nelson Aldrich at the Hoboken Station in New Jersey. They were instructed to arrive separately to the station. They were to avoid curious onlookers and questions from reporters. They were to pretend as if they didn't know each other and use first names only to maintain anonymity. Secrecy was thick in the air like a heavy fog. As the train pulled away from the station, the shades were drawn for their long journey to Jekyll Island.

In the early 20th century, Jekyll Island was an exclusive privately-owned club for the wealthiest in America. Families such as the Morgans, Vanderbilts, Rockefellers, and Pulitzers were just some of its elite members. In preparation for this clandestine meeting, word was sent to all of Jekyll's members that the club would be closed for two weeks. Even the staff were sent on leave so temporary workers could fill their duties. Every detail was thought of to ensure seclusion and anonymity. It was absolutely vital that the meetings remained a secret. If the public discovered that the most powerful financiers in America had gathered to design the framework for a central banking cartel, it would mean utter failure for their plans. The few residents of Jekyll Island were told that these men had gathered for a duck hunt. This was partially true; they were in fact assembled to kill something… but it wasn't ducks!

These "six men" and those they represented, were the industry "Titans" who controlled oil, railways, communication and banking in America. In total, these "six men" were estimated to represent one-fourth of the world's wealth. Their identities have since come to light years after their furtive gathering.

1. Nelson W. Aldrich, Republican "whip" in the Senate, Chairman of the National Monetary Commission, business associate of J.P. Morgan, father-in-law to John D. Rockefeller Jr.;
2. Abraham Piatt Andrew, Assistant Secretary of the U.S. Treasury;
3. Frank A. Vanderlip, president of the National City Bank of New York, the most powerful of the banks at that time, representing William Rockefeller and the international investment banking house of Kuhn, Loeb & Company;
4. Henry P. Davison, senior partner of the J.P. Morgan Company;
5. Benjamin Strong, head of J.P. Morgan's Bankers Trust Company;

6. Paul M. Warburg, a partner in Kuhn, Loeb & Company, a representative of the Rothschild banking dynasty in England and France, and brother to Max Warburg who was head of the Warburg banking consortium in Germany and the Netherlands.[5]

These men were headstrong individuals with firm opinions of how a banking cartel should be structured. Tension filled the air as they hotly debated issues. Senator Aldrich was undoubtedly the one driving the agenda and Paul Warburg was largely responsible for drafting the plan. It took nine days for the framework of the Federal Reserve to emerge from their rendezvous. That fateful November changed the course of our nation; it set us on a path toward destruction.

Now that we have been debriefed on the facts, we can set out on our investigative journey. Were the seeds of the Federal Reserve planted in the soil of Jekyll Island long before the birth of our nation? In order to address this question, we need to set our watches back thousands of years. Let's go.

Archaic People, Antiquated Secrets

Jekyll Island has a culturally diverse history. It is marked by the footprints of numerous groups of people. Unfortunately, most traces of its earliest inhabitants have disappeared from the rising sea level. But we won't let this obstacle derail our investigation. Fortuitously, there are significant archaeological discoveries on nearby islands that will provide traces of the historical roots of Jekyll Island. So come with me, let's travel 54 miles north to Sapelo Island, another one of Georgia's coastal islands.

In 1872, the Sapelo Shell Ring Complex was discovered by William McKinley who was a lawyer, plantation owner, and Georgia state legislator. He wrote a letter to the Smithsonian Institute describing this shell complex.

"South of High Point there are three mound circles. These circles are surrounded by hundreds of shell mounds, about 3 feet high, on bases of 20 to 50 feet, which crowd without visible order, a field of one hundred acres or more... On all these shell mounds... are found fragments of Indian pottery, both plain and ornamented."[6]

Over the next several decades, the Sapelo Shell Rings (see Figure 2) were explored by different teams of people. In the 1950s a more thorough scientific investigation was conducted by archaeologists, Lewis Larson and Antonio Waring. The excavations revealed an ancient city featuring three neighborhoods delineated by large circular walls that were 20 feet tall and constructed from seashells. Archeologists found that the original occupation of these rings date back between 4200–3000 BC (Archaic Period).[7] Some of the oldest pottery found in North America was discovered at the Sapelo Shell Ring Complex. This suggests that the indigenous people on Sapelo Island were among the first people in North America to settle in more permanent villages.[8] These shell ring complexes raise many questions. How did the indigenous people of the Archaic Period, who were thought to be hunter gatherers, suddenly become an agricultural society with the technology to make pottery? Were these early inhabitants of Georgia's coastal islands already a civilized people group who migrated from another land? Who were these indigenous people that constructed the shell rings?

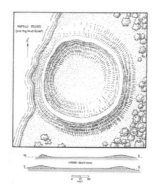

Figure 2. Sapelo Shell Ring. Clarence Bloomfield Moore collection, #9181. Division of Rare and Manuscript Collections, Cornell University Library.

One of the major debates among archaeologists is whether the shell rings were formed intentionally as a wall to protect the village or formed as a result of gradual accumulation of household middens (domestic waste). Victor Thompson, an archaeologist from the University of West Florida, has conducted numerous excavations at Sapelo Shell Complex. He concluded, "regardless of how the shell rings were formed, it is evident from the remains within the deposits that the rings served both as places of daily life and as sites for sacred ceremonies."[9]

In Thompson's research, he has discovered anomalies within the center of the largest ring (Sapelo Shell Ring III) using ground penetrating radar. It's not clear yet what the archaeological deposits within the center of this ring consist of, but it does point to the usage of a particular design during Archaic period construction. These circular formations with a point in the center, or a circle within a circle, were common structural designs of ancient civilizations even from geographically diverse locations (i.e. Great Britain, Egypt, the Levant). Let's investigate other ancient sites with circle formations to see if it can give us some clues as to the purpose of the shell complex and its significance in uncovering the historical roots of Jekyll Island. But first, it's important to dissect the meaning of the circle with the point in the center.

Prolific Megalithic Circumpuncts

While the formation of a circle with a point in the center and/or the circle within a circle is an ancient symbol dating back thousands of years, the terminology to describe this symbol has recently changed. Dan Brown, author of *The Lost Symbol,* coined the term "circumpunct" to identify the circle with a point in the center. For simplicity sake, I will refer to both these symbols as a circumpunct (see Figure 3). Now that we got that squared away, you may be wondering, what meaning does this symbol hold?

Figure 3. Circumpunct by Laura Sanger.

A circumpunct has carried sacred meaning across diverse cultures since the Archaic/ Neolithic Period. It has been an enduring symbol used in both pagan and occult rituals. Its most ancient roots are found in the Egyptian worship of the sun god where it was employed as a "solar-phallic symbol used to represent the eternal nature of the sun god Ra."[10] Accordingly, the Egyptian hieroglyph for the sun is a circumpunct (see Figure 4).

The circumpunct is a two-dimensional phallic symbol with the dot representing the penis and the circle the womb. Egypt has a great many obelisks, towers, and pyramids covering its landscape, all of which are symbolic expressions of sun worship. These structures represent the erect male organ pointing toward the sun, which pagans believed was the source of life. Two prominent locations that will play heavily into our investigation of the Federal Reserve are Rome and Washington, D.C., both with conspicuous obelisks within a circle, or a circumpunct. The obelisk which was erected in St. Peter's Square in 41 A.D., once stood at Heliopolis, the ancient center of Egyptian sun worship (see Figure 5).

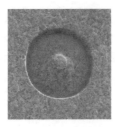

Figure 4. Close up sun hieroglyph. Wikimedia commons.
https://commons.wikimedia.org/wiki/File:Karnak_Tempel_03.jpg

Figure 5. St. Peter's Obelisk Rome, Vatican. Free photo from Pixabay. https://pixabay.com/photos/st-peter-s-square-obelisk-rome-1352770/

Every continent has remnants of ancient circumpuncts, which suggests that this symbol carries a universal spiritual significance. While universal in appearance, the meaning varies across cultures and religions. It's commonly understood that the megalithic civilizations used this symbol as an astrological/astronomical sign for the sun. The circle and the point represent earth's orbital path around the sun and is tied to the expression of sun worship. Philosophical proponents consider the sphere of the circumpunct to be a perfect shape that represents wholeness, unity, spirituality and oneness. Pagans view the circle with the point as associated with a divine collective consciousness. Manly P. Hall, a 33rd degree Freemason, described the significance of the circumpunct in one of his lectures on Ancient Philosophy: "The keys to all knowledge are contained in the dot, the line and the circle. The dot is universal consciousness, the line is universal intelligence, and the circle is universal force – the threefold, unknowable Cause of all knowable existence."[11]

Ouroboros is an ancient Egyptian symbol depicting the serpent eating its tail (see Figure 6) symbolizing the union of Ra and Osiris in the underworld. The symbol was adopted into Greek magical tradition and later became widely known as a symbol for alchemy.

Figure 6. Magical Symbol of Ouroboros by MSSA. https://www.shutterstock.com/image-vector/magic-symbol-ouroboros-tattoo-snake-biting-324809066

Within the realm of magic, the circle represents a sacred space, a boundary. "Some magical action was necessary to transform the ordinary to the sacred and casting a circle is a quick and effective way of doing that."[12]

In the book, *The Lost Symbol*, Dan Brown provides an insightful summary of the significance of the circumpunct:

"In the idiom of symbology, there was one symbol that reigned supreme above all others. The oldest most universal, this symbol fused all the ancient traditions in a single solitary image that represented the illumination of the Egyptian sun god, the triumph of alchemical gold, the wisdom of the Philosophers Stone, the purity of the Rosicrucian Rose, the moment of Creation, the All, the dominance of the astrological sun, and even the omniscient all-seeing eye that hovered atop the unfinished pyramid. The circumpunct. The symbol of source. The origin of all things."[13]

While *The Lost Symbol* is a fictional book, Dan Brown gives an accurate account of the sacred significance of the circumpunct. Simon Cox, the author of *Decoding the Lost*

Symbol: The Unauthorized Expert Guide to the Facts behind the Fiction, writes: "Egyptian obelisks were seen by their builders as a metaphorical connection between heaven and earth, with their topmost pyramidions symbolizing the rays of the sun as they fall to earth. The Washington Monument, the obelisk structure that holds the key to the lost word in *The Lost Symbol*, is revealed to be a circumpunct: the circular plaza surrounding the monument provides the physical setting for the symbol."[14]

The lay out of the city of Washington D.C. is steeped in Freemasonry symbolism. We will discuss this in more detail later in our journey, but for now, it's important to understand that obelisk in Washington, D.C. (and the one in St. Peter's Square) share something else besides the circumpunct in common. Both are strategically positioned in close proximity to a domed building (see Figures 7 & 8).

Figure 7. Aerial view of Washington, D.C. 15525v.jpg.
https://commons.wikimedia.org/wiki/File:Aerial_view_of_Washington,_D.C._15525v.jpg#filelinks

Thomas Horn writes in *Unearthing the Lost World of the Cloudeaters*, "Modern people, especially in America, may view the symbols used in this magic – the dome representing the habitually pregnant belly of Isis, and the obelisk, representing the erect phallus of Osiris – as profane or pornographic (and for good reason). But they were in fact ritualized fertility objects, which the ancients believed could produce tangible reactions, properties, or "manifestations" within the material world. The obelisk and dome as imitations of the deities' male and female reproductive organs could, through government representation, invoke into existence the being or beings symbolized by them. This is why inside the temple or dome, temple prostitutes representing the human manifestation of the goddess were also available for ritual sex as a form of imitative magic. These prostitutes usually began their services to the goddess as children, and they were deflowered at a very young age by a priest or, as Isis was, by a modeled obelisk of Osiris' phallus… temple prostitutes were offered in coitus to divine goats. Through such imitative sex, the dome and obelisk became "energy receivers," capable of assimilating Ra's essence from the rays of the sun, which in turn drew forth the "seed" of the underworld Osiris. The seed of the dead deity would, according to the supernaturalism, transmit upward (through the portal) from out of the underworld through the base (testes) of the obelisk and magically emit from the tower's head into the womb (dome) of Isis where incarnation into the sitting pharaoh/king/president would occur (during what Freemasons also call the *raising [of Osiris] ceremony*). In this way, Osiris could be habitually "born again" or reincarnated as Horus and constantly direct the spiritual destiny of the nation."[15]

Figure 8. Aerial drone view of Saint Peter's square in front of world's largest church - Papal Basilica of St. Peter's, Vatican - an elliptical esplanade created in the mid seventeenth century, Rome, Italy by Aerial Motion. https://www.shutterstock.com/image-photo/aerial-drone-view-saint-peters-square-1233231403

Now that we understand the deeper meaning of the circumpunct, we can continue our search for these structures within ancient civilizations to see if it helps inform us on the origins of the Federal Reserve.

Stone Circles

Megalithic civilizations were prolific in their construction of circumpuncts between 5000 BC – 2000 BC. One of the most well-known examples can be found in England, on a stretch of land that has approximately 1000 stone circles dotting its countryside. The most famous of the stone circles is Stonehenge. Stonehenge is located in Salisbury

Plain, and it's formation dates back to sometime between 3100 BC–2750 BC. (See Figure 9) Advanced technology has allowed archaeologists to make interesting new discoveries regarding the area surrounding Stonehenge. Ground penetrating radar has uncovered 17 monuments that researchers think were Neolithic shrines, with several in the form of a circumpuncts (see Figure 10). This indicates that Stonehenge had been a sacred site long before the monolithic monument was erected. Vincent Gaffney, an archaeologist from University of Birmingham and the project leader of the Stonehenge Hidden Monuments Project, made this statement regarding their discoveries: "Stonehenge is undoubtedly a major ritual monument which people may have traveled considerable distances to come to, but it isn't just standing there by itself. It's part of a much more complex landscape with processional and ritual activities that go around it. That's very different from how this had been viewed before. The important point is that Stonehenge is not alone. There was lots of other associated ritual activity going on around it."[16]

Figure 9. Arial view of Stonehenge in summer, England. Photo by Alexey Federenko. Adobe Stock photo file #265552575

As archaeologists began putting the puzzle pieces together, they realized that other Neolithic remains in Salisbury Plain are linked to Stonehenge. The Cursus, a massive enclosure to the north of Stonehenge that runs 1.8 miles long, has two pits on either end. These recently discovered pits line up with the sunrise and sunset of a midsummer solstice with Stonehenge as its reference point.

Additionally, a long barrow was discovered which housed a large timber building thought to have been used for ritual inhumation and defleshing of the dead. These two structures are connected with Stonehenge along a processional avenue. As mentioned earlier, the Stonehenge complex is just one of over 1,000 stone circles found in England. Other circumpuncts have been discovered off the coast of Norfolk.

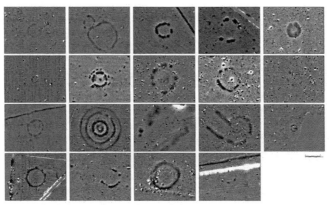

Figure 10. Stonehenge New Monuments by LBI ArchPro. https://www.lbiarchpro-imagery.at/stonehenge2014_images/h1c4dadbd#h1c4dadbd

Seahenge and Holme II are two Neolithic circular monuments discovered within the last twenty years. Seahenge comprises 55 oak posts submerged in the ground with a large inverted, gnarled oak stump. Holme II was centered around two oak logs with oak posts circling around the center. Unfortunately, storms have washed the two center logs and have eroded some of the other features of Holme II. Archaeologists have determined the dates of these two circular monuments as 2049 BC. David Robertson, Historic Environment Officer for Norfolk County Council and Holme II project manager stated: "As the timbers used in both timber circles were felled at the same time, the construction of the two monuments must have been directly linked. Seahenge is thought to have been a free-standing timber circle, possibly to mark the death of an individual, acting as a cenotaph symbolizing death rather than a location for burial. If part of a burial mound, the second circle would have been the actual burial place."[17]

The appearances of over 1000 stone/timber circles within England are quite intriguing, but even more intriguing is that these Neolithic circular monuments can be found in Egypt, France, Ireland, Malta, Morocco, Portugal, Scotland, Spain, Sweden and Turkey. This begs the question, what was the purpose of these circular monuments?

One theory is that they represented burial sites or sites for death rituals. Another theory is that have astronomical purpose. It's possible they were used for both. Alexander Thom, a professor of Engineering at Oxford University, surveyed 300 of Great Britain's megalithic circles. He found a unit of measurement that he termed the "megalithic yard." He published his findings in 1955 after discovering that this unit of measurement was utilized in constructing all the stone circles he surveyed.[18]

Additionally, Thom discovered that many of them were oriented to the sun and the moon. Thom concluded that these stone circles were observatories, places to view the stars from. He believes the stone circles served as astronomical calendars. Over half a century later, researchers have expanded on Thom's theories by looking at the way the standing stones are aligned in relation to the sun, moon and stars.

Gail Higginbottom and her team from the University of Adelaide, Australia studied more than 100 of Scotland's stone circles. They published their findings in the *Journal of Archaeological Science: Reports* in August of 2016.

"By 3000 BCE, in the late Neolithic, there had been a significant change in the way people materialized their cosmology across Scotland with the introduction of free-standing stones that continued to be erected almost until the end of the Bronze Age... Significantly, a series of astronomical patternings have been empirically verified for many Bronze Age monuments that were erected in the latter Bronze Age... Through innovative statistics and software we show that visible astronomical-landscape variables found at Bronze Age sites on the inner isles and mainland of western Scotland were actually first established in stone nearly two millennia earlier, likely with the erection of two of the earliest dated British 'great circles': Callanish on the Isle of Lewis and Stenness on the Isle of Orkney. In particular, we introduce our new statistical test that enables the quantitative determination of astronomical connections of stone circles. It is seen that whilst different standing-stone monuments were created over time... with a mixture of landscape variables... we nevertheless see that highly relevant landscape markers and other aspects remained unchanged through these years. This suggests that there is some continuity of this cosmological system through time, despite the various radical material and social changes that occurred from the late Neolithic to the Late Bronze Age."[19]

The oldest reliably dated stone circles in Scotland are Stenness and Callanish and were the basis of the astronomical patterns that Higginbottom found. This pattern was replicated over the next 2,000 years among the other stone circles erected across Scotland. Higginbottom proposed that the Neolithic people must have understood the specific cycles of the sun and moon. Not everyone shares Higginbottom's perspective.

Kenneth Brophy of the University of Glasgow, Scotland has proposed a much different purpose behind these megalithic monuments. He critiques the application of modern mathematical techniques to prehistoric people and argues that there are no other instances where prehistoric people demonstrate a highly mathematical view of the world. Instead, he suggests that these megalithic stone circles were built with attention to the land itself rather than the celestial world. Research has shown that the stone circles were built in such a way that you can view one stone circle while standing amidst another, a ley-line so to speak. Brophy suggests that the circles represented power and ritual. He believes that the specific location for each monument was chosen because of previous events that took place on the land. In other words, the land represented something sacred for the Neolithic architects and builders. The archaeological evidence demonstrates that these monuments provided a place for social rituals, especially those rituals performed to honor the dead.[20]

Gordon Noble of the University of Aberdeen has collaborated with Kenneth Brophy in several archaeological projects focusing on stone and timber circles within Scotland. He suggests that the design for many of the stone circles in Scotland are similar to the structures people built for their everyday living at that time. However, instead of these stone and timber circles serving the living, they served the dead. In his words, "they're essentially very large houses for the dead and spirits."[21]

Uncovering Ancient Pathways

Brophy speaks about stone circles being created in relation to a ley-line, but what exactly are ley-lines? Were megalithic monuments aligned with intentionality? To answer these questions, it's important we understand ancient pathways. Alistair Petrie, in his book *Releasing Heaven on Earth,* describes ancient pathways as follows:

"Ancient pathways…were really the first migration routes and points of entry into any given geographical area. Even at those early moments in human history, the influence of stewardship was at work, defined by who those people were, what their religious worldview involved, and what covenants and pacts they had established among themselves and with the gods they worshiped…In discovering the ramifications of this early influence, and its subsequent generations of stewardship, we learn what still may be affecting us today."[22]

Along ancient pathways, it was common for people to set up monuments to mark sacred spaces. Alfred Watkins, an amateur archaeologist, photographer, and historian, coined the term "ley-lines" in his thesis proposed in 1921. Ley-lines, as he described them, are alignments of ancient burial mounds, monuments, barrows, ditches, castles, ponds and trackways.[23] Watkins observed that the alignment of these sites was unmistakably intentional. He stated: "Imagine a fairy chain stretched from mountain peak to mountain peak, so far as the eye could reach, and laid out until it touched the high places of the earth at a number of ridges, banks and knolls. Then visualize a mount, a circular earthwork, or clump of trees, planted on these high points, and in low points in the valley, other mounds ringed round with water to be seen from a distance. Then, great standing stones brought to mark the way at intervals, and on a bank leading up to a mountain ridge or down to a ford the track cut deep so as to form a guiding notch on the skyline as you come up. In a bwlch or mountain pass, the road cut deeply to show as a notch afar off. Here and there, and at two ends of the way, a beacon fire used to lay out the track. With ponds dug on the line or streams banked up into "flashes" to form reflecting points on the beacon track so that it might be checked when at least once a year the beacon was fired on the traditional day. All these work exactly on the (ley) line."[24]

If these megalithic monuments were intentionally aligned along a ley-line, it raises the question of how the location of each ley-line was determined. Brophy intimated that the location of a ley-line was determined by monuments marking significant events that occurred on the land. Watkins spoke about high places dotting the landscape in such a way that they are connected to form a ley-line. Unfortunately, British archaeologists are only able to speculate about what significant events might have occurred on the land because there is no written record of these ancient events. Fortunately, we can learn a lot from the biblical record of the Ancient Near East during the Bronze Age (3300 B.C.–1200 B.C.).

The book of Leviticus dates back to approximately 1446 B.C. when the Israelites were in the wilderness following their exodus from Egypt. We find the first biblical mention of high places in Leviticus.

Leviticus 26:30 (NIV) *"And I will destroy your **high places**, and cut down your images, and cast your carcasses upon the carcasses of your idols, and my soul shall abhor you."*

In Hebrew, the word for "high place" is '*bamah*' which means "high place, ridge, height, funeral mound."[25] This sounds strikingly similar to Watkins' definition of high places that connect to form ley-lines. Further understanding of the word '*bamah*' comes from the Gesenius' Hebrew-Chaldee Lexicon which suggests that "the ancient

Hebrews (when they fell into idolatry), like many other nations, regarded sacred rites performed on mountains and hills as most acceptable to the gods… and they erected their sanctuaries or chapels."[26] We can see that high places were sacred sites where monuments, mounds, sanctuaries or other markers were established on elevated land that were visible from a distance. There are 91 instances throughout the Biblical Old and New Testament where the term "high place" is referred to, which adds support to the theory that megalithic monuments were built as a place of worship.

The visibility of a high place served multiple purposes. It was a physical declaration that the land itself was dedicated to a certain deity. It also made the pilgrimage to a location easier, because the worshippers could set their sights on the high place from quite a distance away. Depending on how far worshippers traveled, it is conceivable that they would have erected other monuments along their journey as sacred stations of worship. Ezekiel 6 lends some credence to this theory:

Ezekiel 6:3 (KJV) *"And say, Ye mountains of Israel, hear the word of the Lord God; Thus saith the Lord God to the mountains, and to the hills, to the rivers, and to the valleys; Behold, I, even I, will bring a sword upon you, and I will destroy your high places."*

In Ezekiel's day (597 BC), high places were erected on mountains, hills, rivers and valleys. This is consistent with what Alfred Watkins experienced of the ancient pathways in Hereford, England. Ancient peoples of the Near East and of the British Isles had similar sacred practices in establishing high places of worship. When these high places, or power points, are aligned and form a ley-line, it intensifies the spiritual power in a region.

Ley-lines are established from occult practices or pagan forms of worship. George Otis Jr. has defined ley-lines as "geographic continuums of spiritualized power that are established—or at least recognized—by the early inhabitants of an area" (Otis, n.d. as cited in Petrie, 2000, p. 158).[27] Over the course of time, these ley-lines are reinforced by ongoing worship at high places, ritualistic bloodshed and additional power points established along its path.

Another way to think about a ley-line is it's a spiritual pathway established by geographically aligned power points. Several ley-lines can be connected with each other forming a spiritual grid over a territory or region. Inhabitants living amidst this grid can come under the spiritual forces of darkness or light that operate within the spiritual grid. People may be completely unaware of the existence of such ley-lines or spiritual grids, but still experience the ill effects.

You might be asking yourself, "how does this relate to Jekyll Island and the Federal Reserve?" The connection will become clear if you look at a dollar bill (see Figure 11).

The circumpunct, also known as the all-seeing eye, within the pyramidion is heavy laden with symbolism. We will unpack in greater detail the meaning of the symbols found on the Federal Reserve Note toward the end of our investigation. Let me just say, I don't think it's a coincidence that the circumpunct is displayed on the dollar bill.

Figure 11. Close up of one-dollar bill. Photo taken by Laura Sanger.

We are going to take a brief pause on our journey back in time, to travel to Torino, Italy. This jaunt is necessary in laying the foundation for understanding the importance of ley-lines and how power grids transcend time.

Key Points
- Circumpunct found at Sapelo Shell Rings 54 miles north of Jekyll Island.
- Circumpunct is a prominent symbol in ancient civilizations.
- Ancient monuments often found in alignment with other sacred sites form ley-lines.
- Ley-lines can connect to form a spiritual power grid over a territory.

Chapter 2

Portals, Gates, and Grids, Oh My

Torino, Italy is a city replete with ley-lines and spiritual grids. In 2006, I had an opportunity to partner with the local Christian churches in Torino as they prepared for the 2006 Winter Olympics. When I first arrived, the spiritual darkness over the city was tangible to me. It felt like a thick blanket of oppression. Within moments of entering the city, my body felt the ill effects. I developed nausea and a headache. The spiritual atmosphere was unlike anything I had ever encountered. Even the surrounding countryside was impacted by the spiritual forces of darkness at work within the city.

Portals

I stayed with some good friends who lived in Pecetto Torinese, about 20 minutes outside of Torino in the countryside marked by picturesque rolling hills. After unloading suitcases, I was given a tour of their house and the property. My friend explained that since moving in, they had experienced strange occurrences having to do with witchcraft curses (George Otis' book *The Twilight Labyrinth* provides numerous stories of encounters with witchcraft powers). They found fetishes (objects with curses attached) on their property, their children had several serious injuries while playing in the yard and guests staying in one of their guestrooms reported nightmares that had recurring themes. Through prayer and discernment, they determined there was a portal in their guestroom. This was confirmed by a handful of people over the course of several months.

A portal is a passageway connecting the spiritual realm with the earth realm. A biblical example of a portal can be found in Genesis 28 when Jacob saw a ladder with angels descending and ascending. The portal in their house was defiled with demonic activity and was the source of the intense nightmares their guests experienced while staying in that room. All this was uncovered within my first few hours in the Piedmont Region of Italy! It was an eventful 10-day trip, but I will limit my sharing to the highlights pertinent to understanding ley-lines and spiritual grids.

Gates

Torino is the intersection of two witchcraft triangles, the black magic triangle and the white magic triangle. The differences between black magic and white magic can be a bit complex. In general, practitioners describe white magic as magic utilized for the good of others and black magic as magic used at the expense of others to benefit the magician. White magic is often couched in warm, fuzzy terms such as "healing the souls of others." It's important to expose it for what it is – magic! Describing the difference between white and black magic, Anton LaVey, founder of the Church of Satan, says: "White magic is supposedly utilized only for good or unselfish purposes, and black magic, we are told, is used only for selfish or "evil" reasons. Satanism draws no such dividing line. Magic is magic, be it used to help or hinder. The Satanist, being the magician, should have the ability to decide what is just, and then apply the powers of magic to attain his goals."[28]

The cities that form the triangle of black magic are London, San Francisco, and Torino. Lyon, Prague and Torino form the triangle of white magic. As the apex of these two triangles, Torino has earned a reputation of being the witchcraft capital of the world.[29]

Capitalizing on this reputation, local tour guides enchant tourists with the "Magic Turin Tour." Stops along this tour uncover the hidden, and not so hidden, spiritual power points within the city. I decided to take this tour as a way to collect valuable spiritual mapping information regarding the roots of witchcraft and spiritual darkness in the region. The tour commenced at the Piazza Statuto, a.k.a. "the black heart" of Torino. (See Figure 12)

Locals believe that this is the heart of the city's satanic influence and the location of the "gate of hell." This monument is shaped like a pyramid with a dark angel at the top. The tour guide said that many locals believe this dark angel to be Lucifer. Around the base of the monument are statues of men known as Titans, who exhibit agony and various stages of the dying process. This monument was constructed in 1864 to commemorate the Frejus Tunnel, the first railway to create a passageway underneath the Alps linking Italy with France.

Figure 12. Monumento al Traforo del Frejus Torino. From Wikimedia Commons
https://commons.wikimedia.org/wiki/File:Monumento_al_Traforo_del_Frejus_Torino_23072015_14.j
pg

The construction of this tunnel proved deadly for many workers. While it was constructed to commemorate the workers of the tunnel, the monument has layers of esoteric meaning. (See Figure 13) The dark angel has a five-pointed star, or pentagram that is inverted on top of its head. The pentagram is a symbol used in paganism and black magic to represent the perversion of the natural order by "placing matter over the spirit world."[30] At the base of the monument is a sealed grate which is believed to be the gate to hell. Even for skeptics, the dark occurrences that have happened in this location over the centuries cannot be explained by mere coincidences.

The monument lies just outside the old city, Augusta Taurinorum, which was founded in 28 B.C. The city is protected on two sides by the Po and Dora rivers. During the Roman Empire, it became the center for the Roman network of highways. Control of the Po River Valley became increasingly important for the Roman Empire. Consequently, battles were fought on the land to defend the newly found Roman city.

This is an example of the high places we spoke about in Chapter 1, that has years of bloodshed on the land which strengthens the power of death. Piazza Statuto, the location of the dark angel monument, used to be the site of a pre-Roman necropolis. It was in close proximity to the bloodshed from the Theban Legion massacre in 287 A.D.

The essence of the massacre was that Theban soldiers, who were Christian, refused to burn incense to the statue of Emperor Maximilian. They were martyred for their choice. Piazza Statuto was also the place where the medieval-era gallows took the lives of countless victims.

Bloodshed releases curses on the land in conjunction with a higher concentration of demonic activity.[31] This piazza is known as the gate of black magic in the city and the vertex of the black magic triangle. The statue of the dark angel is looking down Via Garibaldi toward Torino's gate of white magic—Piazza Castello.

Piazza Castello is the central square of Torino and is known as the heart of the Savoy influence in the city. The Palazzo Reale and Palazzo Madama are the royal residences of the Savoy dynasty (1003 AD–1946 AD) which surround the piazza. The Duomo (cathedral) connected to the Palazzo Reale houses the Holy Shroud, one of the world's most famous relics. The Holy Shroud is a sacred linen believed to be the burial cloth that Jesus was placed in following his crucifixion. The power of this relic gives Piazza Castello the central power of white magic in the city. At different points throughout history, the Holy Shroud has been placed on display. In the late 1500's, tens of thousands of worshipers gathered in line for hours just to have the chance to touch the Holy Shroud. Many believed that a single touch of the cloth Jesus was buried in had the power to supernaturally heal and release blessings. The shroud was placed on display in the gate leading to the Palazzo Reale which is flanked on either side by equestrian statues of the Greek mythological underworld deities, Castor and Pollux.

These statues align the power centers in the city. Pollux, the twin on the right, has an inverted pentagram on the top of his head and faces the dark angel at Piazza Statuto. (See Figure 14) Castor faces in the direction of another significant power point in the city, the Gran Madre. These horsemen, Pollux and Castor, positioned at the gate to the Palazzo Reale are said to be the dividing point between black and white magic within the city. Italian journalist, Elena Perotti, writes of the tradition of Piazza Castello as it relates to white magic by saying: "Tradition has it that Maria Cristina of France, the daughter of Henri IV and wife of Vittorio Amedeo I of Savoy, decided to build the Savoy residence in that particular place on the advice of master alchemists. Historians tell us that the Savoy family was always interested in alchemy. It seems that when Cristina became regent after the death of her husband in 1637, she was made privy to the secret concerning the location of the alchemical caves of Torino. It was on that site that she commissioned the castle, which was built between 1646 and 1660, nearby."[32]

Figure 13. Palazzo Reale. Wikipedia Commons.
https://commons.wikimedia.org/wiki/File:Palazzo_Reale.JPG

Figure 14. Pollux Palazzo Reale by Yanez_61
https://commons.wikimedia.org/w/index.php?curid=1086000

The Gran Madre is an ostentatious structure that lies just across the Po River. (See Figure 15) It was built between 1818 and 1831 with a neoclassical architectural design similar to the Pantheon in Rome. It was constructed to celebrate the return of Vittorio Emanuele I after the Napoleonic rule. The location of the Gran Madre is strategic in that it falls along the ley-line, and also is believed to have been built upon the ruins of the temple of Isis.[33] Legends prevail about the ancient history of the city prior to the Romans establishing it as an outpost. One such legend is that the city was built by Phaeton, the son of Isis in 1529 BC. Centuries later it became a gathering place for the Druids, who would gather at the confluence of the Po and Dora Rivers to celebrate the summer solstice. According to esoteric beliefs, the Po River represents the sun (a male deity) and the Dora represents the moon (a female deity).

Figure 15. Chiesa della Gran Madre di Dio.
https://commons.wikimedia.org/wiki/File:Chiesa_della_Gran_Madre_di_Dio_(Torino).JPG

Alchemy

The Savoy family was deeply intrigued by alchemy and became a gateway for the practice of it in Torino. Alchemy is an ancient practice combining philosophy and mysticism. It is considered the precursor of chemistry. The practice of alchemy has its roots in ancient Egypt. The word itself originates from the Arabic name for Egpyt, 'Al-Khemia' which means "black land." This reference describes the rich, black, fertile soil of the Nile Delta.[34] Alchemy in its simplest form is the practice of turning base metals into gold. Egyptian alchemists used their esoteric knowledge to mix potions for healing and prolonging life. They were also known for producing alloys, perfumes and substances to embalm the dead. Ancient Egyptians believed that the cosmos was an "act of divine conscious creation." The mysteries of ancient Egypt were accessed by the elite, those initiates who had obtained higher levels of consciousness on their journey toward transformation.

The primary goal of alchemy is to obtain divinization, that is, to transform human life into divine life. The basic tenets of alchemy are believed to have been written on the

Emerald Tablet by Hermes Trismegistus. The Hermetic Law states, "that which is below is like that which is above and that which is above is like that which is below"; this summarizes the knowledge contained on the Emerald Tablet.[35] The secrets written on this tablet are said to contain seven steps of transformation to obtain the "philosopher's stone." As with most mystic philosophies, alchemy is rich in symbolism. It has long been the pursuit of alchemists to discover the "philosopher's stone." This is not a tangible stone but rather a magical substance obtained through wisdom that is achieved at the highest level of enlightenment. This wisdom is believed to have the power to transform a decaying physical being into an immortal being. The transmutation of lead to gold represents the transformation of mortal to immortal. Base metals are believed to be both impure and immature in development, and gold is a reflection of purity and maturity. Gold is associated with the perfection of all matter, even that of the mind, soul, and spirit. Therefore, gold was the most prominent symbol for alchemy, the shape of which was the point within the circle, or the circumpunct. Are you starting to see a pattern emerge? It seems that cultures engaged in sun worship utilized the symbol of the circumpunct. As we progress in our investigation, we will need to keep this pattern in mind to see if we can validate our hypothesis.

Alchemists were drawn to Torino, primarily because the Savoy family invited them and strongly encouraged their work. It was also believed that Apollonis, a Greek neopythagorean philosopher in the first century AD, deposited a powerful, magic talisman within one of the underground caves in Torino. Many alchemists came to Torino in search of this talisman with hopes of discovering the "philosopher's stone." In 1556, Nostradamus moved to Torino at the request of Emanuele Filiberto and Margherita of Valois to cure their infertility through his practice of alchemy.

Guiditta Dembach, author of *Torino Città Magica*, interviewed Torino's most well-known 20th-century magician, Gustavo Adolfo Rol. His knowledge and usage of the alchemists' cave was the most extensive among locals. He described an intricate underground system accessed through cellars, that led to secret temples and portals where alchemists believe it is possible to "manipulate matter, time, and coincidences."[36] The location of these alchemists' portals are under Piazza Castello or in the near vicinity. Dembach described the alchemists' caves (portals) as "a point of contact between the known earthly dimension and that of the spirit, between our world of thinking beings and "paralleled" worlds, where existence runs on different but contemporary plans to ours."[37] Interestingly, while crews were preparing for the 2006 Olympics, by excavating portions of the Garden of Palazzo Reale, they uncovered underground walls with strange markings on them near the Fountain of Tritons and Nymphs. Following this discovery, funding for the project quickly dried up. This area of the royal gardens has been closed to the public.

Before we move on let's recap our journey in Torino so far. Our origination point was Piazza Statuto, the "gate of hell." As we followed the ley-line from this point straight down Via Garibaldi, we arrived at Piazza Castello, the gate of white magic in the city. The dark angel with the inverted pentagram on its head at Piazza Statuto faces Pollux with the inverted pentagram at Piazza Castello. Castor, the other twin on horseback, faces the Gran Madre down Via Po. While Via Po isn't perfectly in line with Via Garibaldi, it maintains the general axis of the ley-line. It's important to note that ley-lines do not have to be exactly straight.

Spiritual Grids

In following this ley-line further into the nearby countryside and villages, we come to Pecetto Torinese. (See Figure 16) This is where my friends lived. One day during my visit, I went for a walk near their house with a few people from our ministry team. We ended up in farmland that was in a valley below their house. It was on this walk that I experienced a spiritual power grid for the first time. I had a strong sensation that particles, objects, or beings were quickly moving away from me. The best way to describe it is to picture the scene in Star Wars when the Millennium Falcon goes into hyperdrive, only picture it in reverse. That's what I saw in the valley of Pecetto. Thankfully, I was not the only one to experience the spiritual grid, all the others I was walking with experienced different aspects of the grid. It was unmistakable. One friend, while she couldn't see things moving, she could feel the movement pass through her body. One sensation we all experienced was the presence of a distinctive, foul odor much like sulfur. We knew that the Lord had drawn us to this location to cleanse the land through prayer and sever the connection along the ley-line. We invited the presence of the Holy Spirit to fill the void once we separated the connectivity of the ley-line. Immediately, the smell changed, a refreshing pine smell permeated the area replacing the smell of sulfur. When we returned to my friend's house, I shared our experience. She wasn't surprised. She told us that many of the locals talk openly about the energy field in the valley. In fact, people travel great distances to experience the energy flow first-hand.

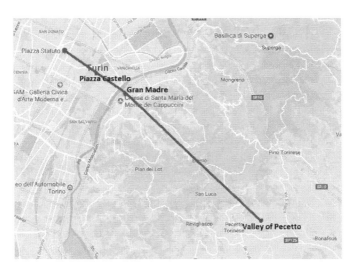

Figure 16. Ley-line extending to valley of Pecetto

Piazza Statuto, Piazza Castello, the Gran Madre and the valley of Pecetto are only a handful of significant power points within Torino and its surrounding areas. There are hundreds of locations within the Piedmont region that are sacred sites for white and black magic. I will draw attention to five prominent structures built by the Savoy family. As you can see, these structures encircle the city of Torino, forming a pentagram within a circle. (See Figure 17) They are: Basilica Superga, Rivoli Castle, Palace of Venaria, Moncalieri Castle, and the Palace of Stupingi. The location of these buildings were not chosen by coincidence. The Savoy family was known for consulting master alchemists for direction on architectural design and geographical positioning to maximize the convergence of power. These are just a few examples of ley-lines that connect with each other to form a spiritual grid across the Piedmont region.

A majority of the locals understand the history of the city and are familiar with these power points around the city. Whether or not they engage in witchcraft, they are exposed to the repercussions of the spiritual grid, simply because they live within the boundaries of this grid. One such repercussion that became a national tragedy occurred at the Basilica of Superga. The Basilica was built in 1706 as a monument to "Our Lady, the Virgin Mary" for providing victory for the Piedmontese Armies over the French Armies. On May 4th, 1949, the entire Torino Football team died in a plane crash on the hillside of the Basilica. Thirty-one lives were lost that day. What seemed like a tragic accident may not have been an accident at all. These kinds of occurrences involving bloodshed are not uncommon along ley-lines or within spiritual grids, especially those involving witchcraft.

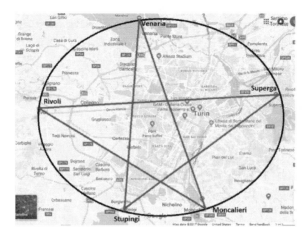

Figure 17. Map of Torino with circle and pentagram overlay aligning Savoy buildings.

As I mentioned earlier in this chapter, bloodshed brings defilement to the land. It can be the original offense leading to a curse on the land, or it can be used to strengthen the grip of darkness in the land.

Numbers 35: 33-34 (NIV) "*Do not pollute the land where you are. Bloodshed pollutes the land, and atonement cannot be made for the land on which blood has been shed, except by the blood of the one who shed it. Do not defile the land where you live and where I dwell, for I, the Lord, dwell among the Israelites.*"

Stewardship of the land by ancient peoples can release curses or blessings over the land. We see in Deuteronomy 29 that the attitudes of people's hearts can cause the land to be cursed.

Deuteronomy 29:23-27 (NIV) "*The whole land will be a burning waste of salt and sulfur—nothing planted, nothing sprouting, no vegetation growing on it. It will be like the destruction of Sodom and Gomorrah, Admah and Zeboyim, which the Lord overthrew in fierce anger. All the nations will ask: 'Why has the Lord done this to this land? Why this fierce burning anger?' And the answer will be: 'It is because this people abandoned the covenant of the Lord, the God of their ancestors, the covenant he made with them when he brought them out of Egypt. They went off and worshiped other gods and bowed down to them, gods they did not know, gods he had not given them.*"

Therefore the Lord's anger burned against this land, so that he brought on it all the curses written in this book."

Ley-lines can be cleansed of defilement and become highways of holiness. We see a description of this in Isaiah 35:

Isaiah 35:1-2a, 7-9 (NIV) *"The desert and the parched land will be glad; the wilderness will rejoice and blossom. Like the crocus, it will burst into bloom; it will rejoice greatly and shout for joy. The burning sand will become a pool, the thirsty ground bubbling springs. In the haunts where jackals once lay, grass and reeds, and papyrus will grow. And a highway will be there; it will be called the Way of Holiness; it will be for those who walk on that Way. The unclean will not journey on it; wicked fools will not go about on it… they will not be found there. But only the redeemed will walk there."*

Isaiah describes land that was once cursed, will become blessed with life and will be a pathway for those walking in holiness.

Isaiah 40:3-5 (NIV) *"A voice of one calling: 'In the wilderness prepare the way for the Lord; make straight in the desert a highway for our God. Every valley shall be raised up, every mountain and hill made low; the rough ground shall become level, the rugged places a plain. And the glory of the Lord will be revealed, and all people will see it together. For the mouth of the Lord has spoken."*

Both of these passages speak of a highway for the Lord within the topography of the land. The enemy is not able to create but instead tries to pervert and twist what God has established. Ley-lines are not something the enemy invented, instead he copied the idea from the Most High and has defiled the land with these passage-ways.

We can glean several valuable insights from our jaunt to Torino that will help us understand the spiritual landscape that underlies the roots of the Federal Reserve. Portals, gates, ley-lines and grids are either redeemed or defiled. They are either open to angelic activity and the agenda of heaven, or they are closed to it. Defiled ley-lines form power corridors that connect sacred sites, thereby establishing a demonic stronghold over a territory.

Ley-lines span time. They don't expire with the passing of a generation. It is imperative in the pursuit of cleansing and redeeming the land that history is researched and the root causes of defilement in the land are revealed. Alistair Petrie, an Anglican vicar and noted expert on ley-lines, has found that bloodshed, broken covenants, idolatry, and immorality/fornication are the primary root causes of strongholds within the land.[38] These root issues send out shoots that attract further acts of defilement, which then strengthen the demonic entanglement over the land and its inhabitants. A way to envision this is to picture the "field bindweed" (often mistaken for morning glory). The root system is deep within the soil, but it sends shoots up that grow and choke out other plants. Picking the weed from the surface does nothing to eradicate the problem. Only striking at the root, will kill this weed.

The good news is that the power emanating from a ley-line can be broken through strategic intercession informed by research and discernment. Targeted prayer can strike at the root eliminating it from the land. We will discuss this in more detail later.

Armed with these concepts of ley-lines, gates, portals and grids from Torino, let's venture back to the Neolithic Period in Europe to see how the megalithic structures, circumpuncts and ley-lines lead us on a trail to Jekyll Island.

Key Points
- Portals, gates, grids and ley-lines are either redeemed or defiled.
- Defiled spiritual grids can have a deleterious effect for people living among its boundaries.
- Broken covenants, bloodshed, idolatry, and immorality/fornication create strongholds.
- Most prominent alchemical symbol is the circumpunct which represents gold and the worship of the sun.

Chapter 3

Civilizations of the Megalithic Architects

The circumpuncts constructed in the Neolithic period throughout Europe seem to resemble the Sapelo Shell Rings constructed in the Archaic period (dated to approximately the same time frame). How did the indigenous people of the Archaic Period, who were thought to be hunter gatherers, suddenly become an agricultural-based society with the technology to make pottery? Were these early inhabitants of Georgia's coastal islands already a civilized people group who migrated from another land? Were these indigenous people, who constructed the shell rings, connected to the architects of the megalithic circumpuncts in other parts of the world? It seems likely that the indigenous people who constructed the Sapelo Shell Rings may have migrated from regions that had a more progressive civilization. The pottery artifacts found on Sapelo Island would suggest these inhabitants were not the hunter gatherers historians originally thought they were. Let's continue to explore these questions to see if we can determine if the indigenous people of the coastal islands of Georgia may have migrated from more ancient, yet advanced civilizations.

Engineering Feats

One of the most mysterious aspects of the civilizations that produced the megalithic monuments is their advanced understanding of architecture, engineering, astronomy, and technology. Across the globe, there are thousands of megalithic structures that leave scholars, archaeologists, scientists, and engineers mystified. In pondering the tremendous feat of building these structures, it certainly stirs curiosity, awe and wonder. Let's take a closer look at a few of these megalithic monuments in hopes of gaining greater understanding of the ancient inhabitants of Sapelo Island and nearby Jekyll Island.

Baalbek

In modern day Lebanon, the megalithic stones of Baalbek emerge from the surrounding landscape in awe. It is one of the most impressive ancient megalithic monuments known to mankind. The ancient ruins found at Baalbek date back to approximately 9000 B.C. It was an important religious site for the Canaanites as a central location for their fertility cult. Centuries later, the Phoenicians (a Semitic tribe of Canaanites) expanded the city.

The grand structure found in Baalbek was originally a temple for Baal and Astarte (the Queen of Heaven or Asherah). Baal and Astarte were the primary deities in the Canaanite fertility cult. Baal was known as the sun god, and Astarte as the moon goddess. Worshipers would make pilgrimage to this temple to engage in ritualistic ceremonies like shrine prostitution and human sacrifice in worship to these deities. Baal was considered to be god of the sky responsible for wind, rain, fertility, and agriculture. The Canaanites believed that they could appeal to Baal by performing ceremonial rituals involving shrine prostitution, ritual homosexual acts, orgies, and child sacrifices (often the firstborn male). By engaging in these forms of worship, they believed Baal would extend his favor by sending the rains to bless their crops. The Canaanites also believed that engaging in the temple prostitution and orgies would arouse the sexual union of Baal and Astarte, thus ensuring fertile crops and fertile families.

Baalbek was established as a high place with spiritual power that held the inhabitants of that region in bondage. As we learned from Torino, the spiritual power emanating from high places becomes a magnet that attracts new forms of false worship that spans the millennia. This is how adaptive deceptions are formed. Adaptive deceptions are changes made to traditional structures of false worship when those structures are in danger of "losing their spiritual potency."[39] Historical records uncover several layers of adaptive deceptions that have operated on the land of Baalbek. In 334 B.C., Alexander the Great conquered the city and renamed it Heliopolis after the Egyptian city. Heliopolis translates to "city of the sun." The false worship at Baalbek during the Hellenistic period was directed toward the Greek sun god, Helios. This is a slight variation from the Canaanite worship of Baal, a hallmark of an adaptive deception. During the era of the Roman Empire, the foundation of the great temple of Baal became the foundation of a Roman temple built in honor of Jupiter. In the Roman mythology, Jupiter is the sky god. Sound familiar? Jupiter was responsible for the weather and storms. This is another example of the spiritual power that is generated from false worship at high places perpetuating from one generation to the next.

If you find yourself confused from time to time about how the gods of different cultures interrelate, you are not alone. As a reference point, let me lay out a simplistic list of the gods from ancient cultures that will be pertinent to our investigation.

Baal	Canaanite/Phoenician sun god
Helios/Kronos	Greek sun god
Mithras	Persian sun god
Ra	Egyptian sun god
Sol Invictus	Roman sun god
Shamash	Babylonian and Assyrian sun god
Saturn	Chaldean, Babylonian, Assyrian "star of the sun"
Moloch	Ammonite sun god

I will refer back to these gods throughout our journey together. Keep in mind that this list is a high-level overview. Depending on the time period of each culture, the sun god could have been designated by different names. For example, in predynastic Egypt, Atum was the name of the sun god. During the early dynastic years, Ra was established as the sun god. Centuries later, Horus replaced or merged with Ra to become the sun god.

Turning our attention to the physical remnants of the temple at Baalbek, we find stones of gargantuan proportion (see Figure 18). It's clear from the archaeological evidence that the Romans did not remove the foundational stones of Baalbek. It would have been impossible to move these stones. The cornerstones alone weigh over 100 tons (224,000 lbs) and the monoliths that form the retaining wall weigh approximately 300 tons each (672,000 lbs). Astonishingly, there are three stones in the base of the temple. These stones are referred to as the "trilithon" and weigh approximately 800 tons each (1,792,000 lbs). The ancient architects who positioned these stones did so with such precision that not even a blade of grass can pass between them. As staggering as this is, there are even larger stones found in the Baalbek complex. A monolith called the "Stone of the Pregnant Woman" (see Figure 19) was thought to be the largest quarried stone ever found. It weighs over 1000 tons (2,240,000 lbs). Archaeologists recently discovered an even larger monolith quarried below the "stone of the pregnant woman." Its weight is estimated to be 1200 tons (2,688,000 lbs).[40] Did you catch that? It weighs over 2 million pounds! That's more than the weight of six Boeing 767's combined. Let's take a moment to let that sink in.

Figure 18. Ancient columns in Baalbek, Lebanon. Photo by iryna1. Adobe stock photo file #213358336

Figure 19. Foundation Stone Baalbek Ancient City in Lebanon. Photo by P. Baishev. Adobe Stock Photo File #187173954

Who could have quarried stones of these immense proportions? What tools did they use? How could they move these stones from the quarry to the temple site about 1 kilometer away? How were they able to position the stones with such precision as they built the temple at Baalbek?

It's difficult with our Western mindset to comprehend the ancient civilization that could produce the megalithic wonder of Baalbek. Some theorize that megalithic monuments were constructed by extra-terrestrial species. Others suggest that the architects themselves were giants. Both may see farfetched, but let's look at some interesting clues.

Baalbek is about 50 miles south of Mt. Hermon. We know, that at one point in history, a giant ruled from Mt. Hermon. His name was Og, king of Bashan.

Joshua 12:4-5 (NIV) "*And the territory of Og king of Bashan, one of the last of the Rephaites, who reigned in Ashtaroth and Edrei. He ruled over Mt. Hermon, Salekah, all of Bashan to the border of the people of Geshur and Maakah, and half of Gilead to the border of Sihon king of Heshbon.*"

There is an important phrase in this scripture that gives us a clue to a potential key piece of evidence. The phrase "*one of the last of the Rephaites*" refers to a lineage of giants recorded throughout scripture. Og is mentioned six times in the Old Testament. One interesting side note is that the Bible provides specific measurements of the bed that Og used.

Deuteronomy 3:11 (NLT) "*(King Og of Bashan was the last survivor of the giant Rephaites. His bed was made of iron and was more than thirteen feet long and six feet wide. It can still be seen in the Ammonite city of Rabbah.)*"

It is reasonable to deduce from this that Og was between 10–12 ft. tall if his bed was just over 13 ft. long. His size was certainly noteworthy for Moses to include it in the Pentateuch. Josephus, the great Jewish historian, records this in his writings: "Now Og had very few equals, with in the largeness of his body or handsomeness of his appearance. He was also a man of great activity in the use of his hands, so that his actions were not unequal to the vast largeness and handsome appearance of his body: and men could easily guess at this strength and magnitude when they took his bed at Rabbath, the royal city of the Ammonites; its structure was of iron, its breadth four cubits, and its length a cubit more than double thereto."[41]

The Ammonites thought his bed was of such renown that they brought it to their capital city, Rabbah, which is the current day Amman, Jordan. The passage in Deuteronomy mentions that Og was the last of the Rephaites or also called Rephaim in some translations. This word Rephaim is often translated as the Hebrew word for giant. Was he truly the last of the giants or was he the last of a lineage of giants? We will explore the origin of giants in more depth in upcoming chapters, but hopefully I have wet your whistle to continue the journey with me. Next stop...Golan Heights, Israel.

Gilgal Rephaim

We are closing in on the land of the giants. Gilgal Rephaim (or Gilgal Refaim) is located approximately ten miles from the ancient Canaanite city of Ashtherot, which is in current day Golan Heights. This stone circle monument has several alternate names: Israel's Stonehenge, Wheel of Giants, Circle of Og, Rujm el-Hiri, and Circle of Refaim. The surrounding area is covered with thousands of dolmens (monolithic structures with two vertical megaliths supporting a horizontal megalith). These megalithic monuments are in a region that was once inhabited by giants like Og.

The monument contains five concentric circles with a diameter of 155 meters (about 500 feet). The most preserved portion of the monument is the outer ring. The best view of the monument is an aerial perspective (see Figure 20). Archaeological researchers, Aveni and Mizrachi (1998), describe Gilgal Rephaim in the following way: "The site has been variously described as a ceremonial center, a defense enclosure, a central storage facility, a large burial complex, and finally, as a center for astronomical observations and a calendrical device. The builders of Rujm el-Hiri brought no less than 37,500 metric tons of basalt stones to the site, making the Rujm el-Hiri complex one of the most impressive archaeological stone monuments in the Levant. Hundreds of dolmens as well as straight low stone walls that surround the monument, along with petroglyphs on the monuments and in neighboring areas, form one of the most impressive megalithic complexes in the southern Levant."[42]

It has been challenging for archaeologists to accurately date Gilgal Rephaim because of the scarcity of artifactual debris. However, of the ceramics found at the site, 95% of them consist of material dating to the Late Bronze Age (1550 B.C.–1200 B.C.) with a much smaller sample dating to the Early Bronze Age (3150 B.C.–3000 B.C.). Researchers have suggested that the cairn and tumulus (mound of stones used as a grave) found in the center of the rings were built upon the pre-existing complex. The remains of earlier construction found beneath the tumulus support this notion. This suggests that the larger portion of the monument consisting of the outer concentric circles was built during the same time period as Stonehenge.

Figure 20. Gilgal Refaim. https://commons.wikimedia.org/wiki/File:Gilgal_Refa%27im_-_Rujm_el-Hiri.JPG

The research conducted by Aveni and Mizrachi (1998) examined the ceremonial complex of Rujm el-Hiri in hopes of providing insight regarding its purpose. They analyzed the architectural structure and layout of the complex. They compared it to celestial bodies and events, landscape markers, and considered the calendrical aspects of the monument. They found that the alignment of the walls (amidst the concentric circles) with celestial bodies was statistically significant. They drew the following conclusions from their results:

"These observations lead us to conclude that, like the main avenue of Stonehenge, the aperture in the outer wall would have made a reasonable anticipatory observational device for demarcating the solstice around 3000 B.C… The outermost opening in Wall 1 was constructed as a marker for the June solstice and the inner aperture in Wall 2 may have functioned as a processional entryway. We suspect that the NW alignment to the June solstice may have been associated with the cult of Dummuzi-Tammuz, the consort of the Sumerian goddess Inanna. Dummuzi figured prominently in the annual fertility rituals of the Sacred Marriage (between the two gods) and on death became a god of the underworld… We see the function of Rujm el-Hiri primarily as a ritual center and/or a temple in which religious ceremonies and ritual observations were attended by the urban populations who inhabited the newly emerged Golan 'enclosure' sites…The design and execution of the alignments associated with the burial chamber shows no relation to astronomical events. This again suggests that the construction of the central cairn with its NW tomb orientation was not coordinated with that of the rest of the site and that this building effort should be interpreted as a chronologically and functionally distinct cultural phase."[43]

Aveni and Mizrachi (1998) also considered the alignment of the structure to markers in the surrounding landscape. They found that Mt. Hermon, the second tallest mountain in the Levant, was located almost due north (0°49' of north). The proximity of the complex as it's aligned with Mt. Hermon raises the questions.

What are the symbolic implications of this apparent deliberate alignment? The researchers acknowledged that the phenomenon of sacred mountains is well-known within the literature addressing cosmology and the origin of religion. Mountains were considered to be the dwelling places of gods. In fact, Aveni and Mizrachi (1998) comment about the significance of Mt. Hermon within the Enochian texts.

Mt. Hermon is the location where the fallen "sons of God" descended from heaven and pursued sexual relations with human women impregnating them with the hybrid race of Nephilim (Genesis 6). Given the historical significance of Mt. Hermon, and that Gilgal Rephaim is aligned almost due north to this landmark, it's possible that this site was significant to the offspring of the Nephilim.

The cairn and tumulus located in the center of the monument are widely known to have been common structures used for burial mounds (see Figure 21). There is a growing body of evidence that this may have been the location in which Og was buried.

Let's consider for a moment an intriguing possibility. The concentric circles were built during the antediluvian period, but the center burial mound was constructed approximately 1500 years later. We know from scripture that King Og died after the Flood (Deuteronomy 3:11) and he was considered one of the last of the Rephaim. Perhaps he requested to be buried at this sacred ceremonial place so that he could be joined with the Nephilim that had lived in this region before him.

In their book, *On the Path of the Immortals*, Thomas Horn and Cris Putnam hypothesize that Gilgal Rephaim was a portal used to access the Nephilim.

"We speculate that the Wheel of Giants served as a necromantic portal for the deceased Nephilim kings of Bashan, of whom Og was the last of their kind…Gilgal Rephaim's design as a megalithic stone circle seems suitable for necromantic magic. According to the *Encyclopedia of Occultism and Parapsychology,* a "magic circle" drawn on the ground is essential to successful necromancy. The circle serves to protect the necromancer as he invokes the underworld spirit…the very center of the megalithic circle contains the dolmen laid corpse, making the portal all the more powerful."[44]

Figure 21. Rujm el Hiri entrance to chamber.jpg photo taken by Ani Nimi.
https://commons.wikimedia.org/wiki/File:Rujm_el_Hiri_entrance_to_chamber.jpg

The Great Pyramid

We would be remiss in our investigation of the engineering feats of the megalithic civilization if we didn't discuss the Great Pyramid of Egypt. The sheer volume of information about the Great Pyramid could fill an entire library. It's in a league of its own and is still considered one of the greatest mysteries in the world. My approach in investigating this enigma, is not to exhaust every angle or turn over every stone, but to capture the most important discoveries in order to grapple with the bigger picture. This requires a chapter unto itself. As we journey to Egypt, you will discover that there are more questions than answers, more mysteries than solutions, more conjecture than evidence; but as we explore the questions, mysteries and conjecture you might find yourself at the precipice of a paradigm shift. As Westerners, we were taught the traditional theories of Egyptologists in our World History classes. Many of us have come to accept that the pyramids are megalithic tombs once containing the mummies of pharaohs. While this may be true of the stepped pyramids, is it true of the Great Pyramid of Giza?

Key Points

- Baalbek was a high place for the worship of Baal.
- Baalbek is the site of the largest monolith weighing 2 million pounds.
- Gilgal Rephaim is a circumpunct monument with orientation almost due north of Mt. Hermon.
- Baalbek and Gilgal Rephaim were located in the ancient land of Bashan, home to giants.

Chapter 4

The Mysteries of an Ancient Wonder

The Great Pyramid complex located on the Giza plateau dominates the skyline on the outskirts of Cairo (see Figure 22). The Great Pyramid holds the distinction as being the only one of the seven wonders of the ancient world to survive. It is no wonder that countless archaeologists, historians, Egyptologists, and scientists have long studied the mysteries held within the Great Pyramid. There are many theories that have emerged over the centuries to address questions like: who built the Great Pyramid, why was it built, and how was it built? We are going to examine some of the mainstream theories, while also considering theories that challenge the confines of traditional thinking. But first let's take a look at some of the facts that make this such an unfathomable engineering feat.

Figure 22. Full View of the Pyramids in Giza, Egypt..
https://www.goodfreephotos.com/egypt/giza/full-view-of-the-pyramids-in-giza-egypt.jpg.php

Just the Facts

At its zenith, the Great Pyramid towered 481 feet above the Giza plateau. It was the tallest man-made structure for nearly 4000 years with 201 courses (40 stories). With the pyramidion missing, it now stands at 449.5 feet, still an impressive sight to behold.

The base of the pyramid is over 13 acres which is roughly 8.5 city blocks or about the length of 10 football fields.[45] Each side is 756 feet long. In 1881, Flinders Petrie conducted the first in-depth survey of the Great Pyramid using precision tools, such as the theodolite, to produce measurements within 1/100th inch of accuracy. Petrie's legacy is that his precise measurements of the Great Pyramid serve as the standard today. He was the first to discover that the Great Pyramid is oriented to true north within 0.05 degrees.[46] In fact, the pyramid's alignment to the cardinal points is more accurate than most of our modern observatories. There are an estimated 2.3 million stones that form the Great Pyramid with the majority of them weighing anywhere between 2 to 20 tons each.[47] The granite slabs within the "King's chamber" are monstrosities weighing between 25 to 85 tons (50,000–170,000 lbs).

It's no surprise that the geometrical shape of the Great Pyramid is pyramidal, but what is surprising is the little-known fact that it has more than four sides. This was first discovered by Flinders Petrie in the late 1700s. In 1940, British airman, P. Groves captured the concave sides of the Great Pyramid in a photograph from his plane. The satellite image in Figure 23 emphasizes the eight sides. Pier Luigi Copat, an architect/consultant for Berlin Potsdamer Platz, said that our modern technology is not capable of replicating such a feat as an eight-sided pyramid with accuracy within a millimeter.[48] This begs the question, how could the ancient architects accomplish such an amazing feat using only the purported hand tools that Egyptologists have determined were available?

Figure 23. The Shadows of the Pyramids. Photo by Kahled Dewidar, Ph.D.

Historical Conjecture

It is commonly thought that the Great Pyramid was constructed in approximately 20 years. This notion can be attributed to the writings of Herodotus, a Greek historian. Herodotus travelled to Egypt around 450 B.C. to gather historical information about the great and mysterious structures of Egypt. He wrote about the causeway leading up to the Great Pyramid and the pyramid itself: "Of this oppression there passed ten years while the causeway was made by which they drew the stones, which causeway they built, and it is a work not much less, as it appears to me, than the pyramid; for the length of it is five furlongs and the breadth ten fathoms and the height, where it is highest, eight fathoms, and it is made of stone smoothed and with figures carved upon it. For this, they said, the ten years were spent, and for the underground chambers on the hill upon which the pyramids stand, which he caused to be made as sepulchral chambers for himself in an island, having conducted thither a channel from the Nile. For the making of the pyramid itself there passed a period of twenty years; and the pyramid is square, each side measuring eight hundred feet, and the height of it is the same. It is built of stone smoothed and fitted together in the most perfect manner, not one of the stones being less than thirty feet in length."[49]

As we consider Herodotus' writings of the Great Pyramid, it's important to keep in mind that he was in Egypt more than a millennium after the pyramids were allegedly built. The stories he collected from the Egyptians were not firsthand, second hand or even third hand accounts. They are best described as folklore tales passed down through the generations. Even Herodotus recognized this when he provided this caveat for his writings: "Now as to the tales told by the Egyptians, any man may accept them to whom such things appear credible; as for me, it is to be understood throughout the whole of the history that I write by hearsay that which is reported by the people in each place."[50]

Whether they are tales or not, Herodotus provides us with the oldest historical records of the Great Pyramid. We are able to take this historical record and compare it to evidence that has since been discovered, to determine the accuracy in which Herodotus wrote.

Before diving into the more complicated questions such as who built the Great Pyramid, when and for what purpose, first we should consider whether we accept Herodotus' record that the Great Pyramid was built in 20 years. Let's consider this from a practical standpoint. If crews worked 12 hours a day, 365 days a year, for 20 years, the rate at which crews would have to quarry, carve, haul, and position 2 million blocks in place would be one block every 2 ½ minutes. This seems like a superhuman feat (but then again so does moving the 800-ton trilithons of Baalbek). For some reason, traditional Egyptologists don't have a problem with this rate of production being achieved with hand tools. In my perspective, it takes a greater leap of faith to believe they accomplished this with hand tools than it does to consider the possibility that ancient civilizations utilized machinery that we have yet to discover or understand. One reason traditional Egyptologists vehemently oppose such a notion is because it would mean that they would have to seriously rethink what ancient civilizations were capable of and this would undermine the theory of the ascent of man. Would this not be a major blow to evolution? Just by looking at the Great Pyramid and considering some of the jaw dropping facts, we simply cannot conclude that these feats were just accidentally accomplished. Yet that is what traditional Egyptologists want us to believe.

Who Built the Great Pyramid?

Now let's dive into the deep end. Experts in various scholarly disciplines have found it difficult to agree on who built the Great Pyramid and for what purpose. Herodotus was the first to record that the Great Pyramid was built for the 4th Dynasty Pharaoh Khufu (Cheops to the Greeks) around 2550 B.C. Manetho, an Egyptian priest and historian two centuries after Herodotus, also claimed that Khufu was the honored pharaoh for which the Great Pyramid was built. This testament has become widely accepted among traditional Egyptologists. For millennia, the association of Khufu with the Great Pyramid was untested. Archaeological explorations in the 19th century began to give this theory evidentiary credence.

Sir John Gardner Wilkinson was one of the first to conduct in-depth, on-site studies in Egypt beginning in 1821; he is regarded by many to be one of the fathers of Egyptology. A pivotal breakthrough in academia came in 1826 from Jean-François Champollion when he broke the code for the hieroglyphics found on the Rosetta Stone. In doing so, he provided a template for deciphering the ancient Egyptian language and handed the academic community a key to unlock ancient mysteries. This new-found understanding propelled scholars such as Wilkinson, Ippolito Rosellini (Professor of Oriental Languages at the University of Pisa and founder of Egyptology in Italy) and Samuel Birch (British Museum's hieroglyphics expert) to improve the accuracy of their linguistic analysis of this ancient Egyptian language.

In 1832, Ippolito Rosellini transliterated the hieroglyphic form of the abbreviated name of Khufu and the full name Khnum-Khuf. (See Figure 24) He published this work in a tome called *l'Monumenti Dell'Egitto e Della Nubia*. This was the first publication of the cartouches for Khufu and Khnum-Khuf. Khufu's cartouche is marked by the number 2 and Khnum-Khuf's cartouche is marked by the number 3 in Figure 24. These three scholars, Wilkinson, Rosellini, and Birch, applied their new found understanding to the analysis of an intriguing discovery by Colonel Vyse that seemed to substantiate the claim that the Great Pyramid belonged to Khufu.

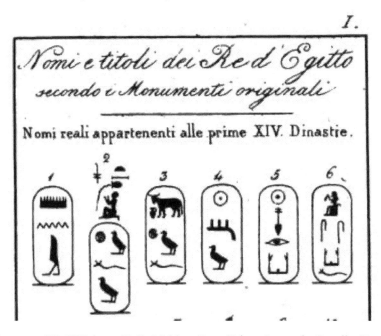

Figure 24. l'Monumenti Dell'Egitto e Della Nubia—Parte Prima. Image by Ippolito Rosellini, 1832.

Khufu Cartouche Quarry Marks, Legit or Hoax?

In 1837, Colonel Howard Vyse, a British soldier, anthropologist, and Egyptologist, discovered crude hieroglyphs marked with red ink (see Figure 25) inside the Great Pyramid. His team found these markings within the "relieving chambers" above the "King's Chamber."[51] It was thought these chambers relieved the weight of the building materials from the roof of the "King's Chamber." The area in which these markings were found were only accessible after utilizing gunpowder to create an opening to these chambers. As Colonel Vyse and his crew blasted their way into each of the four chambers, they measured and examined the contents of these spaces. Upon examining each chamber, red "quarry marks" were discovered. These marks are informal hieroglyphs thought to come from the stones that were quarried from Mokattam (about 17 miles away) rather than the quarry located on site.

Figure 25. Hieroglyphic inscription that includes the cartouche of Khufu found in Campbell's Chamber by Robert M. Schoch. Inset: Drawing of a hieroglyphic inscription that includes the cartouche of Khufu found in Campbell's Chamber by Vye, 1840.

There are several puzzling aspects to Colonel Vyse's discovery of quarry marks. Let's examine one perplexing aspect. There are a total of five relieving chambers within the Great Pyramid; Colonel Vyse discovered four of them. He named the chambers after his colleagues and close friends. They are in order of discovery: Wellington's Chamber, Nelson's Chamber, Lady Aruthnot's Chamber, and Campbell's Chamber. The famous Khufu's cartouche was discovered in Campbell's Chamber, the last chamber to be discovered by Vyse. In 1763, more than 50 years before Colonel Vyse set foot in the King's Chamber, Nathaniel Davison discovered the first relieving chamber, which is known as the Davison Chamber. Interestingly, Davison made no reference to finding hieroglyphs or "quarry markings" in the first relieving chamber. This was verified by Vyse's subsequent examination of Davison's Chamber. Here is an excerpt from Vyse's journal on February 12th, 1837: "Mr. Perring and myself passed most part of the night in examining the interior of the Great Pyramid; particularly Davison's chamber, the passage leading to it, and the excavation made by M. Caviglia on its southern side."[52]

Vyse makes no mention of quarry marks upon his examination of Davison's Chamber. Curiously, Vyse records quarry markings in each of the four relieving chambers he discovered. Why would 4 of the 5 chambers have quarry marks? There has been much speculation that these markings were not written during the reign of Khufu, but instead, added by Vyse's team. We will examine these allegations in a moment. But first let's hear what today's leading experts have to say about the quarry markings.

Egyptologist Mark Lehner and Dr. Zahi Hawass, Egypt's premier archaeologist and former Antiquities Director, have examined the graffiti on the reliefs in the "King's Chamber." The red markings of Khufu's cartouche shown in Figure 25 have been deciphered to say "the companions of Khufu." In an interview conducted by Nova, Dr. Zahi Hawass responds to questions others have posed that perhaps the markings in the relieving chambers *were not* written during the time of Khufu. He states: "They say that these inscriptions were written by people who entered inside. And if you go and see them they are typical graffiti that can be seen around every pyramid in Egypt, because the workmen around the Pyramid left this. I would like those people who talked about this to come with me. I will take them personally to the rooms. First of all, they say that only the second room is inscribed. It's not true—**all the five relieving chambers are inscribed**. Number two there are some inscriptions there that could not be written by anyone except the workmen who put them there. You cannot reach those spots. It had to be the men who put the block there."[53] (emphasis mine)

I find it curious that Dr. Hawass claims that "**all the five** relieving chambers are inscribed," especially since neither Davison nor Vyse recorded that there were markings in the first chamber. If quarry marks were found in Davison's Chamber by Hawass, where did they come from? From the historical records, it would suggest that at some point between 1837 and 2016 someone forged quarry marks in Davison's Chamber. Dr. Hawass seems certain that these inscriptions are located in areas that only the builders of the Great Pyramid could have reached on their way out. In 1996, Hawass took detailed photographs of all the markings in each of the chambers, including Davison's Chamber, but has never made these photographs public.[54] Is this truly the case, are there markings in all five relieving chambers that could only have been inscribed by the builders? Scott Creighton in his book *The Great Pyramid Hoax* addresses these questions and arrives at quite different conclusions than Dr. Hawass and Mark Lehner.

Creighton makes a strong argument that Vyse's team forged the quarry marks... a weighty accusation. "Vyse had the means, the motive, the key knowledge, and the opportunity to perpetrate such a hoax."[55] Creighton suggests that Vyse was a man of dubious character. One example of this was when Vyse committed election fraud by bribing voters in a parliamentary election in 1807. An election committee confronted Vyse with his illegal acts, but he denied any wrongdoing. While this information brings to light Vyse's questionable character, we simply cannot presuppose that he and/or his team members forged the quarry marks in the relieving chambers. We need more substantial evidence. For example, did he have a possible motive to forge a Khufu cartouche?

Archaeological exploration on the Giza Plateau in the 1800s was rife with personalities looking to make the next big discovery. Vyse was no exception to this. In his published work, Vyse writes, "extremely desirous, after all the expense incurred, and inconvenience experienced, to endeavor at least to make some discoveries in the Pyramids before I returned to England, which I wished to do without further delay."[56] Perhaps Vyse was seeking to have his name etched in the history books. This is a potential motive.

Surprisingly, the best evidence actually comes from Vyse himself. Discrepancies have been found in in his journals, particularly in the way he described the discoveries in Wellington's Chamber. His published journal entry for March 30, 1837 says, "Mr. Perring and Mr. Mash having arrived, we went in the evening into Wellington's Chamber, and took various admeasurements, and in doing so we found the quarry marks."[57] His private journal mentions that the only marks found were on the **east** wall near the entrance and they looked "nothing like hieroglyphics." Whereas in his published journal, the entry from May 9, 1837 recorded the quarry marks were found on the **west** wall. He asked his assistant to replicate the quarry markings in Wellington's Chamber for the purpose of sending them to the British Museum for examination. Interestingly, Mr. Hill only copied the quarry marks on the **west** wall of Wellington's Chamber. These markings were purported to be a gang name of the quarry workers along with the Khnum-Khuf cartouche. This would suggest that Khufu was the one responsible for the grand building project of the Great Pyramid. Wasn't this the big discovery Vyse was hoping for? This doesn't add up though. In his private journal,

Vyse recorded that the quarry marks were found on the east wall and that "nothing like hieroglyphics" were discovered inside the chamber.

If Vyse was so desirous of a notable discovery, something that would secure his name in history, why wouldn't he have made a bigger deal of discovering quarry marks that were a royal cartouche? After all, these were the first quarry marks found in a relieving chamber. Not only that, but the first royal cartouche to be found inside the Great Pyramid. This was his big moment... the moment he had been waiting for! Why was he relatively inexpressive about the discovery in his journals? This was not consistent with his personality. There are other instances in his journals, when he is much more expressive and detailed about seemingly less pertinent issues, such as how much he paid a laborer.

The mystery continues to unfold as we examine Vyse's account of the quarry marks found in Campbell's Chamber. On May 27, 1837, the date of their first entry into the chamber, he recorded in his published journal, "there were many quarry marks similar to those in the other chambers"[58] But in his private journal, Vyse makes two different sketches of the Khufu cartouche, one with a plan disc and one with three striated lines in the disc (see Figure 26). This begs the question, why are there two different sketches of Khufu's cartouche on the same journal page? Which one is right? The sketch with the cartouche containing the plain disc is not the actual cartouche found in Campbell's Chamber today (see Figure 25).

The discrepancy in sketches gives us a window into Vyse's deliberations of what the cartouche should look like. But there really was no need for deliberations, if in fact, he discovered an authentic cartouche. The task would have been simple, just sketch a replica of the cartouche as it appeared in Campbell's Chamber. End of story. Astonishingly, his own sketches incriminated him as the author of a hoax. Creighton concludes:

"So here it is, in his private journal, that we find the very essence of Vyse's doubt, his contradiction, and his deliberation; here on this journal page we observe Vyse contemplating a necessary change to what he once believed was the correct spelling of Khufu. The original plain-disc version of the cartouche that he had written twice into his diary and had copied into the Great Pyramid actually required three horizontal lines to be added—or so it seems he believed. It is right here on this page of Vyse's journal that we find the evidence that lays bare the hoax of all history."[59]

Figure 26. Private Journal of Colonel Vyse, June 16, 1837. Original photo
http://myblog.robertbauval.co.uk/. Alterations to original photo made by Laura Sanger.

The theory that Vyse forged the Khufu cartouche brings into question the credibility of the previously untested belief that Khufu is the pharaoh responsible for the building of the Great Pyramid. This hoax may never have been discovered if it weren't for the scrupulous investigative work of Scott Creighton. Vyse certainly covered his tracks well. For nearly two centuries, Egyptologists, historians, and archaeologists have been all too easily convinced that the quarry marks "discovered" by Vyse, legitimize Khufu as the builder of the Great Pyramid. Of course! His findings fit beautifully within the traditional narrative of the date of construction for the Great Pyramid. But if Creighton is correct, which I believe he is, Vyse pulled off the biggest hoax in archaeological history. So, if Khufu didn't build the Great Pyramid, then who did? In order to address this question, we need to investigate the origins of the Great Pyramid.

Origins of the Great Pyramid

As I mentioned, before we embarked on this journey to Ancient Egypt, there are more questions than answers, more speculation than hard evidence, and more mysteries than solutions. The theory of the Great Pyramid belonging to Khufu has been contested on many fronts; an alternative theory offered by independent Egyptologists is that Khufu was not the originator of the pyramid, but instead was the king responsible for the repairs of the Great Pyramid. This would place the date of origin of the Great Pyramid significantly older than during Khufu's reign. The Inventory Stela found in 1858 by Auguste Mariette, a French archaeologist and Egyptologist, lends support to this theory. While it is far from conclusive, it certainly suggests that the Great Pyramid existed before Khufu. Written on the stone tablet known as the Inventory Stela and translated in 1906 by Gaston Maspero, Director General of Excavations and Antiquities for Egypt, is the following inscription:

"Long live The King of Upper and Lower Egypt, Khufu, given life. He found the house of Isis, Mistress of the Pyramid, by the side of the hollow of Hwran (The Sphinx) and he built his pyramid beside the temple of this goddess and he built a pyramid for the King's daughter Henutsen beside this temple. The place of Hwran Horemakhet is on the South side of the House of Isis, Mistress of the pyramid.

He restored the statue, all covered in painting, of the guardian of the atmosphere, who guides the winds with his gaze. He replaced the back part of the Nemes head-dress, which was missing with gilded stone. The figure of this god, cut in stone, is solid and will last to eternity, keeping its face looking always to the East."[61]

There are several interesting clues documented in the Inventory Stela. Most pertinent to our investigation, is that a pyramid already existed on the Giza plateau when Khufu discovered this sacred landscape. It also records that Khufu built two pyramids next to the Temple of Isis. There is uncertainty as to what structure is referred to as the Temple of Isis. Some believe it to be the Great Pyramid, and some believe it to be the temple near the Sphinx. Unmistakable though is that this translated segment of the stela explains that the Sphinx was already in existence during the reign of Khufu and that he was responsible for its restoration. This directly contradicts the timeline of traditional Egyptologists, who purport that Khufu's son, Khafre was the builder of the Sphinx.

Further evidence of an alternative timeline is provided by the investigation of a Boston University Geologist, Robert Schoch, Ph.D (www.robertschoch.com). Schoch has extensively studied the weathering patterns of the limestone on the Sphinx and the surrounding enclosure. From his research, he has found evidence that the Sphinx demonstrates not just weathering from wind (which we would expect, especially since it was nearly covered in sand as late as the 1800's with only the shoulders and head protruding from the sand), but weathering also from water largely produced by rain. Major rain events on the Giza plateau date back much further than the time of Khafre in the Fourth Dynasty. In addition to the weathering patterns of the Sphinx and its enclosure, Schoch conducted low energy seismic experiments on the rocks and weathering layers of the Sphinx. The results were conclusive, Schoch stated, "there is no doubt in my mind that the seismic data alone, independent of any other evidence—such as surface weathering and erosion, strongly support the hypothesis that the origins of the Great Sphinx predate dynastic times by many millennia."[62] Schoch partnered with Robert Bauval to write *Origins of the Sphinx*, in which they present sound reasons for the origin of the Sphinx to be approximately 10,500 BC. I recommend reading their book if you are interested in understanding these reasons, they are too detailed to include here.

If we consider the Inventory Stela and Dr. Schoch's research findings, the evidence is gaining credibility that the Sphinx is much older than traditional Egyptologists would have us to believe. In rethinking the timeline of the Sphinx, it calls into question the timeline of the Great Pyramid. Can we reasonably conclude that the Great Pyramid was built by Khufu in the 4th Dynasty? I think not. The mounting evidence provided by Creighton, Schoch and the Inventory Stela propel us to consider alternative theories. We need to think outside of the constructs of mainstream theories.

What is the Purpose of the Great Pyramid?

Let's start with a common question posed by many independent Egyptologists... if the Great Pyramid was built as a tomb for Khufu, why has there never been a body found? The sarcophagus in the King's Chamber is empty and so the natural conclusion made by traditional Egyptologists, is that grave robbers came and removed the mummy. This simple answer does not seem to line up with other clues, such as, the absence of inscriptions upon the walls of the Pyramid as well as no trace of decorative funerary objects. Absolutely no remains of Khufu have been found, no shards of pottery, not even the smallest shred of evidence that treasures were ever stored within the Great Pyramid. In contrast, the Step Pyramid of Saqqara, which is believed to be the tomb for the Third Dynasty Pharaoh Djoser (2670 B.C.), is highly decorated with blue tiles and over 40,000 stone vessels with inscriptions upon them. Grave robbers did in fact pillage Djoser's tomb, taking his body and many of the treasures stored in his burial chamber. Despite the attempt of the grave robbers to empty the tomb of its valuables, archaeologists were able to find remains of Djoser's mummified foot as well a few valuables.[63] This is what we might expect to find in tombs where grave robbers have gone before. It's unlikely that grave robbers would be so meticulous in their pursuit that they would leave the tomb void of any evidence that a pyramid was in fact a tomb. Yet this is what traditional Egyptologists would like us to believe.

So, if the Great Pyramid was not, in fact, built to be a tomb, why was it built? Over the centuries, this question has largely remained unanswered, but as you can imagine, many theories abound. Theories range from it functioning as a transducer of energy, a portal to the afterlife, a gateway to other dimensions, a celestial calendar, a sacred monument for the worship of Isis and Osiris, a prime meridian for ancient time keeping, a key to higher levels of knowledge, a critical power point along geodetic ley-lines, and on and on. While it's not within the scope of this book to address all of these theories, I will highlight a few.

In the previous chapter, I laid a foundation to understand ley-lines, portals, gates, and spiritual grids. We are going to pick up on these concepts to interpret some of the possible reasons the Great Pyramid was constructed. For millennia, the Great Pyramid has been a high place for occult practices and beliefs. We can find evidence of this across multiple cultures, lands, and epochs. The pyramid has become an iconic symbol for New Age and Freemasonry worshipers, which we will discuss in more detail in upcoming chapters. As we consider potential explanations for the purpose of the Great Pyramid, it's important to know that hundreds of pyramids dot the globe. The sacred geometry utilized in the construction and placement of Egyptian temples was a "science directed toward the embodiment of spiritual knowledge, toward the internalization and corporeal expression of intellectual and spiritual powers."[64] It seems that for Egyptians and other ancient civilizations, the alignment of their monuments, temples and pyramids had geodetic significance. Are these pyramids somehow connected? Are they connected in a way that will assist us in our investigation of the roots of the Federal Reserve?

Pyramids can be found on every continent as well as below the surface of the waters. Some are visible in plain sight, others are disguised as mountains, others are covered with landscape to appear natural. But one thing that is clear, there are more pyramids than can be properly identified. Year after year, it seems that newly discovered pyramids are surfacing. Stephen Quayle and Thomas Horn, authors of the book *Unearthing the Lost World of the Cloudeaters,* pose some thought provoking questions.

"The styles of pyramids differ slightly from region to region, but the fact that these structures are so prevalent begs the question: How could so many cultures, separated by time and distance, as well as by physical barriers like bodies of water and vast land distances, all have in mind to build pyramids? This is particularly an interesting question when the old narrative of "ancient peoples" is attributed with their construction. If these so-called ancient people didn't travel, didn't fly, and had never seen other pyramids, how did they know to build a pyramid?"[65]

Quayle and Horn propose that the Great Pyramid has been utilized as a "star gate." In other words, the Great Pyramid is a portal to other dimensions. I know this sounds farfetched, but it might actually be closer to the truth than the theory that the Great Pyramid was a tomb for Khufu.

Allow me to introduce a few concepts related to quantum physics to provide some building blocks of understanding for interdimensional realities. We live in a four-dimensional world: length, height, width, and space-time. But quantum physicists believe that there are more than just the four dimensions we are accustomed to, in fact, string theorists propose that there are ten dimensions. String theory postulates that the basic building block of the quantum world are minute strings of vibrating energy.[66] Phil Mason in *Quantum Glory* describes string theory as follows:

"According to string theory, these strings are extra-dimensional fields of energy which are the building blocks of sub-atomic particles…each string vibrates at a different frequency… String theory is based upon solid mathematical equations…they describe a universe in which as many as six other dimensions exist "curled up" within the four dimensions that we observe at a macroscopic level."[67]

For most people, quantum physics can be difficult to conceptualize, but an allegory written by the 19th century British novelist, Edwin Abbot, provides a way to grasp the quantum world. *Flatland: A Romance in Many Dimensions,* was a two-dimensional world in which there was no up or down. Everything, as you might imagine from the title, was flat. The inhabitants were known as Flatlanders and appeared as two-dimensional shapes such as, triangles, circles, squares, etc. They could not conceive of a three-dimensional figure. One day, a Flatlander was visited by a three dimensional being, a ball. When the ball entered Flatland, it was seen as a dot at first (the point at which the ball first intersected the 2D plane), but then in astonishment, the Flatlander watched as the dot grew in size to a circle, then gradually shrink back to a dot which then disappeared. The Flatlander was overcome by wonder and realized that this object must have come from another dimension. When he tried to awaken the Flatlanders to the existence of three dimensions, this revelation was met by accusations of his insanity.[68]

George Otis Jr. in *Twilight Labryinth,* makes some important observations about quantum physics and the Flatlanders allegory. "Limited by their perspective, lower-dimensional creatures are left to draw conclusions about higher reality from incomplete and transient clues…Higher-dimensional beings, on the other hand, are in a position to observe lower realms in an unhindered and absolute manner. Coupled with their superior perspective is their ability to manipulate virtually at will. The options, which are many, include violating the lower dimension's laws of cause and effect, invading and inhabiting familiar images and intervening in the vulnerable inner lives of its inhabitants."[69]

We might consider for a moment, the Flatland allegory as it relates to UFO sightings. The ball appearing in Flatland was an unexplainable event. If the ball happened to bounce up and down, from a Flatlanders' perspective, the ball would appear, quickly disappear and then reappear in a different location. A Flatlander might label the bouncing ball as a UFO. But to a person who lives in the 3D world, a bouncing ball is an easily explainable occurrence commonly seen where children are at play.

Okham's Razor is a problem-solving principle, established by a 14th century Franciscan monk named William of Okham, used to reach a conclusion when there are competing hypotheses. Essentially, the principle says, the simplest explanation that is consistent with the evidence is usually the best. There is no need to make the explanation complicated by introducing new assumptions.[70] Generally, this principle is helpful, but there are times when it's application actually leads to flawed conclusions. George Otis Jr. points out: "Sometimes the best alternative *is* sensational. UFO landings, for example, offered a more plausible explanation at one time for Britain's mysterious crop circles than an opposing theory that vast herds of hedgehogs had trampled them out. But Okham's Razor is not infallible. Sometimes the principle discounts hypotheses that appear extravagant but are correct nevertheless. Misplaced skepticism in the past, for example, has diverted attention from realities like the true shape of the earth and the role of microorganisms in causing disease. Keeping an open mind, therefore, is something we must learn to do, for while extraordinary claims require extraordinary proof, sometimes the evidence we seek is nestled right under our noses. As Sherlock Holmes observed, 'There is nothing more deceptive than an obvious fact.'"[71]

With regard to the Great Pyramid, the extraordinary precision in the measurements of the monument are obvious facts that its builders understood the dimensions of the earth, engineering, mathematics, and astronomy. The evidence has been there all along, but it has taken centuries to discover. Here is just a sample of the mind-blowing mathematical aspects of the Great Pyramid. The Great Pyramid faces true north with only 3 arc minutes (3/60th of a degree) of error, which represents 0.0015% (less than 1/10th of 1%).[72] The purpose for this exacting precision even from the perspective of structural engineers is difficult to understand. The time consuming and expensive challenge to construct something of this magnitude to that standard of precision is inconceivable because to the naked eye even an error of 1% would not be visible. The placement of the Great Pyramid upon the Giza plateau is astonishingly located in the exact center of the earth's land mass. It is almost perfectly aligned with the 30th parallel at a latitude 29°58'51" which again demonstrates that the ancient architects were keeping their surveying and geodetic skills to the highest possible standard (less than 1% error).[73] Of course we can't forget that the Great Pyramid is an 8-sided pyramid (see Figure 20) only visible by air on the vernal and autumnal equinoxes. This is especially incomprehensible given the ancient Egyptians were not known to have flight capabilities. I could go on and on about the mathematical wonders of the Great Pyramid. I will include one more jaw dropping phenomenon.

Archimedes, in the 3rd century BC, is credited by being the first person to accurately calculate the mathematical value of *pi*, 3.14. However, it is clear that the ancient architects of the Great Pyramid, as well as the Pyramid of the Sun at Teotihuacan, Mexico understood and incorporated the value of *pi* at least 2000 years before Archimedes. Graham Hancock, author of *Fingerprint of the Gods* explains: "Where the Great Pyramid is concerned, the ratio between the original height (481.3949 feet) and the perimeter (3023.16 feet) turns out to be the same as the ratio between the radius and the circumference of a circle, i.e. *2pi*. Thus, if we take the pyramid's height and multiply it by *2pi* … we get an accurate read-out of the monument's perimeter (481.3949 feet x *2pi* = 3023.16 feet). Alternatively, if we turn the equation around and start with the circumference at ground level, we get an equally accurate read-out of the height of the summit (3023.16 feet divided by 2 divided by 3.14 = 481.3949 feet).

Since it is almost inconceivable that such a precise mathematical correlation could have come about by chance, we are obliged to conclude that the builders of the Great Pyramid were indeed conversant with *pi* and that they deliberately incorporated its value into the dimensions of their monument."[74]

Graham goes on to point out that the formulae of *4pi* works on the Pyramid of the Sun in the same way *2pi* works on the Great Pyramid. He extrapolates a potential explanation for the commonalities between these two pyramids separated by such a great distance.

"…the very fact that both structures incorporate *pi* relationships (when none of the other pyramids on either side of the Atlantic does) strongly suggests not only the existence of advanced mathematical knowledge in antiquity but some sort of underlying *common purpose*… What could have been the common purpose that led the pyramid builders on both sides of the Atlantic to such lengths to structure the value of *pi* so precisely into these two remarkable monuments? Since there seems to have been no direct contact between the civilizations of Mexico and Egypt in the periods when the pyramids were built, is it not reasonable to deduce that both, at some remote date, inherited certain ideas from a common source?"[75]

This suggestion of a common source of knowledge is intriguing and one that we will explore further in our investigation.

Finally, of interest to our pursuit, is that many of the earth's pyramids were built in alignment with each other. If we start on the Giza Plateau and follow a geodetic ley-line around the globe between the 35th and 20th parallel north (see Figure 27), we will pass through pyramids located in Teotihuacan, Mexico; Canary Islands, Spain; Ur, Iraq; Giza, Egypt; and Xi'an, China.[76]

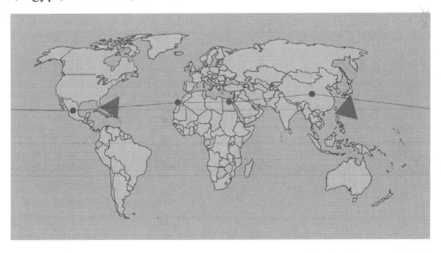

Figure 27. Vintner, J.C. 2018, From an article on Connecting Pyramids with Geographic Mapping, an artist rendition Fg7-10, accessed July 2020 <https://www.mysterypile.com/>

Is the alignment of these pyramids merely a coincidence or were they strategically placed? It would be much easier to say it's a coincidence because to believe otherwise raises even more questions, such as, how would such a feat be coordinated? I believe the answer to this question lies not in the physical realm, but in the spiritual realm.

I imagine this deep dive on the Great Pyramid was an intense chapter to digest. For both our sakes, we need to switch gears a bit, come up for some air, relax and get to know each other better.

Key Points

- Precise measurements of the Great Pyramid defy understanding – oriented to true north, located in exact center of earth's land mass, has eight sides that are only visible by air on the equinoxes, and its mass is related to *pi*.
- Traditional narrative that Khufu built the Great Pyramid cannot be substantiated. Creighton's discovery of Vyse's hoax, Schoch's weathering patterns of the Sphinx and the Inventory Stela all point to the fact that the Great Pyramid was not built by Khufu, instead it originated from an earlier epoch of time.
- Great Pyramid was not used as a tomb – no evidence of any funerary objects nor traces of mummified remains have been found.
- Great Pyramid aligned with other pyramids across the globe suggests it's a high place that acts as a power center along a ley-line forming a spiritual grid.
- It's likely the Great Pyramid has functioned as a portal to other dimensions.

Chapter 5

Let's Talk

Before we go any further on this journey together, I wonder if you and I can spend some time talking. Well to be fair, as the reader, you will spend more time listening while I do the talking, but I think you get what I mean. I realize up until this point, I have been like an investigative tour guide digging into the annals of history to uncover clues that will lead us to understanding the root system that birthed the Federal Reserve. But I would like you to imagine that we just ducked into Pinci Cafe, an inviting cafe in Cairo. Let's place our order, find a table off in the corner, and refuel with great food, refreshing beverages, and good conversation.

Ok now that we can relax a bit, I would like to be more transparent with you. We have traveled together to several countries already, we have even journeyed back several millenniums to ancient times, so I feel this is the opportune time to give you a window into my process.

When I began researching the Federal Reserve, I had no idea where this research would lead me. As I mentioned in the Introduction, I thought I was just going to write a prayer brief. It wasn't until 2017 that I realized investigating the roots of the Federal Reserve was an assignment the Lord had given me.

So why me? I struggled at first with the idea of writing a book like this. It felt like a really daunting task, BUT when we say 'yes' to the Lord, He gives us the grace to accomplish things that are well beyond our current capabilities. As we step out, He increases our capacity. He has definitely expanded my capacity in this process. I have had numerous people over the years encourage me to write a book, not because of my profound knowledge of the economy (wink, wink), but because at heart, I am a storyteller. I envisioned my first book to be a biography of my grandmother's life. She had such a rich, intimate relationship with Jesus which manifested into power encounters, miracles, and salvation for many who interacted with her. Her relationship with Jesus was contagious!! A tribute to her life, would have been a much easier book to write.

I refer to writing this book as an "assignment" because it's the language the Holy Spirit uses with me. As a result of reading *Now, Discover Your Strengths* by M. Buckingham and D. Clifton, I have discovered that one of my top strengths is Learner. My husband, Tom, used to tease me that I would become a professional student. As challenging as graduate school was, I thoroughly enjoyed it. I had thoughts of pursuing a post-Doctorate degree, as if a Ph.D. in Clinical Psychology and a M.A. in Theology wasn't enough. Thankfully, my husband helped me recognize that we didn't need to incur any further debt just because I love to learn. So, I found other ways to feed the learner in me. As a student, I was an obsessive note taker and did everything "by the book," no pun intended. You see, I am not one of those brilliant students that can soak in the material and perform well on tests. I had to work hard at getting good grades, which meant I did all the assignments and didn't try to cut any corners in the learning process. This has become my modus operandi with any assignment I am working on.

I am the type of intercessor that receives assignments from the Lord. When He gives me an assignment, I am wired as a learner to wholeheartedly give myself to what's on His heart and mind. I want to be obedient and faithful with what He's given me. But I want you to know, that right here, right now, in Chapter 5 of this journey, I am unsure where it will take us. The Holy Spirit is only revealing bits and pieces at a time, probably because he knows me all too well. If I saw the full scope of this assignment, I may have said "no thank you, can I have an easier assignment?" But He has shown me that the act of researching and writing is a new form of spiritual warfare. So, I press on with renewed focus and determination, enlisting with thousands of warriors in His Kingdom, to wage war against this creature called the Federal Reserve.

Jesus came so that we may have life abundantly, not a life of enslavement. He wants to set the captives free. So here is my question for you, do you want to continue to join me on this adventurous journey through time and space? It may mean that we are led to the precipice of a few paradigm shifts. My hope is that at the end of our travels together, we will have experienced revelatory truth because we have called upon the Lord to reveal secrets unknown until now.

Jeremiah 33:3 (AMP) *"Call to Me and I will answer you, and tell you [and even show you] great and mighty things, [things which have been confined and hidden], which you do not know and understand and cannot distinguish."*

Personally, I can sense that a paradigm shift is brewing within me and this may be true for you as well. Opening up to a shift in paradigm takes courage and depending on the paradigm, may require some foundational work. People are often hesitant to shift paradigms. Honestly, it can be scary. If how we navigate through life is built upon a foundation of thoughts, experiences, perceptions, and ideologies, when those are shaken, life suddenly feels unsettled. A predominant emotion triggered during this shaking is fear—fear of the unknown, fear of losing control, fear of being wrong. We know our human nature is to avoid fear. Who really enjoys being afraid? So, it's understandable why paradigm shifts are frequently resisted. I think we would be remiss if we didn't acknowledge how much work it takes to allow for a paradigm shift. It requires rethinking ideologies/theologies, recategorizing experiences, and reformulating thoughts. With our fast paced 21st century lives, very few people are willing to engage in this level of effort to allow the shift to occur. But then again, there are those times in life when we don't really have a choice whether we switch paradigms. A new paradigm is thrust upon us that we can't avoid nor deny.

When our youngest son, Zachariah, at 10 months old was diagnosed with kidney failure and failure to thrive, I realized I didn't have a paradigm in my theology for suffering. A simplified description of what I believed is that I and my family are blessed when we walk with God. The Father is good, and He won't allow REALLY bad things to happen to us. While it's true that He is an exceedingly good Father and that we are blessed when we walk in His ways, this doesn't capture the full picture. He never promised a life without sickness, disease, loss, or hardship, but He has promised to never leave us nor abandon us in the midst of our suffering. Life with Jesus is not a guarantee that we will live a life free from hardship. But somehow in the foundation of my faith, I had come to believe this was true. The crisis of kidney failure caused a tremendous shaking in my life. My old paradigm came crashing down. For a while, I was without a new paradigm. I was confused and broken. But brick by brick, the Lord helped me build a new foundation by receiving a paradigm for suffering. One of my favorite quotes is from Charles Spurgeon: "The deep things of life in God are discovered in suffering. If we hold fast to him when all around our soul gives way, then we show that He is more to be desired than all we have lost."

As painful as that season of our lives was, I am grateful that He rebuilt my foundation. In doing so, He expanded my capacity to contend for supernatural healing, to be patient for natural healing, to remain hopeful in the midst of suffering, and to live a life of gratitude for every moment we have together. I would not have been courageous enough to intentionally choose this paradigm shift, but the growth and life that came from it is priceless.

Other times in my life, I have experienced a paradigm shift as a result of a Holy Spirit set-up. Let me explain what I mean…

In 1993, while attending Fuller Theological Seminary, I signed up for a course called "Power Encounter." I was drawn to this course because of an experience I had in 1991, during my first year of graduate school. I was enrolled in a class within the World Missions department taught by Dr. Charles Kraft. As a first-year student, I was an obsessive note taker and as a result, developed carpal tunnel syndrome. It progressively worsened during the year and a doctor said if it didn't improve with the use of a brace, then surgery was my only other option. One day in class, Dr. Kraft noticed I had a brace on my wrist. He asked if he could pray for me during the break. I was a bit stunned by his offer because my only paradigm for student-professor interaction was from U.C. San Diego. I never had a professor demonstrate any care or concern for me before. I accepted his offer to pray for me and remarkably, I was healed.

I no longer needed a brace and I could continue my obsessive note taking pain-free. As you can imagine, this made quite an impact on me. It was the first time I had ever been miraculously healed. Given this experience, I was determined to take whatever courses Dr. Kraft offered that would fit within my degree requirements. This is how I ended up taking the course "Power Encounter," which turns out, was aptly named.

As I have mentioned, I am an obedient student. I don't look for shortcuts in assignments. The course requirements for "Power Encounter" included attending a total of three ministry sessions held two hours before each class. Naturally, I attended the first ministry session offered. In the span of those two hours, I witnessed a power encounter I had absolutely no paradigm for. One of the students being prayed for, manifested a demonic spirit, called a 'spirit of death.' For teaching purposes, Dr. Kraft interviewed this spirit. It was speaking through the student, but its voice was different than the student's normal voice. His eyes changed when this spirit was manifesting. I'm sure my eyes were the size of flying saucers as I was taking in this experience. Up until that moment, my only understanding of the spiritual realm was from reading Frank

Peretti's book *This Present Darkness*. I would casually acknowledge the existence of angels and demons, but I was certain demons only harassed Satan worshipers or atheists. I had no paradigm for demons oppressing Christians. The entry point for this spirit was through the student's involvement in DeMolay when he was a teenager. DeMolay is a Freemasonry organization for young men. After seeing my fellow student, who was a follower of Jesus, be set free from a spirit of death, I realized I needed a paradigm for all this. Thankfully, Dr. Kraft laid out clearly the biblical principles that allowed me to grab ahold of a biblical paradigm for the spiritual realm and spiritual warfare.

During this season of my life, I was really struggling with fear, specifically a "fear of death." I had developed this fear at the age of six when I attended my great grandmother's open casket funeral. It scared me to see her lying dead in a casket. I still get the hibbie jibbies attending open casket funerals. For the most part, this fear laid dormant until I moved to the Greater Los Angeles area for graduate school. Los Angeles news stations regularly reported shootings, stabbings, car jackings, rapes, murders etc. During my first year of graduate school, I lived in a town called Altadena located adjacent to Pasadena. I lived a block from Farnsworth Park, which was a large park where Tom and I would play tennis and volleyball. One day while studying at home, I heard gunshots. It turns out, a young man was shot at Farnsworth Park. Every time I left my house, I had to drive past the blood stains on the road. This really frightened me. From that moment on, the fear of death rapidly intensified to the point of nearly being debilitating. The crime in Los Angeles was a constant trigger, especially helicopters flying overhead. These helicopters weren't giving tourists a scenic ride, these were police helicopters looking for criminals. To make matters worse, Rodney King was living in Altadena when he was pulled over by the LAPD and excessively beaten. Rodney King was an African-American man and the LAPD officers were Caucasians. The beating was caught on video and sparked racial riots. It was a terrifying time. Angry mobs were setting fires to businesses, cars, and homes. I could look across the valley and see fires dotting the landscape. The routes I would take to get around Pasadena where no longer safe. People were getting dragged out of their cars and beaten. I had to be evacuated during a midterm exam at Fuller Seminary because the riots were only a few blocks away. Tom and I were also evacuated from a furniture store in an upscale neighborhood. It felt like no place was safe! It was a violent time to be living in the Los Angeles area which exacerbated the "fear of death" in me. I began having frequent daymares that would practically paralyze me in fear. I would see vivid images of myself being brutally attacked. It was horrible! I didn't know how to shake it.

This is when the Holy Spirit set me up. He had a path to freedom laid out for me in the "Power Encounter" class that I was not aware of. After the experience in the first ministry session, I told myself, I could never volunteer to be prayed for like that other student did. It was way too vulnerable for me to consider doing something like that. So, at the start of the second ministry session, Dr. Kraft asked students to raise their hands if they would like to be prayed for. I had just finished telling myself, "there's no way I am raising my hand," when my hand went up! It was as if my arm and hand were not responding to the signals my brain was clearly sending to NOT RAISE YOUR HAND! I was one of four students selected to receive prayer. In the midst of this prayer time, the power of the Holy Spirit drove out the spirit of the fear of death. The power that's in the name of Jesus, broke the hold that this spirit had on me. I was delivered from the bondage and if that wasn't wonderful enough, the Lord also miraculously healed my heart. I got a two for one that night! I had a heart murmur which had been diagnosed when I was very young. This diagnosis was confirmed every time I had an appointment with a new doctor. During the prayer time in class, I could feel something happening with my heart. I was healed and not one doctor since 1993 has detected a heart murmur! Praise God!! I am so grateful for the power of Jesus' blood, the power in His name, and the power of His resurrection.

The struggle with a spirit of the fear of death was not my only battle with fear. I was plagued with a fear of rejection and a fear of failure. I developed these bondages around the age of 12 through experiences I had in competitive figure skating. I tried to manage this fear by becoming an overachiever. I made an inner vow when I was 12 to never fail, so I could avoid being rejected. This plan worked for a while, but it was exhausting! Little did I realize, the Lord had a better plan for me.

Jeremiah 29:11(NIV) *"For I know the plans I have for you,' declares the Lord, 'plans to prosper you and not to harm you, plans to give you hope and a future."*

In His loving kindness, He paved the way for my freedom.

Galatians 5:1 (GWT) *"Christ has freed us so that we may enjoy the benefits of freedom"*

In the midst of the same prayer ministry in the "Power Encounter" course, I was set free from the spirits of fear of failure and fear of rejection. In a matter of two hours, the power of God knocked the power of fear of death, fear of failure and fear of rejection out of my life. Those stinkin' spirits oppressed me for more than a decade, but that glorious night I was set free. And I have never been the same, HALLELUJAH!!

I share these stories with you to give you a window into how paradigm shifts have occurred in my life. Perhaps these real-life examples will help you embrace a paradigm shift the next time it happens. Over the years, the Lord has had to adjust my paradigms numerous times. It's been helpful for me, as He stretches me and molds me, to remind myself of His words in Isaiah:

Isaiah 55:8-9 (NIV) "*For my thoughts are not your thoughts, neither are your ways my ways' declares the Lord. 'As the heavens are higher than the earth, so are my ways higher than your ways and my thoughts than your thoughts.*"

I would much rather have the mind of Christ than be stubborn in my ways, dig my heels in, and insist on being right. I have experienced so many paradigm shifts that I am able to sense when one is occurring. My process of change generally incorporates the following steps:

1. I refute or reject a new thought/concept/ideology/theology because it is foreign to my tradition, culture, or personal experience.
2. I am flooded with reminders (or what would seem like strange coincidences) of this new thought/concept/ideology/theology over a period of time.
3. I am compelled to research the subject matter because the flooding of reminders and examples becomes ridiculously obvious that the Lord is trying to get my attention.
4. When I am able to vet the thought/concept/ideology/theology using several streams of resources that are not interconnected, I begin to open to the notion that the subject matter may be legitimate.
5. I ponder the ramifications of the paradigm shift and begin to reorganize concepts and perceptions within my schema.
6. I start learning as much as I can about the subject matter so that I can apply it in my life.
7. I intentionally make application of the new paradigm in my life until it becomes a natural expression.*

*When I am thrust into a paradigm shift, my process of change is not as orderly as these 7 steps. In fact, things are rather in an upheaval and I am grasping for anything that feels solid, praying I make it through the paradigm shift without a crash and burn situation.

My personal assessment is that I am between step 3 and 4 right now (you can probably see the psychologist in me surfacing). This assignment of writing about the roots of the Federal Reserve is feeling more and more like a Holy Spirit set-up. I have learned through life experiences walking with the Holy Spirit that He always has my best in mind. It has been my desire to develop a sensitivity to His Presence and His leading. In this journey of writing, it has been no different. I realized from the outset that I have to follow the Holy Spirit's lead. He is uncovering things that have been hidden in darkness and if I relied on my own intuition to find these things, we would still be on Jekyll Island.

I had no intention of writing about megalithic civilizations and certainly no idea I was going to write about the Great Pyramid. When the Holy Spirit first nudged me in this direction, I resisted it. My first thought was "are you kidding me? I know very little about the Great Pyramid and there is such a voluminous collection of books on the Great Pyramid, why would you want me to dive into that?" But His nudging became undeniable, so I began researching and writing about the Great Pyramid 9 months ago. Ugh! Nine months to write one chapter, I never would have gotten through graduate school at this pace. But I keep telling myself "trust and obey for there is no other way." I have to be faithful to follow his nudging even though, right now as I write, I don't know where it's going to lead. I may have just wasted nine months of my life... but I don't think so. I have a strong sense that the Holy Spirit is going to tie it all together. I know deep down that the roots of the Federal Reserve are linked to the mysteries of the Great Pyramid. So, I guess we'll discover together how it all ties together. It's our grand adventure.

A few minutes ago, I mentioned that I can feel a paradigm shift brewing in me. In the research for this book, there have been theories I have come across that I deemed too far beyond the realm of logical reasoning to even consider. The existence of extra-terrestrial beings and UFOs is one such theory. I am a product of being raised with the socially accepted narratives regarding UFOs and extraterrestrial beings. The script for this narrative goes a little bit like this, "people who have seen UFOs are either hallucinating or are attention seeking hoaxsters." Prior to accepting this writing assignment, I never considered examining the body of evidence that refutes the socially accepted narrative. Why bother, right? However, now that I am on this journey of discovering what is hidden in darkness, I have been digging into numerous resources, uncovering treasures hidden in the sands of time and in doing so, it seems that more evidence is pointing towards the possibility that there may actually be extraterrestrial beings than is supporting the socially accepted narrative. As I have been uncovering this evidence, I have been telling myself, "there is no way I am going to include this in my very first book. I would be crazy to do so! I'll be branded as one of THOSE people!" But therein lies my struggle... do I fear man or do I fear God? If the Holy Spirit keeps leading me down a path of collecting stories, documentaries, and eye-witness accounts that suggest that extraterrestrial beings are real, it feels a bit like another Holy Spirit set up.

Now before you completely dismiss me, hear me out for a bit. Extraterrestrial beings can be defined as, living beings outside of the four dimensions of our natural world. It really isn't that big of a stretch to recognize that in other dimensions there could be other beings/entities. After all, Ephesians 6 tells us so.

Ephesians 6:12 (NLT) *"For we are not fighting against flesh-and-blood enemies, but against evil rulers and authorities of the unseen world, against mighty powers in this dark world, and against evil spirits in the heavenly places."*

Even without conducting an exegetical analysis of this passage, we can see that Paul is trying to open our eyes to the reality that there are beings or entities in a realm that we are not able to see with our natural eyes. This is what he means by the "unseen world." It is unseen to our natural eyes, but just because we can't see it, doesn't make it any less real than what we can see. There are times when these beings enter our natural four-dimensional world allowing us to see them with our natural eyes.

My grandmother had several encounters with angels in her lifetime. One time she found herself lost on a rural road in Illinois when her tire went flat on her car (this was long before the conveniences of mobile devices). She prayed asking the Lord to send her someone who could help. Moments after she prayed, two gentlemen in nice suits and ties, walked up and asked if they could help. Mind you, there was no one in sight for miles, and absolutely no cars around. But here were these kind, young, handsome gentlemen ready to help change her tire. After they finished the dirty task, she turned around to thank them, but they had vanished. It was at that moment she realized the Lord had sent her two angels to help her in her time of need.

Thanks to the paradigm shift I experienced during graduate school, I now realize that spiritual beings are real. I have also come to understand that the spiritual realm is, in fact, more real than the physical realm. I took the red pill. I'm a truth seeker. There's a larger reality that exists and that reality is that Yahweh, The Great I Am, the King of all kings, is on His throne. The Creator of the universe, the Almighty Elohim, He's the one that orchestrates everything. I now recognize that there are demons, angels and other spiritual beings that exist in other dimensions. In my mind it's not that huge of a leap to consider there may be other physical beings that either come from outer realms of our galaxy or neighboring galaxies or travel into our four-dimensional world from dimensions beyond.

Let me tell you about a dream I had...

Key Points

- The spiritual realm is real, it exists beyond our four-dimensional physical realm.
- Within the spiritual realm exist angels, demons, and other beings.
- The power in Jesus' name gives us victory over any spiritual force of darkness.

Chapter 6

Titus Dominion

One of the ways the Lord speaks to me is through dreams. There are times when a dream strikes me as particularly weighty in importance. Typically, I don't understand why the dream is significant at first, but then the Holy Spirit will unfold further revelation and understanding.

In the dream, I was in the hospital just after giving birth to a baby boy. It was an unexpected pregnancy which caught my husband and I by surprise. We had not prepared at all for the birth of this child. We did not have a name picked out. We chose the name Dominion, but when I looked at the baby in my arms, I couldn't imagine calling him Dominion. So, Tom and I decided to come up with another name. I asked him if he wanted to name the baby Titus (Tom has always wanted a son named Titus). He said "yes" with a big smile. I said, "how about Titus Dominion"? We both agreed on this name.

I went to the nurses' station to ask if I could change the name and they said "yes, people frequently do." The nurse was fine with the name Titus but really questioned us about keeping the name Dominion. She said, "are you sure you want the name Dominion?" So, Tom and I thought about it and talked a bit more. I shared with him that Dominion represents the authority we walk in as believers, because Jesus has dominion over all things and has given that dominion to us. The nurse still questioned us about the name Dominion and suggested we take some more time to think about it. Tom was starting to get frustrated with the nurse because she was overstepping her bounds. She didn't have a say in the name we chose for our child. I could understand her hesitation because the word dominion can have a negative connotation. Tom and I decided to honor her request, in case it was the Lord telling us to rethink the name. So, we went back into our hospital room to talk. I shared with him that a few days ago I was reading a scripture that used the word dominion, but I couldn't remember the scripture. I felt that the Holy

Spirit was leading us to keep the name Titus Dominion despite some negative connotations. We both felt that this name was important to the destiny of our child…

When I awoke from this dream, I said "dominion, dominion, dominion," repeating it three times then fell back asleep into a continuation of the dream. The 2nd part of the dream has more personal application, so it is not relevant here. As I mentioned earlier, I could tell that this dream was weighty and had the potential of shifting my paradigm, so I set out to gain revelation and understanding.

The name 'Titus' means pleasing; or nurse. In the Greek and Latin, the etymology of the name 'Titus' is associated with the Titans or giants. When I discovered this, it stopped me in my tracks. I suddenly began to see the significance of this dream. I had just finished reading Ron Chernow's book *Titan: The Life of John D. Rockefeller.* I had also just finished watching a documentary *The Men Who Built America.* In this documentary, Alan Greenspan refers to John D. Rockefeller, Andrew Carnegie, J.P. Morgan and Thomas Edison as "Titans." I believe the Lord gave me this dream because it's time we, as the Body of Christ, step into a new identity, one that walks in dominion over the Titans. We are being called to come up to a new level of authority, an authority that has been there all along, but so many of us have not understood our rightful place in the Kingdom of God.

Many of you will agree, the Holy Spirit has a good sense of humor. For several weeks following this dream, I started seeing the words 'dominion' and 'titan' all over the place. For example, my oldest son switched schools and guess what his new mascot is? The Titans! One day, I noticed a large truck driving slowly down our street, the logo on the truck said, "Old Dominion." Our regional gas company changed its name from Questar Gas to Dominion Energy. With increasing frequency, I found myself driving next to or behind a Nissan Titan truck. After about a month of being inundated with reminders from the Holy Spirit of Titus Dominion, I just had to laugh, because the Lord has such a good sense of humor. It reminded me of Evan, in the movie "Evan Almighty," when he would see the numbers 6:14 over and over again until he couldn't escape it, and finally accepted the assignment God gave him to build an ark.

Just today after I finished writing this paragraph, the Holy Spirit had some fun with me. I was on my way to the grocery store and a van passed me in the next lane, it was a company vehicle for Titan Air and Heating. We've explored what Titan means, but what about dominion.

The Dominion Mandate

The first mention of 'dominion' in the Bible is Genesis 1:26.

Genesis 1:26 (NKJV) *"Then God said, 'Let us make man in Our image, according to Our Likeness; let them have dominion over the fish of the sea, over the birds of the air, and over the cattle, over all the earth and over every creeping thing that creeps on the earth."*

The two main points of decision in this divine council meeting were: 1) humankind would be created in the image of God, and 2) humankind would have dominion over the rest of creation. This defines who we are and what our purpose is. We are image bearers. We have the likeness of God in us. We are His representatives on earth. Our purpose as image bearers is to have dominion over all of creation. We are to be stewards over every living part of creation including the earth itself.

Genesis 1:28 records the first instructions God gave to humankind; be fruitful and multiply, and have dominion over creation.

Genesis 1:28 (NKJV) *"Then God blessed them, and God said to them, 'Be fruitful and multiply; fill the earth and subdue it; have dominion over the fish of the sea, over the birds of the air, and over every living thing that moves on the earth."*

God was explaining to Adam and Eve that the first step in walking in dominion authority over all of creation was to be fruitful and multiply. If Adam and Eve weren't obedient with this first command, what is known as the *family mandate*, they would have been unable to accomplish the assignment of having dominion over all of creation.

God established the *dominion mandate* as a principal of great importance. This mandate was to be the hallmark of humanity. But why was this such an important principle to God? In order to answer this question, let's look at the meaning of the Hebrew word for dominion, *'radah.'* It means "to rule, have dominion, dominate, tread down, prevail against."[77] This definition suggests that we will face foes or entities that will resist us as governors. We will need to tread down and prevail against these foes. In order for creation to flourish with abundant life and become heaven on earth as Eden was, it will need to be governed according to the principles of the Almighty God.

God constituted His government on earth and chose us, His image bearers, His representatives, to govern creation, not according to our plans but according to His purposes. He gave Adam and Eve the authority to govern His creation effectively. But before Adam and Eve could give their inaugural speech, a foe showed up on the scene. This cunning creature was seething with hatred and jealousy because he once held high levels of authority. In the heavenly realms, Lucifer once had great power and great authority. He was a beautiful, magnificent spiritual being who became enamored with his own glory. He sought to outshine the glory of the Holy One.

Isaiah 14:13-14 (NIV) *"You said in your heart, 'I will ascend to the heavens; I will raise my throne above the stars of God; I will sit enthroned on the mount of assembly, on the utmost heights of Mount Zaphon. I will ascend above the tops of the clouds; I will make myself like the Most High."*

His punishment for this was being cast out of heaven and stripped of his authority.

Isaiah 14:12 (NIV) *"How you have fallen from heaven, morning star, son of the dawn! You have been cast down to the earth, you who once laid low the nations!"*

Luke 10:18 (NKJV) *"And He said to them, 'I saw Satan fall like lightning from heaven."*

While Satan lost his authority, he still maintained a level of power.

When God established Adam and Eve as his first governors of planet earth, he did so under the existence of free will. Adam and Eve were free to choose what to do with this authority. Creator God was taking a great risk in giving humanity free will, but the alternative would have been unbearable. Being a witness to creation, the foe developed a plan to usurp the dominion authority given to Adam and Eve. He connived a devious plot to trick earth's first governors into thinking they could become even more powerful and wise by eating the fruit from the "forbidden tree." They walked right into the trap. Their hunger for power was greater than their desire for obedience and fear of the Lord. Tragically, they relinquished their God-given dominion authority to the enemy of us all, Satan. Not only that, Adam and Eve placed all of humanity under the dominion of Satan. John 14:30 reminds us of this by describing Satan as "ruler of this world."

Ephesians 2:2 (NKJV) *"in which you once walked according to the course of this world, according to the **prince of the power of the air**, the spirit who now works in the sons of disobedience."*

The dominion mandate was not the only directive destroyed that day.

The Family Mandate

The family mandate was given to Adam and Eve shortly after their creation when the Lord told them to be fruitful and multiply. Before the fall, Adam and Eve could have reproduced eternal beings because they themselves were eternal beings comprised of body, soul, and spirit. Creator God planted a garden in the East, the Garden of Eden. It was the place of His Presence and Glory on earth and was established as the home for Adam and Eve. In it, God planted trees that provided good and pleasing food. In the center of the garden were two trees, the Tree of Life and the Tree of the Knowledge of Good and Evil. Adam and Eve were free to eat of any of the trees, but the Father made it clear to never eat from the Tree of the Knowledge of Good and Evil because it would not be to their benefit. It's a bit like a parent telling a child, don't ever drink bleach because you will die from it. The Father lovingly created the most beautiful garden for them all to live in. They enjoyed walking and talking together in the cool of the day, that is until Satan launched his attack.

Up until that time, Adam and Eve were wholly content, living in peace and harmony with the heavenly Father in the most beautiful place on earth. There was no hint of dissatisfaction. They had absolutely everything they could possibly need or want. They were well taken care of and greatly loved. Satan, a spectator in all this, was seething with jealousy at this symbiotic relationship between the Father and His kids (2 Corinthians 6:18). He devised a plan so wicked; it could only be thought of by someone of his lowly stature. He introduced dissatisfaction in the Father's love and planted seeds of doubt that the Father had their best interest in mind when He instructed them not to partake of the fruit from the Tree of the Knowledge of Good and Evil.

Satan convinced Eve that by prohibiting them to eat of its fruit, the Father was keeping them from obtaining the ultimate wisdom and knowledge that would make them godlike. In the pages that follow, we will circle back to this "pride of life" strategy (I John 2:16) that Satan employs to lure people into the occult. The "pride of life" is a primary component in the seedbed of the Federal Reserve, we will explore this more in upcoming chapters. Tragically, Eve fell right into the trap and talked Adam into doing the same. That was the moment their spirits died.

Yahweh's original plan was that Adam and Eve would be fruitful in procreating and populate the earth with eternal beings who would enjoy a close relationship with Himself, but when Adam and Eve introduced sin into their relationship with the Father, it changed everything! Prior to sin, their relationship was one of intimate communication and oneness, but by the very nature of God's holiness, it precludes sin from being in His Presence. Sin introduced a barrier between the Father and His children. The family mandate was damaged by the consequences of sin. Adam and Eve had to be removed from the Garden of Eden. They could never eat from the Tree of Life (which was intended for them to enjoy and the fruits of which provided eternal life). Their sin nature could not be eternally perpetuated as it would have caused an eternal separation from God—an unbearable possibility for the Father!

The repercussions of the original sin reverberated throughout creation. Adam and Eve had to be evicted from paradise on earth, the place where God dwelt. There was a barrier now in their relationship with the Father. They were no longer able to enjoy the same level of intimacy with the Father they had known prior to that fateful bite. The separation was excruciatingly painful, for both humanity and the Father. The family mandate was in jeopardy. Something had to be done to restore what had been lost.

Restoration of Both Mandates

Thankfully, God already had a grand rescue plan to recover what was lost that fateful day in the Garden of Eden. This plan involved sending His Son, Jesus, with a twofold purpose: to restore the family mandate and restore the dominion mandate.

I Peter 1:20 (NLT) *"God chose him as your ransom long before the world began, but now in these last days he has been revealed for your sake."*

This passage reveals the omniscient nature of Yahweh. We can see that God had foreknowledge that Adam and Eve would mess things up. Jesus, the second Adam, would be sent to restore what the first Adam squandered.

Family Mandate Restored

The first phase of Yahweh's plan was to send His prophets to speak to His children about the state of their hearts and urge them to turn back to the One who loved them unconditionally. The Father longed for the restoration of relationship with His kids. So, He was persistent and sent prophet after prophet for hundreds of years to decree a new covenant, but His children had a strong rebellious streak in them. If they didn't like what the prophets were telling them (which was most of the time), they would kill the prophets.

The final phase of the rescue plan involved the Father sending His only Son. God knew they would kill him too, but unlike the death of the prophets, the death of Jesus would provide a way back into intimate relationship with the Father. While the prophets held an important role as God's messengers, they weren't capable of becoming the ultimate sacrifice for sin, because they themselves were born of a sinful nature. The Father's restoration plan had to involve a resuscitation of the human spirit. Humanity was in need of being born again because our spirits were dead as a result of sin.

Colossians 2:13-14 (NLT) *"You were dead because of your sins and because your sinful nature was not yet cut away. Then God made you alive with Christ, for he forgave all our sins. He canceled the record of the charges against us and took it away by nailing it to the cross."*

God's restoration plan was grounded in love. His deep longing to reconnect with His children provided a way for our spirits to be made alive in Christ.

John 3:3-7 (NLT) *"Jesus replied, 'I tell you the truth, unless you are born again, you cannot see the Kingdom of God.' 'What do you mean?' exclaimed Nicodemus. 'How can an old man go back into his mother's womb and be born again?' Jesus replied, 'I assure you, no one can enter the Kingdom of God without being born of water and the Spirit. Humans can reproduce only human life, but the Holy Spirit gives birth to spiritual life."*

Jesus became the bridge between the sinful nature of humanity and the holy nature of Yahweh. Jesus became the once and for all Passover Lamb, the ultimate sacrifice, whose blood offers us forgiveness. Through the righteousness of Jesus, we can once again approach the Father. Jesus brought restoration to God's family. As His kids, we can now approach the Father without hesitation. A symbiotic relationship is available again for all His children, which encapsulates all of humanity. But the only way back into communion with the Father is through Jesus.

John 14:6 (NIV) *"Jesus answered, 'I am the way and the truth and the life. No one comes to the Father except through me."*

The great news is that not one person is excluded from this opportunity. It is a love gift to humanity from both the Father and the Son. They want us back at the family table for meals no matter how far we have strayed. A place setting with our name on it awaits us. All are welcome at the table! Come, eat and drink at the Father's table.

The family mandate, "be fruitful and multiply," was restored through Jesus. We now have the responsibility, as sons and daughters of God, to not only reproduce earthly offspring but also spiritual offspring.

Mark 16:15-18 (NIV) *"He said to them, 'Go into all the world and preach the gospel to all creation. Whoever believes and is baptized will be saved, but whoever does not believe will be condemned. And these signs will accompany those who believe: In my name they will drive out demons; they will speak in new tongues; they will pick up snakes with their hands; and when they drink deadly poison, it will not hurt them at all; they will place their hands on sick people, and they will get well."*

This is known as the Great Commission. Mark's version of the Great Commission lays out for us our family mandate. The emphasis is on the individual person, it's about rescuing people from their terminal condition of sin which has rendered their spirits dead. It's about restoring the individual to wholeness. This is what C. Peter Wagner refers to as the "pastoral dimension" of the rescue plan. Many theologians consider this dimension of the Great Commission to be the primary reason Jesus came, but we have to remember, God's rescue plan was dual purposed, not only was there a "pastoral dimension" but there was also an "apostolic dimension."[78]

Dominion Mandate Restored

The "apostolic dimension" is about God's kingdom being established within us so that we can exercise dominion authority on the earth and reconcile the world back to God.

Colossians 2:9-10, 15 (NIV) *"For in Christ all the fullness of the Deity lives in bodily form, and in Christ you have been brought to fullness. He is the head over every power and authority. And having disarmed the powers and authorities, he made a public spectacle of them, triumphing over them by the cross."*

Let's consider this for a moment… Jesus is head over every power and authority.

Isaiah 9:6 (NIV) *"For to us a child is born, to us a son is given, and the government will be on his shoulders. And he will be called Wonderful Counselor, Mighty God, Everlasting Father, Prince of Peace."*

This means that Jesus is head over the Federal Reserve, over the State Department, the Department of Justice, the National Security Agency, the Supreme Court and every other agency that has authority in our land. Not only that, He has given us authority.

Let's examine this more closely. The curse uttered from the Righteous Judge in the Garden of Eden was embedded in Satan's memory.

Genesis 3:14-15 (The Message) *"God told the serpent: 'Because you've done this, you're cursed, cursed beyond all cattle and wild animals, cursed to slink on your belly and eat dirt all your life.* **I'm declaring war between you and the Woman, between your offspring and hers. He'll wound your head, you'll wound his heel.***"* (emphasis mine)

A declaration of war was made between the offspring of woman and the offspring of the serpent. Eve's seed would one day crush Satan. When this curse was spoken, there was no reversing it, but the foe established firewalls of protection in an attempt to thwart God's rescue plan. His strategy for take down has essentially been the same since the Garden of Eden (he's not very creative). He looks to tempt God's children with the means to gain godlike wisdom and knowledge, and establish doubt in the Father's love.

Since the time the curse was rendered, Satan has tried to usurp God's purposes and extinguish God's people to prevent the crushing of his head, BUT Satan is no match for God. Satan panicked when Jesus was born. He quickly stirred up jealousy within Herod and devised a wicked plot. A death decree was issued by Herod to slaughter all the boys under the age of two in the region of Bethlehem. When that didn't work to extinguish Jesus' life, Satan tried the age-old strategy of tempting Jesus to sin.

In order to reclaim the dominion authority for which Adam handed over to Satan, Jesus, the second Adam, had to face the accuser and every temptation known to humanity.

I John 2:16 (NKJV) *"For all that is in the world – the lust of the flesh, the lust of the eyes, and the pride of life – is not of the Father but is of the world."*

I John 2:16 (TPT) *"For all that the world can offer us – the gratification of our flesh, the allurement of the things of the world, and the obsession with status and importance – none of these things come from the Father but from the world."*

Eve was faced with these same temptations.

Genesis 3:6 (AMP) *"And when the woman saw that the tree was good for food* [**lust of the flesh**], *and that it was delightful to look at* [**lust of the eyes**], *and a tree to be desired in order to make one wise and insightful* [**pride of life**], *she took some of its fruit and ate it; and she also gave some to her husband with her, and he ate."* (emphasis mine)

As Jesus headed into the wilderness, it was paramount that He overcome the temptations that caused Adam and Eve to stumble into sin. If He gave in to temptation, **ALL** would be lost. The temptations Jesus faced came at the weakest point in His life. Jesus had been in the wilderness for 40 days without food. Yes, He was God, but He was also fully human. The level of hunger Jesus experienced in the desert was unlike anything He had ever experienced. Satan's first attack was to strike Him where He was vulnerable, with the lust of the flesh.

Matthew 4:3 (NIV) *"The tempter came to him and said, 'If you are the Son of God, tell these stones to become bread."*

Satan's strategy was to create doubt within Jesus that God would take care of Him. If the Father knew Jesus was so hungry and on the verge of starvation, why wasn't He providing nourishment for His Son? "Jesus, if you are truly the Son of God, it is within your power to take care of yourself, go ahead, turn that stone into bread," Satan enticed. Jesus responded with a declaration of His complete faith and dependence upon the Father to provide for His needs.

Matthew 4:4 (NIV) *"Jesus answered, 'It is written: 'Man shall not live on bread alone, but on every word that comes from the mouth of God."*

Jesus was unwavering in His faith in God's goodness as provider. In the second temptation, Satan attempted to trap Jesus in the pride of life.

Matthew 4:5-6 (NIV) *"Then the devil took him to the holy city and had him stand on the highest point of the temple. 'If you are the Son of God,' he said, 'throw yourself down. For it is written: 'He will command his angels concerning you, and they will lift you up in their hands, so that you will not strike your foot against a stone."*

Satan was trying to entrap Jesus to prove His divinity by forcing the angels to rescue Him if He were to jump from the temple. Let's imagine for a moment that Jesus leapt from the tallest point of the temple and angels came and scooped Him up before He hit the ground below. This would have created quite a spectacle and drawn attention, wonder, and glory to Himself. It's important to note that this would have been performing the miraculous apart from the glory of God. This is the essence of the pride of life – to make a name for yourself, to place yourself in position above others, and to draw the recognition of others in a boastful, prideful way. Instead, Matthew 4 says,

Matthew 4:7 (NIV) "*Jesus answered him, 'It is also written; 'Do not put the Lord your God to the test.'*

In the third temptation, Satan took Jesus to the peak of a very tall mountain. It was from this vantage point that Satan offered to Jesus **all** the kingdoms of the world, if Jesus would bow down and worship him. The vantage point Jesus had looking at all the kingdoms of the world must have been quite a sight to behold. This temptation was the lust of the eyes, that sinful desire to have everything you find pleasing to the eye. I often experience this temptation when I go to the mall. Our eye gate can be easily enticed, and advertisers know this all too well. Jesus' response to this temptation:

Matthew 4:9-10 (NIV) "*All this I will give you,' he said, 'if you will bow down and worship me.' Jesus said to him, 'Away from me, Satan! For it is written: 'Worship the Lord your God, and serve Him only.'*"

If you notice Jesus' response to Satan, He did not refute that Satan had the authority to give all these kingdoms to Jesus. Jesus was well aware of what was at stake. The first Adam had squandered his rightful authority to govern the kingdoms of the world. Satan had been ruling the kingdoms of the world ever since Adam and Eve were expelled from the garden. If Jesus were to give in to this temptation, dominion authority would have been lost forever. I can't emphasize enough how critical this moment was in cosmic history. If Jesus would have succumbed to the temptation, the grand rescue plan would have failed. We would be without hope, and darkness would reign over all the kingdoms of the world. I am eternally grateful that Jesus did not lift His soul to another and that the Father was the only one worthy of Jesus' worship.

The restoration of the dominion mandate means that you and I, Christ's ambassadors, have a responsibility to exercise our God given authority to govern earth according to His statutes and precepts. Matthew's record of the Great Commission lays out our dominion mandate.

Matthew 28:18-20 (NIV) "*Then Jesus came to them and said, 'All authority in heaven and on earth has been given to me. Therefore go and make disciples of all nations, baptizing them in the name of the Father and of the Son and of the Holy Spirit, and teaching them to obey everything I have commanded you. And surely I am with you always, to the very end of the age.'*"

The emphasis here is on discipling nations. How does one do this exactly? To make disciples of all nations means we apprehend heaven's agenda over a nation and bring it down into the earth realm. We go before the King of kings and inquire about His purposes for a nation. We enter into intercession as Christ's ambassadors, rendering the King's decrees, and become agents of transformation. We steward the land. We change the atmosphere over cities, regions, and nations through prayer. The dominion mandate of Matthew's Great Commission emphasizes releasing wholeness to societies by setting people groups free from oppression and enslavement. This is our responsibility as a citizen of the Kingdom of God. C. Peter Wagner in his book *Dominion Theology* describes it like this:

"God's reign was in the heavenlies, and He created the earth with the thought of extending His reign. Earth was to be a colony of heaven. God was the King of all, and He delegated the human race, represented in the beginning by Adam, as governors over this colony. The visible earth is supposed to reflect the nature and essence of the invisible parent Kingdom of heaven. The second Adam did all that was necessary to put back in place God's original design for the earth as a colony of heaven. Once He did, He then delegated the responsibility of bringing God's plan into being."[79]

Jesus delegated to us the dominion authority He restored through the cross. When He ascended into heaven, the responsibility of governing was placed on our shoulders. This is why He declared in Matthew 16 that we have been given the keys of the kingdom of heaven.

Matthew 16:19 (NIV) *"I will give you the keys of the kingdom of heaven; whatever you bind on earth will be bound in heaven, and whatever you loose on earth will be loosed in heaven."*

In order to govern with dominion authority, it's imperative that we awaken from our passivity. There are spiritual giants in our land that have taken our territory, our inheritance, and our freedom. We must rise up to face the giants with confidence in who we are and who we represent. Let's walk in the same confidence as David when he faced the giant Goliath.

I Samuel 17:45-47 (NIV) *"…You come against me with sword and spear and javelin, but I come against you in the name of the Lord Almighty, the God of the armies of Israel, whom you have defied. This day the Lord will deliver you into my hands, and I'll strike you down and cut off your head. This very day I will give the carcasses of the Philistine army to the birds of the air and the wild animals, and the whole world will know that there is a God in Israel. All those gathered here will know that it is not by sword or spear that the Lord saves; for the battle is the Lord's, and he will give all of you into our hands."*

We need men and women from all generations who are willing to slay the giants in our land. We need to rise up and walk in the dominion authority that we have been given.

Key Points
- Satan usurped the dominion authority that was given to Adam and Eve.
- God declared a war between the seed of woman and the seed of the serpent.
- Jesus restored the family mandate and the dominion mandate.
- Jesus gave His children the keys of the kingdom of heaven to operate in dominion authority.

Section II

Lineage of the Giants

*"If we reject all inexplicable elements of all stories because we have
made up our mind ahead of time that such things simply aren't
possible, we run the risk of shrinking the world down to what
we can comprehend."*
~ Rob Bell

It is human nature to dismiss outlandish stories or eye-witness accounts as myth, folklore, or fabrication. However, caution is needed when we feel the urge to do this simply because we don't have a cognitive schema in which to organize fantastical concepts. Broadening mental capacity involves developing a neural framework, sometimes referred to as cognitive networks, in which new information can be categorized. The tendency is to dismiss outlying information as incorrect, rather than do the work necessary to build the neural framework to contain the new concepts. Certainly, when we are faced with incongruent information, we have a choice to make, either we ignore the data, find problems with it, or substantiate it with corroborating evidence. The discoveries that lie within this section will require us to broaden our mental capacity.

In spanning the globe, we can find folklore from ancient civilizations as well as documented history from recent cultures that all tell a similar story. This story is about an epoch when giants roamed the earth. The fact that giants are a part of human history may not be all that surprising, since many of us are somewhat familiar with the story of David and Goliath. But what you might find intriguing is that we can trace the imprint of giants across virtually every region on earth. We will dig into the history of the giants and look at their lineage as we march toward uncovering the roots of the Federal Reserve.

Logically, our first question should be "where on earth did giants come from"? Well, perhaps their origin wasn't entirely from this earth. When I was growing up, I remember reading fairytales like Jack and the Beanstalk. My concept of giants was almost solely in the realm of fairytale, except of course for the story of David and Goliath. As a child, I never really entertained the idea that giants were real. I thought they were make-believe, but monsters under my bed, now they were REAL! I realize it's a juxtaposition that something I thought was fairytale as a child, I now understand to be real as an adult. Usually the imaginative mind of a child has a large container for what is deemed reality, whereas the mind of an adult scrutinizes the imagination until it is dwindled to the size of a small box. As I have studied the Bible in my adult life, I have discovered that the Bible has a lot to say about the origins of the giants.

In this section, we will use the Bible as our starting point to better understand giants, and then branch out to additional written texts from other cultures. We will be performing archaeological digs on language, so to speak, by examining the meaning of the original Hebrew and Greek words used in scripture and in other ancient languages. Linguist, Aron Dogopolsky, aptly describes it as "looking through the telescope of vocabulary" in order to reconstruct ancient events.[80] By digging into the etymology of words, it will enlighten our understanding, akin to unearthing a treasure that has been buried in the sands of misinterpretation. We simply cannot be satisfied by the definition of words on a surface level, if we are to uncover the roots of the Federal Reserve. We must seriously consider the meaning embedded in the original language, as well as, the context of scripture, extra-biblical texts, and ancient documents.

Chapter 7

The Origin of the Nephilim

Biblical Account

Genesis 6 provides the context for the appearance of giants on earth, or 'Nephilim' as they are called in Hebrew. I have included several translations of this passage to help us gain a better understanding of what is being described:

Genesis 6:1-4 (The Living Bible, TLB) "*Now a population explosion took place upon the earth. It was at this time that beings from the spirit world looked upon the beautiful earth women and took any they desired to be their wives. Then Jehovah said, 'My Spirit must not forever be disgraced in man, wholly evil as he is. I will give him 120 years to mend his ways.' In those days, and even afterwards, when the evil beings from the spirit world were sexually involved with human women, their children became giants, of whom so many legends are told.*"

Genesis 6:1-4 (NKJV) "*Now it came to pass, when men began to multiply on the face of the earth, and daughters were born to them, that the sons of God saw the daughters of men, that they were beautiful; and they took wives for themselves of all whom they chose. And the Lord said, 'My Spirit shall not strive with man forever, for he is indeed flesh; yet his days shall be one hundred and twenty years.' There were giants on the earth in those days, and also afterward, when the sons of God came in to the daughters of men and they bore children to them. Those were the mighty men who were of old, men of renown.*"

Genesis 6:1-4 (AMP) "*Now it happened, when men began to multiply on the face of the land, and daughters were born to them, that the sons of God saw that the daughters of men were beautiful and desirable; and they took wives for themselves, whomever they chose and desired. Then the Lord said, 'My Spirit shall not strive and remain with man forever, because he is indeed flesh [sinful, corrupt – given over to sensual appetites]; nevertheless his days shall yet be a hundred and twenty years.' There were Nephilim (men of stature, notorious men) on the earth in those days – and also afterward – when the sons of God lived with the daughters of men, and they gave birth to their children. These were the mighty men who were of old, men of renown (great reputation, fame).*

Let's dig into this text by considering several noteworthy phrases that require further explanation. First, the phrase *'sons of God,'* begs the question – who are the 'sons of God'? Are they spiritual beings, human or a combination of both? A number of scholars postulate that the 'sons of God' are human in nature and come from the lineage of Seth. Seth was Adam and Eve's son that was born after Cain murdered Abel. In Genesis 4:25-26, it was said that Seth replaced Abel.

Genesis 4:25-26 (NIV) *"Adam made love to his wife again, and she gave birth to a son and named him Seth, saying, 'God has granted me another child in place of Abel, since Cain killed him.' Seth also had a son, and he named him Enosh. At that time people began to call on the name of the Lord."*

The line of thinking is that Seth and his descendants called on the name of the Lord, and therefore, are considered the 'sons of God.' This train of thought then identifies the daughters of Cain as the 'daughters of men,' who were deemed ungodly. The forbidden marriage between Seth's line and Cain's line gave rise to the giants. Personally, I see many flaws in this interpretation of the 'sons of God.' Simply stated, humans beget humans not giants. Furthermore, the text in Genesis 4:26b does not support the notion that it was only Seth's lineage that called on the name of the Lord. *"At that time **people** began to call on the name of the Lord."* This Sethite interpretation of the 'sons of God' negates a supernatural perspective.

To understand who 'the sons of God' are, it's important to look within the Bible itself, since this is where the phrase derives. We can gather several clues about the 'sons of God' by looking at different scriptures where they are referenced.

Job 38:4-7 (NKJV) *"Where were you when I laid the foundations of the earth? Tell Me, if you have understanding. Who determined its measurements? Surely you know! Or who stretched the line upon it? To what were its foundations fastened? Or who laid its cornerstone, when the morning stars sang together, and all the **sons of God** shouted for joy?"* (emphasis mine)

This passage helps us formulate an understanding regarding the identity of the 'sons of God.' They were present before the foundations of the earth were created which means they are not human in nature. If they are not human, they must be spiritual beings. But what kind of spiritual beings? Angels? Other gods? We need to turn to the Hebrew meaning for the phrase 'sons of God,' which is *'beney elohim,'* for the answer to these questions. Michael Heiser, in *The Unseen Realm* defines the phrase this way, "in the ancient Semitic world, 'sons of God' is a phrase used to identify divine beings with higher level responsibilities or jurisdictions."[81] The 'sons of God' have greater jurisdiction than angels. We understand this based on the meaning of the Hebrew word for angel *'mal'ak'* which means a 'messenger, a being that delivers a message'; it comes from a root word which means 'to dispatch a deputy.'[82] Furthermore, we can't overlook the word 'sons' because this gives us an important clue as well, it denotes family. God had an original family before He created Adam and Eve. The 'sons of God' were created by God; they are divine beings under His authority. There was no confusion in the minds of the Jewish writers between Almighty Elohim and the other elohim, known as the 'sons of God.'

Exodus 15:11 (NIV) *"Who among the gods [elohim] is like you, Lord? Who is like you – majestic in holiness, awesome in glory, working wonders?"*

Psalm 97:9 (NIV) *"For you, Lord [Yahweh], are the Most High over all the earth; you are exalted far above all gods [elohim]."*

Job 1:6-7 (NKJV) *"Now there was a day when the sons of God came to present themselves before the Lord, and Satan also came among them. And the Lord said to Satan, 'From where do you come?' So Satan answered the Lord and said, 'From going to and fro on the earth, and from walking back and forth on it."*

These passages highlight the differentiation in the minds of the followers of Yahweh. He is the one true God, the Supreme Elohim, that reigns above all other elohim.

Just as Adam and Eve were rebellious, Psalm 82 reveals that the 'sons of God' were also rebellious. They of course took the rebellion further than Adam and Eve, in that they ruled the nations with a corrupt governing oversight.

Psalm 82 (NIV) *"God presides in the great assembly; he renders judgment among the 'gods': 'How long will you defend the unjust and show partiality to the wicked? Defend the weak and the fatherless; uphold the cause of the poor and the oppressed. Rescue the weak and the needy; deliver them from the hand of the wicked. The 'gods' know nothing, they understand nothing. They walk about in darkness; all the foundations of the earth are shaken. I said 'You are 'gods'; you are all sons of the Most High.' But you will die like mere mortals; you will fall like every other ruler.' Rise up, O God, judge the earth, for all the nations are your inheritance."*

We see in Psalm 82 that the Most High calls the 'sons of God' (or 'sons of the Most High') 'gods.' This is astounding for people who do not have a supernatural worldview. The Supreme Elohim, Yahweh, created other elohim which became His sons ('*beney elohim*'). The gods were created with the purpose of defending the weak and the fatherless, to uphold the cause of the poor and oppressed, and to rescue the weak and needy. But the gods were rebellious sons, and instead of fulfilling their role, they defended the unjust, showed partiality to the wicked, and walked about in darkness. Therefore, the Almighty Elohim, rendered a judgement. The gods would die like mere mortals. In contrast to the rescue plan for humanity, the Almighty Elohim provided no rescue plan for the rebellious elohim. They are spiritual beings and their rebellion was treasonous. Samuel defines the root of rebellion when explaining to Saul why he lost his kingship.

I Samuel 15:23 (NKJV) "*For rebellion is as the sin of witchcraft, and stubbornness is as iniquity and idolatry. Because you have rejected the word of the Lord, He also has rejected you from being king."*

In Genesis 6, we see that the 'sons of God' were wicked and rebellious. They subverted Yahweh's governing plan for His human family by introducing a hybrid race through sexual perversion. We will see on our journey to Jekyll Island that this strand of sexual perversion is existent in all forms of the occult. It originated in the DNA of the Nephilim .

Another noteworthy phrase from Genesis 6 that requires further explanation is "*there were Nephilim on the earth in those days.*" It's imperative at this point in our investigation that we understand the origin of the Nephilim. The first clue we need to look at is the meaning of the word 'Nephilim' or '*nĕphiyl.*' It is a Hebrew word that has been translated to mean "giant, bully or tyrant."[83] It derives its meaning from the Hebrew root word '*naphal*' which means "fallen ones, cast down, fugitive, kingdoms that are overthrown, to fail, to fall away, to desert, to cause someone to fall away, to fall down from heaven, to cast yourself upon another." [84] These descriptors give us a window into the character and nature of the fallen 'sons of God.' We can deduct from these definitions that the giants ('*něphiyl*') have their origins in the fallen 'sons of God'('*naphal*'). The Nephilim are the offspring of the ungodly union between the 'sons of God' and human women. Michael Heiser describes the supernatural view of Genesis 6 in his book *Reversing Hermon*. He states:

"…divine beings came to earth, assumed human flesh, cohabited with human women, and spawned unusual offspring known as Nephilim. Naturally, this view requires seeing the giant clans encountered in the conquest as physical descendants of the Nephilim."[85]

At this juncture, it's important to note that there is some confusion among biblical scholars regarding the origin of the Nephilim. Some scholars conclude that the '*beney elohim*,' the fallen 'sons of God,' are the Nephilim and that the offspring created by the union of the Nephilim with the women referenced in Genesis 6 are the Rephaim. The primary premise for this interpretation comes from the meaning of the word '*naphal*' as 'fallen ones.' I am not able to draw the same conclusion from the biblical text as these scholars. Instead, my exegesis of Genesis 6 aligns me with Dr. Heiser, in that the Nephilim are the **offspring** of the '*beney elohim*' and the daughters of men. This is substantiated in the Enochian texts, the Mesopotamian accounts, and the translation of 'Nephilim' as 'giants' in the Septuagint.

Extra-Biblical Accounts

While the Bible's account of the origins of the Nephilim is only mentioned briefly in Genesis 6, we can turn to extra-biblical texts as a source for more information. For example, the Book of Enoch, or more accurately referred to as I Enoch, is a valuable resource that will uncover important clues for us. While I don't consider these extra-Biblical texts to have the same authority as canonized scripture, I do recognize that Peter and Jude, who were inspired Biblical authors, considered I Enoch to be worthy of referencing in their books. I believe this lends credibility to these extra-Biblical texts. I Enoch was written during the Second Temple era, also known as the Intertestamental Period, which was between 500 B.C. – A.D. 70. While the author is unknown, the main character in I Enoch is not surprisingly, Enoch.

Enoch was one of the ten patriarchs to rule before the Flood. In the Bible, Enoch is mentioned briefly, yet notably.

Genesis 5: 21-24 (AMP) *"When Enoch was sixty-five years old, he became the father of Methuselah. Enoch walked [in habitual fellowship] with God three hundred years after the birth of Methuselah and had other sons and daughters. So all the days of Enoch were three hundred and sixty-five years. And [in reverent fear and obedience] Enoch walked with God; and he was not [found among men], because God took him [away to be home with him]."*

This passage emphasizes the faithfulness of Enoch. It's the first occurrence of ascension in the Bible. Enoch was unique, both in his life and in his departure from this physical world. He walked in continual communion with the Lord, a level of intimacy that not many of us have known. He did not taste death. The Biblical writers, while they did not give extensive details about his life, certainly recognized that his faithfulness was exemplary. The author of Hebrews included Enoch in the "Hall of Faith."

Hebrews 11:5 (AMP) *"By faith [that pleased God] Enoch was caught up and taken to heaven so that he would not have a glimpse of death; and he was not found because God had taken him; for even before he was taken [to heaven], he received the testimony [still on record] that he had walked with God and pleased Him."*

I Enoch describes, in more depth, the experiences Enoch had in the spiritual dimension. The scrolls containing the books of I Enoch were among the writings found in the Dead Sea Scrolls. There are eight distinct sections in 1 Enoch, but for our purposes, we will examine the first section found in chapters 1 – 36. This section is called the Book of Watchers.

'Watchers' is the Enochian term for the 'sons of God.' I will include portions from the Book of Watchers to provide a context for the birth of the Nephilim. These excerpts parallel the story in Genesis 6.

I Enoch 6:1-6 *"And it came to pass when the children of men had multiplied that in those days were born unto them beautiful and comely daughters. And the angels, the children of the heaven, saw and lusted after them, and said to one another: 'Come, let us choose us wives from among the children of men and beget us children.' And Semjâzâ, who was their leader, said unto them: 'I fear ye will not indeed agree to do this deed, and I alone shall have to pay the penalty of a great sin.' And they all answered him and said: 'Let us all swear an oath, and all bind ourselves by mutual imprecations not to abandon this plan but to do this thing.' Then sware they all together* and bound themselves by mutual imprecations upon it. And they were in all two hundred; who descended in the days of Jared on the summit of Mount Hermon, and they called it Mount Hermon, because they had sworn and bound themselves by mutual imprecations upon it."

I Enoch 7:1-4 *"And all the others together with them took unto themselves wives, and each chose for himself one, and they began to go in unto them and to defile themselves with them, and they taught them charms and enchantments, and the cutting of roots, and made them acquainted with plants. And they became pregnant, and they bare great giants, whose height was three thousand ells: Who consumed all the acquisitions of men. And when men could no longer sustain them, the giants turned against them and devoured mankind."*

We find in these passages that one of the sins of the 'children of heaven' (or 'sons of God') was that they lusted after the beautiful women that lived on earth. Lust is most often manifested through unrestrained sexual pleasure or an intense desire for power. We will uncover in the following chapters how lust is deeply rooted within the elite banksters of the Federal Reserve.

This passage in Enoch provides more detail than the account in Genesis 6. The 'sons of God' found the daughters of men sexually appealing and were willing to commit treasonous acts to fulfill their lustful desires. The leader of the 'sons of God' wanted assurance from the other elohim that they were in this together and that he would not be the only one to engage in treason. Misery loves company. This begs the question, why would the elohim risk everything just to fulfill a lustful desire? Their desires were not just lustful, their desires were for every form and shadow of wickedness. A coup d'etat was in motion. The elohim banded together to attempt a takeover of the Supreme Elohim's kingdom through corrupting the seed of the woman so that the promised Messiah could never rescue humanity. In the midst of their wicked plots, the elohim sought out glory unto themselves. As the 'sons of God' defiled themselves with women, their offspring were wicked to the core.

The corruption of the 'sons of God' extended beyond defiling the human genome with the hybrid offspring of the Nephilim. 1 Enoch records the wicked practices of the 'Watchers' in that they taught the dark arts to humans.

I Enoch 8 *"And Azâzêl taught men to make swords, and knives, and shields, and breastplates, and made known to them the metals (of the earth) and the art of working them, and bracelets, and ornaments, and the use of antimony, and the beautifying of the eyelids, and all kinds of costly stones, and all colouring tinctures. And there arose much godlessness, and they committed fornication, and they were led astray, and became corrupt in all their ways. Semjâzâ taught enchantments, and root-cuttings, Armârôs the resolving of enchantments, Barâqîjâl (taught) astrology, Kôkabêl the constellations, Ezêqêêl the knowledge of the clouds, (Araqiêl the signs of the earth, Shamsiêl the signs of the sun), and Sariêl the course of the moon. And as men perished, they cried, and their cry went up to heaven."*

These teachings from the fallen 'sons of God' were the secrets of heaven. Could this account in I Enoch 8 explain how the megalithic civilizations demonstrated a rapid progression from hunter/gatherer societies to highly sophisticated, organized societies with architectural wonders and technological advancements beyond 21st century innovations?

Chapter 9 of I Enoch continues with the cries of the people that are perishing reaching up to heaven catching the attention of the archangels Michael, Uriel, Raphael, and Gabriel who see the bloodshed and lawlessness of humanity.

I Enoch 9:5-7 *"Thou hast made all things, and power over all things hast Thou: and all things are naked and open in Thy sight, and Thou seest all things, and nothing can hide itself from Thee. Thou seest what Azâzêl hath done, who hath taught all unrighteousness on earth and revealed the eternal secrets which were (preserved) in heaven, which men were striving to learn. And Semjâzâ, to whom Thou hast given authority to bear rule over his associates."*

It's worth noting the phrase, the "men were striving to learn." Men were striving to learn the eternal secrets that were revealed by the fallen 'sons of God.' It makes me wonder in what ways were they striving? Did they traffick their mothers, wives, and daughters to the fallen 'sons of God' for access to knowledge that would unlock mysteries? Did the antediluvian women have a choice in the matter? This "striving to learn" the eternal secrets is at the core of every occult endeavor, it's the trap the elite lay for their initiates. You see, the enemy has no new tricks. It's the same trap that was laid for Eve. Why does humanity continually take the bait? The pride of life is a powerful lure.

Mesopotamian Account

There are ancient Mesopotamian texts that tell a story which parallels the origin of the Nephilim as portrayed in Genesis 6. In fact, the Mesopotamian account predates the Pentateuch, leaving many scholars to conclude that Moses' account of creation, the Nephilim, the Flood etc. was shaped by the Mesopotamian texts. Michael Heiser, in his book *The Unseen Realm,* tackles this subject in a way that honors the sacredness of scripture, while recognizing that cultural influences shaped biblical writers.

"Genesis 6:1-4, too, has deep Mesopotamian roots that, until very recently have not been fully recognized or appreciated. Jewish literature like I Enoch that retold the story shows a keen awareness of that Mesopotamian context. This awareness shows us that Jewish thinkers of the Second Temple period understood, correctly, that the story involved divine beings and giant offspring. That understanding is essential to grasping what the biblical writers were trying to communicate. Genesis 6:1-4 is a polemic; it is a literary and theological effort to undermine the credibility of Mesopotamian gods and other aspects of that cultural worldview. Biblical writers do this frequently. The strategy often involves borrowing lines and motifs from the literature of the target civilization to articulate correct theology about Yahweh and to show contempt for other gods. Genesis 6:1-4 is a case study in this technique."[86]

This helps to explain the parallels between the biblical account of Genesis 6 and the Mesopotamian account of these same events. In essence, it is two distinct perspectives of the same events formulated by different belief systems, monotheism versus polytheism. In the Mesopotamian religion, the 'Watchers' or 'sons of God' were known as the 'Apkallus.' Michael Heiser describes the 'Apkallus' as: "…a group of sages (the apkallus), possessors of great knowledge, in the period before the flood. These apkallus were divine beings. Many apkallus were considered evil; those apkallus are integral to Mesopotamian demonology. After the flood, offspring of the apkallus were said to be human in descent (i.e. having a human parent) and "two-thirds apkallu." In other words, the apkallus mated with human women and produced quasi-divine offspring."[87]

There were seven antediluvians 'Apkallus' identified from the ancient Mesopotamian cuneiform tablets. They were the teachers of wisdom, sciences, technology, and magic arts. The Sumerian cuneiform texts portrayed the 'Apkallus' as "conjurers, sorcerers, warlocks, and magicians." Additionally, they were known as alchemists, medical doctors, carpenters, stone cutters, goldsmiths, metal workers, as well as the ones who laid the foundations of the antediluvian cities. Graham Hancock, in his book *Magicians of the Gods* says, "indeed, in later times, all crafts used in royal building and renovation projects were attributed to knowledge that had originated with the antediluvian sages."[88]

Could this be the esoteric knowledge that secret societies seek after, the divine knowledge of all mysteries subversively given to the antediluvian civilizations? We may be on to something here. Amar Annus from the University of Tartu in Estonia wrote a superb analysis of the antediluvian wisdom as viewed from both the Mesopotamian and Jewish traditions. He writes: "Very well attested ancient Mesopotamian intellectual tradition gives a divine origin in the antediluvian age to all priestly sciences. The period before the deluge was the one of revelation in the Mesopotamian mythology, when the basis of all later knowledge was laid down. The antediluvian sages were culture-heroes, who brought the arts of civilization to the land. During the time that follows this period, nothing new is invented, the original revelation is only transmitted and unfolded. Oannes and other sages taught all foundations of civilization to antediluvian humankind."[89]

Let's take in for a moment, the significance of what Annus is saying here. The 'Apkallus,' the 'Watchers,' the 'sons of God,' took the divine knowledge that was intended to remain within the boundaries of the heavenly dimensions, and gave it to human beings as a way to entice them toward craving knowledge instead of longing for relationship with God. Again, it is the same trap that the serpent set for Eve when he enticed her to eat from the Tree of the Knowledge of Good and Evil. I cannot emphasize this enough; **this is the origin, or shall we say, the ROOT, of all mystery religions and occult practices.** We will come to discover how this is also part of the root system within the Federal Reserve.

The Epic of Gilgamesh, a poem that is considered to be one of the earliest surviving literary masterpieces, is another of the Mesopotamian texts that lends confirmation to the presence of the Nephilim. In the *Book of Giants,* several names of giants are listed and Gilgamesh is listed as the offspring of the 'Watchers.' It tells of how Gilgamesh, king of Uruk, oppresses his people. He sexually assaults the Uruk brides on their wedding night. He was said to be 1/3 human and 2/3 divine, a hybrid like the Nephilim. The epic poem depicts the relationship between Gilgamesh and Enkidu. The oppressed people of Uruk cry out to their gods to be delivered from the harsh practices of Gilgamesh. The gods oblige by sending a wild man named Enkidu who can match

Gilgamesh's strength. The two engage in a brief battle with one another. This battle ends with the two having mutual respect for one another. Some translations of the Epic of Gilgamesh record the height of Gilgamesh as 11 cubits (approximately 14 ft 8 inches).[90] By inference, Enkidu must have also been a giant to have matched the strength of Gilgamesh. Interestingly, the pattern of sexual perversion evident in the Nephilim bloodline was also recorded in the life of Enkidu. It was said that he was first initiated through successive sexual acts with a temple prostitute before he met Gilgamesh. What dark doors did Enkidu open as a result of his sexual acts?

Annus concludes that within the Mesopotamian culture, sexual encounters between divine beings and humans were considered a fixed part of the sacred marriage. The sacred marriage was a critical part of agrarian societies. It was believed that the ritual magic performed during the cultic intercourse between the goddess and king would secure abundance and fertility for the people.[91] For the most part, the Mesopotamian perspective was that these sexual encounters were for the betterment of humanity. But for the Second Temple Jewish writers of the Enochian texts, this transgression of boundaries between the divine and human was sacrilegious and was the cause of the corruption of the human genome.

As we have considered three different accounts of the origins of the Nephilim, we now must pose two questions for further investigation. Did the antediluvian knowledge from the teachings of the fallen 'sons of God' transmit to the post-Flood world? And if so, how?

Key Points
- Nephilim are the offspring of the 'sons of God.' They are hybrids.
- Within the bloodline of the Nephilim is sexual degradation.
- Ancient Mesopotamian texts parallel the biblical and extra-biblical accounts of antediluvian transmission of divine knowledge.
- 'Apkullas' or 'Watchers' enticed humans with divine knowledge to lure them away from relationship with Yahweh – origin of the occult.
- Gilgamesh listed as offspring of 'Watchers' which means he was a Nephilim.
- Sacred marriage involves ritual magic through cultic intercourse between goddess and king.

Chapter 8

An Age-Old Question

Anyone who sets out to gain understanding of the giants in biblical scripture will find themselves asking the age-old question… if the Flood (Genesis 7) was meant to rid the earth of the Nephilim, why does Genesis 6:4 say *"the Nephilim were on the earth in those days – and also afterward"*? Did God fail in His attempt to annihilate the Nephilim? Some scholars have attempted to answer this question by interpreting that "those days and also afterward" don't refer to the time period following the Flood, but actually refer to the days after Jared. Who's Jared?

Jared was Enoch's father and Noah's great, great grandfather. Using the genealogy of Genesis 5, along with the fact that Noah was 600 years old when the floodwaters came, we discover that Jared was born 1,196 years before the Flood. He died at the age of 962, leaving 234 years between the time of his death and the onset of the Flood. The scholars who propose that the epoch of the giants was before and after the days of Jared conclude that this time period was before the Flood, thus supporting the incursion (invasion from the 'sons of God') described in Genesis 6 as the only incursion. This explanation quickly breaks down given accounts in biblical scripture that speak about giants present after the Flood.

Numbers 13 describes when the twelve spies were sent out by Moses to gather reconnaissance regarding the Promised Land. Upon their return, Caleb and Joshua had an exceedingly positive report of the abundant provision in the Promised Land, but the other ten spies were gripped by fear. They reported to Moses and the Israelites that there were exceedingly great giants in the land.

Numbers 13:31-32 (NIV) *"But the men who had gone up with him said, 'We can't attack those people; they are stronger than we are.' And they spread among the Israelites a bad report about the land they had explored. They said, 'The land we explored devours those living in it. All the people we saw there are of great size. We saw the Nephilim there (the descendants of Anak come from the Nephilim). We seemed like grasshoppers in our own eyes, and we looked the same to them."*

The ten spies clearly identify that there were Nephilim, or the descendants of Nephilim in the Promised Land. This truth is further corroborated by the length of Og's bed at 13 feet long (Deuteronomy 3:11). Given we know there were giants around after the Flood, we are back to the age-old question – how was that possible?

Many biblical scholars have attempted to answer why the Nephilim were present on the earth after the Flood. The answers polarize into two primary theories: (1) multiple incursion, or (2) single incursion. While it is not within the scope of this book to unpack all the complexities of these two theories, I will summarize some key points. As we move further along on our investigative journey to uncover the roots of the Federal Reserve, a working knowledge of these theories will help us formulate a context for our defiled monetary system.

Multiple Incursion

The multiple incursion theory is the predominant viewpoint of biblical scholars who have studied Genesis 6:4 (NIV) *"The Nephilim were on the earth in those days – and also afterward..."* Michael Heiser describes the multiple incursion theory in his book *Reversing Hermon,* "There are two alternatives for explaining the presence of giants after the Flood who descended from the giant Nephilim: (1) the Flood of Genesis 6-8 was a regional, not global, catastrophe; (2) the same kind of behavior described in Genesis 6:1-4 happened again (or continued to happen) after the Flood, producing other Nephilim, from whom the giant clans descended.

The second option is a possibility deriving from Hebrew grammar. Genesis 6:4 tells us there were Nephilim on earth before the Flood 'and also afterward, when the sons of God went into the daughters of humankind.' The 'when' in the verse could be translated 'whenever,' thereby suggesting a repetition of these pre-Flood events after the Flood. In other words, since Genesis 6:4 points forward to the later giant clans, the phrasing could suggest that other sons of God fathered more Nephilim after the Flood. As a result, there would be no survival of original Nephilim, and so the post-Flood dilemma would be resolved. A later appearance of other Nephilim occurred by the same means as before the Flood."[92]

Simply stated, multiple incursion theory purports that the fallen 'sons of God' mated with human women after the Flood in the same way as they did before the Flood. Even though this perspective is commonly accepted, I see a few problems with this theory.

First, while I highly value Dr. Heiser's supernatural perspective and agree with him in many ways, the Hebrew word *'asher'* can mean "because, as, or since" just as it can mean "whenever."[93] If we translate Genesis 6:4 using 'since' instead of 'when' it reads like this.

*"The Nephilim were on the earth in those days – and also afterward- **since** the sons of God went to the daughters of humans and had children by them. They were the heroes of old, men of renown."* (translation mine, emphasis mine)

To me, it is not a compelling argument for multiple incursions that one can translate this passage as 'whenever' instead of the other possible translations.

Second, when the post-Flood giants are referred to in scripture, they are referred to as the **descendants** of the Nephilim or offspring of another giant, rather than being identified as direct offspring of the fallen 'sons of God.' Only the Nephilim in Genesis 6:4 were identified in this way.

Third, scripture does not provide us with another clear account of the 'sons of God' mating with human women outside of the Genesis 6 passage. There is, however, a passage in I Corinthians 11 that may be a clue that Paul believed there were multiple incursions of the 'Watchers.'

I Corinthians 11:5-6,10, 15 (NIV) *"But every woman who prays or prophesies with her head uncovered dishonors her head – it is the same as having her head shaved. For if a woman does not cover her head, she might as well have her hair cut off; but if it is a disgrace for a woman to have her hair cut off or her head shaved, then she could cover her head... It is for this reason that a woman ought to have authority over her own head, **because of the angels**...but that if a woman has long hair, it is her glory? For long hair is given to her as a covering."* (emphasis mine)

Dr. Heiser provides an insightful and frequently overlooked exegesis of this passage in *Reversing Hermon*. First, it's important to consider the historical and spiritual context for religious women living in the Roman Empire during the 1st century AD. Jewish women were accustomed to being excluded from full participation in their worship gatherings, because they could not be circumcised, which was a requirement for full participation. But women were given a new status within Christianity. They were full participants under the New Covenant. Physical circumcision was no longer the requirement that set a person apart. Instead, it was circumcision of the heart.

The cultural norms in the 1st century A.D. were radically different than our 21st century Western mindset. A woman's hair carried strong sexual connotations; therefore, head coverings were considered a prophylactic measure. In fact, the Greek word *'peribolaion'* used to describe "a covering" has a peculiar meaning in the Greek medical texts. It is the Greek word used for testicles.[94] Now why would the word used in I Corinthians 11:15 referencing a "woman's hair is her covering" be the same word for testicles?

Troy Martin, Professor of Religious Studies at St. Xavier University, Chicago, provides a most unusual explanation. He examined the different literary contexts in which *'peribolaion'* was used in the Greek language. He found that Hippocrates wrote about the association of a woman's hair with a man's testicles. The Hippocratic practitioners believed that hair was hollow and functioned like a vacuum attracting the fluid of a man's semen.[95] This is why Paul said that it is shameful for a woman to cut her hair and for a man to have long hair. It is the man's role to eject the semen and the woman's role to receive the semen in order to procreate.

It's interesting that Paul's concern that women remain sexually modest by covering their hair was not just for the sake of other men, but also "because of the angels."

"The covering for women was commended to protect women from sexual scandal in society and supernatural violation by angels. This dual rationale focused on social boundaries and sexual vulnerability, along with the precedent of angelic violation of women in the past."[96]

Paul was mindful of the incursion of the 'Watchers.' But why? The incursion of Genesis 6 happened thousands of years before Paul was born. It's likely that Paul was familiar with the Enochian texts, as were his contemporaries, Peter and Jude. These texts were written only a few hundred years before Paul's time and lent much more detail to the horrors of what happened during the days of Noah than what is described in Genesis 6:1-4. But we must ask the question, was it really that fresh in Paul's mind or were there subsequent post-Flood incursions that had heightened Paul's concern? We can't really answer this question with certainty given there is no direct biblical reference to subsequent incursions. Or is there?

It's true that there is nothing recorded in history that comes close to what is described in Genesis 6 and the supporting Enochian texts, whereby 200 'Watchers' left their heavenly abode to procreate with human women. There are, however, other not so obvious Biblical references that lend support to multiple incursions.

The direct afront on the human genome recorded in Genesis 6, backfired on Satan. The judgment of the 'Watchers' was severe and the Nephilim were annihilated by the Flood along with every defiled living being. The enemy had to regroup and develop a more insidious strategy; the roll out of this revised scheme, took place in Babel.

Nimrod was arguably the first world leader in recorded history. He fueled humanism among the citizens of Babel; such a self-sufficient pride arose in the post-Flood population that they labored toward reopening a dimensional gateway by constructing the Tower of Babel. Their goal was to achieve wisdom and knowledge through interaction with the gods, the pride of life. George Otis Jr., in *Twilight Labyrinth*, offers a glimpse at the spiritual climate of Babel (he uses Babylon interchangeably with Babel).

"In Babylonia the gods did not descend in order to walk with humans, but to lie with them. This practice involved both men and women and took place inside the ziggurat-crowning temple. In addition to ritual intercourse between a deified human king and the goddess Innana (an annual rite undertaken to ensure fertility for the coming year), there were also high priestesses known as *Entu* who made themselves available to male deities…Although the Babylonians' idolatry and base ambition were deeply troubling, the focus of divine concern was apparently their unity of purpose…the people's moral and physical unity had attracted great attention in the spirit world. The plain of Shinar, which means 'strange power,' was being covered with a swarming darkness…Had He not intervened when He did, it is possible that the power of the collective visualizations would have allowed coalescing demonic forces to imperil the human race. As it was the Tower had already become an alternative source of knowledge – an Edenic *déjà vu*. The Lord God, who had already pledged Himself to refrain from any more mass destruction of life, elected to deal with mankind's unholy alliance through geographic and linguistic separation. Men and women would be confounded rather than consumed."[97]

This is a profound representation of the sinister plan the gods devised to empower the rebellious citizens of Babel to carry out the defilement of the human genome. It didn't take Noah's descendants long before they opened the door to another incursion. The judgment of this second incursion was to bring confusion and disperse the people across the earth.

The account of the Tower of Babel in Genesis 11 is not the only place in scripture where we can find indirect references to the possibility of other incursions. The practice of sacred marriages among the Canaanites, the Sumerians and the Babylonians, as well as the employment of shrine prostitutes, hints at the insidious plot of the gods to corrupt the human genome through sexual rituals.

It seems the preponderance of scholarly opinion is in support of the multiple incursion theory. Occam's Razor, a principle applied for two competing theories, suggests that the simplest explanation is the best. Certainly, Occam's Razor would support the multiple incursion theory, but we don't want to commit one of the weaknesses of Occam's Razor, which is to overlook complex, yet plausible explanations for the presence of post-Flood giants. Therefore, I am compelled to seriously consider the single incursion theory as a probable explanation. What if digging deeper allows us to find plausible alternative explanations that lie beneath the surface? Treasures are often hidden from plain sight.

Proverbs 25:2 *"It is the glory of God to conceal a matter; to search out a matter is the glory of kings."*

The Western mindset often approaches a conundrum of opposing theories by weighing the evidence in favor *for* and the arguments *against* a theory. But it's interesting to note that the ancient Mesopotamian approach to opposing theories is to hold them both as true. The Mesopotamian account of the presence of post-Flood 'Apkallus' attempts to answer the age-old question by providing possible explanations for both theories. Amar Annus writes: "The Gilgamesh epic, with its programmatic first line, 'he who saw the Deep,' presents the hero as the transmitter of the antediluvian wisdom to his contemporary world. There were other thinkable means of preserving the antediluvian knowledge besides making the good survivor the divine source of it and his visitor its transmitter. Still another way was to conceive *apkallus* as amphibious fish-like creatures, capable of surviving in the depths of water, and of re-emerging from there after the inundation was over. One more way to preserve the knowledge was to inscribe pre-Flood wisdom in its entirety on different tablets or stones and either to bury them or to install the knowledge carriers on high places to escape perdition. In Mesopotamian tradition, such a divine source of information was the Tablet of Destinies, which corresponds to heavenly tablets and the *Pargod* in 3 Enoch, on which the divine secrets are written."[98]

Within Mesopotamian mythology lies the possibility that some of the 'Apkallus' survived the deluge because they were part amphibious. Consequently, their survival allowed them to emerge after the Flood to carry on the bloodline of the 'Apkallus' through a second incursion. But the Mesopotamian accounts do not rigidly adhere to the multiple incursion theory. Instead we find that alternative explanations are offered for the presence of giants after the deluge. One is that Noah's family member was the one to transmit the antediluvian wisdom. Another is that the mystery knowledge was written down on stone tablets and later discovered by the post-Flood people. These accounts help to expand our thinking on this topic as we investigate possible ways the giants were around after the flood.

Single Incursion

The single incursion theory purports that the 'sons of God' penetrated women to procreate during a single epoch of history, that is, the antediluvian era. The basis for this theory is that scripture does not record other time periods in which the 'sons of God' mated with human women. Single incursion proponents, such as Rob Skiba, draw upon extra-biblical texts to demonstrate that the punishment for this incursion was so severe that the 'sons of God' would not have engaged in this treasonous act a second time.[99] We find the judgment rendered upon the 'sons of God' in 1 Enoch 13.

1 Enoch 13 *"And Enoch went and said: '**Azâzêl, thou shalt have no peace: a severe sentence has gone forth against thee to put thee in bonds: And thou shalt not have toleration nor request granted to thee, because of the unrighteousness which thou has taught, and because of all the works of godlessness and unrighteousness and sin which thou hast shown to men.**' Then I went and spoke to them all together, and they were all afraid, and fear and trembling seized them. And they besought me to draw up a petition for them that they might find forgiveness, and to read their petition in the presence of the Lord of heaven. For from thenceforward they could not speak (with Him) nor lift up their eyes to heaven for shame of their sins for which they had been condemned. Then I wrote out their petition, and the prayer in regard to their spirits and their deeds individually and in regard to their requests that they should have*

forgiveness and length of days. And I went off and sat down at the waters of Dan, in the land of Dan, to the south of the west of Hermon: I read their petition till I fell asleep. And behold a dream came to me, and visions fell down upon me, and I saw visions of chastisement, and a voice came bidding me to tell it to the sons of heaven, and reprimand them. And when I awaked, I came unto them, and they were all sitting gathered together, weeping in Abelsjâîl, which is between Lebanon and Sênêsêr, with their faces covered. And I recounted before them all the visions which I had seen in sleep, and I began to speak the words of righteousness, and to reprimand the heavenly Watchers. " (emphasis mine)

1 Enoch 14 contains the Lord's response to the petition of the 'Watchers' as delivered by Enoch.

I Enoch 14:4-7 *"I wrote out your petition, and in my vision it appeared thus, that your petition will not be granted unto you throughout all the days of eternity, and that judgement has been finally passed upon you: yea your petition will not be granted unto you. And from henceforth you shall not ascend into heaven unto all eternity, and in bonds of the earth the decree has gone forth to bind you for all the days of the world. And that previously you shall have seen the destruction of your beloved sons and ye shall have no pleasure in them, but they shall fall before you by the sword. And your petition on their behalf shall not be granted, nor yet on your own: even though you weep and pray and speak all the words contained in the writing which I have written."*

I Enoch 68 describes the archangel's response to this judgment given to the 'sons of God.'

I Enoch 68:2-4 *"And on that day Michael answered Raphael and said: 'The power of the spirit transports and makes me to tremble because of the severity of the judgement of the secrets, the judgement of the angels: who can endure the severe judgement which has been executed, and before which they melt away? And Michael answered again, and said to Raphael: 'Who is he whose heart is not softened concerning it, and whose reins are not troubled by this word of judgement (that) has gone forth upon them because of those who have thus led them out?' And it came to pass when he stood before the Lord of Spirits, Michael said thus to Raphael: 'I will not take their part under the eye of the Lord; for the Lord of Spirits has been angry with them because they do as if they were the Lord. Therefore all that is hidden shall come upon them for ever and ever; for neither angel nor man shall have his portion (in it), but alone they have received their judgement for ever and ever."*

The Almighty God, the Righteous Judge, rendered His judgment upon the fallen 'sons of God' with no opportunity for pardon nor forgiveness. This may seem harsh, but the treasonous acts committed by the 'sons of God' required this judgment. You see, the 'Watchers' were well aware of the Seed war initiated shortly after the beginning of time (Genesis 3:15).

This was a declaration of war between the seed of the serpent and the seed of the woman. Contained within the declaration was a prophecy of the coming Messiah. In retaliation, Lucifer unleashed a grand plan with a two-fold strategy to prevent the Messiah from being born, to corrupt the seed of the woman and/or kill the seed of the woman. The 'Watchers' were integral in this strategy by corrupting humanity through defiling the genome.

Genetic Defilement

The Septuagint provides clues that confirm the subversive strategy of the 'sons of God' to corrupt the gene pool of the seed of woman. The Septuagint is regarded as a venerable translation of the Hebrew Old Testament into Greek. With the conquests of Alexander the Great and the spread of Hellenism, the 3rd century BC Jewish scholars recognized the importance of keeping the scriptures relevant and accessible to the growing number of Greek speaking Jews. Septuagint comes from the Latin word *septuaginta* meaning "seventy." Accordingly, it was named for the seventy Jewish elders who were commissioned to translate the Old Testament from Hebrew to Greek. The translators accomplished this arduous task independently of one another. It was clear that they were anointed because the completed work was coherent and unified. The Septuagint was the translation of the Bible that Jesus and the apostles used. The New Testament writers preferred the Septuagint over the Masoretic text (the Hebrew translation of the Old Testament), and many of the citations of scripture found in the New Testament are from the Septuagint.

Notably, for our purposes, the Septuagint Greek translation for the Hebrew word 'Nephilim' in Genesis 6:4 is Γιγαντες or *'gigantes.'*[100] By choosing this word, the Jewish elders created an indelible image for their Hellenistic readers. It was the image of the Titans and other giants within Greek mythology. In Greek mythology, the Titans and/or Gigantes were children of Gê/Gaia, the earth goddess. Gê/Gaia became impregnated when the blood of the castrated Uranus fell on her. In early Greek mythology, the Titans and the Gigantes were different but in later Greek mythology, they were viewed interchangeably. The point I would like to emphasize is that for the Hellenistic readers of the Septuagint, translating 'Nephilim' to Γιγαντες 'gigantes' created a deeper understanding of the nature of the 'Nephilim.'

If we dig deeper, we can see that the translation for Γιγαντες is 'earth born' and derives from the root word '*gê*' as well as from the word '*genetê*.'[101] '*Gê*' was not only the name of the Greek earth goddess but in the Strong's Concordance, it was a Greek word used in the New Testament meaning "earth, land."[102] It is the prefix for English words such as geography, geology, and geometry. '*Genetê*' is defined in Strong's Concordance as 'birth, from birth.'[103] These derivations are the basis for '*gigantes*' meaning "earth born." Now if we dig even further, we find that '*genetê*' is derived from the Greek word '*genea*' which has the following meanings:

1) Fathered, birth, nativity

2) That which has been begotten, men/women of the same stock, a family

   a. Several ranks of natural descent, the successive members of a genealogy

   b. A group of people very like each other in endowments, pursuits, character. Especially in a bad sense, a perverse nation.

3) Whole multitude of people living at the same time

4) An age (i.e. the time ordinarily occupied by each successive generation)[104]

This Greek word '*genea*' is where we get English words such as generation, genes, genetics. Herein lies the brilliance and divine inspiration of the Jewish translators of the Septuagint. The Nephilim agenda of genetic defilement is revealed by using the translated word Γιγαντες or '*gigantes*.' The strategy of Satan was to contaminate the seed of woman by altering the genetic code of humans so that the birth of the promised Messiah would not be possible. The 200 'Watchers' who descended on Mt. Hermon were intent on creating their own human race as an attempt to usurp the Almighty Elohim. Interestingly, the Hebrew word for "Hermon" is '*Chermown,*' it comes from the root word '*charam*' which means "to completely destroy, exterminate, to devote for destruction."[105] We will uncover along our journey that the Nephilim agenda to create their own human race as a way to usurp God's creation, can be found within the globalists' agenda of ushering in the New World Order. It's the same agenda as Hitler had, he wanted to create a perfect Aryan race to supplant humanity. The 'Watchers' in I Enoch 6 engaged in a plot so devious, so treasonous, so evil, it mandated deposing them from their place of authority and evicting them from heaven forever. Never again would the fallen 'sons of God' access the Lord's Presence, for treason is a serious matter with a serious penalty. If we consider that in the days of Noah, humanity was defiled by the hybrid race, which was the seed of Satan, the necessity of the Flood becomes clear. God had to totally annihilate the serpent's seed and restore humanity's genome.

Modern science lends evidence to the potential effectiveness of the Nephilim agenda. Genetic alterations can produce hybrids with supernormal strength and stature. Scientists have discovered that disrupting the myostatin gene doubles the skeletal-muscle mass in mice, cattle, and humans. The myostatin gene is the "growth/differentiation factor 8 (GDF-8) which belongs to the transforming growth factor β superfamily of secreted proteins that control the growth and differentiation of tissues throughout the body."[106]

Schuelke et al. (2004) reported a case study of "myostatin mutation in a child with muscle hypertrophy." The male infant was born to a healthy adult German female who was a former professional athlete. Researchers were not able to obtain any information about the known father. After birth, the infant appeared "extraordinarily muscular, with protruding muscles in his thighs and upper arms." Six days after birth, an ultrasonography verified that the infant had muscular hypertrophy. Interestingly, the researchers noted that several family members of this child have been reported to be unusually strong. For example, one family member was a construction worker and was reported to be able to unload curbstones by hand. At age 4, this child showed increased muscle bulk as well as strength. Amazingly, the child was able to lift two 3kg (6.6lbs) weights in each hand extending his arms in a horizontal suspension. Schuelke at al. (2004) concluded that myostatin gene mutation induces a "double muscling" phenotype not only in mice and cattle, but also in humans.[107]

In response to these findings, Branimir Čatipović, M.D. from the Department of Veteran Affairs in Mason City, Iowa stated,

"Schuelke et al. (2004) describe a child with muscle hypertrophy in association with a mutation in the myostatin gene. Another possible case of a myostatin mutation in an exceptionally strong child was described more than 2500 years ago in Greek mythology, in the story about Hercules. As an infant, Hercules strangled a snake in each hand when the goddess Hera tried to kill him. His legendary strength was obvious from the time of his birth, and it was not the result of any exercise program."[108]

Could this case study of a human gene mutation be an example of the existence of a Nephilim gene? Hold this question close, we will circle back around to it as we journey closer toward Jekyll Island.

Other genetic studies, like this one, might also uncover an answer to a pivotal question in the incursion debate; how does a single incursion theory explain the presence of giants after the Flood? A possible explanation is found within the growing field of epigenetics.

The Epigenetics Key

Epigenetics is a relatively new field within genetic research that has emerged within the past 50 years, but has really gained traction since the 1990s. Simply stated, epigenetics is the impact our thoughts and lifestyle choices have on our body, soul and spirit as well as impacting our future generations. The prefix "epi" means "on top of," so epigenetics means a set of instructions that sits on top of the gene. Epigenetic marks can act like switches "turning on" or "turning off" a gene.

Identical twins have offered scientists a closer examination of epigenetics through the nature/nurture debate. Some of the findings have been puzzling in that identical twins who have virtually the same nature and nurture demonstrate health differences such as autism, asthma, and bipolar disorder in one twin but not in the other. By further investigating these differences, scientists have discovered that there is an epigenetic factor which acts as a 3rd component to the nature/nurture debate. The best way to understand this is to review some of the hallmark epigenetic studies conducted on mice.

The agouti mice studies have shown that epigenetic marks can be influenced by the environment. Here's how it works. Mice have an agouti gene, which if activated, will cause the mouse to develop a yellow coat, become obese and show a higher propensity toward diseases, such as cancer and diabetes.[109] These agouti genes can be passed down from generation to generation through the DNA. Researchers have found that the agouti gene can be turned off if it is surrounded by silencing epigenetic marks. For example, if a pregnant agouti mouse is fed a diet rich in Vitamin B, this methyl group acts as a silencer for the agouti gene. The mother will give birth to a normal pup with the agouti gene switched off.[110] Likewise, in human studies, the diet of pregnant women can have an impact on the health of the child.

Interestingly, researchers have also found transgenerational communication of epigenetic markers. A longitudinal study in Sweden followed the eating and lifestyle choices of pre-pubescent boys and the sequential effects on two generations. Pembrey et al. (2006) found that boys who overate and/or smoked around the age of 10, during the critical stage of sperm development, went on to have sons and grandsons with significantly shorter life spans.[111]

Epigentic markers can also form after birth. The seminal work of Weaver at al. (2006) found that maternal rats who excessively licked and groomed their pups within the first week of life, released the glucocorticoid receptor (GR) gene in the hippocampus allowing the pups to more adequately handle stress as they mature. When rats are born, the GR gene is surrounded by silencing epigenetic marks, but the nurturing interaction of the mother rat with her pups removes the silencing epigenetic markers.[112] Do we see this same process in human relationships? Indeed, scientists have found similar results in humans.

Suzanne King has been conducting the Ice Storm Project since 1998, which is the first human prospective study to use a natural disaster as a way to investigate the epigenetic markers elicited by pre-natal maternal stress. This unique study gives the researchers an opportunity to examine the impact of maternal stress on the development of the offspring. In January 1998, Quebec experienced 5 days of freezing rain which caused the power lines to collapse under the weight of the ice. The electrical grid was disrupted leaving 3 million people without electricity during the coldest months of the year. King and her colleagues recruited 224 women who were pregnant during the ice storm. They assessed the overall stress levels of the mother and the impact on the child in the years that followed. They found that higher stress levels in the mother resulted in more occurrences of autism, metabolic diseases, and autoimmune diseases.[113]

As a psychologist, I can attest to the validity of these results. In my clinical work, I used Attachment Theory as the foundation for my therapeutic practices. Attachment Theory suggests that the early attachments we form in life greatly impact our mental health and the stability of our relationships with others. Secure attachments with a nurturing parent/caregiver in the early formative years can help a person develop into a well-adjusted, mentally healthy adult. Conversely, if there is no attachment or unpredictable attachment in early childhood, a person can develop a myriad of mental health issues, most commonly manifested in personality disorders, anxiety and/or depression.

While scientists view epigenetics as a young field of science, it is actually an ancient science described in the Bible. Dr. Caroline Leaf in her book *Switch on Your Brain* says: "This scientific power of our mind to change the brain is called *epigenetics* and spiritually it is as a man thinks, so is he (Prov 23:7). The way the brain changes as a result of mental activity is scientifically called *neuroplasticity*. And spiritually, it is the renewing of the mind (Rom. 12:2) ... the science of epigenetics, which is tangible, scientific proof of how important our choices are; they bring life or death, blessing or cursing; and they reach beyond us to influence the next generations (Deut. 30:19). This is because choices become signals that change our brain and body, so these changes are not dictated by our genes. Our thinking and subsequent choices become the signal switches for our genes. What's incredible is that genes are dormant until switched on by a signal; they have potential, but they have to be activated to release that potential…your choices might impact the generations that follow: "For the sin of the parents to the third and fourth generation (Exod. 34:7)"[114]

I believe epigenetics is a key that unlocks a plausible explanation for the Nephilim being "on the earth in those days, and also afterward." Let's consider a verse in Genesis 6 that is important in helping tie together the concepts I have laid out in this section. It's a verse that often gets overlooked.

Genesis 6:9 (Koine Interlinear Bible) *"And these are the origins of Noah. Noah was a just man being perfect in his generation; Noah was well-pleasing to God."*

This verse is easily overlooked because much of Genesis 6 is shocking to the reader. With the account of the 'sons of God' mating with human women and producing a hybrid offspring, verse 9 appears insignificant in comparison. It's only by examining the Septuagint translation of this passage that we uncover a critical clue. The Greek word used for "generation" is one we have seen before, '*genea.*' It's the Greek word that forms the English words generation, genes, genealogy. Therefore, "being perfect in his generation" means that Noah's genealogy, his genome, was not corrupted by the

Nephilim. The Hebrew word for "perfect" is '*tamiym*' which means "complete, whole, healthful, unimpaired, sound."[115] Therefore, "being perfect in his generation" means that Noah's genealogy, his genome, was not corrupted by the Nephilim. Noah was 100% pure human, not only that, he pleased God by walking in fear of the Lord. Noah was someone that Yahweh could work with to restart creation. Once every living being was destroyed from the Flood, Noah and his family represented a fresh, new beginning for humanity.

This brings us full circle to the age-old question, how were the Nephilim found on the earth after the Flood? I don't believe the Flood was localized, nor do I believe God's judgment was inadequate in eradicating the Nephilim. The Nephilim are no match for God's judgment! I believe the answer partially lies within our understanding of epigenetics and the principle of blessings and curses. If Noah's genealogy was 100% pure, this means that at the time of the Flood, Noah's genetic pool (himself, his wife and his three sons, Shem, Ham, and Japheth) were without defilement in their genome. We can be assured that the Nephilim gene did not come through Noah. This leaves us to consider Noah's daughters-in-law. Is it possible that one of them had the Nephilim gene? I think it's possible and even probable. Let's examine Ham's lineage more closely given there is biblical evidence that giants were found among his generations.

Ham's Lineage

Noah had three sons, Shem, Ham and Japheth. Of these three, Ham was the one that displayed wickedness in his heart. Shem and Japheth walked with the Lord. Our first indication of Ham's rebellious heart is found in the story of Noah's drunkenness.

Genesis 9:20-27 (NKJV) "*And Noah began to be a farmer, and he planted a vineyard. Then he drank of the wine and was drunk, and became uncovered in his tent. And Ham, the father of Canaan, **saw the nakedness of his father, and told his two brothers outside**. But Shem and Japheth took a garment, laid it on both their shoulders, and went backward and covered the nakedness of their father. Their faces were turned away, and they did not see their father's nakedness. So Noah awoke from his wine, and knew what his younger son had done to him. Then he said: 'Cursed be Canaan; a servant of servants he shall be to his brethren.' And he said: 'Blessed by the Lord, the God of Shem, and may Canaan be his servant. May God enlarge Japheth, and may he dwell in the tents of Shem; and may Canaan be his servant.*" (emphasis mine)

To understand what this story reveals about Ham's heart, we need to dig deeper. You are probably getting used to this by now. After all, that's what makes a good investigation, follow the clues to see what they reveal, right?

When Ham saw the nakedness of his father, his subsequent actions revealed the state of his heart. The Hebrew word for "saw" is '*ra'ah*' which means "to observe, to watch, to gaze upon, to give attention to, to look intently."[116] Instead of quickly covering up his father's nakedness, Ham stared at Noah's indecency for a while, perhaps amused by his father's humiliating condition. Ham's lingering gaze, I believe, revealed a sexual perversion within his heart.

As the story unfolds, Ham proceeded to go outside of the tent and tell his brothers what he just witnessed. The Hebrew word for "tell" is '*nagad*' which means "to be conspicuous, announce, proclaim, report, declare, expound."[117] In other words, Ham was not discreet in telling his brother's what he witnessed. The Hebrew word for "outside" is '*chuwts*' which refers to "being outdoors, on the street or highway."[118] When placed into context, the meaning of these Hebrew words helps us recreate the scene. Ham was more interested in drawing attention to the humiliating state his father was in than being discreet. It's likely that as he was loudly recounting the scene to his brothers outdoors, others may have overheard, further humiliating Noah. Ham was making a mockery of Noah and in doing so deeply dishonored his father. His actions revealed the wickedness in his heart. He was not concerned with protecting Noah's dignity. Conversely, Shem and Japheth were focused on maintaining their father's dignity. They walked in backwards to avoid seeing his nakedness and placed a covering over Noah.

When Noah regained his wits, he recognized the degree to which Ham dishonored him. As a consequence, he spoke a curse over Ham's son, Canaan and his descendants. We know from biblical history that the descendants of Canaan become the enemies of Israel.

Now that we understand Ham's rebellious and dishonoring heart in more depth, it seems reasonable to presume that Ham could have chosen for himself a pagan wife rather than a woman that followed after God. Given the state of humanity at the time, it is also reasonable to presume that, as a pagan, Ham's wife could have been carrying the Nephilim gene. If this is true, then the first question that comes to mind is "why would God have allowed anyone to enter the ark carrying the Nephilim genotype if He was planning to completely destroy the genetically altered humans and animals?"

The answer to this question may lie in our understanding of recessive/dominant genes and epigenetic markers. Solid investigative work requires considering all possibilities and discarding those that are least plausible. Let's consider that Ham's wife was a carrier of a recessive Nephilim gene. It's helpful to first understand recessive and dominant genes. Below is an explanation of how they work:

"Sexually reproducing species, including people and other animals, have two copies of each gene. The two copies, called alleles, can be slightly different from each other. The differences can cause variations in the protein that's produced, or they can change protein expression: when, where, and how much protein is made. Proteins affect traits, so variations in protein activity or expression can produce different phenotypes.

A dominant allele produces a dominant phenotype in individuals who have one copy of the allele, which can come from just one parent. For a recessive allele to produce a recessive phenotype, the individual must have two copies, one from each parent. An individual with one dominant and one recessive allele for a gene will have the dominant phenotype. They are generally considered "carriers" of the recessive allele: the recessive allele is there, but the recessive phenotype is not."[119]

If Ham's wife was carrying the recessive Nephilim gene, but she herself did not have the phenotype of the Nephilim, the fact that Ham did not have the Nephilim gene presented a level of protection from the emergence of Nephilim in their offspring.

To understand this better, we can learn from the activation of sickle cell disease. Sickle cell disease is an inherited disease with a recessive pattern of inheritance. Only those who have both copies of the sickle cell allele have the disease. Those with only one copy are healthy individuals. Ham's wife could have had only one copy of the Nephilim allele and if the Nephilim gene follows a recessive pattern of inheritance, she herself would not have had the phenotype of a Nephilim. We are still left with the problem of explaining how Nephilim were present on the earth after the flood, if Ham's wife had only one copy of a recessive allele.

If the Nephilim gene is instead a dominant gene, then we would expect Ham's wife, a carrier of the Nephilim gene, to have the phenotype of a Nephilim. Remember, with a dominant gene, it only takes one copy of the allele to produce the phenotype of that dominant gene. Given that we have deduced Ham's wife did not exhibit the Nephilim phenotype, does this rule out the possibility of the Nephilim gene being dominant? No, not necessarily.

Genetic inheritance is complex. Another layer to this discussion that we need to consider is epigenetics. We have learned that our thoughts and choices, "turn on" or "turn off" epigenetic markers. These markers trigger an expression of a phenotype that was not previously present. In other words, the epigenetic markers create physical changes in traits such as stature, strength, and appearance. The agouti gene within mice can be "turned off" by environmental factors such as a diet rich in methyl groups like Vitamin B. Dr. Caroline Leaf summarizes it this way:

"Taken collectively, the studies on epigenetics show us that the good, the bad, and the ugly do come down through the generations, but your mind is the signal – the epigenetic factor – that switches these genes on or off… Here is how it works: Epigenetic changes represent a biological response to an environmental signal. That response can be inherited through the generations via the epigenetic marks. But if you remove the signal, the epigenetic marks will fade.

By the same token, if you choose to add a signal – for example, saying something like, 'My mother had depression and that's why I have depression, and now my daughter is suffering from depression'- then the epigenetic marks are activated. The thinking and speaking out the problem serve as the signal that makes it a reality.

Herein lies the key: The sins of parents create a predisposition, not a destiny. Our choices (the epigenetic signals) alter the expression of genes (the epigenetic markers), which can then be passed on to our children and grandchildren, ready to predispose them before they are even conceived. So our bad choices become their bad predispositions."[120]

Is there then an epigenetic signal that "turns on" or "turns off" the Nephilim gene? Yes, I believe we can reasonably deduce that there is an epigenetic signal that activates the Nephilim epigenetic marker. In other words, the expression of the Nephilim gene can be determined by epigenetic signals. This helps us understand that it is plausible that the Nephilim gene is a dominant gene, but can be "turned on" or "turned off" by epigenetic signals such as thoughts, words, and/or behaviors. In our case study of Ham's wife, she could have had epigenetic signals that "turned off" the expression of the dominant Nephilim gene.

Blessings and Curses

Let's dig even deeper to uncover another layer to this discussion that will tie the clues together. The principle of blessings and curses can act as an epigenetic signal. Here again Caroline Leaf's book *Switch on Your Brain* is very helpful in understanding this principle.

"The DNA is zipped up, almost as though it is in a cocoon, until activated or unzipped by the signal. When the DNA is zipped up, it is in a dormant or inert state… So, the zipped-up DNA has to be opened so that the appropriate genetic code needed to build the protein can be read. As it is opened and the code is read, RNA (a type of protein that almost acts like a photocopier) makes a photocopy of the code, which serves as a guide or architectural plan to build the proteins within the machinery inside the cell. This is called "genetic expression." And these proteins you have caused to be built hold the information you have just read as a thought or a memory. You have created substance.

The initiating signals that get the ball rolling come from outside the DNA and are therefore called epigenetic phenomena, which means signals that control the genes…When there is interference with this signal (for example, thinking a toxic thought or eating unhealthy food), genetic expression does not happen correctly and then proteins do not form like they should. So, on a very simplified level, if you have a toxic thought, the resulting proteins look different and act differently than if you had a healthy thought.

…we have a *switch gene* called the "creb gene," which we choose to switch on with our thoughts. Here is a simple explanation of this switch gene: As information in the form of electromagnetic and chemical signals moves toward the front part of the brain, it becomes amplified and highly active. This stimulates the release of specialized proteins inside the cell, turning on the creb gene, which acts like a light switch that we choose to switch on or off by our thoughts. This switch creb gene then activates genetic expression…

Scientists are discovering precise pathways by which changes in human thinking operate as signals that activate genetic expression, which then produce changes in our brains and bodies."[121]

In other words, our thoughts can unzip genes, like a Nephilim gene, that are in a dormant state. This is the scientific explanation of the impact that blessings and curses have over our lives activated by our thoughts, words, and/or behavior.

We see in Genesis 9 that Noah released blessings over Shem and Japheth because they walked with the Lord, but over Ham, he spoke a curse. Blessings and curses do not just impact an individual, they impact their generations.

Exodus 20: 4-6 (NIV) *"You shall not make for yourself an image in the form of anything in heaven above or on the earth beneath or in the waters below. You shall not bow down to them or worship them; for I, the Lord your God, am a jealous God, punishing the children for the sin of the parents to the third and fourth generation of those who hate me, but showing love to a thousand generations of those who love me and keep my commandments."*

Over and over again, scientific research provides confirmation that biblical principles are evident in nature. John Barron in his article *Everything You Need to Know About Epigenetics* summarizes a scientific study by Kaati et al. (2007), which demonstrates that curses last three to four generations, they state: "…the effect does not have to be direct. It can be transgenerational. According to a 2007 Swedish study which tracked food availability between the ages of nine and twelve for paternal grandfathers, food shortages in the grandfathers' lives affected the lifespan of their grandchildren -- but in a surprising way. A shortage of food for the grandfather was associated with an extended lifespan in his grandchildren. Food abundance, on the other hand, was associated with a greatly shortened lifespan in the grandchildren as a result of increased diabetes and heart disease. It would seem that once again, the sins of the parents (in this case "worshipping" rich foods and overeating) are visited upon the children -- even unto the third generation."[122]

The curse spoken over Ham was directed toward Canaan his son, but Ham's iniquity of sexual perversion, mockery, and dishonoring his father was the cause of the curse. This curse then acted as an epigenetic signal that unzipped the Nephilim gene in Ham's children. The clearest example of this is in the life of Nimrod, Ham's grandson.

Nimrod was the son of Cush, the grandson of Ham, and the great grandson of Noah. Within three generations from Noah, we have the emergence of the phenotype of the Nephilim.

Genesis 10:8-12 (NKJV) *"Cush begot Nimrod;* ***he began to be a mighty one on the*** ***earth****. He was a mighty hunter before the Lord; therefore it is said, "Like Nimrod the mighty hunter before the Lord." And the beginning of his kingdom was Babel, Erech, Accad, and Calneh, in the land of Shinar. From that land he went to Assyria and built Nineveh, Rehoboth Ir, Calah, and Resen between Nineveh and Calah (that is the principal city)."* (emphasis mine)

Let's explore the meaning of this passage to understand more about Nimrod. Nimrod's name means "rebellion" or "the valiant."[123] The original text provides an enlightening perspective on the meaning of this passage. The Hebrew word for the phrase "he began" is '*chalal*' which means "to profane, defile, or pollute oneself through ritual or sexual means."[124] The Hebrew word for 'mighty men' is '*gibbowr*' which means "mighty, strong, valiant, strong man, champion, giant, chief, tyrant, impetuous soldier or hunter."[125] It comes from the root word '*gabar*' meaning to "prevail, to be strong, to show oneself mighty, to act proudly toward God."[126] One of the usages of '*gibbowr*' in scripture is to refer to Nephilim and/or giants.

The exegesis of this passage in Genesis 10 sheds light upon the age-old question, how were Nephilim present after the Flood? Nimrod was not born with the phenotype of a Nephilim but he defiled his genome by engaging in ritualistic sexual acts. Nimrod's grandfather, Ham, through his iniquity of disrespectfully gazing at Noah's nakedness, created a predisposition for sexual perversion within his children and grandchildren. Ham's iniquity opened the door for curses to manifest in his generational line. All it took was Nimrod activating it, as we know that "a curse without a cause does not alight" (Proverbs 26:2).

This provides a plausible explanation of how Nephilim were present on the earth after the Flood without the need for multiple incursions. Ham's iniquity, in conjunction with his wife, a likely carrier of the Nephilim gene, and Noah's curse, set the stage for the Nephilim phenotype to emerge after the Flood. Epigenetic signals, such as deviant sexual acts, unzipped the dormant Nephilim gene and the evidence of this is found within Nimrod.

After weighing the evidence for multiple incursion and single incursion, I feel a pull to satisfy my Western mindset by choosing one theory over the other as being more plausible. I am going to resist this temptation and instead, propose that both are true. Yes, there was only one incursion that can be characterized as a massive assault on the human genome. The antediluvian incursion was an onslaught on humanity by a unified front of 200 'Watchers,' giving rise to the Nephilim of renown. They had infiltrated all of humanity, with the exception of one family – Noah's. The incursion unleashed through the Tower of Babel was cunning but not a blatant affront like what happened in Genesis 6. Once confusion and dispersion were rendered from Babel, the enemy's strategy became more insidious. The Nephilim genes were spread through multiple pathways, epigenetics, curses, sacred marriages, and other sexual rituals, just to name a few.

Russ Dizdar, from Shatter the Darkness, a deliverance minister who specializes in working with Satanic Ritual Abuse (SRA) survivors, has a "boots on the ground" perspective on the propagation of the Nephilim genes. Survivors have told him that within the SRA cults, a man and a woman will meet on a Satanic high holy day and invite a demon to join them as they have sex. The intent is that the demon enters at the point of conception to alter the DNA of the baby. This ritualistic sex act is for the purpose of spreading the Nephilim genes.[127]

As I have participated in different prayer initiatives aimed at uprooting wickedness in Utah, I have become increasingly aware of the prevalence of SRA. It's critical to equip ourselves with informed intercession to tear down this pervasive evil lurking in the shadows of our communities. My hope is that throughout the pages of this book, you will be armed with knowledge and understanding mixed with wisdom from the Lord, so that you are equipped to join the spiritual battle to thwart the Nephilim agenda!

Key Points

- The Flood wiped out the Nephilim but did not end the Seed war.
- Multiple incursions of the same magnitude as the original incursion of Genesis 6 cannot be substantiated.
- Both the multiple incursion theory and the single incursion theory explain the presence of post-diluvian giants.
- Sacred marriage within the Mesopotamian cultural between a goddess and king is an example of multiple incursions.
- Epigenetics is the key to single incursion theory explaining the presence of giants after the Flood.
- Noah's daughters-in-law were likely carriers of the Nephilim gene.

- It's plausible the Nephilim gene is a dominant gene that can be "turned on" or "turned off" by epigenetic signals such as thoughts, words, and/or behaviors.
- Ham's sexually perverse reaction to Noah's drunken, naked state released a curse on his descendants.
- Nimrod's participation in sexual rituals and the curse upon Ham's lineage, unzipped the Nephilim gene.
- The Nephilim agenda is to defile the human genome through propagating a hybrid race

Chapter 9

Character Traits of the Nephilim

With the Nephilim on the scene both before and after the Flood, the cosmic battle intensified between the woman's seed and the seed of Satan. Let's review for a moment when the Seed war first began.

Genesis 3:14-15 (The Message) *"God told the serpent: 'Because you've done this, you're cursed, cursed beyond all cattle and wild animals, cursed to slink on your belly and eat dirt all your life.* **I'm declaring war between you and the Woman, between your offspring and hers. He'll wound your head and you'll wound his heel."** (Emphasis mine)

War was declared by the Almighty God in the Garden of Eden, a war between the seed of Eve (humanity) and the seed of Satan. Eve's seed would one day crush Satan. This prophetic declaration sentenced Satan to an existence characterized by a state of alertness, vacillating between pride and panic.

As male and female, we are born in the image of God. We are the seed of Eve.

Genesis 1:27 (NIV) *"So God created mankind in his own image, in the image of God he created them; male and female he created them."*

We are created in God's image which means we are a reflection of Him. My three children share a resemblance to my husband and I. It's unmistakable. All three of them were blessed with my nose and my husband's pinky toe (it faces sideways). We joke that it's better to have gotten my nose and his pinky toe than the reverse. As male and female, we have physical features that reflect our Creator Father, but we also have spiritual DNA that reflects the nature and character of Him. So, if we are created in His image, is it possible that there are beings that are not created in His image? Is it possible for what was once created in the image of God to become so defiled, defaced and genetically altered that there is no longer a resemblance to the Creator Father? I believe the answers to these questions are "yes."

Nephilim Traits

The Nephilim were not created in the image of God, rather they are the seed of Satan. I'm confident Satan swelled with pride at the birth of the Nephilim. These giants bore the resemblance of him. They were born with treason, lust, deceit, rebellion and pride in their spiritual DNA. We will see these same characteristics in the architects of the Federal Reserve; the "six men" that stole away in the dark of night, under a cloak of deception to give birth to the Federal Reserve.

As we consider the traits of the Nephilim and their descendants, a good starting point is to examine the traits of Satan. The apple does not fall far from the tree as they say. Satan is a master deceiver, and one could argue that it is out of necessity. If anyone understood his true character, there is no one on the face of the earth that would follow after him. He is so vile and disgusting, no one would want to resemble him if they caught a glimpse of his true nature.

II Corinthians 11:13-15 (NLT) *"These people are false apostles. They are deceitful workers who disguise themselves as apostles of Christ. But I am not surprised! Even Satan disguises himself as an angel of light. So it is no wonder that his servants also disguise themselves as servants of righteousness. In the end they will get the punishment their wicked deeds deserve."*

Satan has hoodwinked his followers, his seed, into believing that he is the one true God. The fate of those that follow him is that of utter destruction. Jesus articulates this battle between the children of God and the seed of Satan when addressing the Jewish leaders.

John 8:42-44 (NIV) *"Jesus said to them, 'If God were your Father, you would love me, for I have come here from God. I have not come on my own; God sent me. Why is my language not clear to you? Because you are unable to hear what I say. You belong to your father, the devil, and you want to carry out your father's desires. He was a murderer from the beginning, not holding to the truth, for there is no truth in him. When he lies, he speaks his native language, for he is a liar and the father of lies."*

Traits that can be found in the Nephilim and the subsequent offspring of the Nephilim, are that they are deceivers, liars, and they masquerade as servants of righteousness.

Rebellion

At the root of the Nephilim traits, is rebellion. Let's go back to the beginning.

Genesis 3:1 (AMP) *"Now the serpent was more crafty (subtle, skilled in deceit) than any living creature of the field which the Lord God had made. And the serpent (Satan) said to the woman, 'Can it really be that God has said, 'You shall not eat from any tree of the garden'?"*

The Hebrew word for 'serpent' in this passage is 'nachash' which means "serpent because of its hissing."[128] It comes from the root word 'nachash' which means "divination, hiss, whisper a magic spell, an enchanter."[129] It's hard to imagine that Eve was morally seduced by a snake. Would she not have screamed and ran away? This is yet another example of how the translation of this passage lacks the depth of meaning that the original Hebrew offers. It is more plausible that Satan presented himself in an appealing manner, masquerading as an angel of light while whispering magic spells over her. Essentially, Satan engaged in witchcraft to manipulate Eve to walk in rebellion, negating the instructions God gave regarding the Tree of the Knowledge of Good and Evil. After she ate, the Father confronted her.

Genesis 3:13 (NKJV) *"And the Lord God said to the woman, 'What is this you have done?' The woman said, 'The serpent deceived me, and I ate."*

This word 'deceived' in Hebrew is 'nasha' which means "to deceive, beguile, mentally delude, morally seduce, to impose, to cause to go astray" according to Strong's Concordance.[130] But the Hebrew and English lexicon known as Brown-Driver-Briggs (BDB) defines 'nasha' as "to lend on interest, or usury, to become a creditor."[131] Did you catch that? The Hebrew word for 'deceive' means to **make someone a debtor**? Wow. This is a very important insight. In the chapters to come, we will uncover the hidden agenda of the Federal Reserve and how the American people were deceived over a century ago. As citizens, we are buried with so much debt that there is no conceivable way out, short of a miracle or drastic measures. If you want an eye-opening experience, go to USDebtClock.org and watch how fast our national debt rises. As I write this sentence, our national debt is over $22 trillion. When the Federal Reserve Act was passed just before Christmas in 1913, the Congress deviously passed legislation that enslaved American citizens in debt while enriching the coffers of the banking elite. I believe deception, lust, greed, rebellion and pride ruled the hearts of those that birthed the Federal Reserve. Before we conclude our journey together, we

126

will see how this plays out in our everyday lives without our consent. THE TRUTH SHALL SET US FREE!

When Eve was beguiled by Satan and fell into the trap of sin, the consequence was that she owed a debt that could only be paid by death. She was a debtor to her sin.

Romans 6:23 (TLV) *"For sin's payment is death, but God's gracious gift is eternal life in Messiah Yeshua our Lord."*

Stephen Quayle and Dr. Thomas Horn in their book *Unearthing the Lost World of the Cloudeaters* eloquently describe the ramifications of this great deception.

"This is the consequence of the sin of Adam and Eve in the Garden, a consequence that continues to bear bitter fruit in our own sin to this day. The act of rebellion against the Creator's command put humanity into such debt that it could only be satisfied by the blood of Jesus Christ. But Satan was the banker who wrote the note!"[132]

Consider this, we have been beguiled by elite banksters who have been led by the great deceiver, Satan himself. The entire Federal Reserve system is rooted in '*nasha.*' We will see, as we examine the players involved in the creation of the Federal Reserve, that they exuded Nephilim traits. They were master deceivers, skilled at lying to the American people, pretending to have the nation's best interest in mind, while crafting an insidious system of enslavement.

Dishonesty in Trade

Yet another sinister trait of Satan that we also find in the Nephilim and their offspring is dishonesty in trade. What do I mean by this? Let's look at Ezekiel 28.

Ezekiel 28: 12-16 (NIV) *"...You were the seal of perfection, full of wisdom and perfect in beauty. You were in Eden, the garden of God; every precious stone adorned you...You were anointed as a guardian cherub, for so I ordained you. You were on the holy mount of God; you walked among the fiery stones. You were blameless in your ways from the day you were created till wickedness was found in you.* **Through your widespread trade you were filled with violence, and you sinned.** *So I drove you in disgrace from the mount of God, and I expelled you, guardian cherub, from among the fiery stones. Your heart became proud on account of your beauty, and you corrupted your wisdom because of your splendor. So I threw you to the earth; I made a spectacle* *of you before kings. **By your many sins and dishonest trade you have desecrated your sanctuaries…***" (emphasis mine)

While on the surface, this passage is referring to the king of Tyre, but it is commonly understood that Ezekiel is describing a vision he was given of the fall of Satan. The Hebrew word for "trade" used in this passage is '*rěkullah*' which means "merchandise, trade, traffick."[133] It comes from a root word that means to "go about dubiously, trafficking." There are several Hebrew words for trade used in the Old Testament, but '*rěkullah*' is the only Hebrew word that denotes suspicious practices of trafficking merchandise and it is only used four times in the Old Testament, all of them in the book of Ezekiel.

Ezekiel's vision allowed him to understand that the trafficking Satan was involved in led to widespread violence. This is particularly insightful given the current crisis of drugs, weapons, and human trafficking we see in our world. While it's not surprising that trafficking of this nature is evil, this passage reveals that this Satanic trait is one of the reasons Satan was stripped of his splendor and banned from God's kingdom.

Control, Manipulation and Domination

Control, manipulation and domination are traits of Satan that were found within the Nephilim. Satan and the fallen 'sons of God' wanted the glory that was ascribed to the Lord. Their strategy, as we discussed in Chapter 6, was to manipulate God's seed in order to usurp the authority and dominion that was given to Adam and Eve. The strategy called for perversion of the sexual union between a husband and wife that leads to procreation. The sexual perversion involved mixing breeds and was so reprehensible, that the judgment of such an act was death. The plan of the fallen 'sons of God' was to overthrow humanity by corrupting the seed of Eve through the hybrid race of the Nephilim. Satan and the fallen 'sons of God' succeeded with this strategy for a time, but Jesus ultimately won the war through His death and resurrection. Jesus' ability to overcome death was a declaration to all the gods that there is only One True God and He reigns over all!

Sexual Perversion

A clear, identifiable trait of the Nephilim is sexual perversion. Our first indication of this trait is found in Genesis 6 when the fallen 'sons of God' abandoned their boundaries in the spiritual dimensions to commit sexual transgressions with the daughters of men, that ultimately led to their banishment without pardon to Tartarus (the deep abyss). The Nephilim were the result of this unholy union between the 'Watchers' and human women. Some details we haven't touched on yet will give us a deeper understanding of the level of sexual perversion within the Nephilim genes.

The 'Watchers,' as they are aptly revered to, *"saw the beautiful women and took any they wanted as their wives"* (Genesis 6:2; NLT). The Hebrew word for "saw" is *'ra'ah'* which means "to look intently at, to observe, to gaze at, to **watch**"[134] This suggests that they were watching the beautiful women and lusting after them. We don't know how long they were watching, but it was long enough to develop pent up lust, for which they were willing to commit treason in order to fulfill their sexual desires. Even more telling is what we learn from understanding the Hebrew word for "took" in this passage is *'laqach.'* It means "to seize, to capture, to carry off, to take in marriage."[135] In other words, the 'Watchers' captured the beautiful women and carried them off to sexually violate them, force them into marriage, and impregnate them with Nephilim. It's possible that some of the women may have felt honored to have "the gods" choose them as their wives, but the meaning of the Hebrew words used to describe this event suggests otherwise.

Some scholars have even suggested that the men willingly traded the women for the sacred knowledge they were promised from the Watchers. Is it possible that these women were the first trafficked women in human history?

Irenaeus, one of the early church fathers, describes the hidden knowledge that propagated tremendous wickedness and evil among humanity as, "the virtues of roots and herbs, and dyeing and cosmetics, and discoveries of precious materials, love philtres, hatreds, amours, passions, constraints of love, the bonds of witchcraft, every sorcery and idolatry, hateful to God."[136]

It becomes clear that the purpose of passing on the knowledge of cosmetics and dyeing was to enhance the beauty of the women, which in turn fed the lustful desires of the 'Watchers.' The writer of I Enoch includes among the teachings passed on by the 'Watchers': enchantments, sorcery, pharamakeia, divination, astrology, weaponry, and the cutting of roots.

The origins of the Nephilim are marked by sexual perversion and of the most wicked kind—mix breeding. They are the fruit of wickedness. We discussed how sexual perversion can unzip the Nephilim gene through epigenetics. The new genetic revolution of discovering the epigenome helps us understand that genes react to our behavioral choices. Genes can be passed on through a soft inheritance based on how we react to events in our daily lives. Ham's sexually perverse reaction to Noah's drunken, naked state unzipped the Nephilim gene in his descendants.

Blood Thirsty

The Nephilim were violent with no regard for human life. This trait has persisted in their descendants. The Nephilim were blood thirsty creatures, brutally cruel with humans and each other. I Enoch and Jubilees records the bloodshed brought on by the Nephilim.

I Enoch 9:8-10 *"And they have gone to the daughters of men upon the earth, and have slept with the women, and have defiled themselves, and revealed to them all kinds of sins. And the women have borne giants, and the whole earth has thereby been filled with blood and unrighteousness. And now, behold, the souls of those who have died are crying and making their suit to the gates of heaven, and their lamentations have ascended; and cannot cease because of the lawless deeds which are wrought on the earth.*

Jubilees 7:22-23 *"And they begat sons the Naphîdîm, [note: i.e. the Nephilim] and they were all unlike, [note: text probably corrupt] and they devoured one another: and the Giants slew the Nâphîl, and the Nâphîl slew the Eljô, and the Eljô mankind, and one man another. And every one sold himself to work iniquity and to shed much blood, and the earth was filled with iniquity."*

The bloodshed was so great that the cry of the spilled human blood reached heaven. The archangels Michael, Uriel, Raphael, and Gabriel heard the cries of those that had been slaughtered and brought the matter before Yahweh. The judgment rendered by the Ancient of Days was that the 'Watchers' would be forced to watch their children, the Nephilim, slay each other over the course of 500 years.

Cannibalism

Another trait that exposes the brutality of the Nephilim is cannibalism. Numbers 13 gives us our first bit of evidence when the spies report back to Moses and report its *"a land that eateth up all the inhabitants thereof* and all the people that we saw in it are *men of great stature."* The Hebrew word for "eateth" is *'akal'* which means "to devour, consume, eat, burn up, feed."[137] While many commentators may try to skirt around the reality of what was taking place in Canaan, the original Hebrew makes it clear – cannibalism. A little-known etymological clue substantiates the claim that cannibalism was rampant in Canaan. The Canaanites worshiped Baal and their priests were called *'cahna-Bal'* which means "priests of Baal." *'Cahna-Bal'* is where the English word "cannibal" is derived from.[138] The giants in the promised land were cannibals, and the spies most likely witnessed this gruesome act. No wonder they were terrified! This speaks volumes about Joshua and Caleb's trust in the Lord, but I'm getting ahead of myself.

A second clue that corroborates the biblical text that the Nephilim were cannibals can be found in I Enoch 7.

I Enoch 7:3 *"Who consumed all the acquisitions of men. And when men could no longer sustain them, the giants turned against them and devoured mankind."*

The Nephilim had a ravenous appetite. They consumed all of the available food to the point where there was no more food. This passage informs us that the antediluvian people attempted to provide food to satisfy the Nephilim, but when the food was not enough to satiate the giants, the people themselves were hunted down. The Nephilim ate the humans. This demonstrates the utter disregard for the sanctity of another person's life. Cannibalism was and is a wretched sign of the absolute evil agenda of the Nephilim. In the coming chapters, we will discover other tribes of giants and groups of people that perpetuate this Nephilim trait of cannibalism.

Mighty Men Who Were of Old, Men of Renown

In the previous two chapters, we dissected key phrases from Genesis 6:4 *'sons of God'* and *"The Nephilim were on the earth in those days – and also afterward."* Now I want to draw our attention to yet another intriguing phrase, *"mighty men who were of old, men of renown."* Let's look at this passage from several different angles to provide further understanding about the traits of the Nephilim.

Genesis 6:4 (NKJV) *"There were giants on the earth in those days, and also afterward, when the sons of God came in to the daughters of men and they bore children to them. Those were the **mighty men who were of old, men of renown.**"*

Genesis 6:4 (NIV) *"The Nephilim were on the earth in those days – and also afterward – when the sons of god went to the daughters of humans and had children by them. They were the **heroes of old, men of renown**."*

Genesis 6:4 (MSG) *"This was back in the days (and also later) when there were giants in the land. The giants came from the union of the sons of God and the daughters of men. These were the **mighty men of ancient lore, the famous ones**."*

Genesis 6:4 (NLT) *"In those days, and for some time after, giant Nephilites lived on the earth, for whenever the sons of God had intercourse with women, they gave birth to children who became the **heroes and famous warriors of ancient times**."*

Genesis 6:4 (CEB) *"In those days, giants lived on the earth and also afterward, when divine beings and human daughters had sexual relations and gave birth to children. These were the **ancient heroes, famous men**."*

The Nephilim were known as heroes of old, ancient heroes, mighty men of ancient lore, famous warriors. What is being conveyed here?

In dissecting the phrase *"**mighty men who were of old, men of renown,**"* it's helpful to look at the Hebrew words used in this phrase. As we recall from the previous chapter, the Hebrew word for "mighty men" is '*gibbowr*.' The first mention of '*gibbowr*' is in Genesis 6:4 when it is used to describe giants. There are only two times in scripture when '*gibbowr*' is used as a direct reference to giants, this passage is the first and the second is found in I Samuel 17:51 which references Goliath. Other usages of '*gibbowr*' are either indirectly referring to giants (I Samuel 7:15, Judges 5), or describing the mighty men that fought for the Lord (Joshua 6:2, II Samuel 10:7, II Samuel 16:6).

First let's try to make sense of this phrase *"**mighty men who were of old, men of renown.**"* It is all too easy to glance at a phrase in English which was translated from Hebrew and attach some basic meaning or interpretation to what we think it is saying. By digging into the Hebrew meaning of these words, we unlock hidden meaning. As we examine the meaning of the word "old," it uncovers a depth of meaning that we can't casually pick up from just simply reading the word "old." The Hebrew word used in this passage for "old" is '*owlam*.' '*Owlam*' means "ancient, from the most ancient times, everlasting, from a hidden time long ago, eternity."[139] It comes from the primitive root word '*alam*' which means "to conceal, to be hidden, to be a secret."[140] The selection of the word '*owlam*' to describe the giants provides a possible connection between the Nephilim and the builders of the ancient megalithic sites like Baalbek, Gilgal Rephaim, and the Great Pyramid. Moses could have used the Hebrew word 'zaqen' in this passage to convey a similar message; 'zaqen' means "old aged, ancient."[141] But he chose 'owlam' instead. This speaks to an epoch of time that is unknown. It speaks of giants who were from times so ancient that a beginning date cannot be established, *as if* they have been around for eternity.

The giants were "men of renown" which is the Hebrew word 'shem' meaning "name, fame, reputation, glory, memorial, monument."[142] WHAT? Wait a second... MONUMENT? Where have we seen monuments from a time so long ago that its origins are ardently debated by scholars? Yes, you guessed it, some of the ones I just mentioned- Stonehenge, Baalbek, Gilgal Rephaim, and the Great Pyramid. What do these monuments have in common? They are megalithic stone structures considered to be architectural wonders. Could the builders of these ancient monuments have been the Nephilim? There is no way to know for certain, so it remains speculation, but perhaps a reasonable possibility. At any rate, I think this theory is worth holding onto to see if it can tie any future threads together.

So, let's review what we have uncovered about the traits of the Nephilim from digging into the meaning of the Hebrew words used in Genesis 6:4. Nephilim are described as giants with great strength and mighty valor. They are tyrannical champions, certainly a formidable foe for any human. They are from an ancient epoch whose dated origins are unknown. The Nephilim had such striking characteristics that they gained a reputation of great fame. In fact, monuments memorializing them can be found across the earth.

Could it be that the Nephilim are the giants spoken of in the folklore and myths of ancient cultures? In the next chapter we will explore the answer to this question. We will closely examine Ham's grandson Nimrod and how he "became a mighty one." We've talked a little bit about the 'gibbowr.' Given the different usages of this word, it's important to consider the context in which 'gibbowr' is used. Time for a deep dive.

Key Points

- Nephilim are the seed of Satan; they are created in his image.
- Character traits of the Nephilim: treasonous, lustful, deceitful, rebellious, haughty, prideful, vengeful, violent, murderous, masqueraders as servants of righteousness,

dishonest in trade, sexually perverse, traffickers, cannibals, renowned, operate in control, manipulation and domination.

- Nephilim were from an ancient epoch of time that is unknown.
- Nephilim were men of renown with a reputation that was memorialized by monuments, perhaps the megalithic monuments such as Stonehenge, Baalbek, Gilgal Rephaim, and the Great Pyramid.
- The *'gibbowr'* are "mighty men," they are the post-diluvian giants.
- Not every biblical reference of *'gibbowr'* pertains to giants, it's important to consider the context.

Chapter 10

The 'Gibbowr'

In this chapter, we will build upon the information we just gathered about the traits of the Nephilim and study more closely, the character of three post-diluvian men (Nimrod, Goliath, King Saul) identified as '*gibbowr*' to categorize their distinguishable traits. I encourage you to look for patterns that emerge among the traits found in each of them. We will also examine the cultural and spiritual conditions of three cities with ties to the '*gibbowr*' and what disasters befell these cities.

Nimrod

In the chapter 8, I proposed that there are multiple pathways by which the Nephilim genes are propagated, and that Nimrod was a gateway for the spreading of the Nephilim bloodline after the Flood. Let's review for a moment what we have discovered about Nimrod.

Genesis 10:8-12 (NKJV) *"Cush begot Nimrod;* ***he began to be a mighty one on the earth.*** *He was a mighty hunter before the Lord; therefore it is said, "Like Nimrod the mighty hunter before the Lord." And the beginning of his kingdom was Babel, Erech, Accad, and Calneh, in the land of Shinar. From that land he went to Assyria and built Nineveh, Rehoboth Ir, Calah, and Resen between Nineveh and Calah (that is the principal city)."* (emphasis mine)

We learned from the original Hebrew words within this passage that Nimrod **began to be a '*gibbowr*'** because he defiled himself through ritualistic sexual acts. He had the predisposition to become a '*gibbowr*' because of Nephilim genes within his bloodline. The ritualistic sexual acts that he engaged in unzipped the epigenetic markers that activated the Nephilim genes in his genome. Thus, he developed the Nephilim phenotype.

Additionally, he fueled the insatiable hunger of the people of Babel to create a dimensional portal enabling the sexual union between the divine and cult priests/priestesses. As we dissect the above passage further, we will discover fascinating clues that would otherwise go unnoticed.

First of all, the word '*gibbowr*' is used three times in this passage describing Nimrod. This is significant because it alerts us to the substantial impact Nimrod had on the post-diluvian world. The Hebrew word for 'hunter' is '*tsayid*' which means "to chase, to catch food, hunt game, to take provision."[143] The phrase 'he was a mighty hunter before the Lord' is an interesting one. At face value, it does not seem that there is a defiance in Nimrod's hunting. In fact, some translations of this passage say that he became a mighty hunter "by the Lord's help" or because "the Lord blessed him." However, the Hebrew meaning of the phrase "before the Lord" leads us to understand Nimrod's heart motivation with more clarity. The Hebrew word for "before" is '*pariym*' which means "in the face of, in front of, in the presence of" but it can also mean "to say or do anything to anyone's face, to do something 'freely, frankly, and even often impudently and insolently, also, in contempt of.'"[144] The Greek translation of the Septuagint lends further confirmation of Nimrod's modus operandi.

Genesis 10:9 (LXX) "*This one was a giant hunter with hounds before the Lord God. On account of this they shall say, As Nimrod a giant hunter with hounds before the Lord.*"

The Greek word used for 'before' in the Septuagint is '*enantion*' which means "over against, opposite, contrary, hostile, antagonistic in feeling or act, adversary, opponent."[145] So both the original Hebrew and Greek translations of this passage provide evidence that Nimrod's hunting, for which he was so well-known, was a source of pride and an act of defiance in the face of God. Jewish writer R. Gedaliah says Nimrod:

"was called a mighty hunter because he was all his days taking provinces by force and spoiling others of their substance; and that he was 'before the Lord,' truly so, and he seeing and taking notice of it, openly and publicly and without fear of Him, and in a bold and impudent manner in despite of him."[146]

Nimrod was an enemy of the Lord bent on rebellion, which was his namesake. He brashly provoked the Lord to His face. We must understand that rebellion is at the core of all pagan religions because God commands us to have no other gods before Him

(Exodus 20:3). Nimrod's rebellion is also a hallmark trait of the '*gibbowr.*' Let's not stop here though, there are several other Nephilim traits that were evident in his life.

Perhaps we should look into what he hunted. Matthew Henry, the 17th century Biblical commentator provides us with some insight.

"Some think Nimrod did good with his hunting by serving his country in getting rid of wild beasts. Others think that under pretense of hunting, he gathered men under his command, in pursuit of another game he had to play, which was to make himself master of the country and to bring them into subjection. Nimrod was a mighty hunter against the Lord, so the Septuagint, that is (1) He set up idolatry for the confirming of his usurped dominion. That he might set up a new government, he set up a new religion upon the ruin of the primitive constitution of both. Babel was the mother of harlots. Or (2) He carried on his oppression and violence in defiance of God himself, daring heaven with his impieties, as if he and his huntsmen could out brave the Almighty."[147]

I think it's quite possible that Nimrod began hunting wild beasts, but quickly realized his prowess in hunting could be applied toward the domination of others and a rise to power. In John Gill's exposition of Genesis 10:9, he points out that Nimrod ingratiated himself to the people by hunting and killing the wild beasts that would devour them. Nimrod's fame grew quickly, and he was able to attract large groups of men for "hunting which trains men for military exercises whereby they can hunt and destroy men."[148]

The mighty hunter, Nimrod, was driven by a desire for control and domination over others. He used intimidation and fear to suppress his subjects. These are Nephilim traits that we will see in the other '*gibbowr.*'

The Jewish historian, Josephus, supplies us with yet another unique perspective of Nimrod that fills in even more detail for our character sketch.

"Nimrod… was a bold man, and of great strength of hand… He also gradually changed the government into tyranny – seeing no other way of turning men from the fear of God, but to bring them into a constant dependence upon his power. He also said he would be revenged on God, if he should have a mind to drown the world again; for that he would build a tower too high for the waters to be able to reach and that he would avenge himself on God for destroying their forefathers!

Now the multitude was very ready to follow the determination of Nimrod, and to esteem it a piece of cowardice to submit to God; and they built a tower, neither sparing any pains nor being in any degree negligent about the work (Book 1, Chapter 4, 35)."[149]

Nimrod was filled with such pride and arrogance that he believed his own hands could create something that would outmaneuver the Almighty God. He led the people away from a relationship with their Creator and instead taught them to take pride in the works of their own hands.

The Jerusalem Targum says: "He was powerful in hunting and in wickedness before the Lord, for he was a hunter of the sons of men, and he said to them, 'Depart from the judgment of the Lord, and adhere to the judgment of Nimrod!' Therefore, it is said: 'As Nimrod [is] the strong one, strong in hunting, and in wickedness before the Lord."[150]

Our character sketch of Nimrod reveals that he was Satan's first attempt at raising up a type of antichrist. It is widely agreed upon among scholars that Nimrod was the first world leader in human history, the first "globalist" so to speak. Genesis 10 gives a list of the cities he built: Babel, Erech, Accad, Calneh, Nineveh, Rehoboth Ir, Calah and Resen. Interestingly, we can discover a lot about Nimrod's reign through the definition of the names of the cities he built.

- Babel = confusion by mixing
- Erech = lengthen or prolong
- Accad = subtle but comes from unused root word meaning to strengthen
- Calneh = fortress of Anu (supreme god within the Mesopotamian culture)
- Ninevah = abode of Ninus (extrabiblical writings posit that Ninus is Nimrod)
- Rehoboth Ir = wide places or streets
- Calath = vigor, complete, resilient strength
- Resen = bridle used to constrain and control a horse[151]

A composite portrayal of the purpose of Nimrod's kingdom from the above definitions is that Nimrod controlled his subjects by introducing confusion and the mixing of his ways with God's ways. Nimrod subtly strengthened his grip as world leader by prolonging confusion along with the worship of the god Anu. This worship of Anu ushered in multiple pathways to higher beings through the emergence of the Assyrian pantheon.

With the great dispersal of humanity, Nimrod's pantheon of worship was also dispersed among the nations. As the people migrated across the face of the earth, they incorporated the worship from Babel into their new land, using their new language. The false worship offered up at Babel became the root of all pagan religions. The pantheons of Egypt, Babylonia, India, Greece and Rome have their origins in the pantheon birthed in Babel.

Satan's grand plan was to establish an antichrist that had a defiled genome and a Nephilim phenotype that would establish the foundation of paganism. This was accomplished in part through Nimrod. The people were lured away from worshiping the one true God and were led to worship a false, perverted trinity consisting of Nimrod, Semiramis, and Horus. Nimrod had sexual relations with his mother, Semiramis, and then married her (this sexual perversion is further evidence of Nephilim traits). Nimrod became worshiped as the sun god because of the link between his birthday and the winter solstice. The light of the sun grows more dim as the winter solstice approaches, with each subsequent day following the solstice, the sun becomes brighter and brighter signifying the rebirth of the sun. The deified Nimrod, as sun god, has been worshiped by all the cultures of the earth. Here is a shortened list of the different names of Nimrod, the sun god:

- Osiris
- Tammuz
- Moloch
- Baal
- Dagon
- Atlas
- Marduk
- Saturn
- Mars
- Shamash
- Kronos
- Ninurta
- Zeus
- Dionysus
- Mithra
- Ra.

Semiramis also received worship, primarily as the moon goddess, also known as the "Queen of Heaven." Here is a shortened list of the different names of the deified Semiramis:

- Isis
- Ishtar
- Queen of Heaven
- Ashtoreth
- Asherah
- Artemis
- Diana
- Astarte
- Gaia
- Columbia
- Juno
- Hera
- Inanna
- Jezebel
- Lilith
- Mary

I dare say, that many of us in the Westernized world, even Christians, engage in practices and traditions that have their roots in the paganism that Nimrod propagated. Let's explore an example in this next section.

Trap of Syncretism

Nimrod's death marked the intensification of cult worship. His mother/wife, Semiramis, proclaimed that Nimrod's blood fell upon the stump of a dead evergreen tree. The blood of Nimrod brought forth new life in this evergreen and it grew in fullness. Semiramis promulgated the belief that Nimrod came back to life, as symbolized by the birth of this evergreen tree.

Semiramis fueled the worship of Nimrod when she declared a few years after his death, that she had been visited by the spirit of Nimrod for an immaculate conception. She gave birth to Horus, also known as Tammuz/Gilgamesh. She proclaimed that

Horus/Tammuz/Gilgamesh was Nimrod reincarnated. This, of course, is the counterfeit for the virgin birth of the Messiah. Horus and Semiramis were worshiped as the Madonna and Child.[152] Semiramis claimed that on the anniversary of Nimrod's birth, December 25th, the spirit of Nimrod would visit the evergreen tree and leave gifts underneath. This is the origin of the Christmas tree and many of our Christmas traditions have roots in this pagan worship.

This brings up the question, why do Christians celebrate Jesus' birth on December 25th? There is no biblical reference to the time of the year Jesus was born, which is a bit curious given the fact that the Bible is full of specific dates. For example, we know that it was during Passover that Jesus was crucified, and it was during Pentecost that the Holy Spirit was poured out. We know when Ezekiel received the vision of the living creatures and the glory of the Lord.

Ezekiel 1:1 (NIV) *"In my thirtieth year, in the fourth month on the fifth day, while I was among the exiles by the Kebar River, the heavens were opened and I saw visions of God."*

These are just a few examples of specific dates mentioned in scripture. Why is it that the specific date of one of the biggest events and greatest fulfillment of prophecy, Jesus' birth, is not mentioned in scripture? Religious historians would propose it's because the Jews did not celebrate birthdays. The celebration of birthdays is something the pagans engaged in. The Encyclopedia Judaica states "the celebration of birthdays is unknown in traditional Jewish ritual."[153] Rather in Judaism, people are memorialized on the day of their death. The apostles and the followers of Jesus in the early church would not have celebrated birthdays, but rather the day of one's death because it is the moment a person becomes free of the flesh and fully manifest in the spirit.

While the Bible does not clearly articulate the exact date of Jesus' birth, there are many passages ripe with clues that when compiled, point to a likely conclusion of when Jesus was born. Let's take a look at these passages, because in the chapters to follow, we will see how these dots connect to uncover the significance of the timing of the Federal Reserve Act of 1913.

Luke 2:8 (NIV) *"And there were shepherds living out in the fields nearby, keeping watch over their flocks at night."*

Luke provides a clue as he describes that the sheep were out in the fields at night and the shepherds were watching over them. If we consider the weather patterns of

Bethlehem and the cultural traditions of the shepherds, Jesus' birth was most likely not in December. In the book *Daily Life in the Time of Jesus*, Henri Daniel-Rops, a celebrated French academician, notes:

"Palestine may well be a country where clothing and heating do not present very serious difficulties, but the daily and yearly variations are often great. Between midnight and noon, the difference is sometimes 74°F, and the nights often so cold that the Law required the creditor to give the debtor back his cloak, taken as a pledge, at dusk.

The flocks had to spend the greater part of the year in the open air: they were led out the week before the Passover, and they did not come back again until half-way through November, as the first rains of *Hesvan*. They passed the winter under cover, and from this alone it may be seen that the traditional date for Christmas, in the winter, is unlikely to be right, since the Gospel says that the shepherds were in the fields. "[154]

This is corroborated by Adam Clarke's commentary:

"It was custom among the Jews to send out their sheep to the deserts [wilderness], about the Passover [sic], and bring them home at the commencement of the first rain: during the time they were out, the shepherds watched them night and day. As the Passover [sic] occurred in the spring, and the first rain began early in the month of Marchesvan, which answers to part of our October and November, we find that the sheep were kept out in the open country during the whole of the summer. And as these shepherds had not yet brought home their flocks, it is a presumptive argument that October had not yet commenced, and that, consequently, our Lord was not born on the 25th of December, when no flocks were out in the fields; nor could He have been born later than September, as the flocks were still in the fields by night. On this very ground the nativity in December should be given up. The feeding of the flocks by night in the fields is a chronological fact, which casts considerable light on this disputed point."[155]

With the clues offered to us in the above scripture, we can narrow the potential dates of Jesus birth to sometime between Passover and mid-November. The gospel writer, Luke, was a physician with a meticulous writing manner, so it's no wonder he provides the most details out of the gospel writers. Let's see what other clues he provided to help us hone in on the timing of Jesus' birth.

Luke 1:5,8,11-13 (NASB) *"In the days of Herod, king of Judea, there was a priest named Zacharias, of the division of Abijah, and he had a wife from the daughters of*

Aaron, and her name was Elizabeth… Now it happened that while he was performing his priestly service before God in the appointed order of his division, according to the custom of the priestly office, he was chosen by lot to enter the temple of the Lord and burn incense… And an angel of the Lord appeared to him, standing to the right of the altar of incense. Zacharias was troubled when he saw the angel, and fear gripped him. But the angel said to him, 'Do not be afraid, Zacharias, for your petition has been heard, and your wife Elizabeth will bear you a son, and you will give him the name John.''

There is a lot of information in these passages, but I want to draw our attention to the "division of Abijah," because this little detail provides us with a clue regarding the time of the year Zacharias would have been serving his priestly duties.

First, we need to reference I Chronicles 24 as it describes the rotation of the priestly duties by weeks. In verse 10 it says, *"the eighth for Abijah,"* meaning the 8th week was the priestly duty for Abijah and subsequently, his descendants. It was customary for the priests to serve from Sabbath to Sabbath, which was eight days in total because they would overlap their duties on the Sabbath. Additionally, every priest was called to service during the week of the three feasts: Passover, Pentecost, and Tabernacles. Given that Abijah served the 8th week, it would have actually been the 9th week after taking into account the Passover week. The 9th week would have been Iyar 28 – Sivan 5 on the Hebrew calendar. Zacharias would have also stayed to minister during the 10th week because it was Pentecost. Given all this, Zacharias most likely would have been in the temple from Iyar 28 – Sivan 13. Now it's possible that Elizabeth conceived the week Zacharias returned home, which would have been Sivan 14-19, of course, we cannot know for certain the date of her conception. But if she conceived during that timeframe, Elizabeth would have been six months pregnant in Kislev, around the time of Hanukkah.

Luke 1:36-38 (NIV) *"Even Elizabeth your relative is going to have a child in her old age, and she who was said to be unable to conceive is in her sixth month. For no word from God will ever fail.' 'I am the Lord's servant,' Mary answered. 'May your word to me be fulfilled.' Then the angel left her."*

Now if we begin to put some of these pieces together, Elizabeth was about six months pregnant around the time of Hanukkah; when the angel Gabriel gave Mary the news that she will conceive a baby named Jesus. Therefore, it's possible that Jesus was conceived during Hanukkah, also known as the Feast of Lights. Let's take a moment to pause and appreciate the beautiful symbolism of this timing. Jesus, the Light of the World, may have been conceived during the Feast of Lights. Furthermore, if we presume that Mary was nine months pregnant when she delivered baby Jesus, nine months from Kislev is the month of Tishri, the time of the Feast of Trumpets also known as Rosh Hashanah. Once again, the symbolism is beautiful in the timing of Jesus' birth. Immanuel, God with us, was most likely born at the start of the Jewish New Year. Michael Heiser quotes Greg Beale, a New Testament scholar from Westminster Theological Seminary, as he notes the significance of Tishri 1.

"[A] trumpet was to be blown on Tishri 1, which in the rabbinic period came to be viewed as the beginning of the New Year. God's eschatological judgment of all people was expected to fall on this day... The New Year trumpet also proclaimed hope in the ongoing and ultimate kingship of God, in God's judgment and reward according to people's deeds, and in Israel's final restoration."[156]

The blasts of the trumpet on Rosh Hashanah is meant to awaken people that a shift has occurred. In the natural, it's a shift in the Hebrew calendar year, but in the spiritual, it's a shift in perspective. The trumpet sound is meant to awaken people to prepare for the day of atonement, but it also serves as a reminder of when the trumpet blasts sounded drawing Israel to the base of Mt. Sinai. It was at that appointed time that Israel entered into the Mosaic covenant through the law given to Moses. Revelation is released at the sound of the trumpet blasts. It also symbolizes the coronation of a king, in fact, many of the ancient kings were coronated on this day. It seems apropos then that the sound of the shofar on the Feast of Trumpets on Tishri 1 was an awakening for the people to the revelation that the King of all kings had just been born. The Feast of Trumpets in the year of Jesus' birth was on September 11, 3 B.C. The birth of the promised Messiah brought the kingdom of God to earth, marking not just a new day, or a new month, or a new year but a NEW ERA! Blow the trumpets in Zion!

In *Reversing Hermon*, Michael Heiser presents convincing material that the astronomical events and the astral prophecy of Jesus' birth confirm the date of September 11, 3 B.C. For our purposes, I will summarize his argument, but I highly recommend you read his book if you are interested in conducting a deeper dive into the timing of Jesus' birth. I especially appreciate that, in his book, Dr. Heiser compiles the viewpoints and interpretations of many biblical scholars. Psalm 19 proclaims that the heavens declare the glory of God and that day after day, the celestial bodies pour forth their speech revealing the knowledge of the Lord. In sync with this concept, we would expect that the birth of the Messiah would be announced in the heavens as well. This is, in fact, what happened. If we look at the astronomical events, we can pinpoint the day of Jesus' birth. Most of us are familiar with the stories of the "star of Bethlehem" that the wise men followed to find baby Jesus. Well, let's just say that is the tip of the iceberg when it comes to signs in the heavens pointing to the birth of Jesus. The signs in the heavens are connected to what John wrote in Revelation 12. John spoke of great signs in the heavens related to a woman clothed with the sun, the moon under her feet, and 12 stars adorning a crown on her head, giving birth to a male child which the red dragon will try to devour. The symbolism in this passage speaks to the virgin Mary, the birth of Jesus, and Satan's attempt to devour Jesus. Revelation 12 speaks to Jesus' birth but also His second coming. During the time of Jesus birth, the constellations were aligned in such a way to confirm the Messianic prophecies. This is what caught the attention of the Magi, not simply the brightness of the "star of Bethlehem," but rather the significance of the alignment of the stars in their constellations. The only time of the year when the sun would be aligned in such a way within the Virgo (virgin) constellation for the woman to be "clothed" by the sun, is a 20-day window of time. But then to add the detail of the moon located under the feet of the woman narrows the window of time to a 90-minute period on September 11, 3 B.C.[157]

If we consider the time of year that the sheep are out in the fields at night, the time of year that Zacharias served in the Temple, and the astronomical signs in the heavens, we can with more certainty say that Jesus' birth was not on December 25th, as tradition has it. So why do we still celebrate the nativity on December 25th? In one word—**syncretism**. Can you see Satan's strategy? If a day that is venerated by most Christians around the world as being the day that our Lord was born, is not actually rooted in the very nativity it is purposed to celebrate, but rather is rooted in the counterfeit nativity of Semiramis and Horus, then the sacred has been defiled. We must ask ourselves, should we continue to participate in a celebration that has been defiled?

I know this probably shakes the very ground you are standing on to consider walking away from the Christmas traditions. We all grew up with the warm memories of families gathered together around the Christmas tree exchanging gifts, laughing, enjoying one another's company. Believe me, it's hard to walk away. In our family, we are still transitioning away from the cultural traditions of Christmas. For our children especially, it's difficult to discontinue some of these time-honored traditions. We have incorporated celebrating Hanukkah (as it's commonly celebrated in December according to the Hebrew calendar), as we gradually reduce our focus on Christmas. It has become a beautiful time of quiet reflection as our family gathers around the menorah. We each take turns lighting the candles and sharing about the miraculous ways Jesus has moved in our lives. It's simple, peaceful, and beautiful. I love it!

Now, let's transition to an examination of the cultural and spiritual condition of Babel, particularly because it was founded by Nimrod, a '*gibbowr.*'

Babel

The most notable of Nimrod's cities was Babel. Within Babel lies the heart of the mystery religions. There is much to uncover in the sands of time regarding what took place at Babel. Let's first look at the biblical references to Babel.

Genesis 11:1-9 (NIV) "*Now the whole world had one language and a common speech. As people moved eastward, they found a plain in Shinar and settled there. They said to each other, 'Come, let's make bricks and bake them thoroughly.' They used brick instead of stone, and tar for mortar. Then they said, 'Come let us build ourselves a city, with a tower that reaches to the heavens, so that we may make a name for ourselves; otherwise we will be scattered over the face of the whole earth.'*

But the Lord came down to see the city and the tower the people were building. The Lord said, 'If as one people speaking the same language they have begun to do this, then nothing they plan to do will be impossible for them. Come, let us go down and confuse their language so they will not understand each other.'

So the Lord scattered them from there over all the earth, and they stopped building the city. That is why it was called Babel – because there the Lord confused the language of the whole world. From there the Lord scattered them over the face of the whole earth."

The post-diluvian people gathered together in the plain of Shinar, which in Akkadian is Sumer, Mesopotamia, or modern-day Iraq. The entire human population spoke the same language. They began to build a tower in Babel. The word "Babel" in Akkadian means "gate of the gods" but it is also a play on the Hebrew word which means "confusion." What was the purpose of building a tower? Josephus intimated that it was to protect themselves from flood waters again overtaking the earth. The Hebrew meaning of the phrase *"so that we may make a name for ourselves"* is to build a monument or memorial in order to draw fame and glory.[158] This definition exposes the motivation of Nimrod and his followers, they wanted to be known, they wanted glory for themselves so that subsequent generations would revere them—the pride of life. This sounds Luciferian in nature, does it not? This is what the *'gibbowr'* sought after too, to be **men of renown.** Was it just this or was there more to the purpose of the Tower of Babel?

Thomas Horn and Cris Putnam propose in their book *On the Path of the Immortals* that the Tower of Babel was a stargate, similar to the Great Pyramid.

"This was not merely a tower intended to reach heaven due to its height. This was a Stargate, whose design was inspired by forbidden knowledge. Nimrod had deciphered the secret to unlocking a portal – an Einstein-Rosen Bridge that would lead to the heights once envied by Satan: the Sides of the North – the Heavenly Throne.

…the ancient land of Sumer (known as Shinar and later Babylon) produced original accounts by scribes who detailed how certain "gods" descended from Heaven – sometimes in "flying" machines and sometimes through magical doorways associated with specific mountains. These stories were pressed onto Sumerian cuneiform clay tablets using pictographs and other symbols to produce the first known system of writing and recordkeeping. The fantastic encounters told of how visits by the "gods" led to advanced scientific and arcane knowledge, which later was codified in the Babylonian[1] Mysteries and worship of Ishtar, Tammuz, Ashtaroth, and various Baals."[159]

This reminds me of my experience in Pecetto Torinese, Italy with the gates and portals that I wrote about in Chapter 2. It appears that Nimrod had the ability to discern portals and stargates being part man, part divine in his Nephilim phenotype. There is some support to this theory when we remember that the Akkadian definition of Babel means "the gate of the gods." So, if Nimrod was building a tower that would act as a portal, what was he hoping to do with it? Is it possible, Nimrod was trying to open the gate to Tartarus, that woeful abode of the fallen 'sons of God' (II Peter 2:4)? Could he have

---

[1]As a point of clarification, I am in agreement with the preponderance of biblical scholars who link Babel with Babylon. There are some who argue that these cities are in fact different, such as Derek Gilbert in chapter 3 of *The Great Inception*, but for the purposes of this book, I will interchangeably use Babel and Babylon. While they were two distinct cities during different eras, they were both located in the plain of Shinar, and more importantly ruled by the same territorial spirits.

been trying to reach heaven to storm the gates of the kingdom of God to attempt a coup? Of course, this seems preposterous. Who can overthrow God? No Being is more powerful than God, but that hasn't stopped Satan and his throngs from attempting it. Psalm 2 records a conversation between the Trinity regarding an attempted coup that the nations plot.

Psalm 2 (TPT) *Act 1 – The Nations Speak*

"How dare the nations plan a rebellion. Their foolish plots are futile! Look at how the power brokers of the world rise up to hold their summit as the rulers scheme and confer together against Yahweh and his Anointed King, saying: 'Let's come together and break away from the Creator. Once and for all let's cast off these controlling chains of God and his Christ!'

Act II – God Speaks

God-Enthroned merely laughs at them; the Sovereign One mocks their madness! Then with the fierceness of his fiery anger he settles the issue and terrifies them to death with these words: 'I myself have poured out my King on Zion, my holy mountain.'

Act III – The Son Speaks

'I will reveal the eternal purpose of God. For he has decreed over me, 'You are my favored Son. And as your Father I have crowned you as My King Eternal. Today I became your Father. Ask me to give you the nations and I will do it, and they shall become your legacy. Your domain will stretch to the ends of the earth. And you will shepherd them with unlimited authority, crushing their rebellion as an iron rod smashes jars of clay.'

Act IV – The Holy Spirit Speaks

Listen to me, all you rebel-kings and all you upstart judges of the earth. Learn your lesson while there's still time. Serve and worship the awe-inspiring God. Recognize his greatness and bow before him, trembling with reverence in his presence. Fall facedown before him and kiss the Son before his anger is roused against you. Remember that his wrath can be quickly kindled! But many blessings are waiting for all who turn aside to hide themselves in him!"

Satan and his stooges have led one failed coup attempt after another to overthrow Yahweh and the King of all kings. Psalm 2 is a warning to all those earthly rulers who think they can match the strength, wisdom, and power of the Lord. It can't be done! But this is what pride does, it falsely inflates the ego. Nimrod had a classic case of an overinflated ego; he was a narcissist of the highest order.

Michael Heiser in *The Unseen Realm* links the building of the Tower of Babel to the transgressions of Genesis 6:1-4, which is yet further confirmation that Nimrod exhibited the traits of the Nephilim.

"…gods were perceived to live on mountains. The Tower of Babel is regarded by all scholars as one of Mesopotamia's famous man-made sacred mountains – a ziggurat. Ziggurats were divine abodes, places where Mesopotamians believed heaven and earth intersected. The nature of this structure makes evident the purpose in building it – to bring the divine down to earth.

The biblical writer wastes no time in linking this act to the earlier divine transgression of Genesis 6:1-4. That passage sought to portray the giant quasi-divine Babylonian culture heroes (the apkallus) who survived the flood as "men of renown" or, more literally, "men of the name [*shem*]." Those who build the Tower of Babel wanted to do so to "make a name [*shem*]" for themselves. The building of the Tower of Babel meant perpetuating Babylonian religious knowledge and substituting the rule of Babel's gods for rule by Yahweh."[160]

Dr. Heiser points out that when God confused the language and dispersed the people across the earth, He handed over the governing of these burgeoning nations to the gods. He forsook the other nations and sought to establish a nation unto His own, Israel. We see this described in Deuteronomy 32 and Psalm 82.

Deuteronomy 32:8-9 (ESV) *"When the Most High gave to the nations their inheritance, when he divided mankind, he fixed the borders of the peoples according to the number of the sons of God. But the Lord's portion is his people Jacob his allotted heritage."*

Deuteronomy 32:17a (NKJV) *"They* [Israel] *sacrificed to demons, not to God, to gods they did not know..."*

Psalm 82 (NKJV) *"God stands in the congregation of the mighty; He judges among the gods. How long will you judge unjustly, and show partiality to the wicked? Defend the poor and fatherless; do justice to the afflicted and needy. Deliver the poor and needy; free them from the hand of the wicked.*

They do not know, nor do they understand; they walk about in darkness; all the foundations of the earth are unstable.

I said, 'You are gods, and all of you are children of the Most High. But you shall die like men, and fall like one of the princes.'

Arise, O God, judge the earth; for you shall inherit all nations."

To more fully understand these passages, it's helpful to know that there are three tiers of hierarchy in the divine realm. The first and highest tier is the Almighty Elohim, the Father, Son and Holy Spirit. The second tier is the divine council, the '*beney elohim*,' the 'sons of God.' The third level are angels also known as messengers. Almighty Elohim separated the nations and gave them to the '*beney elohim*,' His divine council, to rule over. But we see from the above passages, that the gods governed the nations with wickedness and injustice. Psalm 82 speaks of the judgment they will face for their corruption in administering the nations of the earth.

It's important to note that the 'sons of God' mentioned in Psalm 82 are different from the fallen 'sons of God' mentioned in Genesis 6. We know from Jude, Peter and the Enochian texts that the 'Watchers' of Genesis 6 were bound up in chains for their treasonous acts and are imprisoned in Tartarus until the great day of judgement. Whereas the 'sons of God' described in Psalm 82, are not locked up yet and are still governing some of the nations.

After the dispersion of the people from Babel, the Most High portioned out a people for himself, the nation of Israel. He would be their God and would govern them with love, protection, provision and justice, but they too would rebel and sacrifice to demons while worshiping other gods.

If the Tower of Babel was built to be a portal into other dimensions, it's conceivable that Nimrod was attempting to not only unleash the fallen 'sons of God' from Tartarus, but also release the re-emergence of the Nephilim. If this was the intent of Nimrod and the people of Babel, it certainly explains the urgency for Yahweh to intervene as He did. I believe the globalists, who are driving toward one world government, have the same goal which is to open up a stargate to unleash the hordes of hell. The global leader who will rule the New World Order will be empowered by the hordes of hell to incite every form of wickedness just as in the days of Noah.

What does scripture have to say about the 'Watchers' being released? And will the *'gibbowr'* be released at the same time as the Watchers? First let's look at two passages from Jude and II Peter that give us a better understanding of Tartarus.

Jude 1: 6 (TPT) *"In the same way, there were heavenly messengers in rebellion who went outside their rightful domain of authority and abandoned their appointed realms. God bound them in everlasting chains and is keeping them in the dark abyss of the netherworld until the judgment of the great day."*

II Peter 2:4 (NIV) *"For if God did not spare angels when they sinned, but sent them to hell, putting them in chains of darkness to be held for judgment."*

The Greek word for "hell" used in II Peter 2:4 is *'tartaroō'* which comes from the Greek root word 'Tartarus,' the "deepest abyss of Hell." This is the only place in scripture where *'tartaroō'* is used. Tartarus is the "name of the subterranean region, doleful and dark, regarded by the ancient Greeks as the abode of the wicked dead, where they suffer punishment for their evil deeds."[161] In Homer's Iliad, Tartarus was as, "far below, where the uttermost depth of the pit lies under earth, where there are gates of iron and a brazen doorstone, as far beneath the house of Aides as from earth the sky lies" (Homer Iliad, 8:13 ff). This speaks to the extreme judgment that was rendered upon the 'Watchers' for their treasonous acts. When the fallen 'sons of God' left their proper domain and did not keep their own designated place of power, they were bound in everlasting chains of darkness until the great day of judgment. No Being, human, divine, or hybrid, has the authority to let these 'Watchers' out of Tartarus. They will ultimately be dealt with according to Yahweh's wisdom and power at the appointed time on the great day of judgment.

There are a handful of biblical passages that require a deeper look in order to answer the question. Will the hordes of hell be released in the last days? Isaiah 13 offers some interesting clues. In fact, some scholars have pointed to the Septuagint translation of Isaiah 13 as evidence that there will be a return of the *'gibbowr.'* Horn and Putnam write: "The first oracle against Babylon by the prophet Isaiah opens as the day of the Lord looms over the world (Isaiah 13). The ancient scholars and rabbis who translated the Hebrew into the Greek Septuagint chose the Greek *gigantes* to render the Hebrew *gibborim*, predicting the return of "giants" with "monsters" at the advent of the destruction of Babylon in the final age. From the Septuagint we read:

The vision which Esaias son of Amos saw against Babylon. Lift up a standard on the mountain of the plain, exalt the voice to them, beckon with the hand, open the gates, ye ruler, I give command and I bring them: *giants* are coming to fulfill my wrath… For behold! The day of the Lord is coming which cannot be escaped, a day of wrath and anger, to make the world desolate… And Babylon… shall be as when God overthrew Sodom and Gomorrah… It shall never be inhabited… and monsters shall rest there, and devils shall dance there, and satyrs shall dwell there. (Isaiah 13:1-3, 9, 19-22, Brenton LXX).[162]

Isaiah 13:19-21 (NIV) *"Babylon, the jewel of kingdoms, the pride and glory of the Babylonians, will be overthrown by God like Sodom and Gomorrah. She will never be inhabited or lived in through all generations; there no nomads will pitch their tents, there no shepherds will rest their flocks. But the desert creatures will lie there, jackals will fill her houses; there the owls will dwell, and there the wild goats will leap about."*

Some commentators suggest that Isaiah was prophesying about the fall of Babylon when Cyrus led the Persian army into Babylon in October 539 BC. If we look more closely at what Isaiah prophesied would happen, we have not yet seen these things come to pass. For example, "Babylon shall be as when God overthrew Sodom and Gomorrah." Sodom and Gomorrah were utterly destroyed by burning sulfur falling from the sky. Babylon has not yet experienced total destruction. Many empires have overtaken Babylon, but none have destroyed the city. These things that Isaiah prophesied are speaking of the end of days, the day of the Lord's judgment, which we commonly refer to as the "end times." We find more clues in verses 4-5.

Isaiah 13:4-5 (NIV) *"Listen, a noise on the mountains, like that of a great multitude! Listen, an uproar among the kingdoms, like nations massing together! The Lord Almighty is mustering an army for war. They come from faraway lands, from the ends of the heavens – the Lord and the weapons of his wrath – to destroy the whole country."*

In these verses, we see that a multitude of nations will gather together to rise up against Babylon and these nations will come from faraway lands. If we think about human history, Babylon was overtaken by Cyrus and later by Alexander the Great, neither of which ruled from faraway lands. But more importantly, neither the Persian Empire nor the Greek Empire destroyed Babylon. Both King Cyrus and Alexander the Great had tremendous respect for the wonders of Babylon, therefore they chose not to destroy the city. Even as recent as the reign of Saddam Hussain, there have been building projects to restore ancient Babylon. I believe there will be a time in the near future that Babylon will be re-established as a place of great influence.

Now let me draw our attention to the desert creatures mentioned in Isaiah 13. There are several places in scripture where desert creatures are mentioned, and most often it references desolation and darkness. According to Hebrew terminology, desert creatures were commonly interpreted as demons or gods. Of particular importance to our investigation is the mention of the owl. There are a few times in the book of Isaiah where an owl is mentioned. Similar to Isaiah 13, Isaiah 14 ties the presence of owls in Babylon to the time of its destruction.

Isaiah 14: 23 (NIV) *"I will turn her into a place for owls and into swampland; I will sweep her with the broom of destruction,' declares the Lord Almighty."*

The demonic entities or pagan deities represented by the owl can be found not only in antiquity but also in present-day secret societies. In ancient Babylon and Mesopotamia, Semiramis/Ishtar/Lilith was considered the goddess of the underworld, the "night monster" (see Figure 28). This terracotta clay plaque is a Babylonian relief housed in the British Museum. It originates from southern Mesopotamia during the reign of Hammurabi (1792-1750 BC).[163] Notice that on this relief, Lilith has clawed feet and wings similar to the owls that flank her on either side. Isaiah 34 provides the link between the screeched owl and the goddess Lilith.

Isaiah 34:14 (KJV) *"The wild beasts of the desert shall also meet with the wild beasts of the island, and the satyr shall cry to his fellow;* **the screech owl also shall rest there, and find for herself a place of rest.** *"* (emphasis mine)

The Hebrew word for "screech owl" is *'liyliyth.'* It is the only time this word is used in the Bible and it means "Lilith, the name of a female goddess known as a night demon that haunts the desolate places of Edom."[164] Jackey Colliss Harvey in her book *Red: A History of the Redhead,* provides an explanation of the origins of Lilith.

"The Talmudic *Alphabet of Ben Sira,* of the 8th to 10th century, conjures into being a first wife for Adam, pre-Eve, to explain the fact that in the Book of Genesis a 'wife' is mentioned twice…Out of this minor inconsistency, and a good deal of padding from earlier Jewish and even Babylonian mythology, was created the legend of Lilith, the woman who, seeing herself as her husband's equal, refuses to 'lie beneath,' quarrels with Adam, strikes out into the Babylonian wilderness on her own. Disputatious and disobedient, therefore, and yes, to this day, very often depicted with red hair."[165]

Figure 28. *Burney Relief or "Queen of the Night",* The British Museum, Bloomsbury, London. Photo by Nikoretro. https://www.flickr.com/photos/bellatrix6/167755135/in/photolist-2mW6-fPMKV-m7b6bt-m7c3vs-2mVW-2mW3-2mVS-6P2kY4/ CC by 2.0

Just as in antiquity, symbolism is empowering to those in esoteric circles and they take great pride in displaying their symbols. In Lilith, we have not only the representation of the owl but also the depiction of red hair. As we progress further along in our investigative journey, we will discover the connection between red hair and the Nephilim phenotype, as well as the link between the owl and the Federal Reserve Note.

I want to review some terms for the sake of clarity because it's easy to get confused about the terms 'Watchers,' fallen 'sons of God,' Nephilim, giants, *'gibbowr,'* etc. Let me make several important distinctions. The Nephilim are not the 'Watchers,' rather the Nephilim are the offspring of the 'Watchers.' The term 'Watchers' can be used interchangeably with the fallen 'sons of God' because both terms refer to the same divine beings that descended on Mt. Hermon numbering 200 according to the Enochian texts. These were divine beings that found the daughters of men irresistible and had sexual intercourse impregnating human women with a hybrid race known as the Nephilim. The *'gibbowr'* or giants are the offspring of the Nephilim, also considered hybrids.

Let's review the information we gathered from Isaiah 13 before moving on. The *'gib-bowr'* will return to the earth to be used as God's instruments of wrath when the time has come for the complete destruction of Babylon. From the annals of history, we know that the destruction of Babylon has yet to occur. Therefore, the return of giants spoken of in Isaiah 13, is different from the return of the 'Watchers.' I believe scripture shows us that both will happen in the last days. In order to understand more fully the coming influence of Babylon and the release of the 'Watchers,' we must now turn to the book of Revelation.

Revelation 9:1-11 (NIV) *"The fifth angel sounded his trumpet, and I saw a star that had fallen from the sky to the earth. The star was given the key to the shaft of the Abyss. When he opened the Abyss, smoke rose from it like the smoke from a gigantic furnace. The sun and sky were darkened by the smoke from the Abyss. And out of the smoke locusts came down on the earth and were given power like that of scorpions of the earth. They were told not to harm the grass of the earth or any plant or tree, but only those people who did not have the seal of the God on their foreheads. They were not allowed to kill them but only to torture them for five months. And the agony they suffered was like that of the sting of a scorpion when it strikes. During those days people will seek death but will not find it; they will long to die, but death will elude them.*

The locusts looked like horses prepared for battle. On their heads they wore something like crowns of gold, and their faces resembled human faces. Their hair was like women's hair, and their teeth were like lions' teeth. They had breastplates like breastplates of iron, and the sound of their wings was like the thundering of many horses and chariots rushing into battle. They had tails with stingers, like scorpions, and in their tails they had power to torment people for five months. They had as king over them the angel of the Abyss, whose name in Hebrew is Abaddon and in Greek is Apollyon (that is, Destroyer)."

Much can be written on this passage but for our purposes, we will consider a few important points. During the time when the fifth angel blows the trumpet, there is a fallen star, or fallen angel, that is given the key to unlock the shaft of the Abyss. This brings to memory what Nimrod was trying to accomplish in building the Tower of Babel. Nimrod was building a portal as a key to unlock the Abyss. One of the major differences between what Nimrod was doing in Genesis 10 and what the fallen star will do in the events described in Revelation 9 is that Nimrod was building in defiance of the Lord, trying to unlock the Abyss according to his own timing. It was not directed by the

155

Almighty Elohim, whereas the happenings of Revelation 9 will take place at the appointed time according to the purpose of Almighty Elohim.

Another point we must consider is that the locusts that are released from the Abyss are the imprisoned 'Watchers.' We know from I Enoch 10 that the 'Watchers' were locked up in Tartarus until the day of judgment. The 'Watchers' will be released to wreak havoc on the earth for a period of time. The description of the 'Watchers' as locusts, like horses prepared for battle, with women's hair, faces like that of a human, gold crowns on their heads, and teeth like a lion should not dissuade us from understanding that these are in fact the 'Watchers.' It was common in ancient Jewish literature to describe demonic entities in the form of hybrid creatures. This was and still is, in fact, the purpose of the 'Watchers'—to defile Yahweh's creation by introducing the mixing of species.

What then is the connection between the release of the Watchers in Revelation 9 and the destruction of Babylon? We can find the threads that tie this together in Isaiah 13, Jeremiah 50 and Revelation 17. Jeremiah 50 uses similar language to prophesy the coming destruction of Babylon as in Isaiah 13.

Jeremiah 50:39-40 (NIV) *"So desert creatures and hyenas will live there, and there the owl will dwell. It will never again be inhabited or lived in from generation to generation. As I overthrow Sodom and Gomorrah along with their neighboring towns.' declares the Lord, 'so no one will live there; no people will dwell in it."*

Once again, we see the desert creatures, particularly the owl, inhabiting Babylon following its destruction. The destruction described will be complete and sudden like what Sodom and Gomorrah experienced. As we have determined that the owl represents, Lilith, it's important to now make the connection that Lilith is one of the gods spoken of in Psalm 82. She has corruptly governed over nations.

Are you starting to see the big picture? In the last days, during the destruction of Babylon, the giants will return in the earth realm to be used as instruments of God's wrath (Isaiah 13:3, Septuagint translation), the gods of Psalm 82 (many of these gods are listed in the previous section as deified names of Nimrod and Semiramis) will be found in Babylon, and the 'Watchers' will emerge from the great Abyss. Babylon will become the epicenter of wickedness in the earth.

Revelation 17:3-5 (NIV) *"Then the angel carried me away in the Spirit into a wilderness. There I saw a woman sitting on a scarlet beast that was covered with blasphemous names and had seven heads and ten horns. The woman was dressed in purple and scarlet, and was glittering with gold, precious stones and pearls. She held a golden cup in her hand, filled with abominable things and the filth of her adulteries. The name written on her forehead was a mystery:*

BABYLON THE GREAT

THE MOTHER OF PROSTITUTES

AND OF THE ABOMINATIONS OF THE EARTH."

The woman who rides the beast represents idolatrous religious systems. This woman is considered by some scholars as the Queen of Heaven, Semiramis, the first high priestess of idolatry. All religious idolatry on earth, all forms of the occult, have its postdiluvian roots in Babel/Babylon and its antediluvian roots in the 'Watchers.'

As I conclude this section on Babel, the clues we have assembled point to the significance of the events that happened in antiquity and implicate mystery Babylon as still having influence in the unseen realm, but within the natural realm, it has yet to be reestablished as a great center of influence. Saddam Hussein began the rebuilding of Babylon, but will the work continue at some point? Keep an eye on Babylon!

Sodom and Gomorrah

Given the connections made in scripture between Babel/Babylon with Sodom and Gomorrah, it's essential to examine the cultural and spiritual climate within these cities as well. We will find that there is a link to the *'gibbowr'* that often goes unnoticed.

Most of us, if asked "what was the primary sin of Sodom and Gomorrah," would say homosexuality. After all, the word "sodomy" is derived from the word "Sodom," right? I don't believe that homosexuality was the cause of the utter destruction of Sodom and Gomorrah. I believe it was much more sinister. If there were any remains left of Sodom and Gomorrah, I believe the fingerprints of the Nephilim would have been detected. Given that both cities were relegated to a pile of ashes, instead, we need to turn to the Biblical text for clues about the character and nature of the people from Sodom and Gomorrah. We won't take a deep dive into this topic because it is a bit on the periphery of our investigation, but it is a side trip that is worth taking because it will uncover enough for us to formulate a theory, speculative though it may be.

The Bible mentions Sodom 48 times from Genesis to Revelation. I will draw our attention to some key verses that will help us draw a character sketch of the cultural practices of Sodom and Gomorrah. The obvious place to start is with the account of Sodom and Gomorrah in Genesis 18-19. In Genesis 18, Abraham is greeted by three visitors, two are angels and the third, many scholars believe, was a theophany, a physical manifestation of the Lord Himself. The Lord revealed to Abraham that He was about to destroy Sodom and Gomorrah.

Genesis 18:20-21 (AMP) *"And the Lord said, 'The outcry [of the sin] of Sodom and Gomorrah is indeed great, and their sin is exceedingly grave. I will go down now and see whether they have acted [as vilely and wickedly] as the outcry which has come to Me [indicates]; and if not, I will know."*

An interesting dialogue between Abraham and the Lord ensues. Abraham pleads for Sodom and Gomorrah to be spared if there are righteous people who live in these cities. Abraham bargains with the Lord starting with at least 50 righteous people and continues the negotiations until he narrows it down to ten righteous people. The Lord agrees to spare Sodom and Gomorrah for the sake of ten righteous people. Meanwhile, as Abraham and the Lord are engaged in this discussion, the two angels had left on a reconnaissance mission to gather information about the state of affairs in Sodom and Gomorrah. Lot was positioned at the city gate, as is common for city officials. Immediately, Lot recognized that these two "men" approaching the city gates were angels. The angels communicated their intentions to stay the night in the city square. Knowing the rampant perversion and violence within the city, Lot insisted the two angels spend the night in his home. Word spread rapidly that there were visitors in the city.

Genesis 19:4-5 (NKJV) *"Now before they lay down, the men of the city, the men of Sodom, both old and young, all the people from every quarter, surrounded the house. And they called to Lot and said to him, 'Where are the men who came to you tonight? Bring them out to us that we may know them carnally."*

This particular passage paints a remarkable picture of what took place. The men of the entire city, despite their age, along with all the people from every quarter of the city, surrounded Lot's house. This must have been frightening for Lot and could potentially explain why he offered his two virgin daughters to this mob. He wasn't thinking straight, or was he? Could it be that he recognized that the grievous act of offering his daughters to be raped by a crowd of people was not as grievous as letting the men have sexual relations with angels?

I believe the detestable sin the citizens of Sodom and Gomorrah committed was the mixing of species. Their sexual perversion had become so wicked and defiled that they had crossed over into interbreeding, the vilest of all sexual acts. What may seem like a small, insignificant phrase in the above passage, may actually help us understand what had been taking place in the cities of Sodom and Gomorrah. Not only did all the men of the city surround Lot's house, but it says, "**all the people** from every quarter." The Hebrew word for "all the people" is '`am' which means "nation, people, kinsman, kindred," it refers to a single race.[166] This piece will not make sense until we gather a few more clues in order to form our cultural character sketch of Sodom and Gomorrah.

Ezekiel 16: 49-50 (NKJV) *"Look, this was the iniquity of your sister Sodom: She and her daughter had pride, fullness of food, and abundance of idleness; neither did she strengthen the hand of the poor and needy. And they were haughty and committed abomination before Me; therefore I took them away as I saw fit."*

This passage provides us with an important glimpse into the cultural issues that led to the destruction of Sodom and Gomorrah. It is in this passage that we begin to see the fingerprints of the Nephilim traits emerge. We see that the Sodomites were prideful, neglectful of the poor, idle and haughty before the Lord. Additionally, it is said that they "committed abomination"; the Hebrew word for this phrase is *'tow`ebah'* which means "a disgusting thing in a ritual sense, i.e. mixed marriages; or in an ethical sense, i.e. wickedness."[167]

Let's put these pieces together. Angels from a divine race, showed up in Sodom. Their presence stirred up such licentiousness among the Sodomites, that **all the people**, which included both men and women (of the human race), desired to have sex with them. Their wicked, perverse desires were evidence that they engaged in ongoing practices of abomination before the Lord, and they had committed such acts with haughty attitudes. Their practices included disgusting rituals that included the mixing of marriages. I don't believe this is speaking of interracial marriages, as we think of them today, but rather interspecies marriages—hybrids marrying humans. This would explain the fury in which the Sodomites' passions were stirred at the sight of a divine being. Could it be that the Sodomites were desirous of a sexual orgy with the divine beings to propagate the Nephilim race, the men of renown?

The New Testament book of Jude provides further evidence that the Sodomites were desirous of sexual intercourse with the angels.

Jude 1: 6-7 (NKJV) *"And the angels who did not keep their proper domain, but left their own abode, He has reserved in everlasting chains under darkness for the judgment of the great day; as Sodom and Gomorrah, and the cities around them in a similar manner to these, having given themselves over to sexual immortality and gone after strange flesh, are set forth as an example, suffering the vengeance of eternal fire."*

It is telling that Jude chose to incorporate the example of Sodom and Gomorrah as he was laying out the case against the fallen 'sons of God,' the angels who did not keep their proper domain. Just as the Flood was the example of the punishment for those that engaged in the incursion of the fallen 'sons of God' having sexual relations with the daughters of man, Sodom and Gomorrah became the example of the punishment for those who attempted another incursion. The phrase "strange flesh" in this passage is the Greek word '*heteros*' which means "the other, another, one not of the same nature, form, class, kind, different."[168] This supports the notion that the people of Sodom and Gomorrah were aware that the two visitors were angels and not mere human men. Peter drew a similar comparison as Jude, the Flood was the consequence for the first incursion and the destruction of Sodom and Gomorrah was the consequence for the attempt at another incursion.

2 Peter 2: 4-7 (NKJV) *"For if God did not spare the angels who sinned, but cast them down to hell and delivered them into chains of darkness, to be reserved for judgment; and did not spare the ancient world, but saved Noah, one of the eight people, a preacher of righteousness, bringing in the flood on the world of the ungodly; and turning the cities of Sodom and Gomorrah into ashes, condemned them to destruction, making them an example to those who afterward would live ungodly..."*

There is one more passage I want to draw our attention to, before we move on from Sodom and Gomorrah. In an unlikely way, it links Ham's unzipping of the Nephilim epigenetic marker to the behaviors of the people of Sodom and Gomorrah.

Isaiah 3:9 (NIV) *"The look on their faces testifies against them; they parade their sin like Sodom; they do not hide it. Woe to them! They have brought disaster upon themselves."*

In this passage we are given yet another piece to our character sketch of the Sodomites. *"They parade"* their sin as if it was something to show off like a badge of honor. In the King James Version, it says *"they declare"* which is the Hebrew word *'nagad.'* If you recall, this is the same word used to describe Ham's actions after he saw his father's nakedness. It means to be conspicuous by publicly announcing something. In both cases, it was the public proclamation of sexual perversion, as if it was something to celebrate. This type of behavior exposes the condition of the heart as filled with haughtiness and pride, traits of the Nephilim.

As I have suggested in a previous chapter, Ham's behavior that flowed out of the condition of his heart, unzipped the Nephilim epigenetic marker. In a similar way, I think it's plausible that the Sodomites had unzipped the epigenetic markers of the Nephilim genes and were interbreeding with the hybrids.

Goliath

Goliath is probably the most well-known giant (*'gibbowr'*) recorded in the Bible. His name means "splendor" and comes from the Hebrew root word *'galah'* which means "to expose, to uncover, to remove, to be disclosed, to depart."[169] It's interesting that his name was prophetic in that he was exposed, uncovered, removed, departed from the earth because of the courage of David. The story of David and Goliath contains a plethora of clues for us to discover. The Biblical account of David and Goliath is found in I Samuel 17.

I Samuel 17: 4-11, 32 (NIV) *"A champion named Goliath, who was from Gath, came out of the Philistine camp. His height was six cubits and a span. He had a bronze helmet on his head and wore a coat of scale armor of bronze weighing five thousand shekels; on his legs he wore bronze greaves, and a bronze javelin was slung on his back. His spear shaft was like a weaver's rod, and its iron point weighed six hundred shekels. His shield bearer went ahead of him.*

Goliath stood and shouted to the ranks of Israel, 'Why do you come out and line up for battle? Am I not a Philistine, and are you not the servants of Saul? Choose a man and have him come down to me. If he is able to fight and kill me, we will become your subjects; but if I overcome him and kill him, you will become our subjects and serve us.' Then the Philistine said, 'This day I defy the armies of Israel! Give me a man and let us fight each other.' On hearing the Philistine's words, Saul and all the Israelites were dismayed and terrified."

David said to Saul, 'Let no one lose heart on account of this Philistine; your servant will go and fight him.'"

The Biblical record supplies us with several measurements that give an indication of Goliath's stature and strength. His height was six cubits and a span. We know a cubit to be approximately 16 inches and a span is the measurement from the tip of the thumb to the tip of the smallest finger. In ancient times, a span was known as half a cubit (8 inches). This means Goliath was roughly 8 feet 8 inches tall. His iron spearhead weighed 600 shekels, which is a little over 15 pounds. It was attached to a spear shaft the size of a weaver's beam. His bronze armor scale weighed 5000 shekels, approximately 125 lbs. That is massive! Think about the kind of strength to remain agile in battle while wearing an armor suit weighing 125 lbs.

Scientists may attempt to explain Goliath's stature as a result of "gigantism." It's important to distinguish between traits of the Nephilim and the physical anomaly known as "gigantism." "Gigantism" is a rare disorder defined as: "abnormal overgrowth of the body or a part; excessive size and stature. Generally applied to a rare abnormality of the pituitary gland which secretes excessive growth hormone before the growing ends of the bones have closed. This causes a child to become an unusually tall adult; if the abnormality is extreme, the individual may reach a height of 2.4 meters (8 feet) or more, although the body proportions usually are normal" (Gigantism, 2003).[170]

Statistics show that about 3 in 1 million people develop gigantism. It is not known to be hereditary. While people who suffer from gigantism may have similar stature as some of the giants in the Bible, one of the common symptoms of this disorder is weakness. The weakness can become so pronounced, people need crutches, canes or walkers to assist them in walking. This symptom of weakness clearly differentiates someone with gigantism from the descendants of the Nephilim, the '*gibbowr*.' In other words, the presence of giants with superhuman strength recorded in history cannot simply be explained by the rare disorder of gigantism. Furthermore, the lack of a genetic component found in gigantism could not be used as a possible explanation for the size of Goliath and his four giant brothers.

Goliath knew how to use his mighty strength as a '*gibbowr*' to strike fear in the Israelite soldiers. Goliath hurled insults at them for 40 days and they were absolutely paralyzed by fear. It took an outsider, a shepherd boy, David—one who learned to walk in the fear of the Lord instead of fear of man or fear of the '*gibbowr*,' to have the courage to fight the giant. Retreating in fear was a common response when confronted by the strength of the '*gibbowr*.' In Numbers 13, the Israelites retreat in fear because of the great strength of the people in Canaan, among which were descendants of the giants.

Numbers 13: 28-33 (NKJV) "*Nevertheless **the people who dwell in the land are strong**; the cities are fortified and very large; moreover we saw the descendants of Anak there. The Amalekites dwell in the land of the South; the Hittites, the Jebusites, and the Amorites dwell in the mountains; and the Canaanites dwell by the sea and along the banks of the Jordan.' Then Caleb quieted the people before Moses, and said, 'Let us go up at once and take possession, for we are well able to overcome it.' But the men who had gone up with him said, 'We are not able to go up against the people, **for they are stronger than we**.' And they gave the children of Israel a bad report of the land which they had spied out, saying, 'The land through which we have gone as spies is a land that devours its inhabitants, and all the people whom we saw in it are men of great stature. There we saw the giants (the descendants of Anak came from the giants); and we were like grasshoppers in our own sight, and so we were in their sight.*"(Emphasis mine)

The presence of the '*gibbowr*' in the Promised Land caused a generation of Israelites to cower and subsequently forfeit their inheritance. Those who feared the '*gibbowr*,' instead of the Lord, were banned to the wilderness for 40 years. The '*gibbowr*' seemed to specialize in robbing people of their destiny, especially when the children of God stopped walking in the fear of the Lord. King Saul fell prey to this trap.

King Saul

Earlier, I mentioned that there are instances when '*gibbowr*' is used in scripture as an indirect reference to giants. One of the more telling occasions is the biography of King Saul's life found in I Samuel. Interestingly, a "mighty man," a '*gibbowr*,' is mentioned within Saul's family line.

I Samuel 9:1-2 (NKJV) *"There was a man of Benjamin whose name was Kish the son of Abiel, the son of Zeror, the son of Bechorath, the son of Aphiah, a Benjamite, a **mighty man of power**. And he had a choice and handsome son whose name was Saul. There was not a more handsome person than he among the children of Israel. From his shoulders upward he was taller than any of the people."*

Two things to note about the context of this passage: Saul's father Kish was a '*gibbowr*,' and Saul was markedly taller than anyone else. This usage of '*gibbowr*' in this passage gives us an indication that there were giants in Saul's family line. Within Saul's DNA was the genetic mutation of the hybrids. At first this may be hard to swallow, why would God choose, as Israel's first king, a man with the Nephilim gene? Well, the Almighty, All Powerful, All Knowing Yahweh is not all controlling. In his abounding love for us, He determined at the point of creation to give us free will. The Father was not interested in a race of automatons. He wanted a race of beings that were free to choose whether to love Him and follow in His ways. Free will is risky. It means there can be disappointment, pain, abandonment, and rebellion, but for the Father, it was a risk worth taking.

At two critical junctures in history, the post-Flood repopulation of the earth and the reign of Israel's first king, there were people who had the Nephilim gene. Free will provided them the choice to follow after God, keeping the Nephilim gene dormant, or walk in rebellion, triggering the expression of the Nephilim phenotype. As was previously mentioned, Ham's rebellious heart and Noah's subsequent curse, created the epigenetic signals that activated the Nephilim gene within his children's children. As we will see in Saul's life, he was inclined toward disobedience and pride, showing favor to his fellow '*gibbowr*.'

Throughout Saul's reign, Israel battled the Philistines and/or the Amalekites. Saul is described as warring against the Philistines all the days of his life.

I Samuel 14:52 *"Now there was fierce war with the Philistines **all the days of Saul**. And when Saul saw any strong man or any valiant man ('gibbowr'), he took him for himself."* (emphasis mine)

What does this passage mean? I surmise, that instead of Saul killing the '*gibbowr*' in battle, he took them in, collected them so to speak. The phrase "he took him for himself" is the Hebrew primitive root word '*acaph*' which means to "gather, receive, collect, assemble."[171] Saul's behavior toward the '*gibbowr*' demonstrates a fascination or even an affinity toward the giants. This led to his downfall.

In a battle against the Amalekites, Saul was instructed by the prophet Samuel to totally destroy the Amalekites including the men, women, children, infants, and animals.

I Samuel 15:3 (NKJV) "*Now go and attack Amalek, and utterly destroy all that they have, and do not spare them. But kill both man and woman, infant and nursing child, ox and sheep, camel and donkey.*"

The phrase "utterly destroy" is the Hebrew word '*charam*,' which we defined in Chapter 8 as "to completely destroy, exterminate, to devote for destruction." It is a term that denotes Yahweh's absolute disdain for particular acts of sin or for the defilement of the hybrid race of giants. When God commanded '*charam*,' He was calling for punishment by total annihilation.

Now I have to digress for a moment. I am a mercy driven person with a tender heart toward the pain of others. To think that the loving Father would command '*charam*' regarding certain tribes of people is challenging for me to reconcile. It was not until I examined this further that I was able to come to terms with this command. '*Charam*' is about cleansing the genetic defilement of God's creation. Therefore when '*charam*' is commanded, it is of utmost importance, **for the sake of all creation**, to remove these living creatures from the face of the earth. The word '*charam*' is used 52 times in the Old Testament, 33 of these instances refer to the Israelite conquest of the land of Canaan. We will discover in the pages that follow, that the land of Canaan was filled with the descendants of the Nephilim.

As I mentioned, Saul was given a word from the Lord by Samuel, the prophet, to '*charam*' the Amalekites. This is the first time Saul was instructed to '*charam*,' even though he had previously engaged in numerous battles against the Philistines as king of Israel. It was a crucial assignment given to Saul, but he treated it lightly. He disregarded the importance of full obedience. He disobeyed the instruction to '*charam*' the Amalekites.

I Samuel 15:7-11 (NIV) "*Then Saul attacked the Amalekites all the way from Havilah to Shur, near the eastern border of Egypt. He took Agag king of the Amalekites alive, and all his people he totally destroyed with the sword. But Saul and the army spared Agag and the best of the sheep and cattle, the fat calves and lambs – everything that*" *was good. These they were unwilling to destroy completely, but everything that was despised and weak they totally destroyed."*

King Agag was most likely a giant. His name literally means "I will overtop."[172] His tall stature was spoken of by Balaam when he was prophesying about Saul.

Numbers 24:7 (AMP) *"Water [that is, great blessings] will flow from his buckets, and his offspring will live by many waters, and his king will be higher than Agag, and his kingdom shall be exalted."*

Interestingly, the Hebrew word for "higher than" used in this passage is *'ruwm'* which means "to rise, to be high, to be lofty."[173] It is a word used to describe the stature of other giants, such as the Anakim (Deuteronomy 1:28, Deuteronomy 2:10, Deuteronomy 2:21, and Deuteronomy 9:2).

Now, in order to connect some of the dots as to why God commanded Saul to *'charam,'* we need to understand a bit more about the Amalekites. Amalek was the grandson of Esau. Esau's son, Eliphaz, had a Horite concubine named Timna, who bore Eliphaz a son named Amalek. The Horites are mentioned in Genesis 14 in a list of giant tribes. While it's not thought that the Horites were themselves a tribe of giants, it is commonly thought that they were a tribe of people that intermingled with giants.

If you are not familiar with the Biblical story of Esau, he was the twin brother of Jacob. Esau was the oldest by birthright. He was born with red hair that covered a large portion of his body.

Genesis 25:25 (AMP) *"The first came out reddish all over like a hairy garment; and they named him Esau (hairy).*

There was brotherly competition between Esau and Jacob even from the time they were in Rebekah's womb. Rebekah was unsettled by all the jostling and asked the Lord what was going on in her womb. She was unaware that she was carrying twins.

Genesis 25:23 (NLT) *"And the Lord told her, 'The sons in your womb will become two nations. From the very beginning, the two nations will be rivals. One nation will be stronger than the other; and your older son will serve your younger son."*

We see that even in the womb, Esau and Jacob were jockeying for position. This continued throughout their childhood and into early adulthood. Jacob came up with clever ways to outmaneuver Esau. One example is when Jacob made a stew that tantalized Esau. Jacob seized that moment to negotiate Esau out of his birthright. Esau foolishly gave up his birthright because in the moment, it was more important that his satisfied was stomach. A few years later, when their father Isaac was dying, Jacob tricked Isaac into giving him the blessing of the firstborn. When Esau discovered that Jacob had deceived their father, and that he had been robbed of Isaac's intended blessing, he became so enraged, he let out a blood curdling scream. Esau developed a deep hatred for Jacob and vowed he would kill his brother.

The writer of Hebrews, thousands of years later, mentions this deep seeded hatred that developed into a root of bitterness.

Hebrews 12:15-17 (NLT) *"Look after each other so that none of you fails to receive the grace of God. Watch out that no poisonous root of bitterness grows up to trouble you, corrupting many. Make sure that no one is immoral or godless like Esau, who traded his birthright as the firstborn son for a single meal. You know that afterward, when he wanted his father's blessing, he was rejected. It was too late for repentance, even though he begged with bitter tears."*

The bitter root that grew in Esau's heart opened the door for bitterness to corrupt his generations. We might consider this root of bitterness to be an epigenetic marker that unzipped the Nephilim genes in Esau's bloodline. There are important connections to make with Esau's generations, I will discuss this in more detail in an upcoming chapter. But for now, it's important to highlight that Amalek, not only was a product of Esau's descendants, he was also a descendant of the Horites.

Given that the Horites intermingled with giants, it is reasonable to conclude that Amalek was corrupted with Nephilim genes because his mother was a Horite. Amalek also inherited the extreme hatred of Esau toward Jacob. This strife between Esau's descendants and Jacob's descendants intensified through the generations making the Amalekites, Israel's worst enemy.

The Amalekites were vicious plunderers, they were the first foe to attack Israel as they left Egypt. The Egyptians had handed over their wealth to the Israelites and this caught the eye of the Amalekites. The Amalekites wanted the plunder for themselves, so they attacked Israel. The name Amalek means "blood licker" in the sense of devouring something and licking up the blood.[174] The Amalekites' strategy of attack was to cut off the weak that straggled at the back of the caravan. When the frail, sick, and young were cut off from the rest of the Israelites, they were easier prey for the Amalekites.

Deuteronomy 25:17-19 (NIV) "*Remember what the Amalekites did to you along the way when you came out of Egypt. When you were weary and worn out, they met you on your journey and attacked all who were lagging behind; they had no fear of God. When the Lord your God gives you rest from all the enemies around you in the land he is giving you to possess as an inheritance, you shall blot out the name of Amalek from under heaven. Do not forget!*"

It is reasonable to conclude that the Amalekites were detestable to the Lord for two reasons: the Amalekites were merciless in their attack of the burgeoning nation of Israel as they exited Egypt, and the Amalekites practiced interbreeding promulgating the seed of the '*gibbowr.*' This is why Saul was commanded to '*charam*' the Amalekites, which he failed to do. He did not walk in the fear of the Lord, but instead, gave in to the whims of his fancy. Unfortunately, this was Saul's modus operandi. In his mind, partial obedience equaled obedience. Saul was foolish to disregard the requirements of '*charam*' to preserve King Agag's life. In doing so, he rejected God. Saul's consequence? God rejected him as king of Israel. There are many instances in Saul's life where he demonstrated foolishness.

Was this choice merely a foolish decision, or was there some other reason he chose to spare Agag's life? Josephus, the Jewish historian writes: "He also took Agag, the enemies' king, captive;—the beauty and tallness of whose body he admired so much, that he thought him worthy of preservation; yet was not this done however according to the will of God, but by giving way to human passions, and suffering himself to be moved with an unseasonable commiseration, in a point where it was not safe for him to indulge it; for God hated the nation of the Amalekites to such a degree, that he commanded Saul to have no pity on even those infants which we by nature chiefly compassionate; but Saul preserved their king and governor from the miseries which the Hebrews brought on the people, as if he preferred the fine appearance of the enemy to the memory of what God had sent him about. (Book 6, Chapter 8, 137-138)"[175]

Josephus highlights that Saul developed an affinity toward Agag, a fellow '*gibbowr.*' Saul found Agag more attractive than obeying Yahweh. Samuel, the prophet said to Saul that his rebellion is as the sin of witchcraft. Saul not only had the phenotype of a

Nephilim by being head and shoulders taller than all of Israel, but he also had a rebellious nature which is an identifiable trait within the Nephilim bloodline.

In studying the character of three post-diluvian men, Nimrod, Goliath and King Saul, as well as examining the cultural and spiritual condition of Babel/Babylon and Sodom and Gomorrah, we can now synthesize the traits we uncovered of the *'gibbowr.'* Similar to their Nephilim predecessors, the *'gibbowr'* are controlling, defiant, physically strong, tall in stature, arrogant, intimidating, rebellious, sexually perverse, prideful, and are often tyrannical rulers. While these *'gibbowr'* may have viewed themselves as invincible and the cities they built as indestructible, they were no match for the powerful hand of the Righteous Judge. Justice was served and their plans were thwarted.

Proverbs 19:21 (NIV) *"Many are the plans in a person's heart, but it is the Lord's purpose that prevails."*

Key Points

- The *'gibbowr'* are the post-diluvian offspring of the Nephilim.
- The Lord gives us free will to choose obedience or rebellion.
- Nimrod chose rebellion which triggered his transformation of becoming a *'gibbowr.'*
- Nimrod was the first world leader; he was the original globalist. He fueled pride of life in people of Babel.
- Tower of Babel was a portal to other dimensions.
- Deified Nimrod and Semiramis become Baal and Queen of Heaven.
- Occult origins are found in Babylon.
- Sodom and Gomorrah were destroyed because citizens were desirous of sexual orgy with angels to propagate Nephilim.
- Goliath is classic example of Nephilim phenotype.
- As Israel's first king, Saul had a *'gibbowr'* in his family line. He showed favoritism to fellow *'gibbowr'* instead of carrying out *charam*.
- Traits of the *'gibbowr'* are similar to their Nephilim predecessors: controlling, defiant, physically strong, tall in stature, arrogant, intimidating, rebellious, sexually perverse, prideful, and tyrannical rulers.

Chapter 11

Tribes of Giants

Throughout scripture, there are numerous references to giants, as we have already highlighted. For the sake of clarity, as we move forward in our investigation, it's important to delineate between the tribes of giants mentioned in scripture. The Nephilim are only referenced twice in the Bible, once during the antediluvian epoch in Genesis 6:4 and once post-Flood in Numbers 13:33. There are only two instances when '*gibbowr*' is used to directly reference giants (Genesis 6:4 and I Samuel 17:51). The term most often used to reference giants is the word "Rephaim" (used in 24 verses).

Rephaim

The biblical term "Rephaim" refers to a tribe of old giants and comes from a root word '*rapha*' which means "healer, to be healed." It's where we get Yahweh Rapha, the "Lord our Healer." But another derivative of the Hebrew word '*rapha*' means "ghosts of the dead, shades, spirits."[176] There are a number of different perspectives about the Rephaim. It is all speculation of course, because we don't have any eye-witness testimony or hard evidence proving the nature of the Rephaim. But as with any investigation, there are numerous theories to be tested. We will examine two theories: 1) the Rephaim are the next generation of giants to emerge after the Flood, and 2) the Rephaim are the departed spirits of the Nephilim.

Next Generation of Giants

Many believe that the Rephaim are the descendants of the Nephilim, who were the next generation of giants to emerge after the flood. I will highlight key scriptures that will help us uncover as much information as we can about the character and nature of the Rephaim and to test this theory. In Genesis 14, we have the account of the first world war, the battle between four northern kings of Assyria and the five vassal southern kings.

Genesis 14:5-9 (NKJV) *"In the fourteenth year of Chedorlaomer and the kings that were with him came and attacked the Rephaim in Ashteroth Karnaim, the Zuzim in Ham, the Emim in Shaveh Kiriathaim, and the Horites in their mountain of Seir, as far as El Paran, which is by the wilderness. Then they turned back and came to En Mishpat (that is, Kadesh), and attacked all the country of the Amalekites, and also the Amorites who dwelt in Hazezon Tamar.*

And the king of Sodom, the king of Gomorrah, the king of Admah, the king of Zeboiim, and the king of Bela (that is, Zoar) went out and joined together in the battle in the Valley of Siddim against Chedorlaomer king of Elam, Tidal king of nations, Amraphel king of Shinar, and Arioch king of Ellasar – four kings against five."

If you are scratching your head a bit to try to figure out who's who, you are in good company. Allow me to simplify for our purposes—the king of Sodom, along with four neighboring cities were tired of paying fees to the government of Chedorlaomer. After twelve years of slavery, these five kings decided to rebel by refusing to pay the tributes. Chedorlaomer gathered his allies from the north, which included three other kings, and went to wage war against the five southern kings. En route, the four northern kings came across the tribes of giants, most likely in the region of Bashan and they defeated the giants.

Josephus provides historical context to this war and in doing so, describes the Rephaim as "the offspring of the giants." In essence, Josephus' perspective is that the Rephaim are the next generation of giants following the Flood.

"At this time, when the Assyrians had the dominion over Asia, the people of Sodom were in a flourishing condition, both as to riches and the number of their youth. There were five kings that managed the affairs of this country. Ballas, Barsas, Senabar, and Sumobor, with the king of Bela; and each king led on his own troops; and the Assyrians made war upon them; and, dividing their army into four parts, fought against them. Now every part of the army had its own commander when the battle was joined, the Assyrians were conquerors; and imposed a tribute on the kings of the Sodomites, who submitted to this slavery twelve years; and so long they continued to pay their tribute: but on the thirteenth year they rebelled, and then the army of the Assyrians came upon them, under their commanders Amraphel, Arioch, Chodorlaomer, and Tidal. These kings had laid waste all of Syria, and overthrown **the offspring of the giants**; and when they were come over against Sodom, they pitched their camp at the vale called the Slime Pits, for at that time there were pits in that place; but now, upon the destruction of the city of Sodom, that vale became the Lake Asphaltitis, as it is called."[177] (emphasis mine)

The most well-known among the Rephaim was King Og of Bashan. Og was a contemporary of Moses and ruled over a vast territory which included Mt. Hermon.

Joshua 12:4-5 (NASB) *"and the territory of **Og king of Bashan, one of the remnant of Rephaim**, who lived at Ashtaroth and at Edrei, and ruled over Mount Hermon and Salecah and all Bashan, as far as the border of the Geshurites and the Maacathites, and half of Gilead, as far as the border of Sihon king of Heshbon. Moses the servant of the Lord and the sons of Israel defeated them…"* (emphasis mine)

This area had long been a stronghold of darkness. By now we are familiar with Mt. Hermon, it was the location where the 'Watchers' descended upon the earth to stage their coup d'etat. The aboriginals of Bashan were the Rephaim. The region of Bashan was known as the gate (portal) to the netherworld. The vast area of Bashan was predominately located in what is now Syria and Lebanon. Given the recent conflicts within these nations, archaeological teams have not been able to conduct research. But in the 19th century, an explorer by the name of Josiah Porter, discovered the region of Bashan, Og's kingdom. He recorded his findings in his book *The Giant Cities of Bashan and Syria's Holy Places.*

"Moses makes special mention of the strong cities of Bashan, and speaks of their high walls and gates. He tells us, too, in the same connection, that Bashan was called the *land of the giants* (or Rephaim, Deut 3:13); leaving us to conclude that the cities were built by giants. Now the houses of Kerioth and other towns in Bashan appear to be just such dwellings as a race of giants would build…I measured a door in Kerioth; it was nine feet high, four and half feet wide, and ten inches thick,—one solid slab of stone… The heavy stone slabs of the roofs resting on the massive walls make the structure as firm as if built of solid masonry; and the black basalt used is almost as hard as iron. There can scarcely be a doubt, therefore, that these are the very cities erected and inhabited by the Rephaim, the aboriginal occupants of Bashan…"[178]

Porter's exploration supports the biblical record that the Rephaim inhabited the region of Bashan. Moses and the Israelite army carried out *'charam'* on King Og and his people, just as they had done to Sihon king of Heshbon (thought to be another giant king possibly even the brother of Og).

Deuteronomy 3:6 (ESV) *"And we devoted them to destruction, as we did to Sihon the king of Heshbon, devoting to destruction every city, men, women, and children.*

Deuteronomy 3:11 provides a specific detail about King Og's bedstead (9x4 cubits) that unveils an interesting connection with ritualistic occult practices. I believe this link is what led to the necessity of *'charam.'* Let's dig a little here.

A cubit was an ancient unit of measurement determined by the length from the elbow to the tip of the longest finger. Of course, this varied depending on the size of the person, but there were two standard cubits, a common cubit (approximately 16 inches) and a royal cubit (approximately 20 inches).[179] If we assume the royal cubit (20 inches) was used in measuring King Og's bedstead (9x4 cubits), it would have been 15 ft. long and over 5 ft. wide. Scholars have estimated that based on the size of King Og's bedstead, he may have been as tall as 12 feet. If so, he would have been the largest recorded giant in the Bible. But his height and the fact that he was a giant, does not explain why every man, woman, and child in every city he ruled over was destroyed.

Steve Quayle provides us with a clue to the significance of Og's bedstead by framing the context of how the bed ended up in Rabbath.

"The Ammonites, following behind the Hebrew army as scavengers, found the iron bed in Og's sleeping quarters at either Edrei or Ashtaroth. They took it to Rabbath, the royal city of the Ammonites. There it became a famous "museum piece." It drew curious crowds for many centuries, probably even down to the time of the Babylonian captivity (c. 586 B.C.)."[180]

One can imagine that it was a spectacular piece to behold given its size and strength. But was there more to the fascination with the bedstead? Yes, I believe so, and it has to do with the exact measurements of the bedstead. Michael Heiser provides our next clue, as he explains the significance of Og's bed in *The Unseen Realm.*

"First, the most immediate link back to the Babylonian polemic is Og's bed...Its dimensions (9x4 cubits) are precisely those of the cultic bed in the ziggurat called Etemenanki – which is the ziggurat most archaeologists identify as the Tower of Babel referred to in the Bible. Ziggurats functioned as temples and divine abodes. The unusually large bed at Etemenanki was housed in "the house of the bed"… It was the place where the god Marduk and his divine wife, Zarpanitu, met annually for ritual lovemaking, the purpose of which was divine blessing upon the land.

Scholars have been struck by the precise correlation. It's hard not to conclude that, as with Genesis 6:1-4, so with Deuteronomy 3, those who put the finishing touches on the Old Testament during the exile in Babylon were connecting Marduk and Og in some way. The most transparent path is in fact giant stature. Og is said to have been the last of the Rephaim – a term connected to the giant Anakim and other ancient giant clans in the Transjordan…Marduk, like other deities in antiquity, was portrayed as superhuman in size."[181]

The pieces are starting to come together, Heiser highlighted for us that there is a link between Og's bed and Marduk's bed which was located in the ziggurat connected with Nimrod and the Tower of Babel.

Derek Gilbert, in his book *The Great Inception*, builds upon the connection between Og and Marduk and gives us our final clue connecting Og with ritualistic occult practices. (Note – Gilbert makes a case that Entemenanki was the great ziggurat in Babylon, not to be mistaken for the Tower of Babel).

"Moses was writing to an audience that was familiar with the infamous occult practices of Babylon… Every year at the first new moon after the spring equinox, Babylon held a new year festival called the *akitu*… The highlight of the festival was the Divine Union or Sacred Marriage, where Marduk and his consort, Sarpanit, retired to the cult bed inside the Etemenanki, the House of the Foundation of Heaven and Earth, the great ziggurat of Babylon. Although scholars still debate whether the Sacred Marriage was actually performed by the king and a priestess, it didn't matter to Yahweh…Marduk's bed was…Precisely the same dimensions as the bed of Og. Moses was making sure his readers understood that the Amorite king Og, like the Amorite kings of Babylon, was carrying on pre-Flood occult traditions brought to earth by the Watchers."[182]

Herein lies the significance of the dimensions of Og's bedstead, it was the same size as the cult bed in Babylon. Og was engaging in sexual rituals for breeding purposes, to propagate the seed of the '*nachash.*' The battle between the armies led by Moses and the armies led by Og was an epic battle in the Seed War and precisely why '*charam*' was carried out on Og and his people. The Amorites had a defiled genome and had to be eradicated. On some level, I believe Moses understood the weight of this battle and what was at stake. At the portal to the netherworld, where king Og was engaging in cultic sexual acts to spread the Nephilim genes far and wide, Moses and his army represented the Almighty Elohim, in a monumental battle. The Lord handed Og, the most famous of the Rephaim, into the hands of Moses.

We can take great encouragement from Moses' victory that day. Moses had to face a formidable foe, but with the Lord on his side, he was assured victory! We face giants and formidable foes in our life, but take heart, no matter the size, strength, or power of the giants we face, with the Lord's help we can walk in victory! We will need to keep this in mind as we enter the spiritual battle to eradicate the roots of the occult within the foundation of the Federal Reserve.

Departed Spirits of the Nephilim

Let's turn our attention to the theory that the Rephaim are the departed spirits of the Nephilim. There are several Old Testament references to the Rephaim being inhabitants of the underworld, also known as Sheol, the realm of the dead.

Job 26: 5-6 (YLT) *"The Rephaim are formed, beneath the waters, also their inhabitants. Naked [is] Sheol over-against Him, and there is not covering to destruction."*

Psalm 88:10 (YLT) *"To the dead dost Thou do wonders? Do Rephaim rise? Do they thank Thee?"*

Isaiah 14: 9 (YLT) *"Sheol beneath hath been troubled at thee, to meet thy coming in, it is waking up for thee Rephaim, all chiefs ones of earth, it hath raised up from their thrones all kings of nations."*

Extra-biblical texts such as 1 Enoch provide us with further understanding of the departed spirits of the Nephilim. Heiser points out, in *Reversing Hermon,* that the above scriptures are the "biblical justification for the teaching of I Enoch that demons are the spirits of dead giants."[183]

I Enoch 15:8-16:1 *"and now, the giants, who are produced from the spirits and flesh, shall be called evil spirits upon the earth, and on the earth shall be their dwelling. Evil Spirits have proceeded from their bodies; because they are born from men, and from the holy Watchers is their beginning and primal origin, they shall be evil spirits on earth, and evil spirits shall they be called. As for the spirits of heaven, in heaven shall be their dwelling, but as for the spirits of the earth which were born upon the earth, on the earth shall be their dwelling. And the spirits of the giants afflict, oppress, destroy, attack, do battle, and work destruction on the earth, and cause trouble: they take no food, but nevertheless hunger and thirst, and cause offences. And these spirits shall rise up against the children of men and against the women, because they have proceeded from them. From the days of the slaughter and destruction and death of the giants, from the souls of whose flesh the spirits, having gone forth, shall destroy without incurring judgment – thus shall they destroy until the day of the consummation, the great judgment in which the age shall be consummated, over the Watchers and the godless, yea, shall be wholly consummated."*

From this passage in Enoch, we learn that the death of the Nephilim was the point at which demons emerged on the scene. The Nephilim were the offspring of the divine and the natural, they were hybrids with ineradicable spirits. Their physical nature could be destroyed, but their disembodied spirits lived on. There is no salvation for evil spirits, so they roam the earth in search of host bodies to possess. Let me make a clear distinction, demons are not the same as angels. Angels have bodies but demons do not. I can appreciate that this may be challenging to wrap your mind around because if your experience has been similar to mine, we have been taught for years in the church that demons are fallen angels. But this is inaccurate teaching. Let's look at scripture to iron this out.

Revelation 12:7-17 is a passage that many biblical teachers use to support the teaching that a third of the angels fell when Satan fell and these fallen angels are what we call demons. I do not agree with this interpretation, instead I agree with Michael Heiser that the battle described in Revelation 12 is referencing the time period after the Messiah's birth (Rev 12:5), not the time of Satan's fall. Michael Heiser writes,

"The New Testament is silent on the origin of demons. There is no passage that describes a primeval rebellion before Eden where angels fell from grace and became demons. The origin of demons in Jewish texts outside the Bible (such as 1 Enoch) is attributed to the events of Genesis 6:1-4. When a Nephilim was killed in these texts, its disembodied spirit was considered a demon. These demons then roamed the earth to harass humans. The New Testament does not explicitly embrace this belief, though there are traces of the notion, such as demon possession of humans (implying the effort to be re-embodied)."[184]

Angels and demons are distinctly different, but not just along the demarcation of good vs. evil. When angels appear on earth, they always appear in bodily form. We have already reviewed one such example; the two angels that appeared in Sodom and Gomorrah had bodies like that of men. Another example, and there are many, is when an angel appeared to Daniel.

Daniel 10:5-6 (NIV) *"I looked up and there before me was a man dressed in linen, with a belt of fine gold from Uphaz around his waist. His body was like topaz, his face like lightening, his eyes like flaming torches, his arms and legs like the gleam of burnished bronze, and his voice like the sound of a multitude."*

This passage makes it clear that angels have arms, legs, eyes, and bodies. Tim Sheets, author of *Angels Armies,* builds upon this notion.

"Angels have hands, feet, heads, mouths, hair, faces and voices. This allows them to appear in our three-dimensional realm of length, breadth, and height, looking exactly like us. When their assignment requires it, they can appear in our world or dimension and look just like you and me."[185]

This is why the writer of Hebrews reminds us to be hospitable on all occasions, even to strangers, because we never know when we might be entertaining angels. If we can't distinguish easily between humans and angels, then we can surmise that angels have bodies similar to us.

On the contrary, demons do not have bodies. One place in scripture where this is evident is the account of Jesus' healing the demoniac.

Mark 5:2-13 (NLT) *"When Jesus climbed out of the boat, a man possessed by an evil spirit came out from the tombs to meet him. This man lived in the burial caves and could no longer be restrained, even with a chain. Whenever he was put into chains and shackles – as he often was – he snapped the chains from his wrists and smashed the shackles. No one was strong enough to subdue him. Day and night he wandered among the burial caves and in the hills, howling and cutting himself with sharp stones.*

When Jesus was still some distance away, the man saw him, ran to meet him, and bowed low before him. With a shriek, he screamed, 'Why are you interfering with me, Jesus, Son of the Most High God? In the name of God, I beg you, don't torture me!' For Jesus had already said to the spirit, 'Come out of the man, you evil spirit.'

Then Jesus demanded, 'What is your name?'

And he replied, 'My name is Legion, because there are many of us inside this man.' Then the evil spirits begged him again and again not to send them to some distant place.

There happened to be a large herd of pigs feeding on the hillside nearby. 'Send us into those pigs,' the spirits begged. 'Let us enter them.'

So Jesus gave them permission. The evil spirits came out of the man and entered the pigs, and the entire herd of about 2,000 pigs plunged down the steep hillside into the lake and drowned in the water."

We can learn a great deal about the nature of demons from this passage. First of all, we see that demons search for bodies they can inhabit. If they can't access a human body, they will settle for the body of an animal. Why do they do this? Because they are the disembodied spirits of the Nephilim roaming the earth looking for living beings they can torture. This man had not just one demon, but a legion of demons. At that time in history, a Roman legion consisted of several thousand men, so it was fitting that these 2,000 demons called themselves 'Legion.' The strength of these demons overpowered any human and any contraption meant to contain the man. The torment this man experienced is almost beyond comprehension. The level of his bondage classified him among "the walking dead," he essentially lived in a zombie like state. The only place he could exist was among the graves. This gives us a clear understanding of the motives of demons; they want to torture any living body they inhabit and drive them toward death. When the demons inhabited the pigs, they quickly drove the pigs off a cliff plummeting to their death. Demons suck the very life out of any physical body they possess, as if they feed on the life blood of their host bodies. Stephen Quayle in his book *Genesis 6 Giants* has an interesting perspective on the modus operandi of demons.

"Demons seem to *need* living creatures to survive. The exact mechanism is unknown, but it appears that they may have an almost vampiristic relationship, needing a real body to 'feed' on in order to survive. (This craving may be reflected in the blood sacrifices, need for sexual orgies, cannibalistic acts by 'gods,' and other abominations instigated in the religions the fallen angels and [Nephilim] giants create. As we'll see, this becomes a hallmark of pagan religions.)"[186]

A fascinating detail from this story of deliverance in Mark 5 is that the demons begged Jesus not to send them far away. Why? What were they afraid of? Could it be that they knew Jesus had the authority to lock them up in Tartarus just like their fathers, the fallen 'sons of God'? Hmmm, something to consider.

As we have examined two different theories about the nature of the Rephaim, I think both have merit. The Rephaim are the departed spirits of the Nephilim that roam the earth looking for the most suitable host body. Given the emergence of the Nephilim phenotype in Nimrod and the sacred marriage occult practices in Canaan and Mesopotamia, the giants repopulated the earth after the Flood; the disembodied spirits of the Nephilim were reunited with their phenotype. This is how the Rephaim are known as evil spirits and as a tribe of giants.

In addition to the Nephilim and the Rephaim, we find a useful list of giant tribes in Deuteronomy 2 and Deuteronomy 3.

Deuteronomy 2:10-13, 17-23 (NKJV) *"(The **Emim** had dwelt there in times past, a people as great and numerous and tall as the **Anakim**. They were also regarded as giants, like the Anakim, but the Moabites call them Emim. The **Horites** formerly dwelt in Seir, but the descendants of Esau dispossessed them and destroyed them from before them, and dwelt in their place, just as Israel did to the land of their possession which the Lord gave them.)... that the Lord spoke to me, saying: 'This day you are to cross over at Ar, the boundary of Moab. And when you come near the people of Ammon, do not harass them or meddle with them, for I will not give you any of the land of the people of Ammon as a possession, because I have given it to the descendants of Lot as a possession. (That was also regarded as a land of giants; giants formerly dwelt there. But the Ammonites call them **Zamzummim**, a people as great and numerous and tall as the Anakim. But the Lord destroyed them before them, and they dispossessed them and dwelt in their place, just as He had done for the descendants of Esau, who dwelt in Seir, when He destroyed the Horites from before them. They dispossessed them and dwelt in their place, even to this day. And the **Avim**, who dwelt in villages as far as Gaza – the Caphtorim, who came from Caphtor, destroyed them and dwelt in their place.)"* (emphasis mine)

Deuteronomy 3:8, 10-11 (NKJV) *"And at that time we took the land from the hand of the two kings of the **Amorites** who were on this side of the Jordan, from the River Arnon to Mount Hermon...cities of the kingdom of Og in Bashan. For only Og king of Bashan remained of the remnant of the giants..."* (emphasis mine).

We can identify the offspring of the Nephilim (see Figure 29): Rephaim, Anakim, Emim, Zamzummim, Horites, Avim, and Amorites. Let's try to gather as much information as we can about these tribes in our pursuit toward increasing our ability to identify the traits of giants. This chart may be useful as we try to understand how the tribes of giants interrelate.

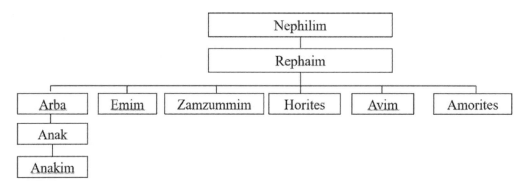

Figure 29. Nephilim offspring. Created by Laura Sanger

Anakim

The Anakim are the tribe of giants that descended from Arba and Anak. The biblical record provides us with some useful information about these giants. First of all, they are described as being "great and numerous and tall" (Deuteronomy 3:21). This may not be surprising given that I just said that they are a tribe of giants, but they seem to be the benchmark by which the other tribes are measured. It's likely the Anakim were exceedingly tall, therefore, if other tribes of giants were as tall as the Anakim, this was worth noting in scripture, as was true for the Emim and Zamzummim. The other tribes of giants were not noted as being tall.

Arba was the father of Anak who ruled the city of Hebron, also known as Kiriath Arba, between the days of Abraham and Caleb. Arba was considered the greatest of the Anakim (Joshua 14:15). The Hebrew word used to describe Arba as "great" is *'gadowl'* which means "large in magnitude and extent, loud, haughty, important."[187] In Hebrew, the name Anak means length of neck or stature. It comes from the root word *'anaq'* which means "necklace, pendant necklace, as if strangling."[188] We know from Numbers 13:33 that the descendants of Anak come from the Nephilim. This a noteworthy detail because it means that the Anakim did not come from the 'Watchers' or fallen 'sons of God,' but rather they came from the Nephilim.

In order to understand the impact of the Anakim in the post-flood world, we need to consider the significance of Joshua's conquests in the land of Canaan. As we know from the report the 12 spies gave, the Anakim lived throughout the land of Canaan. As Joshua and the Israelites conquered cities within the promised land, there were some cities that were devoted to destruction and other cities that were not. You may have already picked up on this from our earlier discussion about '*charam,*' but let me make it clear, Israel was told to '*charam*' those cities where Anakim were known to live. The report from the 12 spies along with details given in the book of Joshua provide information about these cities and which tribes the giants intermixed with.

Numbers 13:28-29 (NLT) *"But the people living there are powerful, and their towns are large and fortified. We even saw giants there, the descendants of Anak! The Amalekites live in the Negev, and the Hittites, Jebusites, and Amorites live in the hill country. The Canaanites live along the coast of the Mediterranean Sea and along the Jordan Valley."*

Joshua 11:21-23 (NLT) *"During this period Joshua destroyed all the descendants of Anak, who live in the hill country of Hebron, Debir, Anab, and the entire hill country of Judah and Israel. He killed them all and completely destroyed their towns. None of the descendants of Anak were left in all the land of Israel, though some still remained in Gaza, Gath, and Ashdod. So Joshua took control of the entire land, just as the Lord had instructed Moses. He gave it to the people of Israel as their special possession, dividing the land among the tribes. So the land finally had rest from war."*

The Anakim interbred with the Amalekites, the Hittites, the Jebusites, and the Amorites as they had spread throughout the land of Canaan, especially in the territory of Bashan where the cities Hebron, Debir, and Anab were located. The purpose of Joshua's military strategy was to eradicate the Anakim from the promised land. Joshua's conquest was impressive in that he eliminated most of the giants from the promised land, BUT he didn't complete the '*charam.*' Michael Heiser in *The Unseen Realm* provides a high-level overview of Israel's conquests led by Joshua and the lasting effects.

"Consequently, in a world governed by other gods who had become hostile rivals in the wake of Yahweh's judgment at Babel, Yahweh's presence was unwelcome. There would be war. There would be death. The land had to be repossessed and made holy. Canaan would be Yahweh's beachhead of cosmic geography from which Israel could fulfill its mission. Israel would be a kingdom of priests, a conduit through which the disinherited nations of the earth would see Israel's prosperity. The surrounding peoples would hear of Israel's God, see his unmatched power, and seek his covenantal love. The nations would be reclaimed, not by force, but by free imagers choosing to turn toward the true God – the creator and Lord of all.

At least that was the plan.

We know that Israel ultimately failed. The seeds of that failure were sown in the events of the conquest. For whatever reasons – lack of faith or lack of effort, or both – Israel failed to drive out their enemies. They allowed vestiges of the targeted bloodlines to remain in the land in the Philistine cities. They chose to coexist (Judg 1:27-36). The visible Yahweh, the Angel, asks the rhetorical question, 'Why would you do such a thing?' and then announces the consequence: 'Now I say, I will not drive them out from before you; they will become as thorns for you, and their gods will be a trap for you' (Judg 2:2-3)."[189]

I don't know about you, but I am left with that uneasy, unresolved feeling like at the end of an intense movie when not everything is wrapped up. There are still "bad guys" out there who didn't face justice, so the potential for more intense battles still linger. Joshua and the Israelites destroyed most of them but it wasn't a total victory. They had the chance to completely eradicate the Nephilim bloodline from the face of the earth, and they fell short. In a way, we are reaping the consequences for their failures. The cosmic war continues…

Amorites

The Amorites were a Semitic speaking people group organized into two main tribes: the Binū Yamina and the Binū Sim'al. They ruled nearly all the major cities of influence in Mesopotamia and the Levant around 1900 B.C. Broadly speaking, their culture was considered Mesopotamian. While they were not a tribe of giants, they had giants living among them interbreeding in their midst. As we have already noted, Og was a giant who was considered an Amorite king. The name "Amorite" stems from the Sumerian word "MAR.TU" which referenced the population living in the region to the west of Babylon and Sumer.

"The Amorites, then are a connection back to Babylon – back to the Mesopotamian context for the biblical "giant talk" that is intimately associated with Bashan and Hermon. This helps us make sense of the prophet Amos' recollection of the conquest of the land centuries earlier. Amos specifically connected the name with giants."[190]

Amos 2: 9-10 (NKJV) "*Yet it was I who destroyed the Amorite before them, whose height was like the height of the cedars, and he was as strong as the oaks; yet I destroyed his fruit above and his roots beneath. Also it was I who brought you up from the land of Egypt, and led you forty years through the wilderness, to possess the land of the Amorite.*"

For quite some time I have been intrigued by the Amorites, particularly by a phrase found in Genesis 15. It's been circled in my bible with a mental note to study it at some point.

Genesis 15:16 (NIV) "*In the fourth generation your descendants will come back here, for **the sin of the Amorites has not yet reached its full measure.**"*(emphasis mine)

What does it mean that "the sin of the Amorites had not yet reached its full measure"? Over the past 20 years, each time I have read this section of Genesis, this phrase consistently jumps off the page at me. But I have not felt the unction to dive deeper in studying the meaning behind this phrase until now. Do you ever get that sense that it's not the right timing to understand something, as if you don't quite have all the pieces in place to grasp the meaning of it? Well this is how I have felt about this phrase. It's as if the Lord has been building in me, over the years, the capacity to grasp the depth of what is meant by this phrase. I am grateful that Derek Gilbert, in his book *The Great Inception*, dissects this very passage, because not only did it answer my lingering questions, but it also connected the fullness of the sin of the Amorites to the Nephilim agenda.

"The sin of the Amorites has multiple layers. They were responsible for founding Babylon and its occult wickedness, which is still infamous today nearly four thousand years later. Moses specifically linked the occult bed inside the temple of Marduk, in Babylon to the bed of the Amorite king Og to make that point clear.

The Amorite kings also apparently considered themselves the descendants and heirs of the Titans (the Watchers) and their children, the Nephilim. The Amorites summoned their venerated dead ancestors, the Rephaim… in rituals to give their kings power in the natural realm."[191]

The Amorites and the Canaanites were the primary inhabitants of the promised land. Yahweh was well aware of the Amorites' wickedness, their occult practices, their idolatry, and their death culture. In the days of Abram (which is the context of Genesis 15), the Amorites had not infiltrated and spread the Nephilim agenda to a great extent. However, 400 years later, or in the fourth generation from Abram, the iniquity of the Amorites had reached its fullness. Moses was led by the providential hand of Yahweh through the Transjordan to eradicate the giant tribes in the region of Bashan. The transition of leadership from Moses to Joshua coincided with the full measure of the iniquity of the Amorites. It was time for the God of Abraham, Isaac and Jacob, the God of Israel, to demonstrate His power and authority over the lesser gods who ruled the other nations. The plan drawn up by the Lord of Hosts was for Joshua to divide and conquer.

The first city Joshua conquered in the promised land was Jericho. Logistically this doesn't make sense. Moses and the Israelites had just come from the battle against Og which was in the northeastern part of Canaan. It would have been more efficient for Joshua to begin his military campaign in the north. But Yahweh's strategy was purposeful. Jericho was a key city inhabited by a tribe of Amorites who worshiped the moon god, some scholars believe that it was the center of moon worship in Canaan.

It's evident from the biblical story of Jericho that the battle was not merely a physical battle, but it was a battle fought in the spiritual dimension. Joshua became aware of this when the Commander of the Army of the Lord showed up with a sword in his hand. The Lord of Hosts was leading the charge and Joshua simply had to follow His lead. The generation of Israelites Joshua was leading had not witnessed Yahweh's sovereignty over the lesser gods, as did those who escaped Egypt. This was the kairos time, the appointed time, for the Almighty Elohim to exert his authority through a power encounter with the moon god, Yarikh, for which Jericho was named after.

Two significant events occurred prior to the march around Jericho that sent a strong message to the moon god ruling over Jericho. First, the Israelite men were circumcised. Imagine this scene for a moment, tens of thousands of adult men had their foreskins cut-off with flint knives. This incapacitated them for several days. In our logical minds, the timing of this mass circumcision does not make sense. But we are quickly reminded that His thoughts are not our thoughts, neither are His ways our ways because His thoughts and His ways are so much higher than ours. There is no comparison! We are limited in our thinking because our perspective often is constrained by our lack of understanding of the multi-dimensional reality we live in. Back to the scene within the camp at Gilgal. The men comprising Israel's military were immobilized from the effects of the circumcision and could not carry out any sort of defense if they were attacked by the army of Jericho. So why didn't the king of Jericho lead his military to attack the Israelites during their time of extreme vulnerability? Our answer lies in the first several verses leading up to the mass circumcision.

Joshua 5:1 (AMP) *"Now it happened when all the kings of the Amorites who were beyond the Jordan to the west, and all the kings of the Canaanites who were by the sea, heard that the Lord had dried up the waters of the Jordan before the Israelites until they had crossed over, their hearts melted [in despair], and there was no [fighting] spirit in them any longer because of the Israelites [and what God had done for them]."*

While the Israelites were incapacitated due to the physical pain of circumcision, the Amorites living in Jericho were incapacitated by their fear of the power of Yahweh.

The second significant event that took place before the conquest of Jericho was the celebration of Passover. It was the fourteenth day of the first month which was when the Israelites were summoned to celebrate the Passover and remember how Yahweh delivered them from the bondage of Egypt. Passover was a sacred time to give thanks to the Lord. It was a time of celebration commemorating the night the angel of death passed over their doorposts because of the blood of the lamb. Instead, the angel of death visited the first-born sons of the Egyptians, marking the culmination of the power encounter between the God of Israel and the gods of Egypt. The timing of the battle against Jericho was a divine set-up. David Livingston highlights the significance of celebrating Passover, the timing of the Israelites march, and the unusual battle strategy given to Joshua. He draws a connection to a Canaanite myth called the *Legend of Keret*. This legend is the narration of a marriage for divine king.

"Let us now look briefly at the Legend of Keret. It is the epic tale of a king who needs an heir to the throne. As Keret weeps in his chamber, El appears to him in a dream and gives him instructions to sacrifice, and then take an expedition to get his wife and, through her, have a son. First Keret provides a great feast for all the people. Then the expedition sets out in order: men of war first, the people following, then the trumpeters last. All are warned to keep quiet until the last day.

Two six-day intervals are recorded in the epic, with the climax on the seventh day in both periods. A tremendous noise is made at dawn on the seventh day, just before arriving at the city (Udum) of the future queen (Hurriya).

All of Israel's actions were commanded by Jehovah as a *travesty, a mockery* of a ritual or pageant known to the Canaanites living in Jericho. It possibly was related to the marriage festival of a "divine" king or had some connection with an annual fertility festival. If so, it should have occurred at the turn of the year—in the spring, possibly April, just when the overthrow of Jericho took place."[192]

Yahweh chose the exact time and place for Israel's first battle in their campaign to conquer the enemies of the promised land. The parallels between the Israelites celebrating the Feast of Passover, and the people of Jericho celebrating the feast connected to the marriage of the divine king are obvious. Yahweh directly attacked the wicked festivals and rituals of their worship to the moon god. The people of Jericho would have gotten the message loud and clear when they watched the Israelite army march around the city in silence for six days. The fear must have been mounting with the anticipation of what would take place on the seventh day when the trumpet blasts were sounded. The utter destruction of Jericho was an epic power encounter between Yahweh and the Amorite gods. It was a victory that solidified the Israelites' faith in the power of the one true God and propelled them to drive out the Amorites from the promised land. In our journey ahead, we will learn strategy from Joshua for facing the giants in our lives by examining another epic battle that took place between Joshua and the Amorites.

Horites & the Link to Edomites

There is a dearth of knowledge about the Horites. Not much is found in the annals of history regarding their origins, their culture, or their extinction, other than a few references found in scripture. It has been suggested by some biblical scholars that the Horites and Hivites are the same tribe of people. If we squeeze as much information as we can out of the few biblical references, we discover a link between the descendants of Esau and the Horites. This link will prove invaluable as we move forward in our investigation. Let's look at this more closely.

Esau married several women who were from the Hittite and Hivite tribes. Isaac and Rebekah were grieved their son, Esau, had not chosen wives who worshiped the one true God, Yahweh. Esau and his wife, Adah, had a son named Eliphaz. Eliphaz married several women and had several children, but he also took for himself a concubine named Timna. Timna bore Eliphaz a son named Amalek. Timna was the daughter of Seir, the Horite, for which Mt. Seir was named. Her brothers were Horite chiefs (Genesis 36:21). Therefore, Amalek was both an Edomite (descendant of Esau) and a Horite. Interestingly, the word "Edom" in Hebrew means red. Genesis 25 provides us with a useful clue.

Genesis 25: 29-30 (NIV) *"Once when Jacob was cooking some stew, Esau came in from the open country, famished. He said to Jacob, 'Quick, let me have some of that red stew! I'm famished!' (That is why he was also called Edom)."*

Have you ever wondered why Moses, the author of the Pentateuch, would include an obscure detail about the color of the stew? Why does the color of the stew matter? Was it the color that enticed Esau or the fact that he was famished? The color of the stew was red probably because of the lentils used in the stew. It's possible that red lentils were Esau's favorite. My guess is that Esau was primarily enticed by the stew because he was weary and faint with exhaustion from being out in the fields so long. Esau was desperate to eat and traded his birthright for a bowl of **red** stew. I don't know about you, but I think there is something more to this little detail of the color of the stew. I am going to go out on a limb here and suggest that Moses was inspired to include this detail to draw our attention to a physical characteristic that set Esau apart from others, that is, he was born with red hair and lots of it! I propose that Esau's descendants were known as the Edomites, not just because the stew was red, but more importantly because of the genetic transmission of red hair in their bloodline. It's highly probable that there were a fair number of redheaded Edomites, which in ancient times, may have been a distinguishable trait.

If we refer back to our text in Deuteronomy 2, we see that the Horites are listed alongside the Emim who are regarded as tall as the Anakim.

Deuteronomy 2: 10-12 (NKJV) *"(The Emim had dwelt there in times past, a people as great and numerous and tall as the Anakim. They were also regarded as giants, like* *the Anakim, but the Moabites call them Emim. The **Horites** formerly dwelt in Seir, but the descendants of Esau dispossessed them and destroyed them from before them, and dwelt in their place, just as Israel did to the land of their possession which the Lord gave them.)* (emphasis mine)

Additionally, the Horites are mentioned alongside three giant lineages in Genesis 14.

Genesis 14:5-7 (NKJV) *"In the fourteenth year Chedorlaomer and the kings that were with him came and attacked the Rephaim in Ashteroth Karnaim, the Zuzim in Ham, the Emim in Shaveh Kiriathaim, and the **Horites** in their mountain of Seir, as far as El Paran, which is by the wilderness."* (emphasis mine)

In these passages, we have an example of a Gentilic adjective in which the ending of the Hebrew word 'Horite' contains a *yod*. The *yod*, which translated in English for this particular usage, is *ite* denoting a distinction that an individual or group of people belong to a certain nation. It's similar to the English ending *an/ian* as in American or Californian. Generally, when giant lineages are mentioned in the Bible, they do not have a Gentilic ending, but rather are simply plural nouns (although some Bible translations errantly list the giant tribes with an *ite* suffix). In these passages, this is precisely how three of the four groups are described. Plural nouns are used to describe the giants: Rephaim, Zuzim, and Emim, whereas a Gentilic ending is used to describe the Horites. Why does this matter? The Horites were a distinct nation, but given they were included in a list of giant lineages it suggests they intermingled with the giants. The various tribes of giants did not form entire nations, but rather lived among the nations and in some situations, were rulers of nations, like King Og. This is consistent with the strategy of the fallen 'sons of God' to corrupt the human genome by interbreeding. It would have been counterproductive for the giants to coalesce into distinct nations. Instead, they infiltrated the nations.

The Genesis 15 and Deuteronomy 2 passages identify that the Horites lived near Mt. Seir and that they were dispossessed of this land by the Edomites. We need to dig a little here before moving on. If you remember Seir, the Horite, was the grandfather of Amalek and the ancestor of King Agag, the *'gibbowr'* that King Saul failed to *'charam.'* We have already established that the Horites intermingled with the giants, and the Edomites intermingled with the Horites. Therefore, it is highly likely that the Nephilim genes were being transmitted among the Edomites as well. But are there any biblical examples of Edomites who were *'gibbowr'*? Yes, his name was Doeg; he was the head shepherd in Saul's camp. Is it any wonder Saul chose the path of the '*gibbowr*'? Here is what David has to say about Doeg,

Psalm 52:1-5 (NASB) "*Why do you boast in evil, O* **mighty man**? *The lovingkindness of God endures all day long. Your tongue devises destruction, like a sharp razor, O* **worker of deceit***. You love evil more than good, falsehood more than speaking what is right. Selah. You love all words that devour, O deceitful tongue. But God will break you down forever; He will snatch you up and tear you away from your tent, and uproot you from the land of the living. Selah.*" (emphasis mine)

David identifies Doeg as a '*gibbowr*,' a man filled with deceit who boasted in evil. We need to remember Doeg, he will re-surface later in our investigation.

Is there any further evidence beyond what the biblical record offers to support the theory that the Edomites intermingled with the giants? It's particularly difficult to ascertain the ethnogenesis of the Edomites, because unlike neighboring ethnic groups, such as the Moabites, there are no "extant historical records from ancient Edom."[193] So we have to look toward the records of the Egyptians, who were by far better historians and who had multiple encounters with the Edomites. Ancient Egyptian documents may lend support to the idea that Nephilim genes were transmitted among the Edomites.

Egyptian texts refer to the Shasu, a term unfamiliar within the biblical text and most likely a term of Egyptian origin. The Shasu were known as a "social group of nomads" referenced as early as 1550 B.C and as late as 747 B.C. The Egyptians reported that the Shasu were from the southern Levant and were not a specific ethnic group tied to one area. Rather they were a nomadic people from a vast area that migrated according to pastoral sustenance, much like the Bedouin culture. With that being said, there are a preponderance of references suggesting that the Shasu were associated with Edom. Levy, Adams, and Muniz (2019) investigated the archaeological record of the Shasu.

"With regard to the region of Edom, he states: Another group of texts places the Shasu in S Transjordan. Short lists of placenames in Nubian temples of Amenhotep III and Ramesses II record six toponyms located in 'the land of Shasu.' Those that can be identified are in the Negeb or Edom. One of the six, Seir in Edom, is found elsewhere in connection with the Shasu. A monument of Ramesses II claims that he 'has plundered the Shasu-land, captured the mountain of Seir'; a 19th Dynasty model letter mentions "the Shasu-tribes of Edom'; Ramesses III declares that he has 'destroyed the

Seirites among the tribes of the Shasu.' From the Egyptian viewpoint, then, the Shasu were a prominent part of the Edomite population."[194]

A specific reference to the Shasu of Edom was found in a document called Papyrus Anastasi VI (lines 51-61) dating back to the reign of Pharaoh Merneptah (1224 B.C.–1214 B.C.). Scholars believe this document is a note between an Egyptian field officer (akin to an army correspondent) named Hori and a scribe named Amenemope. The inscription reads:

"We have finished with allowing the Shasu clansfolk of Edom to pass the fort of Merenptah that is in Succoth ["Tjeku"], to the pools (brkt) of Pi-Atum of Merenptah (that is/are) in Succoth, to keep them alive and to keep alive their livestock, by the will of Pharaoh, LPH, the good Sun of Egypt, along with names from the other days on which the fort of Merenptah that is in Succoth was passed [by such people . . .]. [195]

With the link between the Shasu and the Edomites established through these Egyptian documents, we now can hone in on one particular document, "The Craft of the Scribe," that speaks of the stature of the Shasu. "The face of the pass is dangerous with Shasu, hidden under the bushes. Some of them are 4 or 5 cubits, nose to foot, with wild faces."[196] This text originated during the reign of Ramses II in the 13th century B.C. Scholars suggest that the Egyptian royal cubit was most likely the measurement used in this document, which means the Shasu ranged in height between 6 feet 8 inches and 8 feet 4 inches. While we cannot make a direct correlation to the Edomites from this document, we can consider these Egyptian documents as a whole, lending support to the theory that the Edomites intermingled with the giants.

It's not surprising that the Edomites were longstanding enemies of Israel stemming from the sibling feud between Esau and Jacob. The conflict between Esau and Jacob typified the conflict between the flesh and the spirit. Esau had no concern for the things of the Spirit, whereas, Jacob was steadfast in his pursuit of the blessings of the Lord, so much so that he connived Esau and wrestled with the Lord to get the blessings. Edom was often the focus of prophecies warning of their coming destruction given by Isaiah, Jeremiah, and Obadiah.

Isaiah 34: 8-11, 13-14 (NIV) *"For the Lord has a day of vengeance, a year of retribution, to uphold Zion's cause. Edom's streams will be turned into pitch, her dust into burning sulfur; her land will become blazing pitch! It will not be quenched night or day; its smoke will rise forever. From generation to generation it will lie desolate;*

no one will ever pass through it again. The desert owl and the screech owl will possess it; the great owl and the raven will nest there. God will stretch out over Edom the measuring line of chaos and the plumb line of desolation...She will become a haunt for jackals, a home for owls. Desert creatures will meet with hyenas, and wild goats will bleat to each other; there the night creatures will also lie down and find for themselves places of rest."

Perhaps you noticed the similarities with the prophecies against Babylon that we examined in Chapter 10. The screech owl that will possess Edom is the demon goddess Lilith, the goddess of the underworld. The desolation of Edom renders the land inhabited by demonic entities as represented by the desert owl, screech owl, raven, hyenas, wild goats, and night creatures. There will come a day of vengeance for the enmity of the Edomites toward the children of Israel.

Let's follow the trail of the Edomites into New Testament times and the centuries that followed to gather clues about their role in the roots of the Federal Reserve. As generations progressed, the Edomites continued to play an antagonistic role in the destiny of Israel. David, Joab and the Israelite army struck down 18,000 Edomites in a great victory (2 Samuel 8:13-14). The surviving Edomites became subject to David, which in part, is a fulfillment of the prophetic word Rebekah received while Jacob and Esau were in her womb (Genesis 25:23). Solomon, however, walked in the opposite manner as David with respect to the Edomites. Solomon married Edomite women resulting in a mixture within his bloodline. Solomon's actions were in direct disobedience to the Lord and were the reason the kingdom of Israel was split apart during his son's reign (I Kings 11:1-17).

During the Intertestimental Period, Hyrcanus, a leader among the Maccabean revolt, engaged in a battle against the Edomites (also known by the Greek translation "Idumeans"). Josephus recorded,

"Hyrcanus took also Dora and Marissa, cities of Idumea, and subdued all the Idumeans; and permitted them to stay in that country, if they would circumcise their genitals, and make use of the laws of the Jews; and they were so desirous of living in the country of their forefathers, that they submitted to the use of circumcision, and the rest of the Jewish ways of living; at which time therefore this befell them, that they were hereafter no other than Jews." (Josephus, *Antiquities* 13.9.1)[197]

Hyrcanus converted the Idumeans to Judaism by forcing them to submit to Jewish law if they wanted to stay in the beloved land of their ancestors. We can presume that for most of the Idumeans, their conversion to follow Yahweh was not genuine. Even though during this period of history, the Idumeans appeared to be joined with the Jews, there were still underlying tensions. According to Josephus, Antipater was an Idumean who married Cypros, also an Idumean. They had four sons and one daughter: Phaseal, **Herod**, Joseph, Pheroras, and Salome. Julius Caesar appointed Antipater as Procurator of Judea in 47 B.C. Shortly thereafter, Antipater was killed, and his son Herod rose to power. Herod was disliked by the Jews but used his shrewdness to develop favorable relations with Rome, which in turn led to his promotion as king of the Jews in 37 B.C.[198] Following his appointment as king, Herod killed the priestly line of Hyrcanus along with the last of the Aaronic priesthood. He appointed as high priests, "men of low birth" and deposed them when he desired. The Sadducees were established as high priests through the Herodians. Herod the Great ordered the slaughter of all male infants two years and younger living within the Bethlehem area as an attempt to kill Jesus (Matthew 2:16). He was the one to rebuild the temple in Jerusalem but was not received as a genuine Jew. He was considered "half-Jew" because he was an Edomite. The conversion to Judaism for his parents was not genuine and Herod, himself, was more aligned with the Graeco-Roman religion and culture than Judaism.

This explains the growing antagonism throughout his life toward the Jews culminating in the most horrific of edicts, days before his death.

"He commanded that all the principal men of the entire Jewish nation wheresoever they lived, should be called to him…And not the king was in a wild rage against them all, the innocent as well as those that had afforded him ground for accusations; and when they were come, he ordered them all to be shut up in the hippodrome…they shall place soldiers around the hippodrome…they shall give orders to have those that are in custody shot with their darts." (Josephus, *Antiquities,* 17.6.5)[199]

King Herod was a mad man bent on the destruction of the Jews. He knew the Jews would not mourn his death, but if he ordered the slaughter of one male from every Jewish family at the time of his death, it would force the Jewish nation into mourning. Pure EVIL!

What became of the Edomites/Idumeans after the fall of Jerusalem in A.D. 70? Were they extinguished in the destruction of Jerusalem or did their bloodline live on? History records that there was great turmoil in Jerusalem during the reign of the Roman Empire, culminating in its total destruction in 70 A.D. under the brutality of Titus. The Jews mounted three major revolts against Rome between 66-70 A.D. These rebellions fostered multiple factions among the Judeans and Idumeans over who would regain control of Jerusalem. Josephus identified at least three different factions: Simon bar Giora, John of Gischala, and the Zealots. The Idumeans came under attack by one of their own, Simon bar Giora. Simon promised "liberty for the slaves and rewards for the free" which garnered support from tens of thousands of people. The Zealots were a radical sect of freedom fighters who preached rebellion. Instead of banding together to fight Rome, these factions began the most atrocious infighting, slaughtering each other in great numbers. The Idumeans sent 20,000 of their men to join the Zealots in the fight against Simon and his 40,000 troops that were advancing on Jerusalem. In the early stages of the Jewish-Roman Wars, Josephus was a rebel commander of Galilee, but surrendered to the Romans in A.D. 67. He defected and became a Roman citizen. Josephus does not record history favorably for the other factions.

"Again, therefore, what mischief was there which Simon son of Gioras did not do? Or what kind of abuses did he abstain from as to those very free men who had sent him up for a tyrant? What friendship or kindred were there that did not make him bolder in his daily murders? For they looked upon the doing of mischief to strangers only as a work beneath their courage but thought their barbarity towards their nearest relations would be a glorious demonstration thereof. **The Idumeans also strove with these men who should be guilty of the greatest madness! For they [all], vile wretches as they were, cut the throats of the high priests, that so no part of a religious regard to God might be preserved; they thence proceeded to destroy utterly the least remains of a political government, and introduced the most complete scene of iniquity in all instances that were practicable; under which scene that sort of people that were called Zealots grew up, and who indeed corresponded to the name, for they imitated every wicked work**…Accordingly, they all met with such ends as God deservedly brought upon them in way of punishment; for all such miseries have been sent upon them as man's nature is capable of undergoing, till the utmost period of their lives, and till death came upon them in various ways of torment." (Josephus, *The Wars of the Jews* 7.8.1)[200] (emphasis mine)

Josephus recorded that 97,000 were carried off in captivity and 1.1 million perished as a result of the siege on Jerusalem. (Josephus, *The Wars of the Jews* 6.9.3)[201] Among these, a large portion of Idumeans perished. But in order to investigate whether the bloodline of the Edomites was totally destroyed in the Fall of Jerusalem, we have to follow the trail of those taken into captivity, as well as, those who dispersed. We will continue this part of the investigation in an upcoming chapter.

Other Tribes

As we consider the three other giant tribes from our chart—Emim, Zamzummim and Avim, admittedly it starts to get a bit confusing to figure out whether these are distinguishable tribes or simply different names for the same giant tribes. Depending on how one interprets Deuteronomy 2, they are either distinct giant tribes or the same tribe with different names assigned to them based on the culture describing them. It seems that the various translations of this passage have contributed to the confusion. For example,

Deuteronomy 2:10-11 (ESV) "*(The **Emim** formerly lived there, a people great and many, and tall as the Anakim. Like the Anakim they are also counted as Rephaim, but the Moabites call them Emim.*" (emphasis mine)

Deuteronomy 2:10-11 (NLT) "*(A race of giants called the **Emites** had once lived in the area of Ar. They were as strong and numerous and tall as the Anakites, another race of giants. Both the **Emites** and the Anakites are also known as the Rephaites, though the Moabites call them **Emites***." (emphasis mine)

The New Living Translation clearly distinguishes the Emites (or Emim) as a race of giants that are different than the Anakim, whereas the English Standard Version does not distinguish them as a separate tribe but instead, suggests that they are from the tribe of the Rephaim, which were known as Emim in the Moabite dialect. Clyde Billington in his article entitled *Goliath and the Exodus Giants: How Tall Were They?* provides some clarity as to these tribes.

"If it is assumed that the word "Rephaim" is a proper noun and the name of an ancient people, then "Rephaim" was a general name used for the Emim, Zamsummin, and Anakim. Anakim was a tribal name for the Rephaim who lived west of the Jordan River and Dead Sea, and Emim and Zamsummin were tribal names for the Rephaim who lived east of the Jordan River and Dead Sea in Moab and Ammon. Those Rephaim living east of the Jordan River and Dead Sea, but not in Moab or Ammon, were simply called Rephaim."[202]

While it seems like a viable possibility that the Emim, Zumzummin, and Avim were referring to the same tribe of giants, we don't have conclusive information from scripture to definitively determine whether this is true. It is reasonable to conclude that they are related to the Anakim because of their lineage stemming from the Rephaim.

The meaning of the different names given to the giant tribes (taken from Blue Letter Bible Strong's Concordance) gives us a bit more information about the nature of these giants.

Emim – means "terror," likely because whoever saw them was seized with terror.

Zamzummmim – means "plotters," likely because they were fierce warriors with war strategy purposed to bring forth maximum damage.

Avim – means "those who inhabit desert places, ruins" likely because they inhabited ruins and were themselves brought to ruin.

In our examination of the tribes of giants found in scripture, we can see Nephilim character traits present within their offspring. As a psychologist, I am trained to diagnosis a mental illness based on the preponderance of symptoms present within an individual. The Diagnostic Statistical Manual (DSM-V), now in its fifth edition, is used by psychologists and psychiatrists to delineate mental illnesses based on a cluster of symptoms. While there is not such a manual to determine whether an individual has the Nephilim genes, my hope is that, as citizen-investigators, we can increase the accuracy of our assessment based on the preponderance of Nephilim/giant character traits present within an individual or entity. Although, another aspect to consider, in addition to the character traits is the physical traits of the Nephilim and their giant offspring.

Key Points
- Rephaim are the next generation of giants after the Flood.
- Og was most famous of Rephaim and ruled from the territory of Bashan, considered to be the gate (portal) to the netherworld.
- Og engaged in cultic sex rituals to propagate the seed of the Nephilim.

- Rephaim are also the departed spirits of the Nephilim, known as demons. The Nephilim had ineradicable spirits.
- As disembodied spirits, the Rephaim look for bodies to inhabit.
- Nimrod and Og provided host bodies for the Rephaim spirits to inhabit which reunited the departed spirits of the Nephilim with the phenotype of the Nephilim to birth the post-diluvian giants.
- Giant tribes intermingled with other nations to create a population of hybrids.
- The Lord's righteous judgments came upon the Amorites when their iniquity reached its full measure.
- When Esau sold his birthright for red stew, he was renamed Edom. Edomites intermingled with giants.
- Edomites have been longstanding enemies of Israel because of the deep-seated hatred Esau had toward Jacob.

Chapter 12

Physicality of the Giants

There are a handful of ancient texts that describe the height of the Nephilim and their descendants. As we might imagine, there are conflicting reports. Such is the nature of myths and folklore when held against the backdrop of ancient historical texts. An attribute of the ancient Jewish scribes I have come to greatly appreciate, is that they were meticulous in their transcriptions so as to not change one "jot or tittle." Therefore, I consider the descriptions of the stature of the giants within the Bible to carry more weight than other ancient texts.

Genetic Markers of the Giants

Genetic markers are sequences of DNA that can be traced to specific locations on the chromosome and can be used to readily identify certain groups of individuals or species. We have already discussed the impact of epigenetic markers that are "turned on or off" by epigenetic signals to produce the phenotype of a Nephilim. As we move forward in our investigation, we need to keep in mind the few genetic markers we have discovered that distinguish a Nephilim phenotype. We will continue to search scripture, extra-Biblical texts, historical documents, and scientific studies to uncover additional genetic markers which, taken together, will reduce the degree of our speculation and instead allow us to reasonably point to the presence of the Nephilim genes in the 19th, 20th, and 21st centuries.

Great Stature

The Bible often refers to giants as men of "great stature."

I Chronicles 11:23 (Amp) *"He killed an Egyptian also, a **man of great stature**, five cubits tall. In the Egyptian's hand was a spear like a weaver's beam, and Benaiah went down to him with [only] a staff (rod) and grabbed the spear from the Egyptian's hand and killed him with his own."* (Emphasis mine)

The Hebrew word for 'great stature' is '*middah*' which means "measurement, act of measuring, size, great stature."[203] Interestingly, '*middah*' is used 55 times in scripture and 31 of those times, a literal measurement is given. In this passage, '*middah*' is used not only to describe the Egyptian as being of great stature, but it also conveys the literal height of this giant—five cubits. I will use the common cubit (approximately 16 inches) as a conservative measure when considering the stature of the giants. So, if the Egyptian giant was 5 cubits, then he was about 6 feet 8 inches. We can learn some interesting facts by looking at other places in scripture where '*middah*' is used when describing giants.

1 Chronicles 20: 4-8 says (NKJV) *"Now it happened afterward that war broke out at Gezer with the Philistines, at which time Sibbechai the Hushathite killed Sippai, who was one of the sons of the giant. And they were subdued. Again there was war with the Philistines, and Elhanan the son of Jair killed Lahmi the brother of Goliath the Gittite, the shaft of whose spear was like a weaver's beam. Yet again there was war at Gath, where there was a man of **great stature**, with twenty-four fingers and toes, six on each hand and six on each foot; and he also was born to the giant. So when he defied Israel, Jonathan the son of Shimea, David's brother, killed him. There were born to the giant in Gath, and they fell by the hand of David and by the hand of his servants."* (emphasis mine)

In this '*middah*' passage we find another clue revealing the stature of giants. The description "*the shaft of whose spear was like a weaver's beam*" is used to give the reader an idea of how large this giant must be. This same description is used in I Chronicles 11:23 referencing the Egyptian giant. In fact, there are only four times the phrase "weaver's beam" appears in the Bible and each time, it is describing the stature of a giant (I Samuel 17:7, II Samuel 21:19, I Chronicles 11:23, and I Chronicles 20:5). A weaver's beam is the main beam that supports a loom; there are typically two, one at the top and one at the bottom. These beams had to be strong in order to brace the loom. The size of a weaver's beam varies, but in ancient Israel it was commonly 2 to 2 ½ inches thick and roughly 8 feet long.[204] So how tall would someone have to be to use a spear of this size? Goliath carried a spear with a staff the size of a weaver's beam and his height was roughly 8 feet 8 inches tall. But even Goliath, as menacingly tall as he was, was not the tallest giant recorded in scripture. Remember, that title belongs to King Og, who was likely around 12 feet tall. Although there is another passage in Amos that suggests Og was not the tallest among the giants (Amos 2:9). This passage refers to an Amorite who was as tall as the cedars and as strong as the oaks.

It's not clear from this verse, which giant the Lord is referring to, but it's possible it could have been one of Og's ancestors. This verse uses a simile to make a comparison meant to draw a connection between the stature of the Amorite and the height of cedars. We know from other passages in scripture that cedars were known for being tall (Isaiah 2:13, Isaiah 37:24, Ezekiel 31:3-9), but how tall were they? Estimates range from 75 feet to 150 feet.[205] So are we to believe that there were giants this tall at one time in history or is this simply a metaphor? Let's not draw a conclusion on this one yet.

As I mentioned, there are multiple records, in addition to the Bible, that depict the stature of the giants. Across these records there are discrepancies; one such discrepancy is listed in the extra-Biblical text of Enoch.

1 Enoch 7:2 "*And they became pregnant, and they bare great giants, whose height was three thousand ells.*"

Similar to cubits, an ell is an unfamiliar measurement in modern standards. An ancient ell is roughly equal to 18 inches. If we convert 3000 ells to feet, it equals 4,500 feet tall. This means that the Book of Enoch is suggesting that the 1st generation Nephilim were 4,500 feet tall. WHAT? Let's put that in perspective as it relates to modern day structures—the Eiffel Tower is 1,063 feet, the Willis Tower is 1,450 feet, and the world's tallest building, the Burj Khalifa in Dubai is only 2,722 feet. It is highly unlikely that the measurement of 3000 ells was accurate. What type of measuring standards did the ancients use when measuring something of this magnitude? It is more likely that this measurement was meant to create an indelible image in the mind of the readers, an image of giants so large that they dwarfed even the tallest of humans.

While it is improbable that the Nephilim were 4,500 feet tall, it is conceivable that the stature of the 1st generation Nephilim could have been sizably different than their descendants. If we contemplate our theory that the post-Flood giants were not the direct offspring of the 'sons of God' and the daughters of men, but instead had Nephilim genes that were switched on by epigenetic markers, then it seems reasonable to surmise there could have been significant height variations. Once again, it may be helpful for us to investigate whether scientific studies can corroborate this theory.

Before we turn to science, are there clues in scripture? Yes. Genesis 9 provides an intriguing clue that is easily overlooked. This clue, found in the directive the Lord gives Noah regarding edible things, lends credence to the notion that there were significant changes in the stature of the antediluvian Nephilim versus the post-Flood giants.

Genesis 9:2-3 (AMP) *"The fear and the terror of you shall be [instinctive] in every animal of the land and in every bird of the air; and together with everything that moves on the ground, and with all the fish of the sea; they are given into your hand.* **Every moving thing that lives shall be food for you; I give you everything, as I gave you the green plants and vegetables."** (emphasis mine)

This passage reveals that after the Flood, the Lord changed the diet of humans. Prior to the flood, humans only consumed plants and vegetables, whereas after the flood, the Lord added meat to their diet. This was a significant change and can be a potential explanation for the differences in height between the Nephilim and the post-Flood giants. After all, the epigenetic studies examining the agouti gene in mice demonstrate that changes in diet can change the methylation of DNA, thus producing changes in the phenotype of mice. Diets rich in a methyl group of Vitamin B will change the offspring of an agouti mouse to be normal in size, weight and fur color.

Not only were there changes in dietary practices after the Flood, but the life span drastically changed as well.

Genesis 6:3 (AMP) *"Then the Lord said, 'My Spirit shall not strive and remain with man forever, because he is indeed flesh [sinful, corrupt – given over to sensual appetites]; nevertheless his days shall yet be a hundred and twenty years."*

The antediluvian life span was significantly longer than the life span of those that lived after the Flood. Noah was the last of the antediluvian patriarchs, he died at the age of 950 years old (Genesis 9:29). Over the span of the next 10 generations, the life span significantly dropped to 175 years, which was Abraham's age when he died. It's worth noting that the change in dietary practices after the Flood may have been a factor in the decreasing life span. Recent nutritional studies support this notion. One such study conducted by Richter, Skulas-Ray, Champagne, and Kris-Etherton (2015) was a review of studies examining the effects of animal protein versus plant protein on diseases such as cardiovascular disease (CVD).[206] Richter et. al (2015) showed that plant protein reduces the risk of CVD in humans. Steven Gundry, in his book *The Plant Paradox* advises us, "if you want to be in the game – meaning the game of life – for the long haul, cut down on animal protein or cut it out entirely."[207] He bases this statement on a body of research that has examined the role of insulin like growth factor 1 (IGF-1) in human longevity. In both animal studies and human studies, consuming less sugar and less animal protein correlates to lower IGF-1 which leads to longer life.

Let's ponder these things for a moment. Noah and his family, consisting of eight people in total, experienced significant environmental and physiological changes after the flood. The Nephilim were completely destroyed, animals were part of their diet, and the life span of their subsequent generations was drastically reduced. We have considered the potential impact of epigenetic factors "switching on" the Nephilim gene in Ham's lineage. Is it possible that epigenetic factors may have also significantly altered the size of the post-flood giants in comparison to the 1st generation of Nephilim? Yes, I think this is a definite possibility. Let's look at some scientific studies that examine this phenomenon.

Genetic and epigenetic studies can help us understand a potential explanation for height variation between the Nephilim and their post-Flood offspring. Thanks to the advancements in technology, scientists are able to search the human genome for DNA variants that impact height. It turns out there are roughly 50 genes and areas of the human genome that contribute to the variation in height. McEvoy and Visscher wrote in their article, *Genetics of Human Height,* "resemblances in height between relatives suggest that 80% of height variation is under genetic control with the rest controlled by environmental factors such as diet and disease exposure."[208]

Deepak Chopra and Rudolph Tanzi, authors of *Super Genes*, recognize that the factors contributing to inheritance are far too complex for one factor alone to explain variations. They point out that typically, genetic traits such as height don't favor extremes, instead there is a tendency to revert back to the mean. If we apply this concept to our conundrum of trying to imagine the Nephilim being 4,500 feet tall, we can assume that the height of the Nephilim was an outlier and the subsequent generations of giants began to revert toward the mean. This begins to make sense, especially if we consider that the Nephilim had fathers who were 100% divine. The offspring of the Nephilim had at least one parent that was a hybrid (<100% divine) and one that was human. Over a thousand years, it's reasonable to think that the height variations trended toward more believable heights for giants, i.e. 40 ft, 24 ft, 12 ft, 8 ft.

An interesting study conducted by Randal Olson, a data scientist at Life Epigenetics Inc., analyzed the median height among Dutch males from 1820-2013 (see Figure 30). The sample of data he used was gathered from military records of new recruits. In the 1860's, Dutch men were roughly 5 feet 5 inches and were among the shortest amidst their cohorts from Italy, France, Germany, Sweden, Denmark, and USA. But in a relatively short timespan of approximately 150 years, the Dutch men became the tallest at 6 feet 2 inches among their cohort.[209] An initial explanation offered by Olson was that the variation in height coincides with an increase in wealth within the Dutch population. However, the other cohort countries also experienced similar economic trends, therefore, an increase in wealth cannot explain why the Dutch stand head and shoulders above the rest. Chopra and Tanzi summarize Olson's interpretation: "The sequence of the DNA in Dutch genes is about the same as it was two hundred years ago. It's generally accepted, Olson points out, that our human ancestors were tall. Perhaps the Dutch used to be tall, hundreds of generations ago, but then poor diet caused them to shrink. In that case, a better diet might trigger the ancestral genes, causing a growth spurt."[210]

This brings us back to the theory that the change in diet after the Flood had a significant impact on the height of the giants. I surmise that the height of the Nephilim was significantly greater than the height of the post-Flood giants, but I want to be clear that I am **not** suggesting that the Nephilim were actually 3000 ells tall (4,500 feet).

Superhuman Strength

As noted earlier, the definition of '*gibbowr*' speaks of someone with great strength. This is one of the traits of the Nephilim, as well as their giant offspring. There are several instances in the Bible when the strength of the '*gibbowr*' is recorded.

II Samuel 21:16 (NLT) *"Ishbi-benob was a descendant of the giants; his bronze spearhead weighed more than seven pounds, and he was armed with a new sword. He had cornered David and was about to kill him."*

The author identifies that Ishbi-benob is from giant lineage and then provides a measurement of the bronze tip of the giant's spear. The spearhead weighs about 7.5 pounds (300 shekels, as mentioned in other translations) which implies that the shaft of the spear was large, in order to hold a spearhead of that size. We can reasonably surmise it took great strength to use such a weapon.

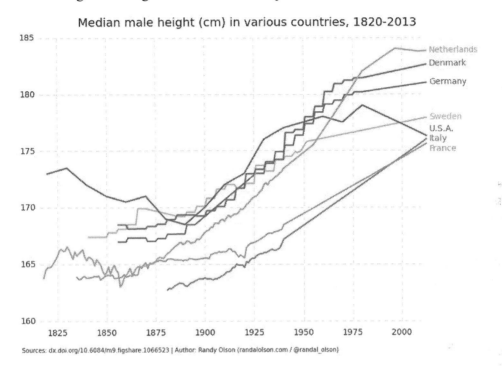

Figure 30. Why the Dutch Are So Tall by Randal Olsen, Ph.D. Retrieved from http://www.randalolson.com/2014/06/23/why-the-dutch-are-so-tall/

Goliath's superhuman strength surpassed that of Ishbi-benob. If you recall, his iron spearhead weighed a little over 15 pounds and was attached to a spear shaft approximately 2 ½ inches thick and 8 feet long. It would have taken great strength to hurl his spear at enemy forces. Goliath's bronze armor scale weighed approximately 125 lbs. Think about the kind of strength that was necessary to remain agile in battle while wearing an armor suit of that magnitude. It's no doubt that Goliath exhibited superhuman strength. It was the primary reason he was the Philistine's best warrior.

Modern science supports the biblical record of superhuman strength found in the hybrid giant species. The Nephilim agenda was to defile the human genome through the mixture of species which effectively created genetic alterations. These genetic alterations produced hybrids with supernormal strength. In Chapter 8, we discovered that scientists found a doubling in the skeletal-muscle mass in mice, cattle, and humans when the myostatin gene is disrupted. The case study we discussed of a German boy born with extraordinary muscle development and supernormal strength by four years of age is a modern-day example of the superhuman strength that results from alterations in the human genome.

Red Hair

We have discovered that great stature and superhuman strength are genetic markers of the Nephilim. Also, if you remember, Esau was covered in red hair when he was born. Given that Esau and his descendants intermingled with the hybrids, we have to consider that red hair may be a potential genetic marker for Nephilim. Now those of you that are redheaded, please don't throw this book across the room. I am not suggesting that you have Nephilim DNA because you have red hair (my grandmother was a redhead, as is my aunt). There are numerous genetic reasons for red hair. Instead, I am proposing that red hair may be a potential genetic marker, because as Esau had red hair and his lineage interbred with giants, it is possible that this genetic trait of red hair became part of the giant lineage.

An article from Science Trends entitled "Redheads: They Have Genetic Superpowers" may be a more accurate description than the author intended. In the 19th century, a French doctor by the name of Augustin Galopin, first started documenting the uniqueness of redheads. He claimed that redheads emit a sensual, alluring aroma. Scientists have since confirmed Dr. Galopin's claim, redheads emit an odor from an acidic film on their skin, but this is not their only "superpower." Redheads have a genetic advantage in that they produce more Vitamin D than the rest of the population. This can be viewed as a "superpower" because it increases their immunity to diseases such as heart disease, autoimmune disorders, diabetes, depression, hypertension and obesity.[211]

In an upcoming chapter, we will discover documentation from the 19th century that describes the presence of red-haired giants in North America. Now it would be foolish to draw conclusions based on this genetic marker alone, just as it would be inaccurate to diagnose someone with schizophrenia based on one symptom alone. Rather the presence of several genetic markers, as well as, several character traits needs to be evident in order to identify the Nephilim DNA.

Polydactyly

An intriguing genetic marker that we have not discussed yet is hexadactyly, that is, someone with six fingers and six toes. This is a physical anomaly found in humans and animals, but notably also found in the giants. If you remember from II Samuel 21:20, there was a giant from Gath that had six fingers and six toes.

Statistics on polydactyly (extra fingers and/or toes) demonstrate that it is not as rare as one might think, especially in the African and African-American population with 1 out of 143 children born with it. It is less common in the Caucasian population with 1 out of 1,339 children born with polydactyly.[212] In fact, polydactyly is the most common birth defect of the fingers and toes. Typically, the extra digits can be removed surgically if they are not fully developed, which explains why it's uncommon to see people with extra digits.

A question we must ask ourselves is, if it is so common, should we even consider it as a potential genetic marker of the Nephilim? While it may seem random that scripture mentions a giant with six fingers and six toes, I don't believe we are to take it as merely an obscure, insignificant detail. Instead, I believe this detail was included to provide us with a clue that this physical anomaly is a genetic marker of the Nephilim, especially if we consider that research has found **bilateral** polydactyly of both the hands and feet to be rare.[213] Let's test this hypothesis. If hexadactyly is a genetic marker of the Nephilim DNA, then are there other examples throughout history of giants with six fingers and/or six toes?

Anthropologists have teamed up with archaeologists to research polydactyly in the Mesoamerican civilizations (Wrobel et al., 2012). Polydactyly appeared within the Mayan culture to such a degree that it required an explanation among the people. It seems that the Mayans believed that polydactyly was a sign of supernatural beings. Even their language depicts this by creating a distinction between humans and supernatural beings. The Mayan word for "human" during the Classic Period (A.D. 200-900) was equivalent to the word for "twenty." Culturally, this signifies the differentiation made between human and supernatural, humans had twenty digits on their hands and feet. If someone had more than twenty, they were not considered pure human. Further evidence that the Mayans believed the six-fingered, six-toed people were not purely human can be found on temples and places of rituals. Wrobel et al. (2012) discussed polydactyly figures found on portions of the Temple of the Sun in

Chiapas, Mexico. It is believed that these figures are representations of supernatural beings.

"Depictions of divinities with six fingers and toes are also found infrequently in several of Mesoamerica's civilizations... It is noteworthy that these examples involve a deified ancestral figure (in the Teotihuacan case) and a particular deity with an avian head-dress (in the Zapotec examples), suggesting that polydactyly indeed served as a distinctive attribute, here perhaps serving as a particular trait, **differentiating between humans and supernaturals**..."[214] (emphasis mine)

The ancient civilizations who recorded polydactyly is not limited to South America. In the United States, we have several native cultures that depict six-toed and six-fingered beings in their artwork, or their fossil remains. Anthropologist, Patricia Crown from the University of New Mexico, conducted research on the prehistoric Pueblo culture (Anasazi), from the high desert of Chaco Canyon, New Mexico. She and her team analyzed 96 skeletons that were previously excavated and found that three out of 96 had polydactyly (3.1%). This is a much higher incidence rate than what is typically found in other Native American populations (0.2%).[215] The petroglyphs from Chaco Canyon depict footprints with six toes and handprints with six fingers. Were these just people with a high incidence of polydactyly or is there more evidence that may link them to the Nephilim?

Chaco Canyon has a rich history of being a congregating place for numerous tribes who engaged in peaceful exchanges of trade and ceremony. The original tribal inhabitants who occupied the territory were admired by their descendants as being "peaceful, happy hunter-gathering, basket-weaving, agrarian people." As time progressed, diversified people groups migrated and established Chaco Canyon as a trading center and ceremonial hub for the practices of different religions. The growing Mesoamerican influence shifted the once peaceful, safe haven into a place where dark rituals ruled the atmosphere. Anthropologist, Christy Turner II, found overwhelming evidence of cannibalism in Chaco Canyon beginning around A.D. 900 and continuing for about 400 years. Turner speculates that the Mesoamerican influence brought human sacrifice and cannibalism to Chaco Canyon as a ritual sacrifice to their god Quetzalcoatl.[216] A Native American legend that sheds further light as to the source of cannibalism is that of the Wendigo, translated as "the evil spirit that devours mankind." Quayle and Horn speak about this legend in their book *Unearthing the Lost World of the Cloudeaters.*

"According to legend, these are evil creatures, sometimes even giants of as much as fifteen feet in height, who at one time were human beings. **But once a person would turn to cannibalism, even under emergency or starvation circumstances, they "changed" forever. They would be overcome with evil spirits who would possess them and permanently transform them into an evil being.** In some instances, the Windigo or Wendigo are different; one is a flesh-and-blood human who is transformed, and in some cases, the other is said to be the evil spirit awaiting a human he can possess and influence to commit cannibalism, sending him on an insatiable, flesh-eating spree....Once a person has tasted human flesh, he or she is overwrought by evil, and passes a point of no return."[217] (emphasis mine)

This lends credence to our theory that epigenetics, in this case, engaging in cannibalism, switches on the Nephilim phenotype. Cannibalism acts as a gateway for the Rephaim spirits to inhabit a host body for the purpose of carrying out the Nephilim agenda.

The Newspaper Rock petroglyphs near Canyonlands, Utah tell a story of the Anasazi encountering giants with six toes. Among the hundreds of petroglyphs, there are human polydactyly feet and giant polydactyly feet. The human footprints are distinguished by an arch and include both normal feet and polydactyly feet. It's important to note that all the giant footprints on Newspaper Rock have six toes. The Anasazi were clearly communicating that the giants they encountered had six toes. This supports our hypothesis that polydactyly is a genetic marker of the Nephilim. Thomas Horn and Chris Putnam in their book *On the Path of the Immortals* make some interesting observations connecting the Anasazi to the biblical account of the polydactyly giant from Gath.

"Note that when the Torah... was written around BC 1300, this would have been the same time when archaeologists believe the Anasazi, across the world from those Bible lands, were drawing giant, six-toed footprints on a slab wall in Utah...When the writings in the Torah are compared with other ancient texts including Enoch, Jubilees, Baruch, Genesis Apocryphon, Philo, Josephus, Jasher...(not counting the accounts of the American Indian tribes on this side of the world), it is clear that this is more than a legend–it is history, a chronicle told through different peoples' methods and worldviews involving giants suddenly infesting the entire world..."[218]

All these examples I have sited are records from centuries ago, but are there any recent discoveries of giants with polydactyly? There was a report of a giant found by an Irish miner in 1895 in County Antrim, Ireland. This giant was said to be over 12 ft tall with six toes on his right foot. It is difficult to confirm the validity of this report, many have considered it a hoax, especially after the body of the giant disappeared. The only evidence is eyewitness accounts and an article published in the *The Strand Magazine*. (See Figure 31) This British magazine was considered to be one of the first, monthly published magazines (founded in 1890). *The Strand Magazine* contained predominantly fictional material consisting of short-stories and serials with illustrations. But mixed among the fiction were factual articles. The magazine became well-known for its Sherlock Holmes stories. Some of the greatest 20th century authors, Agatha Christie, Rudyard Kipling, and Conan Doyle, were regular contributors of *The Strand Magazine*.[219] The section of the magazine that published a photo of the Irish giant was "The Lost Property Office." Essentially it was a public notice of things left on the trains throughout England. These lost property items were held in the local stations for patrons to reclaim.[220] The write-up and accompanying picture of the giant is worth including here.

I will leave you to draw your own conclusions about the authenticity of this giant. I do believe that the article was factual and did appear in *The Strand Magazine* as the archive demonstrates. However, what remains unclear is whether the giant itself is authentic or just a creative attempt by an Irishman to make a shilling or two.

Another interesting finding of six-fingered, six-toed individuals is among the Waorani tribe of Ecuador.[1] They are not tall in stature and it's important to note that the rate of polydactyly is no more common among the Waorani than those in Western civilizations, the difference is that the extra digits are not surgically removed among the Waorani.[221] However, I include the Waorani here because this tribe has several unique qualities that warrant a closer look for the sake of our investigation.

Historically, the Waorani have lived in remote areas of the Ecuadorian Amazon. They were considered the least acculturated tribe in South America. Some of the first known

---

[1] Photos of the Waorani with polydactyly can be found in the article entitled "The Saga of Equador's Secret People: A Historical Perspective," pg. 7.
http://www.lastrefuge.co.uk/data/articles/waorani/waorani_page7.htm

THE MYSTERIOUS COFFIN EMBLEM AT EUSTON.

reproduced here. This monstrous figure is reputed to have been dug up by a Mr. Dyer, whilst prospecting for iron ore in Co. Antrim. The principal measurements are : Entire length, 12ft. 2in. ; girth of chest, 6ft. 6½in. ; and length of arms, 4ft. 6in. There are six toes on the right foot. The gross weight is 2 tons 15 cwt. ; so that it took half-a-dozen men and a powerful crane to place this article of lost property in position for THE STRAND MAGAZINE artist.

Briefly the story is this : Dyer, after showing the giant in Dublin, came to England with his queer find, and exhibited it in Liverpool and Manchester at sixpence a head, attracting scientific men as well as gaping sightseers. Business increased, and the showman induced a man named Kershaw

mechanism inside the coffin, moves its jaws in an indescribably horrible manner, and emits a weird, whirring sound. Behind the skull are seen a scythe and a sexton's spade. In front are a couple of real human bones, kept crossed by a silver snake.

This railway company's sale of lost property takes place at their Broad Street goods station ; and besides passengers' unclaimed luggage, cloak-room parcels, and miscellaneous articles found in the trains and on the platforms, the stock on hand in the goods department is also sold in the same way. This stock consists of merchandize either unclaimed or for which a claim for compensation has been made and paid. Samples figure largely in the unclaimed section. A builder may actually receive a sample case of new fire-bricks, or a grocer a sample of blacklead ; but both may refuse to receive and pay carriage on the consignments. Then, again, a lady may receive a costly dress too late for some social function ; or a bicycle may be damaged in transit, and perhaps in both cases the consignees will refuse to take the goods, and put in a claim for damages. This accounts for the amazing diversity of articles and "lots" that figure in the sale-room.

Pre-eminent among the extraordinary articles ever held by a railway company is the fossilized Irish giant, which is at this moment lying at the London and North-Western Railway Company's Broad Street goods depôt, and a photograph of which is

THE UNEARTHED AT BROAD STREET GOODS STATION.

Figure 31. Photo of Irish Giant by the Lost Property Office of The Strand Magazine, December 1895.

The Roots of the Federal Reserve:

to purchase a share in the concern. In 1876, Dyer sent his giant from Manchester to London by rail ; the sum of £4 2s. 6d. being charged for carriage by the company, but never paid. Evidently Kershaw knew nothing of the removal of the "show," for when he discovered it, he followed in hot haste, and, through a firm of London solicitors, moved the Court of Chancery to issue an order restraining the company from parting with the giant, until the action between Dyer and himself to determine the ownership was disposed of. The action was never brought to an issue, and the warehouse charges, even at a nominal figure, will amount to £138 on Christmas Day, 1895. In addition to this large sum, there is the cost of carriage, and about £60 legal expenses which the railway company incurred. The injunction obtained by Kershaw which prevents the North-Western Railway Company from dealing with the giant is still in force, and the sanction of the Court must be obtained before it can be removed from its resting-place at Broad Street goods depôt; where it remains—a weird relic of distant ages in a vast hive of latter-day industry.

My next visit was to the Great Northern Railway Company at King's Cross, and here is a view of the interior of their depôt for the reception of lost property. The articles are first of all received and registered by clerks on the ground floor, and are subsequently hauled up into this dingy emporium, where, in due time, the auctioneer and his staff arrange things for the annual sale, which takes place in an immense warehouse at one side of the station. The sorting of the articles takes six weeks. In this picture the superintendent of the department is watching his man hauling up part of a small bedstead ; and to the right of him is seen an immense pile of newspapers taken by the porters from the railway carriages. About two tons of newspapers figure in the Great Northern annual

sale. In the illustration are also seen a surprising variety of old clothes, a bicycle, and a string of ladies' muffs ; several bundles of umbrellas, and a fitted luncheon basket.

At the sale the umbrellas are made up into lots of from six to thirty-six, according to quality, and fetch from two guineas a lot downwards. They are bought by Jewish dealers, and are subsequently displayed for sale on barrows in the poorer quarters of London. The sale of lost property realizes quite an insignificant sum. The amount derived from the Great Northern sale last year was £170; and in this sale were included 1,000 walking-sticks and 1,300 umbrellas.

The Midland Railway Company's lost property staff at Derby consists of several men, two of whom are searchers, and are constantly travelling all over this and other systems in quest of missing luggage. During 1894, 17,188 articles were dealt with at Derby. The number of umbrellas found in trains and not claimed was 3,538, besides 1,404 walking-sticks. I am told by Mr. Eaton, the assistant-superintendent of the line—who received me most courteously on the occasion of my visit to the Midland headquarters—that his company also adopt the system of daily reports from every station, advising the Clearing House, and so on. Property is retained at all local stations, including even St. Pancras, for seven days, and if it then remains unclaimed, it is sent on to Derby.

On the next page is seen a queer group. It consists of a couple of barber's chairs found

210

contact with the Waorani was in the 1940s when Shell Oil employees, along with Ecuadorian workers, were speared to death by the Waorani tribesmen. Stories of missionaries making contact with the Waorani began to emerge in the 1950s when Rachel Saint, a Wycliffe Bible Translator, befriended two teenage Waorani girls, Dayuma and Ome, who escaped the violence in their tribe. You may be familiar with this story; Twentieth Century Fox Home Entertainment produced the movie *End of the Spear* based on a true story of the missionaries who dared to make contact with the Waorani. Five missionaries met their untimely death shortly after initial contact was made; Nate Saint, Jim Elliott, Pete Fleming, Ed McCully, and Roger Youderian were speared to death. News of this tragedy made world headlines. Two years following the deaths of their husband and brother, Elizabeth Elliott and Rachel Saint were given an invitation by Dayuma to live among the Waorani, and they accepted. Elizabeth and Rachel were the first to experience sustained peaceful relations with the Waorani largely because they were able to demonstrate forgiveness. Instead of exacting revenge on the Waorani for the murder of their family, they extended kindness along with their forgiveness, which were concepts the Waorani were unfamiliar with. This opened the door for the gospel to reach the Waorani people.

In the 70's and 80's, Dr. James Yost, an American anthropologist working with a mission organization called Summer Institute of Linguistics, spent more than a decade living among the Waorani. He was able to conduct ongoing studies of the tribal people because he developed a trusting relationship with them. James Yost and his colleagues discovered the Waorani were the most violent tribe in the world.

"Unravelling the secrets of Waorani culture, Jim made some amazing discoveries. He found that the Waorani had maintained the highest levels of homicide ever recorded in the annals of human history. Fully fifty percent of all deaths in the preceding five generations had been the result of homicide as the Waorani engaged in a continuous and deadly internal vendetta, pursued mostly at night, in spearing raids. No death, it seemed, whatever the cause, went unavenged. Furthermore, the Waorani were even reputed to kill by spearing any, although only a few instances have been proven, of their old people who no longer had the means to support themselves; and they practised infanticide, either strangling unwanted or malformed babies with vines, or burying them alive."[222]

I find this intriguing, the Waorani, historically an extremely isolated tribe and one of the least genetically diverse tribes on record, have had the highest levels of homicide

211

among their own tribal people. This strikes me as characteristic of the Nephilim traits. Prior to the influence of the Christian missionaries, the Waorani were marked by violence, rage and revenge. In addition to the homicides committed by spearing one another to death, they also practiced infanticide of babies by strangling or burying alive infants that were either unwanted or malformed. They were also known to commit senicide, by spearing to death older tribal people that could no longer care for themselves. These behaviors seem to suggest that the Waorani people had been influenced by darkness and had given themselves over to wickedness. But thankfully, God had a different plan for them and sent a handful of very brave missionaries to teach them about love, kindness, and forgiveness.

Key Points

- Physical traits of giants: great stature, supernatural strength, red hair, and polydactyly.
- First generation Nephilim most likely much taller than subsequent generations of giants.
- Cannibalism acts as a gateway that switches on the epigenetic markers of Nephilim phenotype.

Chapter 13

Classification as a Nephilim Host

At this juncture in our investigation, it's important to amalgamate the character traits of the Nephilim with the physicality of the giants to construct a set of criteria by which to assess the presence of Nephilim traits in an individual. I have coined the term 'Nephilim Host' to describe an individual that meets the proposed criteria for classification. I want to highlight that the character traits are weighted more heavily than the physical attributes in this set of criteria due to the heterogeneity of most populations.

Let me explain this a bit further. Arthur Koestler, in his book *The Thirteenth Tribe*, suggests the heterogeneity in ethnic populations makes it difficult to identify different races based on prominent physical features. For example, it is a common perception that Jewish people are easily identifiable by a distinct nose structure, but he summarizes data that demonstrate this is actually a misperception.

"The type of Jew who can be recognized "at a glance" is one particular type among many others. But only a small fraction of fourteen million Jews belongs to that particular type, and those who appear to belong to it are by no means always Jews. One of the most prominent features—literally and metaphorically—which is said to characterize that particular type is the nose, variously described as Semitic, aquiline, hooked, or resembling the beak of an eagle (bec d'aigle). But, surprisingly, among 2836 Jews in New York City, Fishberg found that only 14 percent—i.e., one person in seven—had a hooked nose; while 57 percent were straight-nosed, 20 percent were snub-nosed and 6.5 percent had "flat and broad noses". Other anthropologists came up with smiilar [sic] results regarding Semitic noses in Poland and the Ukraine. Moreover, among true Semites, such as pure-bred Bedoums [sic], this form of nose does not seem to occur at all."[223]

Similarly, in considering the cluster of traits that identify a set of criteria for classification of a Nephilim Host, I propose that the existence of physical traits alone does not meet the criteria, but rather character traits have to accompany the physical traits to be classified as a Nephilim Host. Furthermore, I propose that it's possible to be a Nephilim Host without the presence of any of the physical characteristics, if there is a preponderance of behavioral characteristics that exist.

Disclaimer—In constructing this set of criteria for classifying an individual as a Nephilim Host, I am drawing upon the concepts found in the Diagnostic and Statistical Manual for Mental Disorders, **BUT I am by no means claiming that this cluster of traits can be used to determine a clinical diagnosis**. This cluster of traits has not been properly scrutinized using research methods involving an adequate sample size to determine by statistical significance the presence of Nephilim traits in an individual. I have developed this set of criteria based upon a literature review of the characteristics of Nephilim and their giant offspring utilizing ancient texts, extra-biblical manuscripts and biblical records as resources (see References section).

Given the ethereal nature of the Nephilim, I am hoping that this set of criteria will help advance our ability to discern the presence of Nephilim traits within an individual. A critical step toward strengthening the body of literature on this subject would be to gather empirical data from a large sample size and apply statistical analysis to test the validity of the proposed criteria. Research of this caliber would require the collaboration of many professionals across various disciplines.

(Proposed) Criteria for Classification as a Nephilim Host

A. Three (or more) of the following physical characteristics:
1. excessively tall (rule out gigantism)
2. extraordinarily strong
3. polydactyly (six fingers and/or six toes)
4. red hair
B. Three (or more), if criterion A has been met, otherwise five (or more) of the following behavioral characteristics:
1. lustfulness in conjunction with sexual misconduct
2. deceitfulness as indicated by repeated lying and purposeful misrepresentation for personal profit and pleasure

3. pervasive pattern of instability in relationships marked by control, manipulation, intimidation, and domination over others
4. rebellious behavior and disregard for the "rule of law"
5. haughty and prideful, as if above reproach
6. vengeful or inappropriate intense anger
7. participation in sorcery, witchcraft, and/or the occult
8. reoccurring violent acts displaying disregard for the rights of others
9. lack of remorse for heinous acts against other living beings
10. excessive focus on death related topics and/or symbolism
11. underlying dark personality that is masked by overinflated self-righteousness
12. dishonesty in trade and business transactions, a propensity toward corruption
13. sexual perversion involving pedophilia, sexual domination of others against their will, and/or bestiality
14. trafficker of humans
15. engage in cannibalism
16. commit treasonous acts
17. pervasive pattern of engagement in sexual and/or blood occult rituals
18. commit human sacrifices
19. enslavement of others

Note: Only need to meet two (or more) regardless of Criterion A, if behavioral characteristics are among criteria #13-19.

I am guessing that as you read through these proposed criteria for classification of a Nephilim Host, several candidates come to your mind. I think we all would be shocked by the sheer number of people that meet this criterion. It's possible that we have even come in contact with people that are Nephilim Hosts, but don't despair, greater is He that is in us than he that is in the world (I John 4:4)! I also want to offer hope to those that may have given themselves over to the Nephilim agenda, Jesus has a path to freedom and deliverance. His kindness leads us to repentance.

Key Point
- The proposed criteria for classification as a Nephilim Host is method of identifying people who have partnered with the Nephilim agenda.

Chapter 14

Giant Slayers

At this point in our journey together, it's crucial for us to tap into the fortitude from heroes of old, so that we can, in turn, become giant slayers. The giants of our day may not have the exceedingly great height that characterized the giants of old; but the power, control and domination Nephilim Hosts wield, reaches to great heights in the global governmental structures. WE THE PEOPLE, COMING TOGETHER IN UNITY, CAN TAKE DOWN THE GIANTS THAT RULE OUR LAND. We can be trained by the renowned biblical giant slayers by studying their battle strategy.

Lessons from Deborah

Deborah was a prophetess, judge, and warrior from the tribe of Ephraim. She governed Israel during a time when they were under the oppression of a foreign king named Jabin. For 20 years, the Israelites were terrorized by Jabin and his military general, Sisera. This violent oppression impacted every area of their lives. They could not travel freely; bandits had overtaken the roadways forcing the closure of trade routes. They were faced with a shortage in their food supply because the farmers' crops were continually raided by Jabin's men and even the watering holes were unsafe due to archers.

Deborah held court under the Palm of Deborah located between Ramah and Bethel, in the hill country of Ephraim. As judge, she settled disputes among the Israelites and governed Israel with wisdom and strength. After 20 years of oppression, the Lord showed her that it was time to overthrow the enemy. She delivered a prophetic word to Barak.

Judges 4:6-9 (NIV) *"She sent for Barak son of Abinoam from Kedesh in Naphtali and said to him, 'The Lord, the God of Israel, commands you: 'Go, take with you ten thousand men of Naphtali and Zebulun and lead them up to Mount Tabor. I will lead Sisera, the commander of Jabin's army, with his chariots and his troops to the Kishon River and give him into your hands.'' Barak said to her, 'If you go with me, I will go; but if you don't go with me, I won't go.' 'Certainly I will go with you,' said Deborah. 'But because of the course you are taking, the honor will not be yours, for the Lord will deliver Sisera into the hands of a woman.' So Deborah went with Barak to Kedesh."*

Barak suffered from a similar problem as Saul, he was stymied by the fear of man. He did not have the courage to lead 10,000 Israelite men into battle, he needed the strength and courage of Deborah to bolster him. This fear of man caused Barak to forfeit the fullness of his destiny. Had he simply believed the word of the Lord and understood who he was and who God is, he would have received honor throughout all of Israel, as the one who delivered them from the enemy. But instead, that honor would go to a little-known woman named Jael, who would drive a tent peg through the head of Sisera.

In contrast to Barak, Deborah walked in the fear of the Lord. She was a warrior without hesitation. She did not fear the battle against Jabin's violent forces; she knew the appointed time had come to be delivered from the enemy. God said it was as good as done, that's all she needed to know. Deborah understood the dominion authority she had.

Judges 5:13 (KJV) *"Then he made him that remaineth have dominion over the nobles among the people: the Lord made **me have dominion over the mighty**."* (emphasis mine)

We are familiar by now with this word "mighty," it is the Hebrew word *'gibbowr.'* Deborah understood that she had dominion over the giants. Jabin's forces, though they were great in number and powerful in warfare, were no match for her because it was the Lord who appointed her to have dominion! She led the way for the Israelites to take action; she inspired Israel to rise up and fight their oppressors. She took her stand at the city gates where violence had commonly erupted over the past 20 years.

Judges 5:7-8 (NKJV) *"Village life ceased, it ceased in Israel, until I, Deborah, arose, arose a mother in Israel. They chose new gods; then there was war in the gates; not a shield or spear was seen among forty thousand in Israel."*

Jabin's forces had removed all of Israel's weapons (not one person was found with a sword or spear) as a means to crush any resistance from the Israelites. Israel was so traumatized by the cruel oppression that fear filled the hearts of the men, and they never once rose up to fight Jabin – until Deborah arose!

The war at the gates of the city was not only a war at the physical gates, but a war at the spiritual gates of the city. As we have discussed, spiritual gates serve as an entry point between dimensions. There was an epic battle, the hybrids and their gods vs. the Israelites and the heavenly hosts of the Lord.

Judges 5:20 (NIV) *"From the heavens the stars fought, from their courses they fought against Sisera."*

This is an interesting depiction of the battle, "the stars fought." What does this mean? Were shooting stars falling from the sky wiping out Sisera and his army? Well, not quite. "Stars" is a biblical term frequently used to describe heavenly beings. One example is in the book of Job, it says,

Job 38:6-7 (ASV) *"Whereupon were the foundations thereof fastened? Or who laid the cornerstone thereof, When the morning stars sang together, and all the sons of God shouted for joy?"*

Deborah declared that the stars fought "from their courses," the Hebrew word for "courses" is '*mĕcillah*' which means "a thoroughfare, viaduct, staircase, highway, path, ladder."[224] This gives us a glimpse into the multidimensional battle that took place. The stars accessed a portal, like Jacob's ladder, to enter into the earth dimension and fight on behalf of Israel. They partnered with Deborah, whom God had positioned at the spiritual gates of the city to take dominion over the hybrids and their gods. When Deborah arose and fought, the heavenly hosts of the Lord fought as well, securing the victory for Israel, just as the Lord had promised. After the victory was won, the Israelites and the land experienced 40 years of peace. Israel received a double portion recompense for the years the enemy had stolen their peace.

Lessons from Joshua

I have always had great respect for Joshua. Caleb and Joshua were the only men among the 12 spies sent out by Moses, who did not return with a negative report. They saw the horrifying sights of the giants in Canaan. In fact, it's probable they witnessed cannibalism as well as other forms of violent oppression among the Canaanites, but they chose to fear the Lord instead of the giants. After 40 years of wandering in the desert, their resolve to defeat the giants grew ever stronger.

Joshua, from the tribe of Ephraim, led the Israelites into the promised land after Moses died. He was Israel's leader as they faced the giants in the land of Canaan. The Lord encouraged Joshua over and over to be strong and courageous because he would lead the people to inherit the land that was promised to his forefathers. Joshua led the Israelites to conquer the land of Canaan and fulfill the promise given to Abraham centuries before.

Joshua and the Israelites had many notable battles, but one that stands out was the battle against the five Amorite kings. It was a battle that they never would have won if it were not for the supernatural hand of God (Joshua 10). Joshua and his best fighting men marched from Gilgal to Gibeon in the middle of the night. It was a grueling journey. They marched about 20 miles and portions of the trek involved steep uphill climbs. Once they arrived, they conducted a surprise attack on the five Amorite kings and their soldiers. We need to remember, these were not just any soldiers, there were giants fighting among the ranks of the Amorites.

Joshua 10:8 (NIV) *"The Lord said to Joshua, 'Do not be afraid of them; I have given them into your hand. Not one of them will be able to withstand you."*

By the Lord's hand, Israel prevailed over their enemy. But this was no ordinary victory, it was a supernatural display of God's dominion and power. As Israel had caught the Amorites by surprise, many fled down the road. The Lord hurled large hailstones down on the Amorites from the sky. More Amorites died from the hailstones than were killed by the sword. The significance of this cannot be overlooked. The Amorites worshiped the sun, moon and stars, so it's fitting that the Creator of the heavenly bodies, took the very objects that the Amorites worshiped, and attacked them with it.

In the midst of the battle, Joshua and the Israelites needed more daylight to completely overthrow their enemy. Astonishingly, Joshua petitioned the Almighty Elohim to halt the rotation of the earth. Never in the history of creation had this happened. The sun stood still over Gibeon for a full day. The impact of this would have been felt all across the planet, and all of creation would have taken notice of this event. It was a declaration to all the other nations that Yahweh fights for Israel. More importantly, this cosmic display of God's power was a statement to all other deities that the one true God, the Almighty Elohim, was superior to all the other elohim.

Joshua was a man of unwavering faith. Joshua was given a prophetic promise from the Lord that the Amorites would be given into his hands. He could have sat back and waited for this word to be accomplished. But Joshua knew that God's promises are fulfilled when met with faith put into motion. Joshua wholeheartedly, without reservation, engaged. He gave every ounce of energy to the battle at hand.

It's important to recognize that Joshua didn't suddenly develop this courage overnight, he had spent more than 40 years developing an intimate relationship with the Lord. He was Moses' right hand man for many years which gave him the opportunity to experience the presence of the Lord. Scripture tells us that Joshua would linger in the presence of the Lord in the Tent of Meeting (Exodus 33:11). This intimacy led to fear of the Lord, incredible courage, and a mighty faith that eradicated the giants. Joshua dared to ask the impossible and did so with boldness in front of the army of Israel because he knew the God they served. May we develop this level of intimacy so that when the day of battle comes, we are not afraid of the giants we face because we know that the Almighty, Powerful God fights on our behalf!

Lessons from Caleb

Caleb was a mighty man of courage, from the tribe of Judah, who walked in the fear of the Lord. He knew that the source of his strength came from the Lord; this gave him extraordinary confidence to face any giant.

Joshua 14:7-8, 10-11 (NIV) *"I was forty years old when Moses the servant of the Lord sent me from Kadesh Barnea to explore the land. And I brought him back a report according to my convictions, but my fellow Israelites who went up with me made the hearts of the people melt with fear. I, however, followed the Lord my God wholeheartedly. So on that day Moses swore to me, 'The land on which your feet have walked will be your inheritance and that of your children forever, because you have followed the Lord my God wholeheartedly.'*

Now then, just as the Lord promised, he has kept me alive for forty-five years since the time he said this to Moses, while Israel moved about in the wilderness. So here I am today, eighty-five years old! I am still as strong today as the day Moses sent me out; I'm just as vigorous to go out to battle now as I was then."

I love Caleb's "can do" attitude; he was not a man who made excuses. After 40 years of wandering in the desert because the 10 other spies stirred up fear in the hearts of the Israelites, Caleb was just as ready to take down the giants in the promised land at age 85, as he was when he was 40 years old. Caleb did not have a retirement mentality, instead he was passionate about possessing his inheritance, even though it meant he would have to face the giants and eradicate them from his land. He valued the prophetic word Moses had given him 45 years earlier. He had waited for the fullness of time regarding his destiny before taking possession of his promised inheritance.

Numbers 14:24 (NIV) *"But because my servant Caleb has a different spirit and follows me wholeheartedly, I will bring him into the land he went to, and his descendants will inherit it."*

Once the Israelites had entered the promised land and began to possess it, Caleb reminded Joshua about his prophetic word. The time of its fulfilment had reached its fullness and he was ready to take the victory at hand! Caleb said to Joshua,

Joshua 14:12-13 (NIV) *"Now give me this hill country that the Lord promised me that day. You yourself heard then that the Anakites were there and their cities were large and fortified, but, the Lord helping me, I will drive them out just as he said.' Then Joshua blessed Caleb son of Jephunneh and gave him Hebron as his inheritance."*

Hebron is located 25 miles south of Jerusalem and is situated high in the hill country of Judah. It is located in the West Bank and today, is largely populated by Palestinians. Hebron has a rich history and has been a city largely contested over the centuries. Hebron was founded around 1720 B.C. and is one of the oldest continually occupied cities in the world.

Hebron was the place where Abram built an altar to the Lord near the trees of Mamre (Genesis 13:18). It was also the place Abraham experienced a heavenly visitation. Three visitors appeared to Abraham to remind him of the promised son that would be born (two were the angels that went on to visit Lot in Sodom and Gomorrah, and the third was most likely the Lord himself). When Abraham saw the three visitors, he ran out to meet them and bowed low to the ground (Genesis 18:2). The Hebrew word for "bowed" is *'shachah'* which means "to bow down, to prostrate oneself in the presence of God in worship."[225] *'Shachah'* is commonly used in scripture to describe worship which helps us to understand that Abraham established Hebron as a place of worship.

When Sarah died, Abraham purchased a parcel of land in order to bury Sarah in Hebron. This was the first property owned by an Israelite in the promised land. Not only did Abraham live in Hebron, but Isaac and Jacob also lived in or near Hebron when they lived in Canaan. Hebron is considered a Jewish holy site because it's the burial place for the patriarchs and their wives: Abraham, Sarah, Isaac, Rebekah, Jacob and Leah. While Abraham, Isaac and Jacob lived in Hebron and its vicinity, there was no mention of Anak, Anakim, or Arba living in Hebron.

The giants took up residence in Hebron following the death of the patriarchs. The hybrids defiled the land, and renamed the city Kiriath Arba, in honor of Arba, who was the greatest among the Anakites (Joshua 14:15). This reveals an age-old strategy of the enemy – steal the inheritance of God's people and defile the land. Hebron had become a place of debauchery and wickedness, a place of violence and intimidation, a place of false worship and idolatry. It grew to become a large, fortified city that seemed impenetrable to the 10 spies. Many biblical scholars believe that Hebron was the primary source of the negative report from the spies.

Numbers 13:28-30 (NIV) *"But the people who live there are powerful, and the cities are fortified and very large. We even saw descendants of Anak there. The Amalekites live in the Negev; the Hittites, Jebusites and Amorites live in the hill country; and the Canaanites live near the sea and along the Jordan. Then Caleb silenced the people before Moses and said, 'We should go up and take possession of the land, for **we can certainly do it**."*

There is that "can do" attitude that Caleb is so well-known for. Despite the fear and unbelief among the Exodus generation of Israelites, Caleb would live up to his word. He took possession of Hebron.

Joshua 15:14 (NIV) *"From Hebron Caleb drove out the three Anakites – Shesai, Ahiman and Talmai – the sons of Anak."*

Once again, Hebron was in the hands of God's people, the tribe of Judah, which was fitting given that Judah means praise. Hebron was re-established as a place of praise and worship. It would later be the location where David was first anointed king of Israel.

Lessons from David

The story of David and Goliath is probably one of the more commonly told biblical stories along with Noah's ark and the Flood. Whether people believe the story to be myth, folklore, or truth, most people can identify some basic details from the story – David was a boy, Goliath was a giant and David slayed the giant with a slingshot. But by now, you know me well, we can't just get by with the basic details of this story. There is much to learn from David's courage and confidence. David was from the tribe of Judah and similar to Caleb, he walked in the fear of the Lord. His confidence came from the strength he found in the Lord.

Goliath, the Philistine giant warrior, hurled insults and utilized every form of intimidation he could. The Israelite soldiers were paralyzed in fear because they had not developed the fear of the Lord, instead they were bound by the fear of man. Onto the scene walks a shepherd boy. David was sent on an errand by his father to provide food to sustain his brothers for the battle. This shepherd boy had been tried and tested on the fields while protecting his sheep. He had spent his days watching over the sheep developing intimacy with the Lord. This intimacy gave David the courage to fight the lion and the bear that came to attack the sheep. When David heard the insults Goliath spewed, he was indignant and perplexed by the lack of courage found among Saul's fighting men. David had not given himself over to fear of man because he knew the Almighty God, the all-powerful Elohim. David had confidence because he was in relationship with the God of Israel:

I Samuel 17:45-47 (NIV) *"David said to the Philistine, 'You come against me with sword and spear and javelin, but I come against you in the name of the Lord Almighty, the God of the armies of Israel, whom you have defied. This day the Lord will deliver you into my hands, and I'll strike you down and cut off your head. This very day I will give the carcasses of the Philistine army to the birds and the wild animals, and the whole world will know that there is a God in Israel. All those gathered here will know that it is not by sword or spear that the Lord saves; for the battle is the Lord's, and he will give all of you into our hands."*

What a declaration of confidence! It reminds me of the scene from Prince Caspian when Lucy is on the banks of the Great River near the Fords of Beruna and the vast Telmarine army is charging toward her. She faces them with courage because she knows who she is and who she is with; Aslan is right behind her. Lucy's strength and confidence comes from Alsan's power. Lucy sought after Aslan and longed to be in his Presence. She often could sense him or see him when the others could not. She developed intimacy with Aslan. This same fearless attitude can be found in David, who had no fear of Goliath, the 8-foot 8-inch giant from Gath, nor the vast Philistine army, because he knew who he was and that the Ancient of Days had his back.

There is a stark contrast between the life of Saul, a *'gibbowr'* who feared men, and David who feared the Lord. Saul lost his kingship and his descendants never ruled over Israel. Saul lost the dynastic aspect of his monarchy because of his fear of man. On the other hand, David shifted the atmosphere when he arrived on the battlefield with the fear of the Lord. Goliath had been hurling insults at the Israelites for 40 days; the soldiers were stymied by these curses and could not imagine their deliverance. But the fear of the Lord enabled David to see a different reality—this pathetic, arrogant giant is no match for the Ancient of Days!

Fear of man causes us to lose our inheritance, whereas fear of the Lord releases an exponential increase in our inheritance. David's lineage would not only include multiple kings of Israel, but the King of all kings was from the line of David, the tribe of Judah. There is no greater inheritance!!

Lessons from Ephesus

The Book of Acts (chapters 19-20) record some of Paul's experiences in the city of Ephesus, the capital of magic during the first century. In particular, Ephesus was the center for the worship of Artemis, the Greek name given for the Roman goddess Diana. The Temple of Artemis was well-known throughout the region, and worshipers would travel great distances to partake in rituals and ceremonies honoring Artemis. Female shrine prostitutes surrounded the temple grounds for worshipers to engage in ritualistic sexual deviances. Spiritual darkness enveloped the city and prior to Paul's visit, only a few followers of Jesus resided in Ephesus.

When Paul arrived in Ephesus for the second time, he sought out the believers. There were only twelve. He discovered that they had not been discipled; they only knew of the baptism of repentance that John brought. Paul taught them about the baptism of the Holy Spirit, and they were eager to receive the Holy Spirit. Paul laid hands on them and they were filled with the Holy Spirit, speaking in tongues and prophesying.

Paul began to teach in the synagogue, he spoke boldly for three months about the kingdom of God. The Jewish leaders began to refute Paul and publicly maligned the Way (later called Christianity). Paul continued his teachings for two years in the lecture hall of Tyrannus, so that all the Jews and Greeks living in the province of Asia could hear the word of the Lord. God did extraordinary miracles through Paul demonstrating the power of the gospel. Light broke through the darkness. Paul engaged in "ground level spiritual warfare" by healing the sick and casting out evil spirits. Paul was a conduit for the power of God; even handkerchiefs he touched transmitted the power of God in such a way that people were delivered from illness and demonic possession.

The demonstration of power through the ground level warfare was so extraordinary that several of the Ephesians tried doing it themselves. The cultural norm in Ephesus was to use magic spells, incantations, and curses to manipulate circumstances and/or people. So, the sons of a Jewish chief priest named Sceva, errantly thought they could use a magic formula to release the power to cast out demons. They went around town trying to drive out demons by reciting the incantation "In the name of Jesus, who Paul preaches, I command you to come out." The sons of Sceva quickly realized that the power of God cannot be accessed by incantation. They were overpowered by the evil spirits and wound up a bloody mess, nearly beaten to death.

Word traveled fast around Ephesus of this power encounter and a great fear fell upon the people. The power in the name of Jesus rendered their methods of witchcraft and sorcery inept. Their occult practices were no match for the power of the One True God. Consequently, the name of the Lord Jesus was greatly honored.

C. P. Wagner, in his book *Confronting the Powers*, describes three levels of spiritual warfare: ground level, occult level, and strategic level. Ground level warfare is casting demons out of people. Occult level warfare is confronting practitioners of the magic arts through power encounters that demonstrate the authoritative power of Yahweh. Strategic level warfare is dismantling the strongholds setup by territorial spirits over a city, region, and/or nation.[226]

Paul engaged in ground level and occult level spiritual warfare while he was in Ephesus, but he did not engage in strategic level warfare. Why? Was the power of God that flowed through Paul not enough to dismantle the strongholds of the territorial spirit Artemis? I believe it was a matter of timing. It wasn't the kairos (opportune) time. C. P. Wagner emphasizes a crucial principle regarding strategic level warfare,

225

"When Paul left Ephesus, Diana of the Ephesians had been thoroughly embarrassed, and her power had been severely weakened... Sometime after Paul left Ephesus, the apostle John went there to live and to minister. We saw that during Paul's ministry there, he did not enter the temple of Diana, nor did he engage the territorial spirit in overt strategic-level spiritual warfare. John did both of these things... An obvious question arises. Why was it that Paul did not go into the temple of Diana, but John did? The answer is simple, because it rests on a principle...***in strategic level warfare, proceed only on God's timing***. Both Paul and John had the discernment and the experience to know this principle well. I would surmise that if Paul had violated the principle and gone into Diana's temple to take her on, he, rather than her altar, might have ended up split in pieces. It is dangerous to trifle with territorial spirits." [227] (emphasis mine)

In order to understand the strategic level warfare that the apostle John engaged in, we need to turn to an apocryphal writing called the Acts of John. This book did not make it into the canonized Scriptures; however, it is useful as a historical document. It informs us about the nature of John's experience in Ephesus prior to banishment to the island of Patmos.

John was in Ephesus during a festival honoring the birthday of Artemis. It was on that day of celebration that the kairos moment came for strategic level warfare. The worshipers gathered at the temple of Artemis in white robes as part of the celebration, but John showed up wearing a black garment. John sensed the magnitude of the moment and told the frenzied worshipers:

Acts of John 40-44: "For now is it time that either ye be converted by my God, or I myself die by your goddess; for I will pray in your presence and entreat my God that mercy be shown unto you. And having so said he prayed thus: O God that art God above all that are called gods, that until this day hast been set at nought in the city of the Ephesians; that didst put into my mind to come into this place, whereof I never thought; that dost convict every manner of worship by turning men unto thee; at whose name every idol fleeth and every evil spirit and every unclean power; now also by the flight of the evil spirit here at thy name, even of him that deceiveth this great multitude, show thou thy mercy in this place, for they have been made to err. And as John spake these things, immediately the altar of Artemis was parted into many pieces, and all the things that were dedicated in the temple fell, and... the half of the temple fell down, so that the priest was slain at one blow... The multitude of the Ephesians therefore cried out: One is the God of John, one is the God that hath pity on us, for thou only art God: now are we turned to thee, beholding thy marvelous works! Have mercy on us, O God, according to thy will, and save us from our great error! And some of them, lying on their faces, made supplication, and some kneeled and besought, and some rent their clothes and wept, and others tried to escape. But John spread forth his hands, and being uplifted in soul, said unto the Lord: Glory be to thee, my Jesus, the only God of truth, for that thou dost gain (receive) thy servants by divers devices. And having so said, he said to the people: Rise up from the floor, ye men of Ephesus, and pray to my God, and recognize the invisible power that cometh to manifestation, and the wonderful works which are wrought before your eyes. Artemis…Where is the power of the evil spirit? Where are her sacrifices? Where her birthdays? Where her festivals? Where are the garlands? Where is all that sorcery and the poisoning (witchcraft) that is sister thereto? But the people rising up from off the floor went hastily and cast down the rest of the idol temple, crying: The God of John only do we know, and him hereafter do we worship, since he hath had mercy upon us!"[228]

We learn from this passage that going into the temple of Artemis had not been on John's radar until that day. He discerned that the kairos time had come, that it was the God orchestrated moment to dismantle the strongholds in Ephesus and evict Artemis from the city. He prayed with authority as one of Christ's ambassadors and took dominion over the principality of Ephesus.

As you may remember, Artemis is another name for the Queen of Heaven (or Semiramis). Semiramis perpetuated the Nephilim agenda through deifying Nimrod who had become a *'gibbowr.'* All throughout scripture, the worship of the Queen of Heaven involves sexual orgies with female shrine prostitutes. The purpose of such vile sex acts is not only pleasure and hedonism, but to carry out a sinister scheme against humanity. The shrine prostitutes act as a proxy for the Queen of Heaven, thus promulgating the Nephilim agenda of Genesis 6—the interbreeding of human and divine. During the sexual rituals, demonic powers are invited to enter at the point of copulation in order to alter the DNA at conception.

Paul began the warfare campaign against Artemis by engaging in ground level and occult level warfare. Through Paul's efforts, the power of Artemis was sufficiently weakened which allowed John to come in and finish the job. The spiritual warfare over Ephesus was successful in lifting the cloak of darkness that had enveloped the city. With the darkness dispersed, the Ephesians were able to receive the gospel message.

There was a great harvest in Ephesus and it later became an important apostolic center for the early church.

We can learn a lot from what took place in Ephesus. At times, the Lord may use us to do some of the initial work of weakening the power of strongholds over regions. We do this through intercession, deliverance, and healing the sick. We also may find ourselves in that kairos moment when the Lord is ready to dismantle the strongholds and evict the territorial spirits. Just like with any military campaign, no matter what role we are given, whether it's on the front lines or behind the scenes, we carry it out with integrity and excellence. The battle for souls is on the line.

Dominion Over the Giants

As followers of Jesus, we are to walk in the dominion authority He has given us. In chapter 6, I spoke about our dominion mandate, but I find it helpful to be reminded frequently of who we are.

We are image bearers. We have the likeness of God in us. We are His representatives on earth. We are stewards of creation. Our purpose as image bearers is to establish **His** purposes throughout the earth. Matthew's great commission gives us the directive to go and make disciples of all nations. As we learned from Paul and John's experience discipling the Ephesians, in order to fulfill the great commission, it requires ground-level, occult-level and strategic-level warfare to remove the shroud of darkness and the territorial spirits so that the light of the gospel can be received. Where there is defilement in the land, we are to appropriate the cleansing blood of Jesus for restoration to be established. We have tremendous power and authority as Christ's ambassadors. It's time to rise up and evict the spiritual forces of evil that have taken our territory, our communities, our nation, and our destiny.

With Christ in us, who is head over every power and authority, we have dominion authority to trample on snakes and scorpions. We can follow the footsteps of Deborah, Joshua, Caleb, David, Paul and John who were giant slayers by taking dominion over the giants of our day and age. As we will see more clearly in the upcoming chapters, the battle against the giants was not just relegated to ancient times. The giants we face (now a days) are very real and must be exposed for who and what they are.

The lives of these giant slayers provide us with strategy of how to conquer the giants we face. A pattern emerged in their stories; did you notice it? Intimacy with the Lord, developed the fear of the Lord which led to supernatural strength and courage to defeat the giants. These character traits fashioned them into giant slayers and allowed them to possess their inheritance.

What is your inheritance? What is your destiny? Has fear of man stolen these from you? Let us be people committed to cultivate intimacy with the Lord by lingering in His Presence, by carving time out of our busy lives to learn to hear His voice. Then we will be people who know who we are and who He is. This revelation infuses our body, soul and spirit with the power that only comes from the Lord. Let us be encouraged to be strong and courageous (Deuteronomy 31:6), not shrinking back from the battle at hand. For our fight is not against flesh and blood...

Ephesians 6:13 (NIV) *Therefore put on the full armor of God, so that when the day of evil comes, you may be able to stand your ground, and after you have done everything, to stand."*

So, I ask you, are you a giant slayer? If you are a follower of Jesus, then unequivocally, YES you are a giant slayer! My hope is that you will discover the truth of who you are, the truth of who Jesus is, and the truth of who our enemy is. May you be equipped from the evidence laid out in our investigation, to face the giants in our land and join the ranks of great warriors and patriots fighting to thwart the Nephilim agenda.

Key Points

- The giant slayers of the Bible understood the importance of timing. Waiting for the fullness of time allowed them to apprehend their inheritance and fulfill their destiny.
- A pattern emerged from the stories of the giant slayers – they developed intimacy with the Lord and walked in the fear of the Lord. This equipped them with great courage and strength to defeat the giants.
- There are three levels of spiritual warfare: ground level, occult level and strategic level. Strategic level warfare requires the kairos timing of God in order to see victory.

Chapter 15

Giants Among Us

We are about to discover fantastical archaeological records that will challenge our cognitive schemas. We will need to do the work of substantiating the claims. If they cannot be substantiated, then we can dismiss them as inaccurate assumptions. But if substantiated, then we must consider building the cognitive network to process these findings. We will explore historical and archaeological records from every continent (with the exception of Antarctica) to demonstrate that giants have walked among us. This is not an exhaustive examination, that would require a book in itself, but rather a look at some of the more well-known discoveries and those that are pertinent to our investigation. As we examine these records, we have to keep in mind that some of the explorers who chronicled their journeys may have had ulterior motives in their reports. Whenever possible, we will look for corroborating records to substantiate their claims.

South America

Paracas

The Paracas region of southern Peru, located just south of the city of Pisco, is home of an archaeological discovery of "elongated skulls" that has created much debate over the years. In 1927, Julio C. Tello, the "father of Peruvian archaeology," discovered 427 mummy bundles in Paracas. Among these mummified remains were over 300 elongated skulls. Artificial cranial deformations (ACD), otherwise known as head binding, has been practiced by ancient civilizations on every continent except Antarctica.[229] So at first, it was not unusual to find elongated skulls and as you can imagine, archaeologists initially determined that the indigenous people of Paracas practiced ACD. This hypothesis was true for the most part; many of the elongated skulls show the typical markings from ACD. However, there is a collection of elongated skulls unearthed in the Chongos burial site that some say are atypical of ACD (see Figure 32). These skulls have several anomalies, which I believe, warrants our consideration for possible evidence that these are the remains of a hybrid race.

Brien Foerster, Assistant Director of the Paracas History Museum (a small privately-owned museum), and author of *Elongated Skulls of Peru and Bolivia* suggests that the elongated skulls found in the Chongos grave site are evidence of a hybrid race. He summarizes the anomalous characteristics of the Chongos elongated skulls. In a small percentage of the skulls, the curvature is complex across the entire surface of the skull with no sign of flattening due to implementation of ACD devices. Foerster reports that all the skulls found at Chongos have complete sagittal suture obliteration. While this can be found in skulls with ACD, it is peculiar that all the skulls at Chongos have 100% obliteration, whereas other Paracas skulls with ACD have varying degrees of obliteration and even some with visible sagittal sutures. He states that in normal skulls with 100% obliteration (which can be a common occurrence with older age), the ossification of the sagittal suture can be detected. However, with the elongated skulls from the Chongos burial site, ossification cannot be distinguished.[230]

Figure 32. Paracus Elongated Skull. Photo by Brien Foerster of www.hiddenincatours.com

Additionally, the Chongos skulls have parietal foramina which is inconsistently present in human skulls. Normally, the human skull has four foramina that can be viewed externally: mental foramen, zygomatico facial foramen, supraorbital notch/foramen, and infraorbital foramen.[231] Unfortunately, Foerster does not provide any data regarding how many of the Chongos skulls had parietal foramen present. He states in his book, "almost all, if not all the elongated skulls of the Paracas area" have parietal foramen. So, if his assessment is accurate that "almost all" of the skulls had parietal foramina, we can compare this to studies demonstrating the prevalence rate of parietal foramen in human skulls.

Yoshioka et al. (2006) studied 20 cranial samples and found parietal foramen in 12 skulls (60% prevalence rate); more specifically they studied 40 parietal regions of the 20 cranial samples and found parietal foramina in 20 of the parietal regions (50% prevalence rate).[232] One flaw in this study was the small sample size. Boyd (1930) used a much larger sample to study the parietal foramen. He "systematically examined 1500 crania" from the Anatomical Museum of University of Edinburgh. His findings indicated that parietal foramina were present on both sides of the cranium in 19.9% of the sample, and absent on both sides in 39.6% of the sample.[233] This corroborates the results from Yoshioka et al. (2006), approximately 40% of human skulls have the absence of parietal foramina. We can extrapolate from these two studies that parietal foramina are present in 60% of human skulls, which means that Foerster's claim that "almost all" the Chongos skulls have parietal foramina, does not seem unusual. If he had quantified the "almost all" for us and it was 90-95%, then we could consider the finding as unusual.

Many questions still linger regarding the nature of the Paracas elongated skulls. Are these above-mentioned anomalies enough to determine the skulls are not 100% human? No, I don't think there is enough evidence to make a determination with confidence. So then are they simply the result of ACD, a well-established practice among indigenous people to distinguish class and tribal distinction? Possibly, but the anomalies do raise questions. One thing we can be certain of—there is much research that still needs to be conducted on the Paracas skulls. Foerster's assessment that the Chongos skulls are evidence of a hybrid race would have more credibility if he provided data demonstrating that systematic examinations of the skulls have been conducted by reputable experts. While he claims that DNA studies have been performed by laboratories in the United States and Canada, these DNA studies have not been published. Therefore, the credentials of the researchers cannot be vetted when their names have not been released. This raises concerns regarding the validity of Foerster's claims.

Before moving on, I will leave you with one more reported finding that will cause you to scratch your head, if it's true. Foerster reported a recent discovery (2017) in which the remains of a red-haired newborn infant, approximately 3 months old, were found. What makes this discovery potentially significant is that the skull is elongated. If the age of the infant is accurate, this suggests the possibility that the child was born with an elongated head. Foerster and others assert that this discovery suggests, "a genetically elongated skull, since the process of artificial cranial deformation takes at least 6 months to produce the desired effect. Since more than 300 elongated skulls have been found over the years in Paracas, it is possible there was a race of people living there that were born with this curious feature."[234]

Yes, it's possible that there were hybrids living among the Paracas people, but with regard to this recent discovery, is this really that uncommon for a newborn to have an elongated skull?

There are several cranial deformations that form as a result of the baby's position within the womb, as well as, the difficulty passing through the birth canal. Daniel Bronfin, M.D. (2001) reviewed the anatomy and physiology of abnormal and normal brain growth. He identified several cranial deformities that might explain the elongated skull of the Paracas newborn.

"*Caput succedaneum* is due to edema of the skin and subcutaneous tissues of the scalp resulting in a "conehead" appearance, which normally resolves in less than 6 days. A *cephalohematoma* is a traumatic subperiosteal hemorrhage that does not cross a suture line. This deformity is initially soft and, with time, becomes firm as it calcifies; it generally requires up to 4 months to resolve entirely."[235]

I find it particularly interesting that Bronfin describes a cranial deformation among newborns that resolves within a week, but has the initial appearance of a "conehead," given the Chongos skulls have been described as "coneheads." There are other cranial deformations, as he mentioned, that produce an elongated skull and take up to 4 months to normalize. His review of the literature suggests that it is not unusual to find cranial deformations within newborns. Therefore, it would be misleading to determine that the skull of the Paracas newborn is evidence of a genetic predisposition to an elongated skull. Instead, rigorous research is needed to determine the probable cause of the elongated skull in the Paracas newborn and with full disclosure of these findings.

As mentioned above, this newborn was found with red hair, which is consistent with some of the other elongated skulls found in Paracas. This piqued my interest given our study of Esau/Edom. The question is whether the red hair is a natural remnant of the hair color while they were alive or the result of dye or of interment. It's not surprising that Foerster and crew say two hair experts have refuted the idea that the red hair is a result of bleach or time.[236] But they don't provide the documentation of who the "hair experts" are. The post-mortem changes the body undergoes cannot be overlooked. The cells rapidly cool, bacteria begin to decompose, and depending on the conditions of the ground in which the body is interred, further chemical reactions take place. This process alone can alter the color of the deceased persons hair. However, the discovery of the Tarim Basin mummies lends credibility that the Paracas mummified remains may naturally have had red hair.

The mummies found in the Tarim Basin, China are the most well preserved mummies to date. The caves in which these mummies were buried provided an exceptionally dry atmosphere lending to ideal desiccation. Among these mummies were those with red hair, blonde hair and brown hair (we will discuss the Tarim Basin mummies in more detail in a moment). Of the 300 plus elongated skulls found in Paracas, only 5 had red hair, all of which were buried in the Chongos grave. However, these were not the only skulls found with hair, skulls with blonde hair found in nearby areas with similar conditions may help to rule out oxidation as a cause for the red hair. [237] Once again, it would be helpful if Foerster published the results from the "hair experts," so the validity of their scientific process could be assessed. We will re-visit the significance of red hair, Edom ("to be red"), and the Nephilim agenda in the upcoming chapters. For now, let's journey further south to the region of Patagonia.

Patagonia

The first recorded exploration to Patagonia was made by Portuguese explorer, Ferdinand Magellan, in 1520 A.D. He and his crew encountered giants on numerous occasions. Here are a few of their accounts, "There we found beside a river, men of the kind called *Canibali*, who eat human flesh. And one of those men, as tall as a giant, came to our captain's ship to satisfy himself and request that the others might come. And this man had a voice like a bull's…And he was so tall that the tallest of us only came up to his waist. Withal he was well proportioned. He had a very large face, painted round with red, and his eyes also were painted round with yellow…In time past these tall men called Canibali, in this river, ate a Spanish captain named Juan de Solis and sixty men who had gone, as we did, to discover land, trusting too much in them…When one of them dies, ten or twelve devils appear, and dance round the dead man. And it seems they are painted. And one of these devils is taller than the others, and makes much more noise, and rejoices much more than the others. And from this the giants took the fashion of painting themselves on the face and body, as has been said…The captain [Magellan] named the people of this sort *Pathagoni*."[238]

In Magellan's account of these *Pathagoni*, he identifies them as cannibals, which aligns with Nephilim traits. The height of these giants, according to Magellan's description, must have been between 10-12 feet tall, but this was disputed by subsequent explorers. In order to verify that the *Pathagoni* were actually giants, we need to review the travel records of other explorers that encountered them.

An Englishmen named Sir Francis Drake, led a circumnavigation in the 1620s, one hundred years after Magellan. His nephew published the account of their voyage and their encounters with the Patagonians in *The World Encompassed*.

"Magellane [sic] was not altogether deceived, in naming them Giants; for they generally differ from the common sort of men, both in stature, bignes [sic], and strength of body, as also in the hideousnesse [sic] of their voice: but yet they are nothing so monstrous, or giantlike as they were reported; there being some English men, as tall, as the highest of any that we could see, but peradventure, the Spaniards did not thinke [sic], that ever any English man would come thither, to reprove them; and thereupon might presume the more boldly to lie: the name *Pentagones,* Five cubits viz. 7. Foote [sic] and halfe [sic], describing the full height (if not somewhat more) of the highest of them. But this is certaine [sic], that the Spanish cruelties there used have made them more monstrous, in minde [sic] and manners, then they are in body; and more inhospitable, to deale [sic] with any strangers, that shall come thereafter."[239]

Drake seemed pleased to discount Magellan's report of the size of the giants but, nonetheless, he found similar attributes as Magellan; the Patagonians had atypical sounding voices and a stature that exceeds that of normal humans.

The following century, Captain John Byron from England landed in Patagonia on December 21st, 1764. The record of his interactions and observations of the indigenous people further supports the claims of Magellan and Drake.

"…who afterwards appeared to be a chief, came towards me: He was of a gigantic stature, and seemed to realize the tales of monsters in a human shape: He had the skin of some wild beast thrown over his shoulders, as a Scotch Highlander wears his plain, and was painted so as to make the most hideous appearance I ever beheld: Round one eye was a large circle of white, a circle of black surrounded the other, and the rest of his face was streaked with paint of different colours: I did not measure him, but if I may judge of his height by the proportion of his stature to my own, it could not be much less than seven feet...There were among them many women, who seemed to be proportionately large...Mr. Cumming came up with the tobacco, and I could not but smile at the astonishment which I saw expressed in his countenance, upon perceiving himself, though six feet two inches high, become at once a pigmy among giants; for these people may indeed more properly be called giants than tall men. Of the few among us who are full six feet high, scarcely any are broad and muscular in height... our sensations therefore, upon seeing five hundred people, the shortest of whom were at least four inches taller, and bulky in proportion, may be easily imagined."[240]

Byron's account helps us understand that there weren't just a few 7 footers in the mix, in which case, they could simply be considered tall men. But the fact that there were 500 Patagonians with extraordinary stature suggests that this was a tribe of giants carrying on the phenotype of the Nephilim.

North America

Giant remains have been discovered all throughout the United States, from coast to coast, stretching from our northern borders to our southern borders. It is beyond the scope of this book to include records from all the findings, because there are hundreds, if not thousands. But I will highlight those that are most pertinent to our investigation. At the outset, I also want to point out that there have been numerous allegations against the Smithsonian Institute for the disappearance of hundreds of skeletal remains collected in the early 1900s. We will touch on this briefly to see if there is any validity to these allegations.

Nevada

In Chapter 12, I alluded to red-haired giants from North America. In order to piece together this discovery, we first turn to the writings of Sarah Winnemucca. She was the first Native American woman to write an autobiography; her father was Chief Winnemucca and her grandfather was Chief Truckee of the Northern Paiute tribe. She was a Native American educator, author, and lecturer. She spoke more than 300 times to American audiences across the nation in hopes of awakening the American people to the plight of her tribe. She also served as an interpreter for the U.S. government as a way to bridge the gap between Native American issues and government overreach. In

1883, her autobiography was published, *Life Among the Piutes*; she recounts the experiences her tribe had with red-haired cannibals.

"Among the traditions of our people is one of a small tribe of barbarians who used to live along the Humboldt River. It was many hundred years ago. They used to waylay my people and kill and eat them…That tribe would even eat their own dead – yes, they would even come and dig up our dead after they were buried, and would carry them off and eat them…My people…made war on them… Their number was about twenty-six hundred... My people killed them in great numbers…At last one night they all landed on the east side of the lake and went into a cave near the mountains. It was a most horrible place, for my people watched at the mouth of the cave and would kill them as they came out to get water. My people would ask them if they would be like us, and not eat people like coyotes or beasts…but they would not give up. Then the poor fools began to pull the wood inside till the cave was full. At last my people set it on fire… they must all be dead, there was such a horrible smell. This tribe was called people-eaters… My people say that the tribe we exterminated had reddish hair. I have some of their hair, which had been handed down…I have a dress which has been in our family a great many years trimmed with this reddish hair."[241]

Sarah Winnemucca's account of this savage tribe of red-haired cannibals has since been corroborated by discoveries of skeletal remains in Lovelock Cave located near Humboldt Lake. The inside of the cave is blackened and charred from a previous fire. While Sarah never mentioned the height of the "people eaters," the skeletal remains suggests that they were a tribe of giants. In 1911, a group of miners were the first to discover the remains in Lovelock Cave as they were digging out bat guano for use in fertilizer. The following year, the University of California, Berkeley sent L.L. Loud, an anthropology student, to excavate the caves. Loud joined with Mark Harrington, an anthropologist with a master's degree from Columbia University. They documented their excavations and published their findings in 1929 in a book called *Lovelock Cave*. They estimated 32 to 45 people died in the cave. Among their findings were artifacts that confirm Sarah Winnemucca's report.

"Tending to confirm the Northern Paiute legend of the assault on the cave are the fire-arrow foreshafts… The inflammable parts are dry reed in one instance and grass in the other… A very large number of arrow fragments were found in the crevices of the rockfall blocking the mouth of the cave, as if they had been shot into it, and in the rare cases where a part of the latest cave floor was found intact, the rushes and grass had been burned to the depth of a foot or so, as if fired by the flaming arrows mentioned in the legend."[242]

Loud and Harrington reported finding evidence of cannibalism with the discovery of three human bones that were artificially split to extract bone marrow. In their writings, they also included a report from the first miners to discover the skeletal remains. The following account is from one of the miners, James H. Hart,

"In the north-central part of the cave, about four feet deep, was a striking looking body of a man 'six feet six inches tall.' His body was mummified and his hair distinctly red... The other mummies all had red hair – I think there were either four or five... the man was a 'giant.'"[243]

John T. Reid was another of the miners to make the first discoveries of the remains and artifacts in Lovelock Cave; his background provides some interesting details. He grew up in the Humboldt Lake area and often spent time with the Paiutes. He spoke their language and had many friends that were Paiute, including Chief Winnemucca's son, Natchez (who later became chief). There was an occasion in Reid's childhood when he was asked to join some of his Paiute friends to round up wild horses. Natchez was among the group; they found themselves near Lovelock Cave in the midst of a storm. They took shelter near the mouth of the cave. Reid wanted to go into the cave, but his Paiute friends were resistant because they feared the "evil spirits."[244] Natchez pointed out to Reid, the scars on the rocks above the mouth of the cave and even the tips of the arrows remaining in the crevices. He proceeded to relay a story very similar to Sarah's account recorded in her biography. This experience stayed with Reid for many years, and he was fascinated by the possibility there may be the remains of the red-haired cannibal tribe in Lovelock Cave.

While Reid was never trained as an archaeologist or anthropologist, he was a mining engineer with a passion for Paiute and Nevada history. When the locals found skeletons in the surrounding area, they would contact Reid; he seemed to be the resident curator of ancient artifacts and skeletons. On June 19, 1931, the Lovelock Review-Miner reported that a skeleton of a "giant" was found in the dry lakebed. The femur measured 16 ½ inches, Reid and his associates approximated that the man must have been "nine and one half or possibly ten feet" tall.[245] Even though Natchez and Sarah never explicitly mentioned to Reid, the red-haired cannibals were giants, he drew this conclusion later in life based on numerous discoveries of skeletons that were seven feet tall and more. Even if we don't agree with Reid's conclusions that the tribe of red-haired cannibals were giants, the characteristics of this tribe, as described by the Northern Paiutes, is consistent with the traits of the Nephilim.

Below are a few excerpts from newspaper articles chronicling the discovery of giant skeletons in the Winnemucca, Humboldt Lake, and Lovelock Cave area (see Figures 33-34).

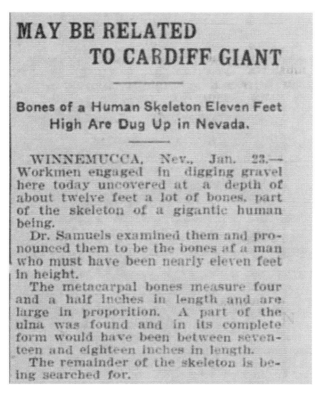

Figure 33. The St. Paul Globe 1904, pg. 28. Retrieved from https://www.newspapers.com/image/84106831/

Georgia

We turn our attention to discoveries made in Georgia as we close in on Jekyll Island. The Golden Isles (St. Simons Island, Sea Island, Jekyll Island, and Little St. Simons Island) are home to several pertinent discoveries. The Wichita Daily Eagle on May 26, 1894 documented the discovery of giant remains on St. Simons Island, Georgia. (See Figure 35) This is of particular interest given St. Simons is only 6 miles north of Jekyll Island. The paper reported the skeletal remains were over 8 feet long.

The Salt Lake Tribune carried a story entitled *"Georgia's Sand-Dunes Yield Startling Proof of a Prehistoric Race of Giants,'* on August 2, 1936 (see Figure 36). The article reported that as excavation began on the Glynn County Airport, Sea Island, workers discovered skulls and skeletons scattered in the sand dunes. It was reported that all the adult skeletons found were between 6 ½ feet to 7 feet tall. Preston Holder was the archaeologist that directed the excavations; his work was sponsored by the Smithsonian Institute. The article states: "One of the nation's leading archaeologists, Dr. F. M. Setzier, of the United States National Museum, was dispatched to the scene. One look, and Dr. Setzier was convinced that the earth beneath the sand dunes would bear importantly upon the history and habits of southern coast aborigines.

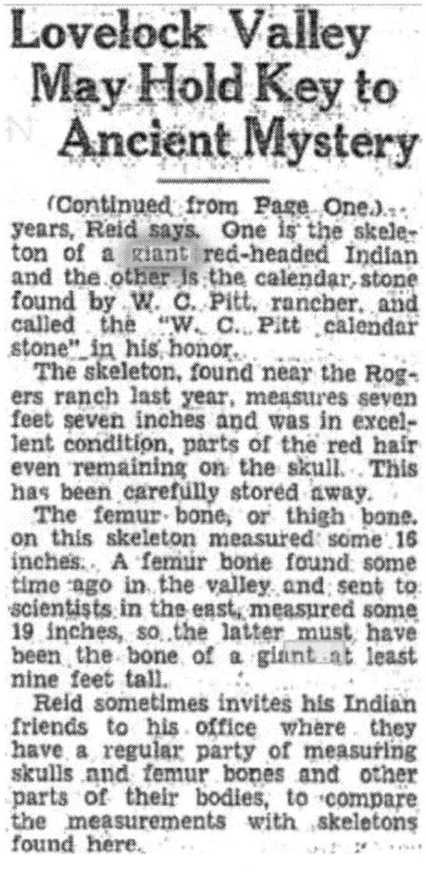

Lovelock Valley May Hold Key to Ancient Mystery

(Continued from Page One.) years, Reid says. One is the skeleton of a giant red-headed Indian and the other is the calendar stone found by W. C. Pitt, rancher, and called the "W. C. Pitt calendar stone" in his honor.

The skeleton, found near the Rogers ranch last year, measures seven feet seven inches and was in excellent condition, parts of the red hair even remaining on the skull. This has been carefully stored away.

The femur bone, or thigh bone, on this skeleton measured some 16 inches. A femur bone found some time ago in the valley and sent to scientists in the east, measured some 19 inches, so the latter must have been the bone of a giant at least nine feet tall.

Reid sometimes invites his Indian friends to his office where they have a regular party of measuring skulls and femur bones and other parts of their bodies, to compare the measurements with skeletons found here.

Figure 34. Nevada State Journal, April 17, 1932. Retrieved from https://www.newspapers.com/image/75282796/

240

ANTIQUITIES.

EGYPTIAN monuments represent hats in nearly the shape of the Mexican sombrero.

IT is estimated that one of the largest stones in the pyramids weighs fully eighty-eight tons.

THE "rock cork" mentioned by Pliny and other ancient writers is thought to have been asbestos.

IN an old Indian burying ground in St. Simon, Ga., the remains of a warrior over eight feet long were excavated recently.

A PREHISTORIC human skull found at Anniston, Ala., in 1800, measured thirty-four inches in circumference just above the ears.

A MAN OF BROAD ACRES.

What Thomas Harrison of North Dakota Owes to Paine's Celery Compound.

Figure 35. Wichita Daily Eagle, Antiquities section. Retrieved from https://www.newspapers.com/image/85661257/

Figure 36. The Salt Lake Tribune, August 2, 1936. Retrieved from https://www.newspapers.com/image/598594082

So systematic work began. Some of the first skulls to be disinterred by Preston Holder have already been examined at the Smithsonian Institute by Dr. Ales Hrdlicka [sic], foremost authority on North American types. According to Dr. Hrdlicka [sic], the Sea Island skulls follow closely the Timucuan characteristics…Archaeological experts declare they are not of the accepted Indian [sic] type…Skulls are unusually large and of the long-headed type."[246]

The description of the skulls being of the "long-headed type" sounds like elongated skulls, but we can't know for certain. Dr. Hrdlička makes a connection with the remains of the giants and the Timucuans, who were the mysterious tribe that inhabited Jekyll Island, the Golden Isles, and parts of Florida. Make note of this, we will return to it in an upcoming chapter. It's clear from this article, that the archaeologists had a heightened sense of anticipation regarding the significance these discoveries would lend toward understanding the coastal pre-historic tribes. What's curious is that, as promising as this archaeological find seemed to be, the trail of it just seemed to vanish.

241

Holder never published the results from his St. Simons and Sea Island excavations. In fact, the Society for American Archeology states:

"Very little information is in print about Preston Holder's extensive, seminal... excavations of prehistoric and early-contact Indian sites on the Georgia Coast...For reasons that remain obscure, his... supervisors in Washington and Georgia did not permit Holder to publish his work-in progress, discouraged the use of his results for his Columbia doctorate, and effectively hid his formal unpublished reports and relevant papers from scrutiny. In some cases, the supervisors expunged the reports and papers."[247]

This is most curious... Was this a pattern for the Smithsonian Institute? Before delving into this a bit, let's consider one more interesting discovery in Georgia.

Naturally, the pre-historic race of giants did not limit themselves to the Georgian coastline; John Wesley Powell, in his expeditions of 1883-1884, discovered giant remains at an Indian burial mound adjacent to the Etowah River near Cartersville, GA. He recorded the height of the skeletal remains to be 7 feet tall with a "heavy" frame.[248] These details help us rule out gigantism because a "heavy" frame is atypical of someone with the rare growth disorder. Rather a "heavy" frame suggests the person was strong and built proportionately to his/her height. The New York Times carried a story on April 5, 1886 entitled "Monster Skulls and Bones."

"Cartersville, GA, April 4 – The water has receded from the Tumlin Mound Field, and has left uncovered acres of skulls and bones. Some of these are gigantic. If the whole frame is in proportion to two thigh bones that were found, their owner must have stood 14 feet high. Many curious ornaments of shell, brass, and stone have been found. Some of the bodies were buried in small vaults built of stones. The whole makes a mine of archaeological wealth. A representative of the Smithsonian Institution is here investigating the curious relics."[249]

Did these curious relics ever make it on display at the Smithsonian? What did the representatives of the Smithsonian determine? Again, the trail seems to vanish once the Smithsonian became involved.

The Smithsonian Institute

As mentioned above, Preston Holder's supervisors from the Smithsonian Institute prevented him from publishing the results of his work in-progress from Sea Island and St. Simons Island. I don't know about you but this seems a bit strange to me. Why didn't they want him to publish any results? Why did they go to the extent of expunging his reports and papers? Did his discovery of giant skeleton remains not fit the narrative of pre-historic North America that the Smithsonian Institute crafted? A brief examination of the character and background of Holder's superior at the Smithsonian, may shed some light.

Dr. Aleš Hrdlička was an anthropolgist known for his studies on Neanderthal man as well as his theories of migration of the Native Americans from Asia. He was a supporter of the pre-Nazism Eugenics movement and his inhumane treatment of Native American cadavers drew quite a bit of negative press. More importantly was his staunch support of the evolutionary theory involving Neanderthal man. Evolutionary science posits that Neanderthal man was shorter than the average male height. It's quite possible that Preston Holder's findings of giant skeletons on the Golden Isles challenged the narrative of the Smithsonian Institute. In fact, not just Holder's discoveries, but hundreds of discoveries across America have been hidden or ignored. If you are intrigued by the possibility of the Smithsonian covering up hundreds of giant discoveries, you are not alone. I encourage you to dig deeper, research it further. A good place to start is Chapter 11 called, "The Truth About the Great Smithsonian Cover-up" (it's 55 pages long) of Quayle and Horn's book *Unearthing the Lost World of the Cloudeaters*.

After weighing the evidence Quayle, Horn and others present, it appears likely to me that the Smithsonian has engaged in rewriting history to fit the theory of evolution. This has necessitated the cover-up of hundreds, if not thousands, of ancient remains that would otherwise corroborate the existence of giants in North America. Perhaps the last scene of *Raiders of the Lost Ark* with the vast warehouse of ancient relics stored in boxes within the bowels of the Smithsonian is not fictional!

Africa

On the continent of Africa, we have a unique situation; the tallest documented tribes are the Watusi of Ruanda and the Dinka of South Sudan. It's not uncommon to find tribesmen between 7 and 8 feet tall. Manute Bol was an NBA player from the Dinka tribe and measured 7 foot 7 inches. John Gunther, an American journalist in the 1950s, wrote about his encounter with the Watusi in his book *Inside Africa.*

"Ruanda [sic] is a fascinating little entity on several counts, but what makes it most distinctive is that it is the home of the Watusi giants. Outside the hotel in Astrida, next to a woman cupping a child's head to her naked breast, we ran into the tallest man I have seen except in a circus. He made the American playwright Robert E. Sherwood, who is six foot seven, look like a dwarf. He must have been at least seven and a half feet tall."[250]

Is there any connection between the height of these tribes and giants carrying the Nephilim genes?

A recent study conducted by scientists from the University of Buffalo (Xu et al., 2017) provides potential evidence of the discovery of hybrids in Africa. Xu et al. (2017) found a variant of the MUC7 gene in saliva among a Sub-Saharan African population which is atypical among the human genome.[251] One of the lead biologists on the study, Omer Gokcumen, interpreted the unusual findings this way,

"It seems the interbreeding between different early hominin species is not the exception – it's the norm…Our research traced the evolution of an important mucin protein called MUC7 that is found in saliva. When we looked at the history of the gene that codes for the protein, we see the signature of archaic admixture in modern day Sub-Saharan African populations. Based on our analysis, the most plausible explanation for this extreme variation is archaic introgression – the introduction of genetic material from a 'ghost' species of ancient hominins…We call it a 'ghost' species because we don't have the fossils."[252]

"Archaic introgression" is a fancy term for two species mating and producing hybrid offspring. Gokcumen is suggesting that human inhabitants of ancient civilizations in Sub-Saharan Africa mated with a species that was not 100% human. He attaches the identifier, 'ghost' species, because there are no fossil remains of such a species. Evolutionists find these results supportive of the existence of ancient hominins in the evolutionary process. However, the results can also provide evidence for the biblical and extra-biblical account of the fallen 'sons of God' mating with the daughters of men.

While Gokcumen may not think there are fossil remains of a hybrid species on the African continent, documented discoveries point to the contrary. We must turn once again to the land of Egypt. First, we search the accounts of Egyptian history recorded by Manetho. Manetho documented a 2nd dynasty Egyptian king, named Sesôchris, whose stature was "5 cubits and 3 palms."[253] If you remember our discussion from Chapter 12, there is an Egyptian royal cubit (approximately 20 inches) and a common cubit (approximately 16 inches). A palm is a measurement we have not discussed yet, it is the equivalent of ½ a cubit. If we use the royal cubit as the measurement applied to Sesôchris, he would have been just over 9' 2" tall. If we use a more conservative measurement of the common cubit, he still would have been 7' 4" tall. Either way, he would have been a towering giant in comparison to the average height of an Egyptian male in those days of just over 5 feet tall. It's unclear though, if Sesôchris suffered from gigantism or if he was a hybrid.

An interesting discovery of giant skeleton's was made in 1881 by "Professor Timmerman." An article about this discovery appeared in the Arizona Silver Belt on November 16th, 1895 (see Figure 37). If true, this was quite a discovery of giants from ancient Egypt. The article refers to these skeletons as evidence of a prehistoric giant race. The sheer number of skeletons found in this tomb that were over 7 feet tall (about 60 skeletons), rules out gigantism (prevalence rate of 1 in 3 million). Unfortunately, it is difficult to corroborate these findings because the article does not give a first name for the professor and an exhaustive search of who Professor Timmerman was does not yield any further clues. We will have to hold this discovery as possible, but not probable. What more can be found in the land of Egypt that points to evidence of giants?

An archaeologist and professor from BYU, Kerry Muhlestein, has been part of a team of archaeologists working on a burial site 60 miles south of Cairo called Fag el-Gamous. Excavations at this cemetery have been ongoing for the past 30 years. The archaeologists have suggested that this grave site dates from the 1st century A.D. to 7th century A.D. An article in the Salt Lake Tribune (January 11, 2015) stated Muhlestein and team have discovered a 7-foot skeleton among the 1700 skeleton's they have unearthed.[254] The researchers admitted that more examination needs to take place on this skeleton to determine whether gigantism was the cause for the extraordinary height but it's unclear if that ever happened.

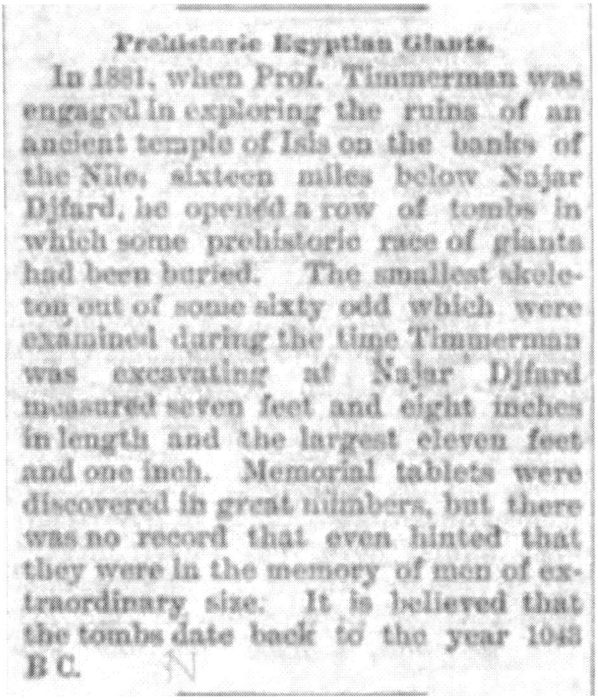

Prehistoric Egyptian Giants.

In 1881, when Prof. Timmerman was engaged in exploring the ruins of an ancient temple of Isis on the banks of the Nile, sixteen miles below Najar Djfard, he opened a row of tombs in which some prehistoric race of giants had been buried. The smallest skeleton out of some sixty odd which were examined during the time Timmerman was excavating at Najar Djfard measured seven feet and eight inches in length and the largest eleven feet and one inch. Memorial tablets were discovered in great numbers, but there was no record that even hinted that they were in the memory of men of extraordinary size. It is believed that the tombs date back to the year 1043 B C.

Figure 37. Prehistoric Egyptian Giants. November 16th, 1895. Arizona Silver Belt retrieved from https://www.newspapers.com/image/42149234

Flinders Petrie, a 19th century British archaeologist, who was considered by many to be the father of Egyptology, made some interesting discoveries that contribute to our investigation. In his book *Naqada and Ballas*, he wrote about a discovery of a "New Race" of people found in the excavation sites between Naqada and Ballas. Petrie developed a reputation for being meticulous in his measurements, as you may remember from our deep dive into the mysteries of the Great Pyramid. Petrie's precision became the standard and his measurements of the Great Pyramid are still being used today. So, we can be assured that when Petrie labels a discovery of a people group as a "New Race," it was not something he proclaimed lightly. To be clear, he was not referring to them as a new race of people, as in hybrids per se, but he and his team determined from the plethora of artifacts, inscriptions, burial rituals, and physical stature of the skeletal remains that they were not Egyptian.

"The remains shew that the New Race were a sturdy hill people, by the massive legs and tall stature often found...They had a great burning at their funerals, though the body was never burnt. But the bodies were often cut up more or less, and in some cases certainly treated as if they were partly eaten."[255]

Petrie was able to construct a potential narrative of this new race from his findings. The remains date between 3300 B.C. and 3000 B.C. It does not appear a process of acculturation took place, instead, the findings suggest that the "New Race" invaded the Thebaid region. He states,

"The relation of these invaders with Egyptians appear to have been completely hostile. The absence in even the later period of their history of any Egyptian objects, and the total disregard (by such artists in pottery) of the potter's wheel which was quite familiar to Egyptians, point not only to an absence of any trade, but to the complete extrusion of the Egyptians from the region."[256]

I find this very intriguing. What would cause the Egyptians to completely disappear from the region? Was it the extraordinary size and stature of the "New Race"? Was it their violent nature which struck terror in the Egyptians who fled for their lives? Ok I might be starting to create my own narrative here, but indulge me for a moment. There are some other clues that Petrie leaves us in his writings that might help us pull some pieces of the puzzle together. Petrie notes that some of the cultural aspects depicted in the artifacts are similar to those found among the Amorites. We know from our study of the giant tribes, that the Amorites engaged in interbreeding with the giants and promulgated the Nephilim agenda. Petrie found evidence of disturbing burial rituals from a grave that was untouched by grave robbers.

"Not only were the ends broken off, but in some bones the cellular structure had been scooped out forcibly, what remained of it being very firm and strong; and beside this there were grooves left by gnawing on the bones. That this disturbance could not be due to any animals that might have got at the bodies, either before or after burial, is proved by the scooping out of the cellular structure of the long bones; and by the heaping together of the bones in a pile, all dissevered and broken."[257]

The evidence of cannibalism among the "New Race" is consistent with the behavior of giants inhabiting other continents and more importantly, it further confirms cannibalism as a characteristic of a Nephilim Host.

Europe

Rich with history, the continent of Europe is where we will turn next to collect further evidence of the presence of giants with Nephilim traits. Historical records can provide us with detailed descriptions of people groups and individuals we might classify as giants. Of particular interest are the Celts and the Gauls, due to their Druidic practices that align with Nephilim traits. Diodorus, the famous Greek historian from the first century B.C., recorded the mannerisms and characteristics of the Gauls.

"For stature they are tall, but of a sweaty and pale complexion, red-haired, not only naturally, but they endeavour [sic] all they can to make it redder by art. They often wash their hair in a water boiled with lime, and turn it backward from the forehead to the crown of the head, and thence to their very necks, that their faces may be more fully seen, so that they look like satyrs and hobgoblins…

These people are of a most terrible aspect and have a most dreadful and loud voice. In their converse they are sparing of their words, and speak many things darkly and fig- uratively… They are apt to menace others… Prophets likewise they have… who fore- tell future events by viewing the entrails of the sacrifices, and to these soothsayers all the people generally are very observant. When they are to consult on some great and weighty matter, they observe a most strange and incredible custom; for they sacrifice a man, striking him with a sword near the diaphragm, crossover Ills breast, who being thus slain, and falling down, they judge of the event from the manner of his fall, the convulsion of his members, and the flux of blood; and this has gained among them (by long and antient usage) a firm credit and belief" (Diodorus, *Bibliotheka Historia,* Book V).[258]

Diodorus also describes the likeness of the Celts, "The women here are both as tall and as courageous as the men. The children, for the most part, from their very birth are grey-beaded; but when they grow up to men's estate, their hair changes in colour [sic] like to their parents. Those towards the north, and bordering upon Scythia, are so ex- ceeding fierce arid cruel, that (as report goes) they eat men, like the Britains [sic] that inhabit Iris.

According to their natural cruelty, they are as impious in the worship of their gods; for malefactors, after that they have been kept close prisoners five years together, they impale upon stakes, in honour [sic] to the gods, and then, with many other victims, upon a vast pile of wood, they offer them up as a burnt sacrifice to their deities. In like manner they use their captives also, as sacrifices to the gods. Some of them cut the throats, burn, or otherwise destroy both men and beasts that they have taken in time of war; though they have very beautiful women among them, yet they little value their private society, but are transported with raging lust to the filthy act of sodomy; and, lying upon the ground on beast's skins spread under them, they there tumble together, with their catamites lying on both sides of them: and that which is the most abominable is, that without any sense of shame, or regard to their reputation, they will readily prostitute their bodies to others upon every occasion. And they are so far from looking upon it to be any fault, that they judge it a mean and dishonourable [sic] thing for any thus caressed to refuse the favour offered them (Diodorus, *Bibliotheka Historia,* Book V).[259]

Diodorus' description of the Gauls and the Celts reveals character traits and mannerisms that meet our proposed criterium for Nephilim Hosts. They meet 3 or more of the physical traits: excessively tall, extraordinarily strong, and having red hair. Even more convincing are the number of behavioral characteristics they meet: lustfulness in conjunction with sexual misconduct, vengeful or inappropriate intense anger, reoccurring violent acts displaying disregard for the rights of others, lack of remorse for heinous acts against other living beings, participation in cannibalism, pedophilia (catamites), and pervasive pattern of engagement in sexual and/or blood occult rituals.

In considering the history and brutality of the Roman Empire, it would not be surprising to find the Nephilim agenda carried out by Roman Emperors who became Nephilim Hosts. For example, history records Emperor Maximus I to be exceedingly tall, measuring 8'6" tall. Not only was his stature great, but he had extraordinary strength as well. It is said that he was able to draw a carriage that two oxen were unable to move.[260] He was born in Thrace; so, what does history say about the Thracians?

Herodotus, the Greek historian, visited Thrace around 450 B.C. and wrote about the characteristics of the Thracians in *Histories*. It's in his writings that we discover that the Thracians meet the criteria for classification as Nephilim Hosts; they participated in polygamy, trafficked their children to slave traders, engaged in cannibalism as a funerary practice for the wealthy, and considered war and plunder the most glorious aspect of life.[261] Additionally other historical records provide us with a clue that some of the Thracians may have been redheads. Clement of Alexandria, commented in his writings that the Thracians depict their gods in their own likeness, "ruddy and tawny."[262] There were many Thracian gravestones with the name 'Rufus' on them, meaning "redhead" in the Roman vernacular. The most famous being Rufus Sita, a

Thracian cavalryman, whose tombstone was discovered in Gloucester, England in 1824.[263]

Interestingly, we see that the Thracians had the presence of both the character traits and physical traits of Nephilim Hosts. In *Historia Augusta*, we find more details about Emperor Maximus I:

"For certainly he was strikingly big of body, and notable among all the soldiers for courage, handsome in a manly way, fierce in his manners, rough, haughty, and scornful, yet often a just man… It is agreed, moreover, that often in a single day he… ate forty pounds of meat… Along with these…went such cruelty that some called him Cyclops… Typhon or Gyges… he hung men on the cross, shut them in the bodies of animals newly slain, cast them to wild beasts, dashed out their brains with clubs… As a matter of fact, he was convinced that the throne could not be held except by cruelty…he had already taken on the life and character of a wild beast, he was made still harsher and more savage."[264]

Of note in this description is that the Romans referred to him by the names of giants, such as Cyclops and Typhon. In Greek mythology, Typhon was the "father of all monsters"; a giant whose head reached to the stars; a god who was also a monster with a torso of a viper. The Cyclops were a race of fierce and lawless one-eyed giants. This gives us a good indication of how the Roman citizens perceived Emperor Maximus I. He had the behavioral characteristics and the physical stature of a giant who carried out the Nephilim agenda during his reign.

Asia

In ancient history, we know the footprints of giants were numerous and vast across the continent of Asia. After all, most of the cast and characters in the biblical accounts of giants inhabited Asia. Is there evidence of the existence of giants in the Common Era? If so, it would illustrate a continuity between the hybrids of ancient history and the giants of modern history. It would support the notion that there is an age-old Nephilim agenda at work that extends into our day and age. Let's dig into the annals of history to see what we find.

Pliny the Elder, a Roman author of the first century A.D. produced a voluminous work entitled *Natural History*; essentially it was the preeminent encyclopedia of the first century. In fact, his work was so brilliant, it became the model for encyclopedias, as well as the premier authority on scientific matters until the Middle Ages.[265] In it, he records eye-witness accounts of several giants,

"The tallest Man that hath been seen in our Age was one named *Gabbara*, who in the Days of Prince *Claudius* was brought out of Arabia; he was nine Feet high, and as many Inches. There were in the Time of *Divus Augustus* two others, named *Pusio* and *Secundilla*, higher than *Gabbara* by half a Foot, whose Bodies were preserved for a Wonder in a Vault in the Gardens of the Salustiani."[266]

This is fascinating, the Arabian giant was 9' 9," but he wasn't even the tallest known at the time. There were two other men (giants) who were 10' 3." Let me put this into perspective, Goliath measured in at 8' 8." In other words, these men would have dwarfed Goliath!

Examining Pliny's work even further, we uncover some critical details that provide an important link, the significance of which will unfold in upcoming chapters. Pliny speaks of the "Seres," who were "famous for the fine silk their Woods would yield"; he was describing the people of the Tarim basin, in the Xingjiang province of China.

"… the Inhabitants themselves exceeded the ordinary Stature of Men, having red Hair, blue Eyes, their Voice harsh, their Speech not fitted for any Commerce."[267]

Pliny's description is corroborated by the 1976 discovery of the Tarim mummies in the Xinjiang province of China, bordering Mongolia. These mummies were pristinely preserved due to the cool, dry climate of the Taklamakan Desert. To date there have been over 100 mummies found in this area. Many of them still with hair and yes, some them with red hair. These mummies date from 1800 B.C. to the 1st century B.C. The tallest of the mummies is "Yingpan Man" who is 6' 6."[268] These mummies were most likely the ancestors of the "Seres."

Australia

Are you still with me mate? We have covered a lot of territory in this chapter. Australia will be our last stop before making our long and methodical journey back to Jekyll Island. Actually, let me clarify just a bit. In our journey around the globe searching for the footprints of giants, we must include the Pacific Islands, because there is more evidence to be found there than in Australia itself.

In 1875, an article in the Timaru Herald from New Zealand reported the discovery of a giant skull (see Figure 38). Xavient Haze wrote about the Maori legends of giants in his book *Ancient Giants.* By his report, "the skull of this giant was supposedly big enough to hold the skull of a normal human just in its mouth alone."[269]

The title of this chapter "Giants Among Us" takes on a literal meaning if we consider the stories that have emerged from the Solomon Islands. This sovereign state of islands, east of Papua New Guinea, is known to have giants who live among the interior portions of some of the islands. There have been numerous eye-witness accounts and it is local knowledge among the villagers on Guadalcanal, one of the larger islands, that giants live among them. Marius Boirayon, an Australian who moved to the Solomon Islands, worked as a pilot and engineer. He married an indigenous woman from Gaudalcanal. After 15 years of living on Guadalcanal, he compiled island folklore, as well as, eye-witness accounts of the giants in his book *Solomon Island Mysteries*.

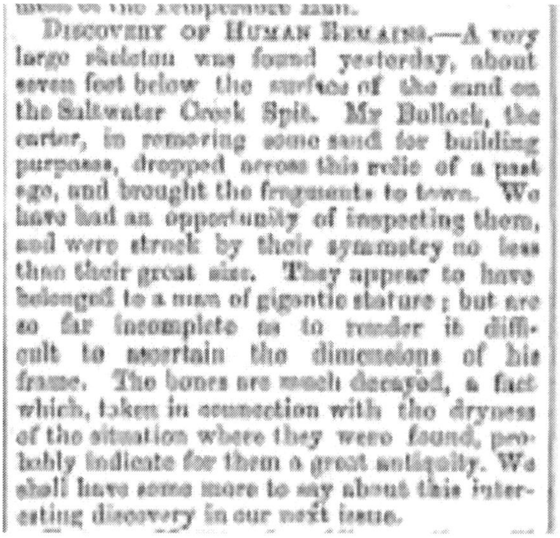

DISCOVERY OF HUMAN REMAINS.—A very large skeleton was found yesterday, about seven feet below the surface of the sand on the Saltwater Creek Spit. Mr Bullock, the carter, in removing some sand for building purposes, dropped across this relic of a past age, and brought the fragments to town. We have had an opportunity of inspecting them, and were struck by their symmetry no less than their great size. They appear to have belonged to a man of gigantic stature; but are so far incomplete as to render it difficult to ascertain the dimensions of his frame. The bones are much decayed, a fact which, taken in connection with the dryness of the situation where they were found, probably indicate for them a great antiquity. We shall have some more to say about this interesting discovery in our next issue.

Figure 38. "Discovery of Human Remains," February 24, 1875, Timaru Herald. Retrieved from https://paperspast.natlib.govt.nz/newspapers/timaru-herald/1875/02/24/3

Boirayon reports that the indigenous people believe these giants have lived on the island for several millennia and estimate the population of the giants to be in the thousands. The locals say the giants live in an elaborate cave system beneath the mountainous rainforest on Guadalcanal. The main entrance to the cave system is Mount Tatuva, where giants have been spotted by the locals, coming and going out of the caves. The height of the giants varies between 10 – 20 ft tall. Boirayon describes one of the types of giants in this way (the locals say there are three different types):

"These giants have long black, brown or reddish hair, or a mixture…bulging red eyeballs, a flat nose, wide-gapped mouth and an unmistakable odour, which the coastal people would once use as a sign of their presence, depending on the wind."[270]

Unfortunately, the indigenous people have been terrorized by the giants throughout the years; many have been abducted and consumed as a meal. There is a well-known account of a woman named "Mango," who was abducted by the giants. After 25 years of being missing and considered dead, she was found pregnant and frothing at the mouth. She gave birth to a "half caste boy," a hybrid, who lived for 5 years before Mango's brother killed him. Mango had lived with the giants for approximately 25 years. She passed away in 2000, after years of mental instability. These stories seem like such tall tales. If it were not for the eye-witness accounts from reputable locals, we would dismiss these reports as imaginations.

Several government officials have had encounters with the giants. Ezekiel Alebua, the 3rd Prime Minister of the Solomon Islands, tells of a time in his childhood that his father took him to a burial site of the giants within one of the caves; he remembers seeing a 15 ft skeleton. Additionally, the Guadalcanal Premier and the Guadalcanal Finance Minister told Boirayon of an encounter they had with two giants. The island is rich in precious metals, such as gold. They took a drive in a 4wd Toyota truck up to one of the mine sites in the mountains, but because of recent rains, their truck slipped off the edge and was stuck in mud. They walked back to the nearest village to gather about 30 men for assistance. When they returned to the truck, they found two 15-foot giants next to the vehicle. It was apparent these giants had lifted the truck and put it back onto the road. The men instinctively screamed and ran from the giants, but when a few of them returned after about 30 minutes, the giants were gone. What remained was their footprints, distinctively marked in the wet soil. The Premier and Finance Minister estimated the footprints to be about 3 to 4 feet in length.[271] These eye-witness accounts of living giants in the 21st century are remarkable and require us to form a new cognitive schema in which to contain this information. This was an unexpected discovery, even for me, as your lead investigator (so to speak).

In our pursuit of collecting evidence to reveal that giants have walked among us, we have uncovered some questionable assumptions researchers have made, particularly

Brien Foerster, but also, we have found credible evidence that giants have continued to populate the earth beyond the boundaries of the ancient biblical accounts. We identified a pattern that emerged in the physical and behavioral characteristics of the giants across numerous continents which lends further support to the criteria for classification as a Nephilim Host proposed in Chapter 13. It is disturbing to realize the Nephilim agenda, like an infectious disease that has become pandemic, has spread across time and land mass; it is no respecter of boundaries. As we close in on the events that took place on Jekyll Island, we will uncover, in more detail, the insidious nature of the Nephilim agenda.

Key Points

- The criteria for classification of a Nephilim Host was corroborated by historical records detailing the physical traits and character traits of giants across the globe.
- Among the Golden Isles in Georgia (Jekyll Island is part of this chain of coastal islands), "proof of a prehistoric race of giants" was discovered. The skulls of some of these giants were described as the "long-headed type" and followed closely the characteristics of the Timucuan tribe who inhabited Jekyll Island.
- There appears to be a cover-up of the remains of giants found in North America and it's likely the Smithsonian Institute is at the center of this controversy.
- Traces of giants can be found on every continent (we did not investigate Antarctica) from the time of the Flood to modern day. The Nephilim agenda has not been eradicated and instead spreads like a global pandemic.

Section III

Return to Jekyll Island

Our journey has taken us back to the dawn of human history. We have spanned the globe in search of evidence hidden in the sands of time, with the goal to uncover ancient layers of deception and bring to light what has been lurking in the darkness. Our investigative research led to the development of preliminary criteria by which to identify a Nephilim Host based on a cluster of traits. As we dug into the accounts of history across six continents, the criteria for classification as a Nephilim Host seems to be supported by the evidence we found. This criteria for a Nephilim Host will become invaluable as we use it to examine the masterminds behind the Federal Reserve.

We are now equipped to traverse from ancient times to the Common Era, to make our return to Jekyll Island.

In this next section, we will follow up on leads, search through historical records, examine archeological evidence, glean from anthropology experts, weigh testimonies from eye-witness accounts, and garner the perspective of insiders, privy to the insidious agendas present within the last several centuries. While in the 21st century, there may not be 15-foot giants roaming the earth (well except on the Solomon Islands), there are still giants in our midst. Lest we be fooled and lulled into slumber, modern-day giants have morphed into spirits of ethos exerting dominion over economic systems, political ideologies, institutions of industry, and globalism. Do you perceive it? The Nephilim agenda still prevails in the seedlings of monopoly continually sprouting up, enslaving all those who fall under its canopy.

Alas, we gain courage and strength to complete our mission to fight for FREEDOM, by remembering the words of a few great men.

But you must remember, my fellow-citizens, that eternal vigilance by the people is the price of liberty, and that you must pay the price if you wish to secure the blessing.
~ Andrew Jackson

Educate and inform the whole mass of people. They are the only sure reliance for the preservation of our liberty.
~ Thomas Jefferson

WE PRESS ON...

Chapter 16

Trail of the Edomites

We have some unfinished business from Chapter 11… we don't know yet what happened to the Edomites after the Fall of Jerusalem. As I have eluded to, the Edomites may not have been annihilated in the 1st century AD, even though there is not much written about them following this time period. Actually, it should not be too surprising that Esau's bloodline survived the Fall of Jerusalem, especially given the prophecies of Edom's impending destruction in the last days. I have a hunch that if we follow the trail of the Edomites, it will lead us to uncover if there are Nephilim at work today.

It's important for us to gather as much information as possible from the scant historical records of the Edomites migration because it may provide us with critical links to the region of Khazaria, Rome and the Zionists. Let's pick up on the trail that we veered off from. In order to do that, we need to retrace our steps a bit and collect more clues along the way regarding the Edomite migration routes.

Edomite Migration

Ezekiel 36:5 eludes to the time the Edomites migrated north from Mt. Seir, a desert and mountainous region, into the fertile land of southern Judah and possibly even further north into the Caucasus. The Edomites were accustomed to migrating given their location along the King's Highway, a major thoroughfare for north-south trade routes.

Ezekiel 36:5 (NIV) *"this is what the Sovereign Lord says: In my burning zeal I have spoken against the rest of the nations, and against all Edom, for with glee and with malice in their hearts **they made my land their own possession** so that they might plunder its pastureland."* (emphasis mine)

Throughout history, the Edomites repeatedly seized opportunities to take advantage of Israel's calamities. True to form, on the day that Jerusalem fell to the Babylonians in 586 B.C., the Edomites chanted "tear it down, tear it down to its foundation" (Psalm 137:7). They celebrated the captivity of the Jews and saw it as an opportune time to occupy their land. A large number of Edomites took up residence in southern Judah claiming it as their new homeland. Hebron became the capitol of Idumea (the Greek term for Edom). It seems that at this point in history, there was a dispersal of the Edomites from Mt. Seir. Some scholars attribute this to the Nabateans, who took up residence in Edom establishing Petra as their capital.[272] While a large portion of the Edomites moved to southern Judah, there were those who relocated along trade routes and those who were swept up in captivity under Nebuchadnezzar.

Around 110 B.C., in the land of Judea, the Edomites were forced to convert to Judaism when John Hyrcanus conquered the Idumean cities of Marissa and Dora. This was unprecedented in Israel's history; never before had a Jewish ruler and high priest forced Judaism upon a conquered people. Not surprisingly, the Idumeans' conversion was ingenuine; in fact, it had deleterious effects on the sanctity of Judaism, the impact of which cannot be underestimated. In the words of Benjamin Freedman, "conversions have often proved to be but 'infiltrations by latent traitors with treasonable intentions."[273]

During this period in history, there was admixture of the Idumeans with the Judeans. The Idumeans became known as Judeans to such an extent that Herod, who was Idumean, was given authority by Rome to govern as king of the Judeans. True to their character, the Idumeans used Judaism as a means by which to achieve their goal of dominion over the usurpers of their inheritance, the Israelites. The strategy was to either cast off Judaism in favor of Hellenism or pervert it into a false Judaism. The Idumeans fit the description of "whitewashed sepulchers."

As we discussed in Chapter 11, the Idumeans were interwoven in the horrific drama that unfolded in Jerusalem and Judea when Rome laid siege in A.D. 70. It's difficult to know with any level of certainty what happened to the Edomites following the fall of Jerusalem. The best we can do is collect tidbits of information from a variety of sources and assemble these pieces to ascertain the whereabouts of the Edomites in the early centuries of the Common Era and beyond.

One such tidbit is offered by C.F. Parker in *A Short Study of the Esau Edom in Jewry,* written in 1949. Parker describes the migration patterns of the Jews and Idumeans.

"Armenian and Georgian historians record that after the destruction of the First Temple…Nebuchadnezzar deported numbers of Jewish captives into Armenia and the Caucasus. These exiles were joined later by co-religionists from Medea and Judea…Jews lived in the Crimea and along the entire eastern coast of the Black Sea at the beginning of the common era…Jews from Crimea moved eastward and northward and became the founders of Jewish communities along the shores of the Caspian Sea…carrying with them a civilisation more advanced than that of the native tribes among which they settled. Under their influence Bulan, the 'chagan' of the Chazars, and the ruling classes of Chazaria adopted Judaism in 731 or 740.

I have indicated something of the complexity of these migratory movements, showing that right up to the last days in the bitterly-contested history of the nation, large numbers of Jews migrated to, or were deported into, regions adjacent to the gateways into Europe through the Caucasus, through which they passed in large numbers for some centuries into the Christian era. Out of any comprehensive analysis of all the ethnic data available there is bound to come one inescapable conclusion, that just as the Idumeans became part and parcel of the Jewish nation after their amalgamation with it in the time of John Hyrcanus, so too they became an integral part in its enforced migrations towards the Caucasus, and subsequently into Central Europe whither they carried Hellenism."[274]

Eran Elhaik (2012), a genetic researcher from Johns Hopkins University, confirms C.F. Parker's description of Jewish migration into the Caucasus.

"Biblical and archeological records allude to active trade relationships between Proto-Judeans and Armenians in the late centuries BCE… that likely resulted in a small-scale admixture between these populations and a Judean presence in the Caucasus."[275]

Elhaik (2012) also confirms Parker's hunch that "ethnic data" or genetic studies supports the Jewish migration into the Caucasus. We will look at this more closely later in this chapter.

Another tidbit of information we should pay attention to, originates from a letter written in the 10th century A.D. by a foreign minister to the Sultan of Cordova named Hasdai. Hasdai wrote a letter to King Joseph of the Khazars (Chazars). He was particularly interested in the origins of the Khazars and their connection with Judaism. Hasdai had first learned about the kingdom of Khazar from envoys along his travels, but he wanted to confirm his understanding by asking the king directly.

"Taking a keen interest in everything relating to the kingdom of the Chazars, Ḥasdai begs the king to communicate to him a detailed account of the geography of his country, of its internal constitution, of the customs and occupations of its inhabitants, and especially of the history of his ancestry and of the state. In this letter Ḥasdai speaks of the tradition according to which the Chazars once dwelt near the Seir (Serir) Mountains." [276]

These "Chazarian Letters," as they are known, have been studied at great length by numerous scholars, some who have determined them to be fake, while others who have proven their authenticity. As a greater awareness of linguistics and a better understanding of the subtleties of dialects expanded over the centuries, scholars have come into agreement by determining that the authenticity of these letters between Hasdai and King Joseph are irrefutable. The significance of these letters cannot be overlooked because they provide a possible link between the Khazars and the Edomites. But I realize you are probably asking yourself, who are the Khazars?

Khazars

Anthropologists have classified the Khazars as Turco-Finns. They were a violent, warlike people from Asia who migrated to the north end of the Caspian Sea. The phallic symbol was prominent in their worship as was the practice of sexual excesses. In the 7th-8th centuries A.D., the moral degradation became so great, King Bulan was compelled to adopt Judaism (Talmudism) as their state religion. Bulan's successor, King Obadiah brought Babylonian rabbis into Khazaria to establish synagogues for the instruction in the Babylonian Talmud.[277]

The Jewish Encyclopedia of 1906 describes the Khazars as: "A people of Turkish origin whose life and history are interwoven with the very beginnings of the history of the Jews of Russia. The kingdom of the Chazars was firmly established in most of South Russia long before the foundation of the Russian monarchy by the Varangians ([A.D.] 855). Jews have lived on the shores of the Black and Caspian seas since the first centuries of the common era."[278]

In this description about the Khazars, we find an important detail, the Jews lived in the Caucasus region beginning in the first centuries of the Common Era. Here we have documentation of dispersion that occurred around the time of the fall of Jerusalem. It is reasonable to deduce that some of these Jews may have been Edomites given the intermingling that happened during the Hasmonean kingdom. Shlomo Sand, an historian and author of *The Invention of the Jewish People,* an international bestseller, writes, "the great mass proselytizing campaign that began in the second century BCE, with the rise of the Hasmonean kingdom, reached its climax in Khazaria in the eighth century CE."[279]

In order to understand the origin of the Khazars and their impact on world history, we must glean from a few of the experts, Benjamin Freedman and Matthew Johnson. Benjamin Freedman held an unparalleled perspective on the Khazars and modern-day Jewry. He was a successful Jewish businessman from New York City in the early 1900s. He was an insider among some of the most influential Jewish organizations in the United States during the first half of the 20th century. His business and social circles intersected with Samuel Untermyer, Jacob Schiff, Bernard Baruch, Woodrow Wilson, Henry Morgenthau Sr., Franklin D. Roosevelt, Joseph Kennedy, and John F. Kennedy. He served as liaison, or in his own words, the "confidential man" for Henry Morgenthau Sr., Chairman of the Finance Committee for the Democratic Party.[280] What makes him so unique is that he defected from his role as a Zionist operative.

Benjamin Freedman walked away from Judaism after the Judeo-Communist Russian victory in 1945. He saw up close and personal, the corruption, manipulation, and tyranny of the Zionist movement and no longer wanted anything to do with it. He spent the remaining years of his life trying to awaken the American people to the truth about the Zionists' agenda, especially with regards to the United States involvement in WWI and WWII. In today's vernacular, he would be considered a "whistleblower." He was privy to information that the public was and still is largely unaware of. One such topic he was well versed in was the history of the Khazars. He brought to light that much of the history of the Khazar kingdom has been kept silent within the history books. Hmmm… I wonder why?

"In the 1st century B.C. the Khazars had invaded eastern Europe from their homeland in Asia… The Khazars were not 'Semites.' They were an Asiatic Mongoloid nation…They were a very warlike nation. The Khazars were driven out of Asia finally by the nations in Asia with whom they were continually at war…The very warlike

Khazars did not find it difficult to subdue and conquer the 25 peaceful agricultural nations occupying approximately 1,000,000 square miles in eastern Europe. In a comparatively short period, the Khazars established the largest and most powerful kingdom in Europe, and probably the wealthiest also.

The Khazars were a pagan nation...Their religious worship was a mixture of phallic worship... This form of worship continued until the 7th century. The vile forms of sexual excess indulged in by the Khazars as their form of religious worship produced a degree of moral degeneracy that Khazar's king could not endure. In the 7th century King Bulan...decided to abolish the practice of phallic worship...and selected the future state religion as... 'Talmudism,' and now known and practiced as 'Judaism.'

King Bulan and his 4000 feudal nobles were promptly converted by rabbis imported from Babylonia...The Khazar kings invited large numbers of rabbis to come and open synagogues and schools to instruct the population in the new form of religious worship...The Khazar kingdom became a virtual theocracy...The religious leaders imposed the teachings of the Talmud upon the population as their guide to living. The ideologies became the axis of political, cultural, economic, and social attitudes and activities throughout the Khazar kingdom. The Talmud provided civil and religious law."[281]

Freedman emphasized the role the Babylonian Talmud had in Khazaria. This begs the question, what exactly is the Babylonian Talmud?

The Babylonian Talmud is what most people are referring to when they speak of the Talmud. It is composed of the Mishnah (written form of the Oral Law compiled around 200 A.D.) and the Gemara (commentaries and interpretations of the Mishnah compiled around 550 A.D.); it is a compellation of ancient rabbinic writings which began before the time of Christ. The final work of transcription was conducted by a group of rabbinic sages under the tutelage of Rav Ashi, a renowned 5th century rabbi.[282] Generally speaking, the Talmud is the Oral Law that was believed to be given to Moses on Mt. Sinai at the time he received the Written Law. Orthodox rabbis believe this oral tradition was passed onto Joshua, the Prophets and finally to the rabbis who transcribed it. It is a complex collection of rabbinic interpretations of the oral tradition meant to guide Jewish life. I have heard it said, "it takes a lifetime to study the Talmud" because one version has 30 volumes and is approximately 15,000 pages.[283] Within Judaism, it has gained a sacred status even surpassing that of Scripture.

"Those who devote themselves to reading the Bible exercise a certain virtue, but not very much; those who study the Mischnah exercise virtue for which they will receive a reward; those, however, who take upon themselves to study the Gemarah exercise the highest virtue." (Babha Metsia, fol. 33a)[284]

It is important to keep in mind that there is a distinction between the Israelite faith of the Old Testament and Judaism. The Khazarian converts were taught the principles of the Talmud instead of Scripture.

"The Khazar theory suggests there is no connection between Israelites and Jews. Yet even if there were, the religion of the modern Jew bears no relationship whatsoever to the Israelite faith, which is vehemently condemned in the Talmud...In adopting the ethic of the Talmud, they adopted the mentality of the Pharisees, whose arrogance served as the early foundation of the Talmud."[285]

Louis Finklestein, a prominent 20th century American-Jew and Talmudic scholar, explains the connection between the Pharisees and the Talmud.

"Pharisaism became Talmudism, Talmudism became Medieval Rabbinism, and Medieval Rabbinism became Modern Rabbinism. But throughout these changes of name, inevitable adaptation of custom, and adjustment of the Law, the spirit of the ancient Pharisee survives unaltered...When the Jew...studies the Talmud, he is actually repeating the arguments used in the Palestinian academies."[286]

To be clear, the Khazarian Jews adhered to pharisaical religious practices. Let's turn now to our other expert who can help us understand the origins of the Khazars and their impact on modern day Jewry.

Matthew Raphael Johnson, Ph.D. is a former professor in the fields of History and Political Science at Penn State University and Mount St. Mary's University. He has specialized in Russian and Ukrainian history for the past 20 years, making him well versed in the history of Khazaria. In agreement with Freedman, Johnson reports that the history of the Khazar empire is rarely discussed in the history books. He attributes this to the less than favorable behavior of the Jews and the intimidating aspect of being labeled an anti-Semite for revealing the truth about Khazaria. Johnson wrote in his essay, *Defending the Khazar Thesis of the Origin of Modern Jewry*, "the Khazar Khanate was one of the most violent, unpredictable and wealthy of the medieval empires. They filled the power vacuum left by the death of Attila the Hun."[287]

He provides an interesting window into the trade practices that shaped the economic policies of the Khazar empire in his essay, *The Regime: Usury, Khazaria and the American Mass.*

"In Russian history, this [usury] was the role of Khazaria. Charging tolls on passing merchants was their primary form of income. Domestically, the top layer of society, mostly Jewish, extracted tribute from their conquered peoples. The Khazar empire had a small but powerful group of Jewish bankers in Kiev as early as the 10th century.

Khazaria existed as a multinational state ruled over by an oligarchy of Jewish converts. Few historians will touch this issue, and with good reason...By controlling the "Great Silk Road," the Khazar Jews fully seized the trade between East and West, between North and South, that is, all the trade routes passing through the Caucasus Mountains. This was the main purpose of their migration to the region...Full control of the caravan routes passing through the Khazar Khanate allowed the Jews to establish a trade monopoly, where they began to control the prices of imported and local goods. As a result, consumers were gouged.

Having come to Kazaria already wealthy, the Jews quickly pushed the gentiles out of the parasitic niches of the economy. According to the testimony of medieval travelers, the main source of income of the Khazar Khanate, except for usury, was the slave trade. Regular raids on neighboring lands (mostly Slavic) gave the Khazars a large number of slaves which were sold all over the world...Trade in general and the slave trade in particular, has always been the traditional source of income for the Jewish entrepreneurs and a source of super-profits, which made it possible to get rich quick, and further strengthen its parasitic power."[288]

Within Johnson's essay lie two invaluable clues. If you'll recall, we discovered the origins of usury from the serpent's deception of Eve.

Genesis 3:13 (NKJV) *"And the Lord God said to the woman 'What is this you have done?' The woman said, 'The serpent **deceived** me, and I ate."* (emphasis mine)

The Hebrew word for 'deceived' used in this passage is *'nasha'* which is defined as "to lend on interest, or usury, to become a creditor."[289] Johnson defines usury as, "the result of a power relation where the superior is able to use that status to extract non-economic rents out of the inferior. This is to say rents that are not based on market, labor or use values."[290]

'*Nasha*' is the basis of our defiled monetary system. The Federal Reserve is built upon usury, lending with interest; the Fed's product is DEBT. King Solomon appropriately summed it up.

Ecclesiastes 1:9 (NIV) "*What has been will be again, what has been done will be done again; there is nothing new under the sun.*"

It's the same root defilement stemming from the beginning of the ages, just repackaged and renamed, to perpetuate the deception. But we are awakening from our slumber; a growing number of Americans want to know what or who's behind the curtain. Just who is this Wizard of Oz controlling our monetary system? As you might have guessed, our investigation will lead us to answer this question, but brace yourself, it's not going to be pretty.

A second clue Johnson provides is that the Khazars amassed great wealth through slave trading. The spirit behind debt is one of slavery. Simply stated, when we are in debt, we do not have the freedom to spend our money as we desire. Debt is bondage, every American is a bond slave because of our national debt. The insidious system characterized by a two headed monster, the IRS and the Fed, robs every American of our freedom. The Fed spends our future. Perhaps you are not aware that every American is on the line for a portion of the national debt thanks to the IRS. As I'm writing this paragraph, each tax paying citizen owes $183,738.00 to cover the national debt according to USDebtClock.org. If that ain't slavery, I don't know what is!

The kingdom of Khazar began to decline as the Russians invaded in the 10th century, but the kingdom was not conquered until Genghis Kahn's sons invaded in the early part of the 13th century. These invasions caused a diaspora of the Jewish Khazars into Russia, Ukraine, Lithuania and Poland, which according to some historians, comprised the establishment of Judaism in Eastern Europe.

Now that we are armed with a greater understanding of the Khazars, thanks to our two experts, let's return to examining the connection between the Khazars and the Edomites. We need to revisit the correspondence from Hasdai to King Joseph. In his letter, Hasdai intimates that the Khazars originated from Mt. Seir, which we know was the land of the Edomites. Charles Weisman in his book *Who is Esau-Edom?* proposes,

"If the Khazars did originally "dwell near the Seir Mountains" then the Khazars, and thus world Jewry, are racially of Edomite stock. But how and when did Edomites get

265

to Khazaria? There is evidence that in the 6th century B.C., some of the Edomites fled their homeland of Seir and migrated north: 'After the fall of Jerusalem, in 586 BC, the Edomites began to press northward (Ezek. 36:5).' The extent and ultimate destination of this northward trek is not found in history, but it is likely that it brought some Edomites to the region of Khazaria."[291]

Weisman makes an intriguing point that the Khazars may have originated from the Edomites. This is an idea worth following up. In order to corroborate this idea, the first logical place to look is at King Joseph's response to the question raised in Hasdai's letter.

"You have asked of what nation and family and tribe we are. Know you that we are of the sons of Japhet and of his son Togarmah... It is said that in his time my ancestors were but a few, and the Lord granted them strength and boldness, and they fought with many great nations mightier than they were, and with God's help drove them out and inherited their country...Many generations passed until a king rose whose name was Bulan, a wise and God-fearing man, who put all his trust in the Lord, and removed all the sorcerers and idolaters from the country and lived under the Lord's wing... This king summoned all his ministers and servants and told them all these things. They were content, and accepted the king's judgment and entered under the wing of the Shekhinah... Then rose a king of his offspring, named Obadiah, a righteous and honest man, who reformed the kingdom and set the Law in proper order, and built synagogues and seminaries and brought in many of the sages of Israel."[292]

King Joseph described his ancestors as being from Noah's son, Japheth and Japheth's son, Togarmah. This account quells the rumor that the Khazarians originated from Mt. Seir and therefore, does not corroborate Weisman's theory. Japheth and his descendants migrated into Europe and Asia's mainland north of the River Don, which later became the region of the Khazar kingdom.[293] The Khazars' ancestors did not migrate south into the region of Mt. Seir. We also know from the Biblical record, the Judeans and the Edomites come from the line of Shem, therefore, the genetic heritage of the Khazarians is not related to the Edomites. Given this understanding, the only potential connection that remains between the Edomites and Khazarians is through the migration of the Judeans into the Caucasus region in the early centuries of the Common Era.

C.F. Parker wrote an historical sketch of the Edomites influence on Jewry. In line with most Jewish historians, he concluded there are two categories of modern Jews in the world: Ashkenazim and Sephardim. (For our investigation, we will hone in on the Ashkenazi Jews because within this subgroup are connections to the masterminds behind the Federal Reserve.) He argued that the Edomite influence within the Ashkenazim, or Central European Jews, may be minimal, but should not be overlooked.

"Ashkenazic Jewry is thus comprised of three elements of not exactly known proportions: (a) those of Judahite descent; (b) those of Idumean origin; (c) proselytes of other origins."[294]

There is a longstanding debate regarding the origins of the Ashkenazi Jews. Many scholars and historians purport that the Ashkenazi Jews hail from Germany. But growing evidence points to Khazaria as the land in which the Ashkenazi Jews trace their roots. For example, a 12th century rabbi recorded in his travelogue that the kingdom of Khazaria comes from the descendants of Meshach, son of Gomer, grandson of Japheth, great grandson of Noah.[295] This confirms King Joseph's report that the Khazars are from the bloodline of Japheth. Notably, this bloodline also produced Magog, Togarmah, and Ashkenaz. The Talmud makes a reference to a town near the Black Sea called Ashkenaz, but this term was also used more broadly to describe the Khazar kingdom.[296] The Scythians are from the bloodline of Magog and Ashkenaz. Of further interest is a passage in the book of Ezekiel which describes the trade practices of the descendants of Meshach and Togarmah.

Ezekiel 27:13-14 (MSG) *"Greece, Tubal and Meshech did business with you, trading slaves and bronze for your products. Beth-togarmah traded work horses, war horses, and mules for your products."*

The descendants of the Khazars were slave traders and warlike people who utilized horses in battle which provides further confirmation to the practices of the Khazars in slave trading.

Let's begin to assemble these tidbits of information we have collected. The Edomites began to migrate north during the Babylonian captivity and took up residence in Judah. The Idumean cities of Marissa and Dora were conquered by John Hyrcanus. Following this victory, Hyrcanus gave the Idumeans an ultimatum—convert to Judaism or leave the region. Their mass conversion led to mixed marriages between the Idumeans and the Judeans. The Idumeans rose in power under Roman rule to become governmental overlords of Judea through the line of Herod. Given the admixture of the Idumeans with the Judeans, historians such as Josephus, referred to the Idumeans, as Judeans

267

(Josephus, *Antiquities,* 13.9.1).[297] A migration of Jews into the Caucasus region occurred about the same time as the fall of Jerusalem. These diaspora Jews were likely to be a mixture of Judeans and Edomites since historical records indicate the Edomites were part of the horrific drama leading up to the last days of Jerusalem. King Joseph reported to Hasdai that the Khazarian King Bulan was a God-fearing man and his son, King Obadiah, converted to Judaism as a result of being proselytized by Jews in the Caucasus. The gradual exposure of the Khazars to Judaism led to a large-scale conversion between the 8th and 9th centuries A.D. Judaism was the primary religion of the Khazar kingdom for more than 200 years; Hebrew was used for written communication and sacred ceremonies.[298]

While we cannot yet make a strong, irrefutable connection between the Khazars and the Edomites, the migration of the Edomites, their conversion and admixture with the Judeans, and the subsequent conversion of the Khazars to Judaism, provides an intriguing link.

Genetic Studies

The debate among historians, Zionists, geneticists, and Jewish scholars regarding the ethnobiology of the Jewish people residing in Israel has been a long-standing contentious argument. I do not wish to get into the middle of this hotly contested debate, but it is useful for the purposes of our investigation to provide an overview of these matters.

There are two primary hypotheses for the origin of the Eastern European Jews: 1) the "Rhineland hypothesis," and 2) the "Khazarian hypothesis." Eran Elhaik (2012), from John Hopkins University, Department of Mental Health and McKusick-Nathans Institute of Genetic Medicine, conducted genetic research to test these two hypotheses, as a way to find the missing link for the Jewish European ancestry.

"The 'Rhineland hypothesis' envisions modern European Jews to be the descendants of the Judeans—an assortment of Israelite–Canaanite tribes of Semitic origin. It proposes two mass migratory waves: the first occurred over the 200 years following the Muslim conquest of Palestine (638 CE) and consisted of devoted Judeans who left Muslim Palestine for Europe... The second wave occurred at the beginning of the 15th century by a group of 50,000 German Jews who migrated eastward and ushered an apparent hyperbaby-boom era for half a millennium.

The competing "Khazarian hypothesis" considers Eastern European Jews to be the descendants of Khazars. The Khazars were a confederation of Slavic, Scythian, Hunnic–Bulgar, Iranian, Alans, and Turkish tribes who formed in the central– northern Caucasus one of most powerful empires during the late Iron Age and converted to Judaism in the 8th century CE… Biblical and archeological records allude to active trade relationships between Proto-Judeans and Armenians in the late centuries BCE … that likely resulted in a small scale admixture between these populations and a Judean presence in the Caucasus. After their conversion to Judaism, the population structure of the Judeo–Khazars was further reshaped by multiple migrations of Jews from the Byzantine Empire and Caliphate to the Khazarian Empire. Following the collapse of their empire and the Black Death (1347–1348) the Judeo–Khazars fled westward, settling in the rising Polish Kingdom and Hungary and eventually spreading to Central and Western Europe. The Khazarian hypothesis posits that European Jews are comprised of Caucasus, European, and Middle Eastern ancestries."[299]

Elhaik's (2012) results supported the Khazarian hypothesis; the best explanation of the origin of Eastern European Jews is that they are from Judeo-Khazarian ancestry. Elhaik (2012) posits the migration of this people group occurred over many centuries beginning in the late centuries B.C. This is substantiated by the flow of trade along the Silk Road and the historical records which document Jewish Radhanite traders venturing beyond the borders of Judea and Israel.[300]

Further substantiating the Khazarian hypothesis is a study conducted by Das, Wexler, Pirooznia & Elhaik (2013) to identify the geographical and ancestral origins of the Ashkenazi Jews (AJ) and the linguistic origins of Yiddish. They were the first to analyze genetic data of Yiddish speakers. Das et. al. (2013) tested the "Rhineland hypothesis" and the "Irano-Turko-Slavic hypotheses for the origins of Yiddish. The historical data and results of their study is revelatory for our investigation.

"An analysis of 393 Ashkenazic, Iranian and mountain Jews and over 600 non-Jewish genomes demonstrated that Greeks, Romans, Iranians and Turks exhibit the highest genetic similarity with AJs. Geographic Population Structure analysis localized most AJs along major primeval trade routes in northeastern Turkey adjacent to primeval villages with names that may be derived from 'Ashkenaz.'

The name 'Ashkenaz' is the Biblical Hebrew adaptation of the Iranian tribal name, which was rendered in Assyrian and Babylonian documents of the 7th century B.C. as *aškūza*, called in English by the Greek equivalent 'Scythian.' Already by the 1st century, most of the Jews in the world resided in the Iranian Empire. These Jews were descended either from Judaean emigrants or, more likely, from local converts to Judaism [possibly Idumeans] and were extremely active in international trade, as evident from the Talmud and non-Jewish historical sources. Over time, many of them moved north to the Khazar Empire to expand their mercantile operations. Consequently, some of the Turkic Khazar rulers and the numerous Eastern Slavs in the Khazar Empire converted to Judaism to participate in the lucrative Silk Road trade between Germany and China, which was essentially a Jewish monopoly. Yiddish emerged at that time as a secret language for trade based on Slavic and even Iranian patterns of discourse...to gain an advantage in trade."[301]

The belief that many of Eastern European Jews originated from Khazaria is not well received among Zionists because it undermines the historical claim the Jews have to the land of Israel; if most of the Jews occupying Israel are not the direct descendants of Abraham, Isaac, and Jacob, is it really their land? This is the crux of the contentious debates about who are the rightful inhabitants of the land of Israel.

In *The Invention of the Jewish People,* Sand provides a thorough review of the history and origin of modern-day Jewish people residing in Israel. He highlights that the Khazarian theory was more readily accepted prior to the 1950s but it went silent until the 1970s, at which point it was considered "scandalous, disgraceful and anti-Semitic" for the next several decades. A resurgence of research has begun in the 21st century; below are two perspectives in support of the Khazarian theory.

"Yitzhak Schipper, a senior socioeconomic historian and a prominent Zionist in Poland, believed for a long time that the 'Khazar thesis' accounted well for the massive demographic presence of Jews in Eastern Europe. In this, he was following a series of Polish scholars, Jewish and non-Jewish, who had written about the first settlements of Jewish believers in Poland, Lithuania, Belorussia and Ukraine. Schipper also assumed that there had been 'authentic' Jews in Judaizing Khazaria who contributed to the development of crafts and commerce in the powerful empire that stretched from the Volga to the Dnieper River. But he was also convinced that the influence of Judaism on the Khazars and the eastern Slavs gave rise to the large Jewish communities in Eastern Europe."[302]

"Israel's minister of education in the 1950s—did not hesitate to… express an unambiguous position regarding the origins of the Eastern European Jews: 'The Russian conquests did not destroy the Khazar kingdom entirely, but they broke it up and diminished it. And this kingdom, which had absorbed Jewish immigrants and refugees from many exiles, must itself have become a diaspora mother, the mother of one of the greatest of the diasporas—of Israel in Russia, Lithuania and Poland.'"[303]

Consider this for a moment, if the Khazarian Jews are the progenitors of the large majority of modern-day Jews, does that mean that the Jewish people living in Israel are considered Jews because their Edomite and Khazarian progenitors converted to Judaism and they are not true descendants of Jacob/Israel?

Admittedly, the link we have established between the Edomites and the Khazars is not a particularly strong connection because of the dearth of information surrounding the Edomite migration following the fall of Jerusalem. Perhaps we need to look at characteristics of the Edomites and Khazars to see if the link can be strengthened.

Character of Edom

As we consider the character traits of the Edomites, there are three Edomites, in particular, recorded in scripture that demonstrate identifiable patterns characterizing the Edomite bloodline: Doeg, Haman, and Herod. Remember Doeg, the '*gibbowr*,' from Chapter 11? His story is recorded in 1 Samuel 21-22. Doeg served Saul as head shepherd. When Saul was in pursuit of David's life, David sought provisions from the priests in Nob. David was in need of food and a weapon to defend himself. The priest of Nob gave David the showbread, as it was the only bread available, and provided him with Goliath's sword. In doing so, the priest saved David's life. Doeg was eyewitness to these events and reported it to King Saul. Enraged, Saul ordered his guards to kill the priests of Nob, but the guards were unwilling to strike down the priests of the Lord. The Edomite, Doeg, welcomed the opportunity and carried out the order with an ungodly vengeance. He not only slaughtered the priests of Nob, but he killed all the women, children, infants, cattle, donkeys and sheep in the town. It was a genocidal blood bath; the streets of Nob flowed with blood. This same genocidal character trait was found in Haman when he secured the king's decree to annihilate the Jews. Haman was an Agagite, a descendant of Esau. Agag was king of the Amalekites and we know from scripture that Amalek was Esau's grandson. This explains why Haman had a deep seeded hatred toward the Jews, it ran deep within his generations; it has its roots in the hatred of Esau toward Jacob. Herod, the Idumean, carried out genocide on all the male infants less than two years old in Bethlehem and its vicinity, as an attempt to kill the infant Messiah. The character traits displayed by these three Edomite men (deceit, hatred, rage, violence, murder and genocide) are all identifiers of Nephilim Hosts. Within the Edomite bloodline were the Nephilim.

C.F. Parker summarizes the history of the Edomites' intentions toward the Jews from the time Esau and Jacob were wrestling in Rachel's womb.

"Esau purposed to kill Jacob (Gen. xxvii, 42). The progeny of Esau repeatedly sought to destroy Israel: after the Exodus; in the time of the siege of Jerusalem; in the time of Esther; they even tried to destroy the infant Christ; they pursued Him to the Cross; they destroyed the Aaronic Priesthood, and created their own heretical hierarchy above which they were supreme to symbolise that they were above the God of Israel."[304]

In considering identifiable traits of Edomites, we cannot overlook the unique description of Esau's physical traits at birth, i.e. being born of red hair (and possibly ruddy complexion). This physical trait became a defining aspect of Esau's identity and subsequently that of his bloodline. Let me explain…

To Be Red

The color red is indelibly linked to the Edomites. The first mention in scripture of the Hebrew word for red, '*admoniy*,' is when Esau was born; it means 'reddish, of the hair or complexion.'[305] (Interestingly, this Hebrew word is only used three times in scripture, once to describe Esau and twice to describe David). A transformation took place when Esau became Edom. The Hebrew word for Edom is '*adam*' which means '**to be red.**'[306]

Hmmm… To be, or not to be, that is the question…

Esau chose **to be RED**. This choice had substantial ramifications upon his generational line. Esau branded himself RED (Edom), when he willingly traded his birthright for red stew. Something much deeper than just a desire for lentil soup was at work here. Esau sealed a transaction, one that would constrict his allegiance to a particular seed. In essence, he aligned himself with RED, the seed of Satan, and rejected the birthright blessings of Abraham and Isaac. On that fateful day, he declared himself to be separate from Yahweh, the God of his fathers, Abraham and Isaac.

What does it mean **to be RED?** First, let's consider the biblical meaning of the color red. An obvious connection with red is to the blood of sacrifice; the blood of Jesus which cleanses us from sin. This is an example of red being linked to the seed of God. But there are numerous connections of red aligning with positions that are antithetical to Yahweh, positions that align with the seed of Satan. Here is just a sample:

Isaiah 1:15-16,18 (NIV) *"When you spread out your hands in prayer, I hide my eyes from you; even when you offer many prayers, I am not listening. Your hands are full of blood! Wash and make yourselves clean. Take your evil deeds out of my sight; stop doing wrong… 'Come now, let us settle the matter,' says the Lord. 'Though your sins are like scarlet, they shall be as white as snow; though they are red as crimson, they shall be like wool."* **Red = sin, blood of evil deeds**

Revelation 6:4 (NIV) *"Then another horse came out, a fiery red one. Its rider was given power to take peace from the earth and to make people kill each other. To him was given a large sword."* **Red = chaos, death, destruction**

Revelation 12:3 (AMP) *"Then another sign [of warning] was seen in heaven: behold, a great fiery red dragon (Satan) with seven heads and ten horns, and on his heads were seven royal crowns (diadems)."* **Red = Satan**

Revelation 17:3-6 (GNT) *"The Spirit took control of me, and the angel carried me to a desert. There I saw a woman sitting on a red beast that had names insulting to God written all over it; the beast had seven heads and ten horns. The woman was dressed in purple and scarlet…On her forehead was written a name that has a secret meaning: 'Great Babylon, the mother of all prostitutes and perverts in the world.' And I saw that the woman was drunk with the blood of God's people and the blood of those who were killed because they had been loyal to Jesus."* **Red = the beast, Mystery Babylon, martyrdom**

Red carries connotations of intense emotion – passionate love, eroticism, seduction, danger, power, violence, anger, and rage. It's not a coincidence that areas known for prostitution and sexual perversion are called the "red-light district." Red is also associated with death. Red is equated to Satan, observable by the vast majority of artists' renditions of the devil. Occultists uses red candle wax in preparation for black magick. Below is an excerpt explaining this,

"Red incites accidents, fires, and injuries. It is used in spells to invoke power and intensity before workings of black magick. Red is inflammatory and is used in spells for revenge, anger, courage, determination, and dealing with enemies…The color red is firmly rooted in the physical world. The burning of red candles is said to put one in touch with the power of the flesh. Red represents temporal pleasures."[307]

What strikes me about the above description is that the use of red candles in black magick closely parallels the character traits of the three Edomite men we reviewed, vengeful and angry. Interesting.

The Hunter

Additional characteristics of Esau can be found in scripture. We learn from Genesis 25:27 that Esau was a cunning hunter, a man of the field. To understand this better, let's look at the meaning of the Hebrew words for cunning hunter; cunning is '*yada*`' which means 'to be skillful at, to know how, to be wise.'[308] Esau was a hunter, '*tsayid*,' which means 'prey taken in hunting,'[309] it comes from the root word '*tsuwd*' which means 'to lie in wait, to chase, to take provision.'[310] Esau was a rugged man, an outdoorsman who was skilled at hunting and probably enjoyed the thrill of the hunt, the stalking of an animal and then moving in for the kill. Intriguingly, the root word '*tsuwd*' is used figuratively to describe someone who lies in wait to catch a human, in other words, to entrap someone with the intent to exploit for personal gain. The discovery of these character traits helps us develop a character sketch of Edom. Edom was a rugged, gruff, strong and burly mountain man who was cunning and skilled in hunting down prey. He likely was a man driven by the thrill of the kill and had very little interest in the tradition of his fathers. Additionally, he was intelligent and wise, willing to be patient in stalking his prey, but quick to pounce when the time was right.

We have wrung out the characteristics of Esau found in scripture, but if we expand our resources to include the extra-biblical texts, the Book of Jasher provides some interesting details.

Jasher 26:17 "*And the boys grew up to their fifteenth year, and they came amongst the society of men. Esau was a designing and deceitful man, and an expert hunter in the field, and Jacob was a man perfect and wise, dwelling in tents, feeding flocks and learning the instructions of the Lord and the commands of his father and mother."*

This passage adds to our understanding of Esau's personality; he was designing and deceitful. Jasher provides a more thorough background to the events that transpired leading up to Esau trading his birthright for lentil stew. But before we look at Jasher 27, it's important to point out the Hebrew word to describe Esau as a hunter, '*tsayid*,' is the same word used to describe one of the '*gibbowr*' we have discussed before... Nimrod! With that little nugget, let's look at a telling event in Esau's life.

Jasher 27: 1-5, 7 "*And Esau at that time, after the death of Abraham, frequently went in the field to hunt. And Nimrod king of Babel, the same was Amraphel, also frequently went with his mighty men to hunt in the field, and to walk about with his men in the cool of the day. And Nimrod was observing Esau all the days, for a jealousy was formed in the heart of Nimrod against Esau all the days. And on a certain day Esau went in the field to hunt, and he found Nimrod walking in the wilderness with his two men. And all his mighty men and his people were with him in the wilderness, but they removed at a distance from him, and they went from him in different directions to hunt, and **Esau concealed himself for Nimrod, and he lurked for him in the wilderness**...And Nimrod and two of his men that were with him came to the place where they were, when **Esau started suddenly from his lurking place, and drew his sword, and hastened and ran to Nimrod, and cut off his head**.*" (emphasis mine)

This story is incredible in that it contains valuable details about Esau's character. It brings to life the conniving, designing, deceitful, murderous aspect to his personality. Esau must have been very confident in his hunting skills that he would stalk Nimrod, a deified '*gibbowr*,' who himself had a reputation as a mighty hunter of men. This hunting expedition led up to the familiar passage in Genesis 25 when Esau comes in from the field faint, weary, and famished. He exerted a tremendous amount of energy killing Nimrod and two of his guards. He was on the run from the rest of Nimrod's men who were intent on avenging the death of Nimrod. In this state, Esau finds Jacob in the tent making lentil stew. Kimberly Rogers, in *The Esau Effect*, explains the significance of the exchange.

"Jacob was at home performing the ritual that was the responsibility of the firstborn son, Esau. What ritual was that? It was the traditional meal of comfort that the eldest son made for his father when the grandfather died. Red lentil stew was the

TRADITIONAL middle eastern meal of comfort that Isaac deserved to have cooked for him by his firstborn son. But Esau was so self-concerned that his only thought, upon the death of his grandfather Abraham, upon whose knees he sat, was to go kill things. His thoughts were not toward the grieving Isaac and caring for him."[311]

This is the backdrop to the transformation of Esau to Edom. Esau chose **to be red** by covering his hands with murderous blood, instead of fulfilling his role as a loving, firstborn son caring for his grieving father. Unbelievable! Now we understand why God says, Jacob I love, Esau I hate.

But is this enough to determine there is a strong link between the Edomites and Khazars? I don't know about you, but I am not yet satisfied. Let's dig further. In case you are asking yourself at this moment, is it really necessary to dig further? I want to remind you of a caveat I mentioned at the outset, that is, our investigative journey will take twists and turns in unexpected ways. Sometimes, those twists and turns will not be as fruitful as others, but if we are to uncover the roots of the Federal Reserve, we must keep digging…the roots run very deep.

Edom-Khazar Connection

Scripture tells us that the Edomites were wise (Jeremiah 49:7), hateful and bitter (Genesis 27:41, Hebrews 12:15-16), cruel inflictors of terror (Jeremiah 49:16), prideful and arrogant (Jeremiah 49:16), vindictive and vengeful (Ezekiel 25:12), occultists (Jeremiah 27:3,9), idolaters (2 Chronicles 25:14), opportunists (Ezekiel 36:5), murderers (Matthew 14:6-11), genocidal (1 Samuel 21-22, Matthew 2:16), and hybrids (Numbers 24:7, 1 Samuel 15:8). We also know from Josephus' historical account that the Idumeans were syncretistic; they embraced Judaism when it was in their best interest but held onto elements of polytheism. Now that we have solidified our character sketch of Esau and the Edomites, we can compare what we are able to uncover about the Khazars, to see if there are any similarities.

The writings of a 10th century Rabbi Saadia Gaon, supply us with a window into some of the characteristics of the Khazars. He described them as being tough warriors who rode on horses; they were heavily engaged in slave trading and periodically executed their own kings. Again, this confirms the description of the descendants of Meshach and Togarmah given in Ezekiel 27. Rabbi Saadia Gaon called the Khazarian Jews, "wild Jews." The Khazars had a peculiar practice of empowering a Kagan (the king);

he is throttled with a silk cord until he is near death from suffocation. At that moment, he is asked how long he wishes to reign. The length of time declared by the newly appointed Kagan essentially determines the length of his life. If he dies prior to the end of his reign, so be it, but if he lives to the end of his term, then he is executed the day after his term ends.[312] What else can we learn about the characteristics of the Khazars?

The Khazars seemed to be tolerant of other religions as evidenced by the structure of their supreme court; there were seven justices appointed to this high court, two for the Muslims, two for the Jews, two for the Christians and one for the pagans.[313] It is not entirely clear the extent to which the Khazars' conversion extended across the massive sociopolitical kingdom. Was it only the elite that converted or did the majority of the citizenry convert? There is some indication that by the 9th century, a large portion of the Khazars had converted to Judaism and the Talmud became central in the political, economic, and cultural life in Khazaria. We will peer into the implications of the Talmud guiding economic and financial policies in an upcoming chapter. Benjamin Freedman lends strength to the connection between the character of the Edomites and the character of the Khazars in that he described the Khazars as very warlike. In fact, there were times in their history when they were continually at war driven by a desire for plunder and revenge. Johnson quotes from the Georgian and Armenian chronicles in which the Khazars were interpreted to be Gog and Magog, they were described as "wild men with horrible faces and the manners of wild beasts, feeding on blood."[314]

A surprising connection between the Edomites and the Khazars can be found in the origins of the Khazars. Earlier in this chapter, I mentioned that Elhaik (2012) noted that the "Khazars were a confederation of Slavic, **Scythian**, Hunnic–Bulgar, Iranian, Alans, and Turkish tribes" (emphasis mine).[315] Why is this important? Jacky Colliss Harvey, author of *Red: A History of the Redhead* explains the importance. First, she points out that the Scythians are referred to in the New Testament.

Colossians 3:11 (NIV) *"Here there is no Gentile or Jew, circumcised or uncircumcised, barbarian, Scythian, slave or free, but Christ is all, and is in all."*

In Strong's Concordance, '*Skythēs*' means "rude or rough." The Scythians who lived in what is now modern-day Russia, were considered "as the wildest of the barbarians."[316] Harvey reveals that Herodotus wrote about the inhabitants of Gelonus, a city in northern Scythia along the Volga River; he described the Scythians as having "deep blue eyes and bright **red hair**."[317](emphasis mine) Can you see the link between the Edomites and the Khazarians strengthen before our eyes? One of the tribal groups of the Khazarian confederation, the Scythians, were reported to have red hair. Furthermore, Kevin Allen Brook, historian and author of *The Jews of Khazaria*, records a description given by a 10th century Arab geographer. "The Khazars were described by ibn-Said al-Maghribi as having blue eyes, light skin and reddish hair."[318]

Interestingly, Harvey discusses the possible backstory of the Scythians as reaching eastward to Mongolia and parts of modern-day China. This is consistent with historians' reports that the Khazars originated from parts of Asia along the Silk Road. This also reminds me of the archaeological discoveries from the Tarim Basin. Is it possible that the Tarim mummies were the ancestors of the Scythians who later became the Khazarians? Remember the description Pliny the Elder gave of the people from Tarim? "These people, they said, **exceeded the ordinary human height**, had flaxen hair, and blue eyes, and made an uncouth sort of noise by way of talking…"[319]

This 1st century account of red-haired people of extraordinary height in Asia provides a possible link to the origin of the Khazars. After looking more closely at the trail of the Edomites into the Caucasus region, we can more assuredly surmise that the Khazars and Edomites were similar in many ways. They were wild, redhaired, rugged, exploitive, barbarians, murderous, syncretistic, vengeful, and opportunistic. But we must recognize there was not a singular trail of migration for the Edomites; they spread out to other regions besides the Caucasus. There may be a possible connection in Rome.

Key Points
- John Hyrcanus forced the Idumeans (Edomites) to convert to Judaism.
- Admixture of Idumeans with Judeans occurred.
- Edomites migrated into the Caucasus at several points in history: after the destruction of the first temple by Nebuchadnezzar, as a result of trade routes of the late centuries B.C., and during the fall of Jerusalem in A.D. 70.
- Khazar kingdom was a vast, powerful empire in the Caucasus from 1st century B.C. to the 10th century A.D.
- The Khazars were a mysterious people who originated from Asia. They were a violent, war-like people who engaged in sexual excesses, usury (*nasha*), and slave trading.
- Khazars had a mass conversion to Judaism in 8th century A.D. and were taught from Babylonian Talmud.

- Ashkenazi Jews most likely originated from Khazaria.
- Esau chose to be red by aligning himself with the seed of Satan and rejected his birthright blessings.
- Khazars and Edomites shared similar characteristics. They were wild, red-haired, rugged, exploitive, barbarians, murderous, syncretistic, vengeful, and opportunistic.

Chapter 17

The Roman Connection

~All roads lead to Rome~

We are circling back once again to the land of the Roman Empire, present day Italy. Isaiah 34 provides an interesting connection between Edom and Rome, one that is easily overlooked if it weren't for Clark's commentary. Clark quotes the venerable medieval Rabbi Kimchi who had this to say about Isaiah 34,

"This chapter points out the future destruction of Rome, which is here called Bosra; for Bosra was a great city of the Edomites. Now the major part of the Romans are Edomites, who profess the law of Jesus. The Emperor Caesar (qy. Constantine) was an Edomite, and so were all the emperors after him. The destruction of the Turkish empire is also comprehended in this prophecy."[320]

What's curious about Kimchi's perspective is that Isaiah 34 makes no reference to Rome. Yet he seems to draw a substantial connection between Edom and Rome, why? I believe it's due, in part, to Edom being considered a type of antichrist. A great many eschatological scholars believe the antichrist will arise out of Rome, perhaps Kimchi shared a similar view. But if we investigate further the Jewish tradition connecting Edom with Rome, we come across a useful resource written by William Beeston in 1858, entitled *The Roman Empire the Empire of the Edomite*. Within this resource lies valuable information elusive within 20th and 21st century books. Unfortunately, history can be rewritten for the benefit of optics; examples of this abound in our U.S. history books regarding atrocities, such as, the Trail of Tears or the Bear River Massacre, to name only a few. George Orwell confronted this trending reality by warning us of the mind control of Big Brother.

"And if all others accepted the lie which the Party imposed – if all records told the same tale – then the lie passed into history and became truth. 'Who controls the past,' ran the Party slogan 'controls the future: who controls the present controls the past.'"[321]

Great historical institutions, such as the Smithsonian Institute, are substantial contributors to the rewriting of history, especially as it pertains to the skeletal remains of giants found in North America, as we discovered in Chapter 15.

Beeston presents an alternative historical account of the founding of Rome; most history books do not provide a similar account. His discovery through etymological linguistic study, in conjunction with Rabbinic tradition and Bible prophecy, reveals a key link for our investigation. Beeston writes,

"…the story of the foundation of Rome, and the people from whom THE ETERNAL CITY sprung, are admitted to being the very points about which the learned are most ignorant. Unspeakable, then, must our astonishment be, when we perceive, that this grand secret was certainly discovered, and disclosed, more than twelve hundred years ago; that the true answer to the question WHENCE CAME THE ROMANS? may have been returned, and even registered in writing, before the birth of Christ; that the response proceeded neither from Greek nor Roman, but from the DESPISED JEW; that it has been preserved to us in the JEWISH TARGUMS;… that it may be comprehended in these twenty words: THE ROMANS CAME FROM ESAU, WHO IS EDOM; AND ITALY IS THE IDUMEA, ROME THE BOZRAH, OF THE HEBREW PROPHETS.

'The descendants of Esau,' say the JEWISH RABBINS, 'the sworn enemies of the descendants of Jacob, even to the end of the world, were at first a small nation, inhabiting Mount Seir and the adjacent country, contiguous to the land of Canaan. They were easily confined within their own limits, so long as the Israelites enjoyed a great and formidable empire in Canaan: but, after that the powerful republic of the twelve tribes had been destroyed by the Assyrians and Babylonians, they wonderfully increased in numbers and in strength; extended their dominion in the West; subjugated Italy; founded Rome, and the Roman Empire; and at length entirely overturned the Jewish state, the Second Temple being destroyed by Titus Vespasian; and, professing the religion of Jesus Christ, which they were the first of all nations to embrace…' The Rabbins further assert, that the prophecies of the prophets against Esau, Edom and the cities of Edom have as yet received but a partial accomplishment; and that they will obtain their fulfillment in the punishment and destruction of ROME CHRISTIAN…

such is the TRADITION OF THE RABBINS; and PAPAL ROME has done her utmost to suppress it: but without success."[322]

Let's unpack these two paragraphs as it pertains to our investigation. Beeston refers to the Jewish Targum as containing pertinent clues linking Edom and Rome. The Targum is the Aramaic translation of the Hebrew scripture. When the Israelites were taken into captivity, the society at large spoke Aramaic. Out of necessity, most Jews became bilingual; they spoke Aramaic in their social and business transactions, but continued to speak Hebrew at home and at their religious gatherings The Targum became part of Jewish traditional literature with its inception dating to the Second Temple period.[323] Beeston's deep dive into the lingual analysis of Greek, Latin, Aramaic and Hebrew lends support to the Jewish tradition of the Idumeans being the ones who founded Rome. His analysis is meticulous and complex, well beyond the scope of this book. However, one aspect of his research I must highlight is his reference to the translation of Lamentations 4:22 by Johannes Buxtorf. Elder Buxtorf was a 16th–17th century Hebraist who was greatly revered and known as the "master of the Rabbis." He translated the Targum passage of Lamentations 4:22 into Latin, "Isto tempore visitabo iniquitatem tuam, ROMAM IMPIAM, quas aedificata es in Italia, et repleta es turbis hominum EX POSTERIS EDOM."[324]

For those who don't read Latin (myself included), an English translation of this reads as follows, "And at that time I will punish your iniquities, wicked Rome, built in Italy and filled with crowds of Edomites."[325]

As Beeston sought to corroborate Buxtorf's translation, his research led him to a copy of the first edition of the Biblia Hebraica Rabbinnica. This Bible was printed in the years 1517-1518 (prior to the King James Bible) by Bomberg of Venice; Beeston located a copy of it in the Bodleian Library at Oxford. Within its contents, the passage as translated by Buxtorf was found. Beeston concluded that the Bomberg Bible is a genuine translation of the Targum; the Targumist was most likely Jonathan Ben Uzziel, a disciple of the venerable Hillel who lived approximately 100 years before the destruction of Jerusalem.

Beeston's work provides a history of the western Edomite migration during the Assyrian and Babylonian captivities. The Edomites increased in number and spread out across the West. The Jewish tradition, as recorded by the rabbis, credits the Edomites with founding Rome. Beeston provides confirmation of this assertion through his in-depth analysis of linguistics. While not all Romans were Edomites, their influence certainly increased over the centuries.

Kimberly Rogers, author of *The Esau Effect*, points out the influence of Edom within the ranks of the Roman soldiers.

"…the Romans were conquering peoples. And when the armies needed more recruits, they hired them from outside their culture. Enter the Edomites, the descendants of Esau. Esau, who it was said would live by the sword! The ranks of the Roman Empire became filled with enlisted Edomites. These particular Edomites…were the original Edomites from the area of Mount Seir. Edom came under the control of the Arabs in the 5th century B.C. The mercenary Edomites among the Assyrians that moved north to Rome enlisted in large numbers into the Roman army…historians and Rabbis alike agree that Rome and Edom became one and the same entity."[326]

Let's review the clues we have just uncovered: Kimchi's assertion that Constantine was an Edomite, the Jewish Targum translation linking Edom with Rome, Rabbinical tradition that Rome was founded by Edomites, Beeston's research corroborating the founding of Rome by the Edomites, and Rogers' assertion that Edomites continued their migration to Rome and joined the ranks of the Roman military. If we take all these clues to mean, that in fact, "Rome and Edom became one and the same entity," then we should expect to see similarities between Edom and Rome.

Edom was bloodthirsty; it was an archenemy of the Israelites. The Edomites (among which were the Amalekites) used brutal acts of violence toward the Israelites because of the deep-seated hatred toward Jacob. The Edomites engaged in genocide. Likewise, Rome was considered one of the most bloodthirsty empires in history evidenced by the brutality of the Roman legions, but even more so, by the Roman games held in the Colosseum. Roman citizens were entertained by observing the ever-increasing grotesque mauling of humans by ravenous beasts. The bloodier the event, the more riveted the spectators were.

The Roman Empire engaged in genocide when they decimated Carthage in 146 B.C. It was common practice for the Roman military to destroy cities, killing thousands in their wake, but what makes the atrocities of Carthage stand out is the Romans' desire to eradicate Carthage, its people, and its culture. The Roman legions systematically went door to door slaughtering everyone they found. Conservative estimates record 150,000 Carthaginians were killed and another 30,000-50,000 were enslaved. After the massacre, the Romans burned the city and then proceeded to remove, brick by brick, the foundations that remained. The destruction of the Carthaginians was described by Polybius as 'immediate and total.'[327]

Finally, if we compare our list of Edomite characteristics (wise, hateful, bitter, cruel inflictors of terror, prideful, arrogant, vindictive, vengeful, occultists, idolaters, opportunists, murderers, genocidal, syncretistic, and hybrids) with what we know of the Roman Empire, I think you will agree that there is a substantial overlap. We need only to remember what we uncovered in Chapter 15 about Emperor Maximus I to corroborate the link between Edomite characteristics and the Romans. Maximus was strikingly tall with extraordinary strength and he was fierce, haughty, violent, scornful and cruel.

At this point in our investigation, we are drawing close to being able to connect the dots between the Edomites, Khazars, Ashkenazi Jews, Rome (Vatican) and Zionists. But what does this have to do with the Federal Reserve? Were there individuals behind the creation of the Federal Reserve that we need to investigate? The Rothschilds come into focus as we look at the overlap between these people groups. We will soon discover that *all financial roads lead to the House of Rothschild*.

Key Points
- Emperor Constantine may have been an Edomite.
- The translation of the Jewish Targum for Lamentations 4:22 states that Rome is Edom.
- Rabbinical tradition records the Edomites as the founders of Rome.
- Similarities between Rome and Edom: haughty, bloodthirsty, cruel, and engaged in genocide.

Chapter 18

Rise of the Rothschilds

Let me issue and control a nation's money
and I care not who writes the laws.
~ Mayer Amschel Rothschild

The tentacles of the House of Rothschild reach into the monetary policy of 85% of the countries worldwide (164 central banks owned and controlled by Rothschilds as of 2016 report), our country is no exception.[328] For this reason, we must investigate the Rothschilds and their modus operandi.

Mayer Amschel Rothschild was the patriarch of the most powerful dynasty of financiers the world has ever seen. Mayer Amschel Bauer, an Ashkenazi Jew, born in Frankfurt, Germany in 1743, developed an interest in money when he was just a boy. His father, Moses, ran a small family bank and often enlisted Mayer's help to exchange money for the business. It is said that Moses Bauer hung a red shield with a hexagram on the front of his house denoting his banking business.[329] The family later incorporated the hexagram into the Rothschild Coat of Arms (see Figure 39). Rothschild means 'red shield' in German.

This really should come as no surprise at this point in our investigation, but it still strikes me as uncanny that we see yet another connection to **red.** I guess a way to interpret this connection resurfacing again and again, is that it's like a calling card or a signature mark of the Edomites and/or Nephilim Hosts. These signature marks, or symbols, will help us ascertain the web of connectivity that form the roots of the Federal Reserve.

Figure 36. Great coat of arms of Rothschild family by Mathiew Chaine. CC by- SA 3.0
https://commons.wikimedia.org/w/index.php?search=Rothschild+shield&title=Special:Search&go=Go
&ns0=1&ns6=1&ns12=1&ns14=1&ns100=1&ns106=1#/media/File:Great_coat_of_arms_of_Rothschi
ld_family.svg

Mayer Amschel Rothschild

Mayer Amschel grew up in the Jewish ghetto of Frankfurt. The Jews in Germany were not allowed to have family surnames. Therefore, it was common for a family to identify themselves by a symbol associated with their house or take the name of the town in which they lived. The Rothschild Archive describes the history of the Rothschild name,

"Like most of the other inhabitants of the Frankfurt Judengasse, the Rothschilds took their name from their house. Although their civil status was uncertain, the inhabitants of the Judengasse derived a proud sense of identity from their ancestral homes. Pictorial representations of names were engraved or painted onto keystones and doors, and people often retained their names, and emblems, when they moved to another house."[330]

When Mayer was 12 years old, both his parents died from smallpox. He was sent to Hanover to apprentice with a prominent Jewish banking house, Oppenheimer. It was during his training with Oppenheimer that Mayer learned the ins and outs of finance, particularly foreign trade and dealing in rare coins. His time there proved fruitful as it opened doors for him when he returned to Frankfurt. Mayer took over the family banking business and greatly expanded it by doing business with dignitaries such as, Prince William of Hanau. It is noteworthy to understand whose coattails Mayer Amschel clung to; Prince William was a human trafficker. Frederic Morton, author of the biography *The Rothschilds,* wrote the following,

"William conscripted his male subjects and processed them for the auction block. He refined and perfected his troops; he shined and sharpened them on the parade grounds; he made sure of the officers' pigtails and the enlisted men's muskets. And when a batch was ripe and enticingly packaged, he sold the lot to England, which used "the Hessians" to keep peace in the Colonies.

William's merchandising of the peacekeepers brought him enormous wealth. Every time a Hessian was killed, the prince received extra compensation to soothe him for the victim's trouble. The causalities mounted, and therefore his cash."[331]

Prince William's complete disregard for human life, seemingly all in his quest to attain power and wealth, became the seedbed upon which Mayer Amschel cultivated the Rothschild banking dynasty. F. Tupper Saussy, author of *Rulers of Evil,* provides some critical clues for our investigation.

"Aware that the Rothschilds are an important Jewish family, I looked them up in *Encyclopedia Judaica* and discovered that they bear the title "**Guardians of the Vatican Treasury**." The Vatican Treasury, of course, holds the imperial wealth of Rome. Imperial wealth grows in proportion to its victories in war – as the Jesuit empowerment *Regimini militantis ecclesiae* implies, the Church-at-War is more necessary than the Church-at-Peace. According to H. Russell Robinson's illustrated *Armour of Imperial Rome,* Caesarean soldiers protected themselves in battle with shields painted red. Since the soldiery is the State's most valuable resource (the Council of Trent admitted this in preferring the Jesuits to all other religious orders), it is easy to understand why the **red shield** was identified with the very life of the Church. Hence the appropriateness of the name *Rothschild,* German for 'red shield.' The appointment of Rothschild gave the black papacy absolute financial privacy and secrecy. Who would ever search a family of orthodox Jews for the key to the wealth of the Roman Catholic Church? I believe this appointment explains why the House of Rothschild is famous for helping nations go to war. It is fascinating that, as Meyer Rothschild's sons grew into the family business, the firm took on the title *Meyer Amschel Rothschild und*

Söhne, which gives us the notariqon MARS. Isn't Mars the Roman God of War, whose heavenly manifestation is 'the **red planet**'?"[332] (emphasis mine)

Are you having an aha moment right now like I am? It's "elementary my dear Watson, elementary." ALL ROADS LEAD TO ROME…and…ALL FINANCIAL ROADS LEAD TO THE HOUSE OF ROTHSCHILD. We see unfolding before us the layers of occult meaning in the chosen name, Rothschild. The Rothschilds are Ashkenazi Jews, which from our discovery in Chapter 16, means they are descendants of the Khazarians. This yields an increasing probability that the Rothschilds are Edomites with a connection to Rome! After all, **RED** is the calling card of the Edomites.

Mayer Amschel had five sons whom he grafted in to the family banking business when they turned 12. Mayer developed a stalwart business strategy that would prove virtually impenetrable. He positioned his sons in five strategic locations across Europe to establish powerful banking houses in Vienna, Naples, London, Paris and Frankfurt. It didn't take Mayer long to realize that there was enormous profit in the business of war, especially if his proxies fund both sides of the war. Mayer Amschel was not a nationalist; he was a globalist in search of dominance. It was of no consequence to his conscience to fund both sides of a war because he had no loyalty to any one nation. This attitude and unscrupulous method of amassing great wealth was woven in the fabric of the Rothschild empire. For the past two centuries and counting, the Rothschilds have implemented this policy. They are the wealthiest family on the planet, aside from the Saudi Princes (who are no longer in power, causing their net worth to plummet).

Mayer Amschel Rothschild seized an opportunity to finance the start of a secret order that would develop into a world dominating force—the Illuminati. Mayer recognized that in order to control Europe, he had to wrest power from the Roman Catholic Church. In 1770, he procured the help of Adam Weishaupt, a Bavarian Jew who converted to Catholicism after being educated by the Jesuits, but later developed such disdain for the Jesuits, he became an atheist. In the eyes of Mayer Amschel Rothschild, Adam Weishaupt was the perfect person to establish a secret order that would destroy the Church and one day rule the world. This secret order was named the Illuminati in honor of Lucifer as the pathway to enlightenment.[333]

Just prior to his death in 1812, Mayer Amschel Rothschild drew up his will with edicts dictating the structure of the House of Rothschild. All key positions were to be held by members of the family and only the males in the family could manage the business. Unless otherwise voted on by the majority, the eldest son was to be the head of the family.[334] He asserted that marriages remain within the family, meaning cousins were to marry each other. The second and third generations followed this edict closely with 29 marriages among cousins.[335] In his will, Mayer insisted the value of his estate remain private. He forbade any public inventory of his estate by the courts. Mayer instructed the five brothers to work closely in order to establish a dominate dynasty that would survive for centuries. In essence, the five formed a multinational banking institution in which they could manipulate and control monetary systems to gain power and amass unfathomable wealth. In the 19th century, the House of Rothschild gained a firm grip, or should I say, a strangle hold on the European nations.

The immense power of the House of Rothschild can not be underestimated. The Weekly Register, a 19th century national magazine published in Baltimore described the reach of the House of Rothschild,

"The Rothschilds are the wonders of modern banking…The Rothschilds govern a Christian world. Not a cabinet moves without their advice. They stretch their hand, and with equal ease, from Petersburgh to Vienna, from Vienna to Paris, from Paris to London, and from London to Washington. Baron Rothschild [James de Rothschild], the head of the house, is the true king of Judah, the prince of captivity, the Messiah so long looked for by this extraordinary people. He holds the keys of peace and war, blessing or cursing. The lion of the tribe of Judah, Baron Rothschild, possesses more real force than David – more wisdom than Solomon. They are the brokers and counsellors of the kings of Europe and of the republican chiefs of America."[336]

Nathan Mayer Rothschild

Nathan Mayer Rothschild, the third born son, received the majority vote from his brothers to be appointed as head of the House of Rothschild following the death of Mayer Amschel Rothschild. Nathan was the most astute among the brothers, not to mention, the one who imbued Machiavellian tactics in the ethos of their business. His unscrupulous dealings earned him the reputation of being "without a soul," a characteristic that swiftly became a hallmark of the Rothschild business practices.

Arguably, one of the most fiendish maneuvers Nathan orchestrated was the manipulation of intelligence regarding the outcome of the Battle of Waterloo, which enabled him to single handedly take control of the London markets.

The Napoleonic Wars were financed by the Rothschilds. Nathan supplied gold to Wellington's army through the House of Rothschild in London. Simultaneously, Jacob Mayer Rothschild supplied Napoleon's army with gold from the House of Rothschild in Paris. Twenty-three years of Napoleonic wars came to a head at the Battle of Waterloo. With the Rothschild banks spread across Europe, they were in the enviable position to secure a network of secret routes for their couriers to pass quickly through blockades that thwarted other couriers. The Rothschild emissaries were stealthy, outpacing all other messenger systems, with vast modes of transportation at the ready. During the Battle of Waterloo in 1815, the tipping point of nations laid in the balance; all the while Nathan Rothschild was poised to pounce on the prey locked in his sight...

Nathan had his courier, a man named Rothworth, positioned to receive news of the outcome at Waterloo. Word that the British defeated Napoleon reached Nathan Rothschild a full 24 hours before Wellington's couriers delivered the news. This advantage granted Nathan the ability to manipulate the British markets. Consistent with his conniving methods, Nathan instructed his agents on the floor of the stock exchange to start dumping the British bonds called consuls. This triggered frantic selling by other traders, who believed that it was a sign the British had lost the battle. As the value of the consuls plummeted, Nathan's traders discreetly bought them up at fire sale prices. When Wellington's courier delivered the news that the Brits had won, it was too late. Nathan had swooped in for the kill. The price of the British consuls skyrocketed, yielding Nathan a handsome return of approximately 20 to 1 on his investment. Nathan declared that same year,

"I care not what puppet is placed on the throne of England to rule the Empire. The man who controls Britain's money supply controls the British Empire and I control the British money supply."[337]

Nathan Mayer Rothschild became the most powerful financier in England's history. Through his stealth maneuvering of the British consul, he essentially took control of the Bank of England. His wealth was greater than that of the Queen. The Rothschild empire, with it's five multinational banks, yielded great influence over heads of state and governments. But Nathan's insatiable appetite for power, control and dominance was not satisfied by his enormous wealth. He, like his father, had his sights on forming a world government to subjugate the citizens of the world to Rothschild dominance. The Congress of Vienna was the arena in which Nathan tried to wrest control through the bargaining tool of debt instruments created by the Rothschilds during the Napoleonic Wars. Most European nations were indebted to the House of Rothschild with the exception of Russia. Nathan envisioned a European Federation (the predecessor of the EU) but the Russian Tsar, Alexander I, stood in the way. Russia was not interested in having a Rothschild owned central bank and Nathan held no leverage over the Tsar to force the issue. Instead, Alexander I created The Holy Alliance Treaty; a coalition linking the monarchs of Russia, Austria and Prussia in unity through the governance of Christian principles. Nathan's plans were foiled and he was incensed with the Russian Tsar. It has been said that Nathan Mayer Rothschild threatened that one day the Rothschilds or their proxies would destroy the Tsar and his entire family.[338] While it's difficult to corroborate this statement with eye witness accounts, history shows that this is in fact what happened. Jacob Schiff, a proxy of the Rothschilds, orchestrated the demise of the Romanov dynasty.

Jacob Schiff

Jacob Henry Schiff was born in 1847 in Frankfurt-on-the-Main, Germany, in a five-story home shared with Mayer Amschel Rothschild's family. Jacob's father, Moses Schiff, was a broker for the House of Rothschild. It was common for Jewish families to share housing in those days. Jacob followed in his father's footsteps by immersing himself at the young age of 14 in the Frankfurt banking realm and later becoming a Rothschild broker. This proved advantageous for the Rothschilds who were trying to expand their banking dominance upon the shores of America.

Schiff arrived in New York when he was 18 years old with prescribed tasks from the Rothschilds: 1) gain control of the monetary system for the purpose of establishing a central bank; 2) recruit men who, for a price, are willing to serve as agents of the Rothschilds, then promote them into high places within government; 3) create racial tension especially among blacks and whites; 4) fuel a movement to destroy religion, especially Christianity.[339] Fresh from training at the Rothschild's London Bank, he established himself with Kuhn, Loeb & Co. and had a meteoric rise within the banking institution. He fulfilled the bidding for the Rothschild empire in the United States and carried out his prescribed tasks dutifully.

Jacob Schiff became the purveyor of capitalism and American expansionism. His innovative leadership propelled the United States into becoming an economic powerhouse with few rivals. Ron Chernow, in his biography *The Warburgs* said,

"One observer said of the Schiff era, 'hardly any enterprise of a Jewish philanthropic or educational nature was launched…without first consulting that dominant figure in the leadership of American Jewry.' When the commanding Schiff strode into a charity meeting, a respectful silence fell over the room; he was always first among equals."[340]

In 1913, the same year the Federal Reserve Act was signed, Jacob Schiff established the Anti-Defamation League (ADL). This organization was established to insulate the Rothschild agenda. It's primary method of protectionism for the globalists was to accuse those who challenge the Rothschild agenda as being "anti-Semitic."[341]

The Schiff era, from 1880 to 1920, was so named for the powerful dominance this "titan" had, not only over the economic sector in the United States, but also over international affairs. Schiff despised the Romanov dynasty to the extent he used his influence to thwart the Russian Tsars at every turn. The infamous Kishinev pogrom of April 1903 fueled Schiff's animosity toward the Tsars after angry mobs massacred 45 Jews and injured hundreds more. He boasted to Lord Rothschild in 1904,

"I pride myself that all the efforts, which at various times during the past four or five years have been made by Russia to gain the favor of the American market for its loans. I have been able to bring to naught."[342]

One example is during the Russo-Japanese War, Schiff was instrumental in funding Japanese war bonds. This newly found economic backing strengthened Japan's hand against Russia. Schiff positioned Japan to be a "vessel of divine retribution" for the Russian pogroms.[343] He fomented the seedbed for the Bolshevik Revolution by spreading propaganda among tens of thousands of Russian soldiers who were prisoners of war. Schiff bank-rolled the cost of printing 1.5 tons of Marxist doctrine which was distributed among the Russian prison camps. This insidious plan used mind control to indoctrinate the prisoners and plant seeds of treason deep in their psyche. When the Russo-Japanese War ended and 50,000 Russian prisoners were released to their homeland, seeds of treason spread across Russia.[344] It only took a few sparks to ignite the flames of rebellion. Leon Trotsky was one such spark; a Schiff plant within the tinderbox of Tsarist dissenters. Trotsky was influential in organizing the Bolsheviks, led by leftist revolutionary Vladimir Lenin, who murdered the entire Romanov royalty.

The Bolsheviks would later form the **Reds** (the Edomite calling card), a.k.a., the Communist Party.

If we take a step back to consider the course of history, we see that Jacob Schiff, a Rothschild proxy, was instrumental in ushering in Red Communism, the significance of which cannot be understated. He carried out Nathan Mayer Rothschild's death threat to the Romanov dynasty. Furthermore, Communism is responsible for the deaths of 100 million people in the 20th century alone. This scale of human destruction has not been seen before in history, not even from the brutal forces of the Roman Empire.

"Communism denies the existence of a soul, and its adherents normally punish those that would say otherwise. The brutal brainchild of Karl Marx, the Communist Manifesto, promised utopia on Earth. All one needed to do was overturn society and throw off the ruling class through violent revolution. The road to paradise was red, built on a new social order built by destroying traditional beliefs, social structures, property ownership, and governance." 345 (emphasis mine)

You may be wondering, what does this have to do with the Federal Reserve? Great question, it's always good to keep this question at the forefront of our investigation. Jacob Schiff was one of the main U.S. Rothschild agents at the turn of the century. His influence extended far and wide. He had the power and personality to sway decision makers in multiple areas of society, including the President of the United States, heads of state, business moguls, and other banking elites. Unknown to many, his rudder was maneuvered by the Rothschilds. Jacob Schiff was instrumental in providing a platform for Paul Warburg, such that within eight years of moving to America, Paul would be one of the "six men" on that furtive train to Jekyll Island.

Paul Warburg

The Warburgs were a prominent Jewish banking family from Hamburg, Germany; they were contemporaries of the Rothschilds. Unlike the ghettos of Frankfurt, Hamburg was more tolerant of Jews, which allowed the Warburgs to freely conduct business. They were Court Jews similar to the Rothschilds. The Warburgs and Rothschilds were a microcosm of a larger societal norm during the 18th and 19th centuries. European noblemen were prohibited by the Church to engage in lending money on interest; this was the practice of "sinners." But the economic landscape of Germany, with it's kingdoms, city-states, and principalities, required this type of financial transaction.

Therefore, Court Jews were appointed to conduct money lending. It's important to distinguish that Jews were not innately brilliant with money, instead, their propensity toward money lending was more a factor of a society that funneled them in that direction, primarily because they were banned from other occupations, such as, farming and crafts within the medieval guilds.[346]

Max Warburg, Paul's older brother, was head of the family bank, M. M. Warburg & Co. In 1814, M. M. Warburg & Co. dealt extensively in silver stock which allowed them to intersect with the Rothschilds, who were masters in metals trading. As we know, the Rothschilds had profited immensely from the Napoleonic wars and were considerably wealthier and more influential than the Warburgs. Max so highly valued the relationship forming with the Rothschilds, that he went so far as to hire a gentleman who was exceptionally good at penmanship for the sole purpose of writing important communiques with the Rothschilds. But what proved more advantageous for the Warburgs were providential marriages with Rothschild agents. These unions kept M. M. Warburg & Co. afloat during dicey financial times. Two marriages in particular changed the course of the family business, the marriage of Felix Warburg to Frieda Schiff, Jacob Schiff's daughter, and the marriage of Paul Warburg to Nina Loeb, Solomon Loeb's daughter, of Kuhn, Loeb & Co. Ron Chernow, in *The Warburgs,* captures the importance of these marriages,

"Paul's and Felix's marriages guaranteed that the Warburgs would avoid the great strategic error of the Rothschilds, who had failed to build a major presence on a burgeoning Wall Street…These love matches would prove more beneficial to future Warburg prosperity than the family's shrewdest business calculations. The Warburgs had arrived in America on the eve of its industrial and financial preeminence."[347]

Both Paul and Felix were given positions within the prestigious Kuhn, Loeb & Co. banking institution. Of the two brothers, Paul was the astute banker; a serious and intelligent person not given to frivolity, like his brother Felix. Max leaned on Paul as a partner in M. M. Warburg & Co., so even though Paul's departure for America was difficult for Max, it turned the tide of M. M. Warburg & Co. The Warburg banking house now had a strong presence on two continents. The constant communication between Paul and Max allowed M. M. Warburg & Co. to be one of the few banking houses privy to critical developments within the financial sector of American-European relations. Paul Warburg was not a domineering personality like Jacob Schiff but through his shy, mild mannered persona, he conducted a bloodless revolution…

Rothschild Infiltration into American Banking

Jacob Schiff and Paul Warburg were not the first Rothschild influencers in American banking. We have to go back to the formation of America's first several central banks; there we will find the tentacles of the Rothschilds.

Bank of North America

We begin with America's first chartered banking institution, The Bank of North America. It was chartered in 1781 by the Continental Congress and became a de facto central bank; yes, America had a central bank even before the Constitution was signed. Robert Morris, a member of Congress, was the architect of the Bank of North America. He patterned it after the Bank of England (Nathan Mayer Rothschild was four years old at the time); although the Bank of North America was never given the authority to directly issue the nation's currency, it was given monopoly status, so that virtually no other currency was allowed to circulate.[348] From its origins, the Bank of North America was fraught with deceitful practices. Morris used his political clout to fraudulently maneuver the assets and liabilities of the Bank.

"In a maneuver that was nothing less than legalized embezzlement, he took the gold that had been lent to the United States from France and had it deposited in the Bank. Then, using this as a fractional-reserve base, he simply created the money…and lent it to himself and his associates. Such is the power of the secret science."[349]

By 1783, two years after its inception, the experiment of the first de facto central bank had come to an end, but not without drawing the attention of Alexander Hamilton. Hamilton, a former aide to Robert Morris, closely studied the affairs of the Bank of North America. Hamilton had great respect for Morris' financial prowess and wanted to demonstrate his own intellectual capacity as a financier, so he drafted a 30-page letter in which he argued the raison d'être for a national bank. Hamilton penned,

"A national debt, if it is not excessive, will be to us a national blessing. It will be a powerful cement of our union."[350]

I wonder what constituted "excessive" in the mind of Alexander Hamilton? Would $23.2 trillion be considered "excessive"? The weight of our current national debt is certainly not a blessing, it feels more like being buried alive in "cement."

The period of time between the operation of the Bank of North America and United States of America's first central bank was no insignificant period of time; rather it was a momentous time in our national history. In 1787, the Constitution was signed and ratified by nine states to become the binding law of the land in 1788. The new government under the United States Constitution began on March 4, 1789.[351]

First Bank of the United States

Alexander Hamilton used his letter to Robert Morris to build a base of support with hopes to one day propose the chartering of a central bank. That day came shortly after he was appointed our nation's first Secretary of the Treasury in 1789. Hamilton took on this newfound role with breakneck speed, thrusting his plans for a central bank on the newly formed government.

"Hamilton, wanted the bank to remain predominantly in private hands, advanced a theory that became a truism of central banking- that monetary policy was so liable to abuse that it needed some insulation from interfering politicians: 'To attach full confidence to an institution of this nature, it appears to be an essential ingredient in its structure that it shall be under a *private* not a *public* direction, under the guidance of *individual interest*, not of *public policy*.'"[352]

Hamilton had taken a great liking to the structure of the European central banks and attempted to convince the Congress that the survival of the United States depended upon such a bank. In 1791, less than ten years after the Bank of North America was dissolved, a 20-year charter was granted by Congress; the First Bank of the United States (BUS) was born, but not without a vociferous debate between Alexander Hamilton and Thomas Jefferson. Jefferson strongly opposed Hamilton's proposal for another central bank, stating,

"A private central bank issuing the public currency is a greater menace to the liberties of the people than a standing army. We must not let our rulers load us with perpetual debt."[353]

Hamilton rebutted, "No society could succeed which did not unite the interest and credit of rich individuals with those of the state."[354]

The acrimonious debate over the constitutionality of a central bank continued for a decade. Chief Justice John Marshall contends that the origins of political parties in our country is linked to this dispute.[355] The charter of our nation's first central bank was a defining moment in the burgeoning republic. The structure of the BUS, with 80% of its capital from private investors, of which, foreign investors were not restricted, created an opportunity for the long arm of the Rothschilds to become shareholders. In *History of the Great American Fortunes*, turn of the century American journalist and historian, Gustavus Myers wrote, "Under the surface, the Rothschilds have long had a powerful influence in dictating American financial laws. The law records show that they were powers in the old Bank of the United States. August Belmont and Company were their American representatives."[356]

The repercussions of the First Bank of the United States followed closely Thomas Jefferson's predictions. The U.S. government relied too heavily on the central bank for loans, and by 1796, they were in over their heads to the tune of $6 million. Mayer Amschel Rothschild tightened his grip on American interests by demanding partial payment for the loans. Over the next several years, the government was forced to sell all its shares, liquidating their 20% ownership and effectively, shifting the BUS to a **100% privately owned central bank**.[357] Rothschild was the primary shareholder and conducted the ebb and flow of monetary policy in the United States. In 1811, the charter was set to expire, and Jefferson vehemently opposed its renewal. Stephen Mitford Goodson, in *The History of Central Banking and the Enslavement of Mankind*, describes the practices of the BUS and the vote that denied renewal of its charter.

"The bank was concealing its profits, operating in a clandestine manner and was believed to be unconstitutional...What particularly irked the legislators was the fact that the bank was now 100% in the ownership of foreigners. The press variously described the central bank bill as a 'great swindle,' 'a vulture,' 'a viper,' and 'a cobra.' Furthermore, they contended that it was the constitutional right of Congress to regulate weights and measure and issue coined money. The bill was defeated by a wafer-thin margin of 65 to 64.

When the principal shareholder of the First Bank of the United States, Mayer Amschel Rothschild heard about the deep dissension regarding the renewal of the bank's charter, he flew into a rage and declared that 'either the application for renewal of the charter is granted, or the United States will find itself involved in a most disastrous war.' He also said that 'I will teach those impudent Americans a lesson and bring them back to colonial status.' Rothschild tried to influence the British Prime Minister Spencer

Perceval into declaring war on the United States in order to resurrect his privately-owned central bank."[358]

We see the fingerprints of the Rothschilds all over the First Bank of the United States, especially in its practice of "concealing profits" and "operating in a clandestine manner"; these are hallmark characteristics of the Rothschilds. While it may be harder to prove, it is likely that the War of 1812 was instigated by the Rothschilds. At the conclusion of the war, the United States were victorious in their second war of independence, but not without paying a heavy cost. The war claimed the lives of 15,000 Americans and strapped the country with the hefty burden of $105 million in war debt. Who swooped in for the kill? None other than a Rothschild proxy, Nicholas Biddle.

Second Bank of the United States

Government officials were convinced the only viable solution for the mountain of war debt was the creation of yet another central bank. Congress approved a 20-year charter for the Second Bank of the United States (BUS) on April 10, 1816. Nicholas Biddle was instrumental in the establishment of this second central bank. He was considered the foremost banker of his time; a ruthless master of the science of money.[359] Biddle was a brilliant, arrogant, aristocrat who graduated valedictorian from the College of New Jersey (Princeton) at the age of fifteen. Biddle first crossed paths with the Rothschilds in 1804 when he was conducting government business in Paris, France. His connection with James de Rothschild, the first manager of the Paris House of Rothschild, proved mutually beneficial. James de Rothschild became the primary shareholder in the Second Bank of the United States, and Biddle was appointed as president of the bank. Biddle acted on behalf of the interests of James de Rothschild by expanding and contracting the flow of money for the profit of the bankers.

One such episode of money manipulation was the artificial panic of 1819-21. The Second Bank tightened the money supply so that loans were no longer available. A financial crisis ensued followed by an economic depression. Of course, this was by design, it created the perfect condition for the Rothschilds to do what they always do after they create financial havoc... swoop in for the kill. The Rothschilds purchased vast amounts of assets at rock bottom prices.[360] The ruthlessness of these bankers to profit off the destruction of people's livelihoods is despicable; businesses went under, farmers were forced into foreclosure, and many people lost their life savings. The public sentiment toward central banks became increasingly negative and Andrew

Jackson was convinced that the only way to avoid these types of financial crises was to get rid of the Second Bank.

In 1828, Andrew Jackson ran for president with slogans like "the monster must perish" and "Jackson and No Bank." Andrew Jackson was the "people's President." He ran on the doctrine of minimal government and the necessity for reform. Previous administrations had expanded governmental reach leading to rabid political ideologies; corruption spread to every corner of government with the BUS as one of the biggest offenders. Jackson saw the evils of the central banking system. He had the tenacity and conviction to go head to head with the Rothschild banking empire. Jackson proclaimed to the Rothschild cabal, "You are a den of vipers. I intend to expose you and by Eternal God I will rout you out. If the people understood the rank injustices of our money and banking system, there would be a revolution before morning."[361]

When Nicholas Biddle forced the issue of re-charter four years before the BUS was set to expire, it emboldened Jackson to annihilate the monetary beast. In 1832, the bill to re-charter the BUS narrowly passed in the Senate, but convincingly passed in the House. Now it was up to Jackson to decide the fate of the BUS. Jackson vetoed the bill. He drove a stake through the heart of the monster, with this explanation for his veto,

"The Act seems to be predicated on an erroneous idea that the present shareholders have a prescriptive right to not only the favor, but the bounty of the government…for their benefit does this Act exclude the whole American people from competition in the purchase of this monopoly. Present stockholders and those inheriting their rights as successors be established a privileged order, clothed both with great political power and enjoying immense pecuniary advantages from their connection with government. Should its influence be concentrated under the operation of such an Act as this, in the hands of a self-elected directory whose interests are identified with those of the foreign stockholders, will there not be cause to tremble for the independence of our country in war…controlling our currency, receiving our public monies and holding thousands of our citizens independence, it would be more formidable and dangerous than the naval and military power of the enemy. It is to be regretted that the rich and powerful too often bend the acts of government for selfish purposes…to make the rich richer and more powerful. Many of our rich men have not been content with equal protection and equal benefits but have besought us to make them richer by acts of Congress. I have done my duty to this country."[362]

For this resolute act, President Jackson was rewarded with a resounding victory in his run for a second term; clearly the American sentiment was behind him. In his second term, Jackson orchestrated the eradication of the national debt, a Herculean feat, no doubt. Robert Remini, biographer and author of *The Life of Andrew Jackson*, records the attitude of the nation on January, 1835 as it was captured at a gala of "extraordinary magnificence" celebrating the nation's freedom from debt.

"It was a glittering affair, but President Jackson declined to attend. The purpose of the occasion was to celebrate a historic moment and he did not wish to subvert it by his presence. He wanted no personal glorification. It was far more important that the nation celebrate its deliverance from 'economic bondage.' In that, and that alone, Andrew Jackson would have all the satisfaction and honor he needed... 'This month of January, 1835,' Benton continued, 'in the fifty-eighth year of the Republic, ANDREW JACKSON being President, the NATIONAL DEBT is PAID! and the apparition, so long unseen on earth, a great nation without a national debt stands revealed to the astonished vision of a wondering world!'"[363]

The freedom from the heavy burden of debt and the impending closure of the BUS, earned Jackson a hero status from the majority of Americans. How did James de Rothschild respond? He hired a mentally unstable stooge to attempt to assassinate President Jackson.[364] Miraculously, the assassin's pistols misfired. But Jackson would not be the only President to have his life threatened by the "powers that be" for daring to defy their monetary monopolistic rule. At this point in our investigation, the Rothschilds have become the primary suspects for being the masterminds behind central banking, the system which has ushered in the death of the American dream and the enslavement of humanity. How did we arrive at this? Let's review the trail of clues (see Figure 40).

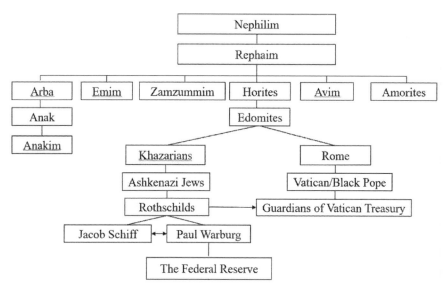

Figure 40. Trail of the Edomites. Created by Laura Sanger

Key Points

- Rothschilds are a powerful banking dynasty who dominate economic policies in 85% of the countries of the worldwide through their central banking system.
- Rothschild means "red shield" in German. A red hexagram marked the Rothschild home in Frankfurt, Germany.
- Red is a calling card for the Edomites and possibly Nephilim Hosts.
- Rothschilds are Ashkenazi Jews and most likely descendants of Khazars.
- Rothschilds are the "guardians" of the Vatican treasury.
- Rothschilds are globalists who fund both sides of war to enslave citizens in debt.
- Mayer Rothschild orchestrated the creation of a secret society called the Illuminati.
- Modus operandi of Rothschilds: 1) use unscrupulous tactics to usurp the authority of heads of state, 2) gain control of a country's money supply to gain control of the country, 3) conceal profits, 4) use of clandestine transactions, 5) exact revenge upon national leaders who reject their control, 6) form a world government to subjugate the citizens of the world to Rothschild dominance.
- Rothschilds have infiltrated the U.S. monetary system through central banking.
- Jacob Schiff and Paul Warburg were the most influential Rothschild agents in American banking.

Chapter 19

Hidden Agenda of Zionism

If an offence comes out of Truth, better it is that the offence comes
than that the Truth be concealed.
~ St. Jerome

To round out our investigation, as well as, close the loop on clues that we gathered in Chapter 16 (Edomites → Khazarians → Ashkenazi Jews → Zionists), we need to peer into the origins of Zionism and examine the Zionist agenda to see if it can be found within the fabric of the Federal Reserve. At the outset, I want to acknowledge that Zionism is a topic which stirs passionate debates among just about everyone, and especially between biblical scholars, rabbis, Messianic Jews, Christians, Orthodox Jews, Zionists, and historians. The complexities of Zionism seem innumerable, so we must narrow our scope to only that which will further our investigation. Hence, we will focus on the origins of Zionism, the Zionist agenda, the Rothschilds influence upon Zionism, and the Talmudic precepts related to banking.

Origins of Zionism

Nathan Birnbaum, one of the first Zionist intellectuals, coined the term "Zionism" in 1890.[365] Generally speaking, Zionism refers to a national movement marked by 'aliyah,' the return of the Jewish people to the Land of Israel, and for Jewish sovereignty through the creation of a nation state.

Birnbaum was influential in the early foundation of Zionism. His life was marked by three distinct phases. The first phase was one of political Zionism, in which his ideologies closely resembled those of Theodor Herzl (whom most consider to be the "Father of Zionism"). It was during this phase that Birnhaum served as Secretary

General of the First Zionist Congress in 1897. The second phase of his life was characterized by a Jewish cultural emphasis in which he strongly advocated for the autonomy of the Jewish culture and the rise in prominence of the Yiddish language. In the final phase of Birnhaum's life, he became a devout orthodox Jew, which led him to reject Zionism. It was in his later years that he became acutely aware of the differences between Zionism and Judaism. Birnhaum purported that "Jewish authenticity" could only be found in the adherence and practice of the devout Jewish faith.[366]

A foundational pillar of Zionism was the restoration of the Jewish State. The basic problem that Zionism tried to solve, simply stated by Herzl, was "the misery of the Jews." Herzl penned a work called *The Jewish State* in which he laid out the premise of Zionism.

"It is useless, therefore, for us to be loyal patriots... If we could only be left in peace…But I think we shall not be left in peace. Oppression and persecution cannot exterminate us. No nation on earth has survived such struggles and sufferings as we have gone through… The infiltration of immigrating Jews, attracted to a land by apparent security, and the ascent in the social scale of native Jews, combine powerfully to bring about a revolution. Nothing is plainer than this rational conclusion… I shall now put the Question in the briefest possible form: Are we to "get out" now and where to? Or, may we yet remain? And, how long?"[367]

Herzel proposed that the creation of a State for the Jewish people would allow those Jews who wished to assimilate in their host nations to do so in peace, as the greater portion of Jews would leave. With this mass departure, Herzl believed that anti-Semitism would end, because any remaining Jews would be so thoroughly assimilated in their host nations, that the citizenry would have no use for slogans such as "Don't buy from the Jews" and "Out with the Jews." History proves that his convictions regarding anti-Semitism were short-sighted. He underestimated the intensity of anti-Semitism and who benefits from it.

As Zionism gained momentum, its political agenda strengthened and, dare I say, overpowered the religious undertones. Shlomo Sand, in *The Invention of the Jewish People*, articulated the underbelly of Zionism.

"Zionism from its inception was an ethnocentric nationalist movement that firmly enclosed the historical people of its own invention and barred any voluntary civil entry into the nation its platform began to design. At the same time, any withdrawal from the "people" was depicted as an unforgivable offense, and "assimilation" as a catastrophe, an existential danger to be averted at all costs. No wonder, then, that to bind together the frangible secular Jewish identity, it was not enough to write a history of the Jews, so culturally disparate, so chronologically fragmentary. Zionism had to resort to another scientific discipline, that of biology—which was conscripted to reinforce the foundation of the "ancient Jewish nation."[368]

As Sand aptly described, Zionism was conceived in nationalism, and as we will discover, blossomed into a full-blown political agenda. Henry Morgenthau Sr., a prominent American Jew born in Germany, who served as head of President Woodrow Wilson's Committee on the pogroms of Poland, condemned Zionism.

"Zionism is the most stupendous fallacy in Jewish history…Where it is not pathetically visionary, it is a cruel playing with the hopes of a people blindly seeking their way out of age-long miseries.

The very fervor of my feeling for the oppressed of every race and every land, especially for the Jews, those of my own blood and faith, to whom I am bound by every tender tie, impels me to fight with all the greater force against this scheme, which…can only lead them deeper into the mire of the past, while it professes to be leading them to the heights.

Zionism is a surrender, not a solution. It is a retrogression into the blackest error, and not progress toward the light. I will go further, and say that it is a betrayal; it is an eastern European proposal, fathered in this country by American Jews, which, if it were to succeed, would cost the Jews of America most that they have gained of liberty, equality, and fraternity."[369]

Even though Zionism experienced a tide of resistance prior to 1948, its proponents worked incessantly toward fulfilling the strategy. Since its inception, there have been many offshoots of Zionism such as "Religious Zionism" and "Christian Zionism," which have caused great confusion among people of faith. Religious Zionism has the basic premise that the establishment of the State of Israel for the Jewish people hastens the return of the Messiah. It promotes the fusion of Jewish nationalism with the resurgence of Jewish religious practices. Christian Zionism is the belief that the establishment of the State of Israel as the homeland for the Jews, fulfills Bible prophecy. ChristianZionism.org, an opponent of Christian Zionism, summarizes the movement this way: "Christian Zionists believe that modern Israel is a continuation of the Biblical Israel and therefore should enjoy special privileges. They declare that it is the responsibility of Christians to support the State of Israel and its policies."[370]

Is this a fair assessment? Here is how Reverend Malcolm Hedding, a spokesperson for International Christian Embassy Jerusalem (ICEJ), summarizes Christian Zionism, "Christian Zionism teaches from the scriptures that God's covenant with Abraham is still valid today. There remains a national destiny over the Jewish people and her national homeland is her everlasting possession in fulfillment of God's plans and purposes for her. The New Testament scriptures not only affirm the Abrahamic covenant, but they confirm the historical mission of Israel and that Israel's gifts and calling are irrevocable.

Thus, Christian Zionism is not based on prophecy or end-time events. Most Christian Zionists would agree, however, that Israel's reemergence on the world's scene, in fulfillment of God's promises to her, indicate that other biblically-predicted events will follow."[371]

One thing that is undeniable is the intensity of the debate when it comes to Israel. For anyone who has been caught in the crosshairs of the Zionism debate, you know exactly what I mean. It brings out a viciousness in people that, otherwise, are mild mannered individuals. At the core of the issue is a passionate belief in the rights of a people group and their right to occupy a homeland, whether they be Palestinian or Israeli. It can be stated with almost certainty that the Jewish people have been the most persecuted people group in history, so polemics is not an uncommon reality for the Jews. But does this give the Zionists license to occupy land that, in our modern era, rightfully belonged to the Palestinians?

While I don't enjoy being in the crosshairs, I will share some of my thoughts regarding the State of Israel, so you are not left wondering.

I believe both the land of Israel and the people of Israel have a redemptive purpose in God's kingdom. There is a remnant in Israel that are God-fearing, Messianic believers (Romans 9:27). As Gentile believers, we have been grafted in to the olive tree (Romans 11:17-21) and our salvation is meant to create envy for the people of Israel, so that one day they will step into the fullness of relationship with the Messiah, Jesus Christ (Romans 11:11-12).

I believe the United States of America also has a redemptive purpose (as does each nation), despite the fact that a great number of our Founding Fathers were Freemasons.

Similarly, even though a great number of Zionists, instrumental in the formation of the State of Israel, inserted wicked schemes in its foundation, this does not negate the redemptive purposes of God for Israel.

Psalm 33:10-11 (NIV) *"The Lord foils the plans of the nations; he thwarts the purposes of the peoples. But the plans of the Lord stand firm forever, the purposes of his heart through all generations."*

While the majority of Zionists were not God-fearing people and even outwardly displayed fruits of wickedness in their hearts (we will dig into this shortly), I believe one day there will be a turning back because God's call upon Israel is irrevocable!

Romans 11:25-29 (NIV) *"I do not want you to be ignorant of this mystery, brothers and sisters, so that you may not be conceited: Israel has experienced a hardening in part until the full number of the Gentiles has come in, and in this way all Israel will be saved. As it is written: 'The deliverer will come from Zion; he will turn godlessness away from Jacob. And this is my covenant with them when I take away their sins.' As far as the gospel is concerned, they are enemies for your sake; but as far as election is concerned, they are loved on account of the patriarchs, **for God's gifts and his call are irrevocable.**"* (emphasis mine)

Jesus is the mediator of the New Covenant and came to fulfill the Old Covenant. The New Covenant does not cancel the Old Covenant, but rather enlarges its tent pegs. God still loves the land of Israel and the children of Israel; they have not been rejected or replaced under the New Covenant. Instead, the enlargement of the New Covenant means that all races are welcome to be called children of Abraham through faith in Jesus, who is the rightful heir of Abraham – the MESSIAH. All nations have a redemptive purpose within the Kingdom of God. I don't believe that Israel has special privileges or gets a pass on upholding the principles of the Kingdom of God.

The Zionist agenda has propagated atrocities toward the Palestinians that are undeniable, but the same can be said of the Palestinians. I do not presume to know the answer to this geopolitical crisis, nor do I presume to know whether the creation of the modern State of Israel is, in fact, fulfillment of biblical prophecy. As I examine the fruit (or the fallout), I see carnage on both sides. I consider the possibility that Zionists took it upon themselves to create the State of Israel by force and manipulation, instead of letting the God of Israel regather His people in the land of Zion. Sometimes we can force prophetic fulfillment in appearance only, while the heart of the prophecy is subverted. Is this such an instance?

Zionist Agenda

Of utmost importance is to understand that all Jews are not Zionists. Furthermore, not all Jews living in Israel are Zionists. We cannot hold Jewish people, as a whole, responsible for the Zionist agenda. In fact, the Jews unbeknownst to them, have been pawns in the Zionists' master plan. It is true that most Zionists are Jews, but this harkens back to our discussion about the true identity of the Jews. The Zionists are not fond of the Khazarian hypothesis as an explanation for the origin of Eastern European Jews; it violates the foundational premise of Zionism—**Israel belongs to the Jews**.

The agenda of Zionism is convoluted because there are many layers to it. I liken it to secret societies such as, Freemasonry. On the surface, Zionism is a nationalistic movement characterized by the slogan, "a land without a people for people without a land," but beneath this layer of public awareness, lies an insidious agenda for global domination by the Zionist elites. This agenda can only be unveiled through meticulous research coupled with discloser from insiders who are privy to this plot, as well as, a close examination of symbols. Afterall, we have discovered through our investigation thus far that a key which unlocks mysteries, things hidden in darkness, is scrutiny…particularly scrutiny of occult symbolism.

Star of David

At this juncture, we are compelled to research the "Star of David" (see Figure 41) to understand how it became the prominent symbol for Jewish solidarity. This hexagram is also known as the "six-pointed star," "Shield of David," or the "Seal of Solomon." The word "hex" means to practice witchcraft or place an evil spell on someone,[372] it is the base word for hexagram. This is our first clue that this symbol is not what we think it is.

The Star of David was found on the front cover of the Leningrad Codex, the oldest complete copy of the Hebrew Bible dated to 1008 A.D. (see Figure 42). This suggests that the six-pointed star had some level of significance in 2nd century Judaism. The Talmud speaks of the Seal of Solomon as an in-signet ring given to Solomon by God for the subjugation of demons. Solomon used this ring to exploit demons to labor on the construction of the temple.[373] But are there any historical references to the six-pointed star that can be attributed to King David? It seems that a stronger case can be made that there is no connection between the Shield of David and King David himself. David declared in several of the Psalms that God is His shield (Psalm 28:7, Psalm 119:114, Psalm 144:2).

Figure 41. Flag of Israel. Photo by Zachi Evenor, CC by 4.0 https://commons.wikimedia.org/wiki/File:Flag-of-Israel-01sq-Zachi-Evenor.jpg

Figure 42. Leningrad Codex https://en.wikipedia.org/wiki/Leningrad_Codex -/media/File:Leningrad_Codex_Carpet_page_e.jpg

Psalm 3:3 (NIV) *"But you, Lord, are a shield around me, my glory, the One who lifts my head high."*

Gershom Scholem, a Jewish mysticism scholar, in his 1949 essay entitled *"The Curious History of the Six-Pointed Star"* states,

"Actually, the six-pointed star is not a Jewish symbol; *a fortiori* it could not be "the symbol of Judaism." It has none of the criteria that mark the nature and development of the true symbol. It does not express any 'idea,' it does not arouse ancient associations rooted in our experiences, and it is not a shorthand representation of an entire spiritual reality, understood immediately by the observer. It does not remind us of anything in Biblical or in rabbinic Judaism. Indeed, until the middle of the 19th century, it did not occur to any scholar or Cabalist to inquire into the secret of its Jewish meaning, and it is not mentioned in the books of the devout or in all of Hasidic literature."[374]

This begs the question… if it is not a Jewish symbol originating from King David, where did it come from?

O.J. Graham, a journalist and theologian, suggests that the origins of the six-pointed star are found in ancient Egypt during the time of the exodus. He points to Amos 5:25-26 and Acts 7:37-43 as biblical references to the six-pointed star.

Amos 5:25-26 (KJ21) *"Have ye offered unto Me sacrifices and offerings in the wilderness forty years, O house of Israel? But ye have borne the tabernacle of your Moloch and Chiun your images, the star of your god which ye made for yourselves."*

Acts 7:43 (KJ21) *"Yea, ye took up the tabernacle of Moloch and the star of your god Remphan, images which ye made to worship them. And I will carry you away beyond Babylon."*

While, these passages don't necessarily specify a six-pointed star, it does suggest that the Israelites worshiped the star of the god Chiun/Remphan. Chiun is the Hebrew translation and Remphan is the Greek translation of Set (Egyptian god), a.k.a. Moloch (Canaanite god), a.k.a Saturn (Roman god), a.k.a. Kronos (Greek Titan). In other words, these passages demonstrate that the Israelites created a symbol representing Saturn. According to Matthew Henry, the Israelites carried with them "pocket-idols" of Chiun, representing Saturn, the highest of the planets.[375] Could this pocket idol have been a six-pointed star?

Let's consider some attributes of Saturn (some of which we know thanks to modern technology); it's the 6th planet from the sun; the north pole of Saturn forms a hexagon, the shape inside a six-pointed star; and Saturday is the 6th day of the week, named in honor of Saturn. In *The Two Babylons,* Alexander Hislop writes, "Rhea or Cybele… was the female counterpart of the…deity [that] was Ninus, or Nimrod, we have still further evidence from what the scattered notices of antiquity say of the first deified king of Babylon, under a name that identifies him as the husband of Rhea…That name is Kronos or Saturn."[376]

I guess we shouldn't be surprised that the origin of the six-pointed star can be connected to Nimrod. Just as all roads led to Rome and all financial roads lead to the House of Rothschild, all occultic roads lead to Nimrod. Kronos and Saturn were worshiped as representations of the deified Nimrod. This false deity was worshiped through cannibalism, sexual orgies, and human sacrifice. Sounds familiar doesn't it? Once again, we see the criteria for classification as a Nephilim Host in these acts of false worship. This further reveals the agenda of the Nephilim throughout the ages; these dark lords seek to lure worshipers into a trap to use them as a host to do their bidding. Graham traced the progression of this occult symbol in his book *The Six-Pointed Star,*

"the six-pointed star made its way from Egyptian pagan rituals of worship, to the goddess Ashteroth and Moloch, to King Solomon when he went into idolatry. Then it progressed through the magic arts, witchcraft, astrology, through Cabala to Isaac Luria, a Cabalist, in the 16th century, to Mayer Amschel Bauer, who changed his name to this symbol, to Zionism, to the Knesset of the new State of Israel, to the flag of Israel and its medical organization equivalent to the Red Cross."[377]

The Masonic Dictionary defines the Seal of Solomon as follows: "The Seal of Solomon or the Shield of David, for under both names the same thing was denoted, is a hexagonal figure consisting of two interlaced triangles, thus forming the outlines of six-pointed star. Upon it was inscribed one of the sacred names of God, from which inscription it was opposed principally to derive its talismanic powers.

These powers were very extensive, for it was believed that it would extinguish fire, prevent Wounds in conflict, and perform many other wonders. The Jews called it the Shield of David in reference to the protection which it gave to its Possessors."[378]

Now that we are armed with a greater understanding of the occultic, pagan origins of the Star of David emblazoned on the Israeli Flag, and its ties to the Rothschilds, we are ready to peer further into the dealings of the Rothschilds with regard to the establishment of the State of Israel.

Rothschild Influence of Zionism

At first, the Rothschilds were not unified in their support of Zionism. The privileges they were afforded living as Jews in their respective countries did not make the premise behind Zionism very appealing. Why would the Rothschilds forfeit the control they held in each of the nations in which they lived, to make 'aliyah' to a land in Palestine? Another deterrent was that the Rothschilds were not fond of Theodor Herzl. After Herzl passed away and Chaim Weizmann led the charge for Zionism, the benefits became clearer to the Rothschilds. The primary benefactors of Zionism were Edmond de Rothschild, Dorothea de Rothschild, and Lionel Walter Rothschild.

Baron Edmond de Rothschild, born in 1845, was the youngest son of James de Rothschild. He earned the nickname, "The Benefactor" and "The Father of Israel," primarily for his commitment to establishing settlements for the Jewish people in Palestine. He became a strong supporter of Zionism and one of the largest financiers of the movement. However, his initial plans of developing settlements in Palestine for Jewish immigrants fleeing persecution, should not be mistaken for Zionism. His efforts were primarily in response to the Russian pogroms of the 1880s. In 1882, Edmond set up the first Jewish colony in Palestine, Rishon le Zion.[379] Harvard Professor and historian, Niall Ferguson describes the authoritarian basis upon which Edmond established this colony, "Every new settler at Rishon le Zion had to sign an agreement 'to submit myself totally to the order which the administration shall think necessary in the name of M. le Baron in anything concerning the cultivation of the land and its service and if any action should be taken against me I have no right to oppose it'…every detail supervised by the Baron's 'officials.' Although he insisted all along that he was engaged not in a philanthropy but in creating economically self-sustaining settlements, Edmond's highly paternalistic approach inevitably generated what would now be called a 'dependency culture.'"[380]

It's not surprising that Edmond de Rothschild took a controlling and oppressive approach to establishing the Jewish colonies. The agreement subjected the new settlers to be contractually bound to limited uses of the land. If they altered from what Edmond deemed viable, there were repercussions without recourse. Essentially, it was his way or the highway! Edmond de Rothschild continued his colonization effort for decades.

In 1896, Theodor Herzl published *Der Judenstaat*, arguably the most important document of Zionism. In it, Herzl proposed that the solution for the great Jewish problem of persecution was a State unto their own. Herzl presented his proposal to the House of Rothschild in hopes of securing the financial backing for Zionism, but Edmond rejected the plan. Edmond found Herzl's plan contrary to his own plan for colonization. Edmond had encouraged the Jewish settlers to assimilate into the

Ottoman Empire, as was the pattern for the Rothschilds, instead of establishing a nation state which was Herzl's plan.

In 1906, the Sursock House, an aristocratic Greek Orthodox family from Lebanon, began selling their land holdings in the Jezreel Valley to Baron Edmond de Rothschild's Jewish National Fund. The Sursocks had acquired the land from the Ottoman Empire in 1872 when it was on the verge of bankruptcy. The Sursocks had been absentee landlords for the entirety of their ownership. They owned more than 90,000 acres in the region.

Edmond de Rothschild gradually increased his land purchases to expand the Jewish settlements. After the death of Herzl, Chaim Weizmann led the charge for Zionism. He was considerably more charming and charismatic than his predecessor; Herzl was prone to hostility when his Zionist plans were rejected. Weizmann, on the other hand, established a connection with Dorothea de Rothschild, who was in her teens at the time. She was deeply devoted to the idea of a homeland for the Jewish people. Her contributions to Zionism were critical in that she provided the pathway for Weizmann to establish relations with influential British political leaders, such as, Lord Balfour. Dorothea had prepared Chaim to assimilate into the highest echelons of British society in order to further the cause of Zionism. Her assistance proved invaluable as Chaim was able to persuade Lord Balfour of the importance of establishing a Jewish homeland.[381] He was not only able to skillfully insert himself within the British establishment, Chaim was also able to secure the financial backing of the House of Rothschild, as well as, the Warburg banking family.

As we revealed in the previous chapter, it was common practice for the House of Rothschild to fund both sides of a war. World War I was no different. At this juncture, we must turn once again to the testimony of Benjamin Freedman to uncover a Zionist agenda that operated behind the scenes with regards to WWI.

"World War I broke out in the summer of 1914…war was waged on one side by Great Britain, France and Russia; and on the other side by Germany, Austria-Hungary, and Turkey. Within two years Germany had won that war: not only won it nominally but won it actually. The German submarines, which were a surprise to the world, had swept all the convoys form the Atlantic Ocean. Great Britain stood there without ammunition for her soldiers, with one week's food supply – and after that, starvation. At that time the French army had mutinied. They had lost 600,000 of the flower of French youth…Not a shot had been fired on German soil. Not one enemy soldier had crossed the border into Germany. And yet, Germany was offering England peace terms… 'Let's call the war off and let everything be as it was before the war started.' England…had no choice. It was either accepting this negotiated peace that Germany was magnanimously offering them or going on with the war and being totally defeated.

While that was going on, the Zionists in Germany, who represented the Zionists from Eastern Europe, went to the British War Cabinet and…said: 'Look here. You can yet win this war. You don't have to give up. You don't have to accept the negotiated peace offered…You can win this war if the United States will come in as your ally…We will guarantee to bring the United States into the war as your ally, to fight with you on your side, if you will promise us Palestine after you win the war."[382]

Freedman provides us with a critical testimony from his attendance at the Paris Peace Conference; a perspective we find wanting in our history books. It was the Zionist Jews from Germany who devised a plan to defeat Germany. Is it no wonder a few decades later, Hitler was able to foment heinous acts toward German Jews? Once the United States had entered the war in April of 1917, the British drafted a letter of receipt for the agreement reached with the Zionists. According to Benjamin Freedman, the receipt had cryptic language in it to hide what had transpired behind the scenes. This receipt became the British mandate known as the Balfour Declaration (see Figure 43). It was addressed to Lord Lionel Walter Rothschild, who was considered the unofficial leader of the British Jewish community.

At the Paris Peace Conference, Lord Walter Rothschild submitted a proposal on February 3, 1919 on behalf of the Zionist Organization to advance the establishment of a Jewish homeland within Palestine. The proposal asserted the historic rights of the Jews to Palestine as recognized by the British government in its Declaration from Lord Balfour.[383] The Balfour Declaration changed the course of history for the Jewish people. It paved the way for Edmond de Rothschild to purchase the majority of the Sursock's land by 1926.[384] The Arab farmers who had been tenants on the land were understandably distressed by the sale of the land. The Jezreel Valley was considered to be the most fertile parcel in Palestine; this land grab by the Baron led to nearly a century of displacement for the Palestinians. Herein lies the origin of the hotly debated issue among the Palestinians and Israelis – who does the land belong to?

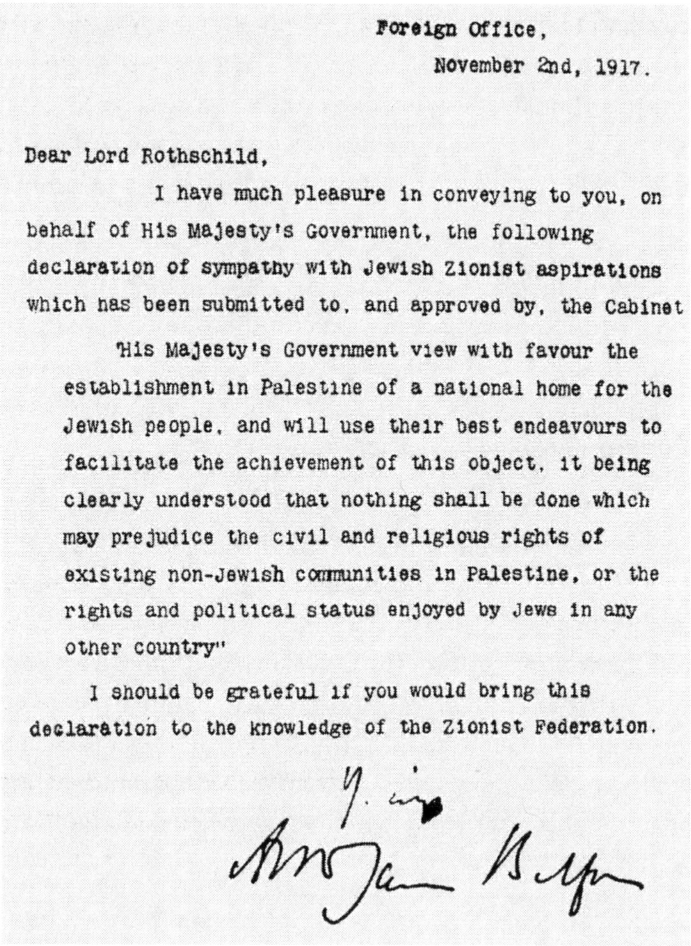

Figure 43. Balfour Declaration.
https://commons.wikimedia.org/wiki/File:Balfour_declaration_unmarked.jpg

In total, the Baron spent $100 million in land purchases and development; he built hospitals, schools and factories. Edmond's contributions to Zionism were so significant that after his death, his remains were transported to Israel for a state funeral led by former Prime Minister David Ben-Gurion. To further honor Baron Edmond de Rothschild, a street in Tel Aviv was named after him, as well as parks and other locations he helped finance.

The Rothschilds have been intricately involved in Zionism and the formation of the State of Israel. Their tentacles reach into the very heart of Israel. We must ask ourselves a series of questions, but before we do, brace yourself, these questions may cause a jolt. Given what we have just uncovered, can we unequivocally conclude it was the Lord's hand that established the State of Israel in 1948? Is the establishment of Israel a fulfillment of biblical prophecy? Is Israel the personal fiefdom for the Rothschilds? Did the Zionists establish Israel to one day become the central power for the New World Order (NWO)? Do Zionists dominate the global banking industry and shape the monetary policies of nations?

I'm guessing these questions triggered an array of emotions for you that may include anger, dismay, indignance, confusion, and/or denial. Some of you may want to throw this book across the room because these questions just trespassed into an area that you have held as a sacred place, you know, those areas in your mind that have been deemed "off limits." But before you walk off this investigation, let me be clear, NOT ALL JEWS ARE ZIONISTS. Consider this perspective held by True Torah Jews.

"Zionism, by advocating a political and military end to the Jewish exile, denies the very essence of our Diaspora existence. We are in exile by Divine Decree and may emerge from exile solely via Divine Redemption. All human efforts to alter a metaphysical reality are doomed to end in failure and bloodshed...Zionism has not only denied our fundamental belief in Heavenly Redemption it has also created a pseudo-Judaism which views the essence of our identity to be a secular nationalism. Accordingly, Zionism and the Israeli state have consistently endeavored, via persuasion and coercion, to replace a Divine and Torah-centered understanding of our peoplehood with an armed materialism."[385]

I also want to be clear that even though most Zionists are Jews, it does not mean that every Zionist understands the hidden agenda of Zionism. It is imperative that we understand this, so we don't falsely assume devious motives for everyone who identifies as a Zionist. Secret societies, occult organizations, and the cabal (global elites) are all structured similarly—a circle within a circle (the circumpunct). Knowledge and understanding are gradually doled out as a person proves him/herself worthy of such knowledge. Initiates who comprise the outer circles are largely unaware of the "knowledge" and "wisdom" held by those in the inner circle. In other words, the puppet masters do not inform the puppets of their role in the strategy for global domination. I want to be crystal clear on this point, so no one is misled to think I am implying that all Zionists are wicked, evil people. There are many wonderful individuals who identify themselves as Zionists and don't operate under a satanic structure. Our investigation is focused on the masterminds behind the Federal Reserve, so when I use the phrase 'Zionist,' I am referring to the global elites, the Zionists within the inner circle. Now that we have that cleared up, I leave you with the aforementioned questions to ponder as we continue our journey. These are the type of questions that can be paradigm shifting, so they are questions for you to wrestle with. I don't want to answer these questions for you. Once we have gathered all the evidence, you will need to decide how you interpret the evidence so as to answer these questions.

One last aspect of Zionism we must consider before moving on is how the Talmud has shaped Zionism.

Intersection of Talmudism and Zionism

I want to revisit an important set of connections we discovered in Chapter 16:

$$\text{Pharisaism} \rightarrow \text{Talmudism} \rightarrow \text{modern Rabbinism} \rightarrow \text{Judaism}$$

The Talmud is the esteemed work of Judaism; it inspires the highest level of sacred study in Judaism. For those who are not Jewish, the Talmud can provide historical insight into early century Judaism; it can be a source of inspiration for daily living; it can be a fountain of wisdom for those that drink from it; but there are portions that can also be quite disconcerting. Often times, it is misinterpreted and therefore, misunderstood.

Within the Talmud, lie some critical clues for our investigation. We will examine the Talmud more closely, especially those tractates related to banking. First, we find an interesting clue in the 1906 Jewish Encyclopedia, "The first complete edition of the Babylonian Talmud was printed at Venice, 1520-23 by Daniel Bomberg, and has become the basis, down to the present day, of a very large number of editions, including... the edition of **Frankfort-on-the-Main**, 1720-22, with its additions, became the model of all subsequent editions of the Talmud."[386] (emphasis mine)

You may recall from Chapter 18, that the Rothschilds and Schiffs were from Frankfort-on-the-Main. The Jewish section known as the Judangasse ("Jews' lane") was 330 meters long (about ¼ mile), 3-4 meters wide and had three gates into the town.[387] The gates were locked at night, on Sunday and on Christian holidays. The Jews lived in tight quarters with houses built right next to each other. As the Jewish population increased, it was common for families to share houses. It is likely that the Rothschilds and Schiffs were deeply influenced by the Babylonian Talmud given the importance of the Frankfort-on-the-Main edition. Furthermore, many of the residents of the Judengasse were money lenders and/or money changers. In addition to the Rothschilds and Schiffs, the Oppenheimers and Kanns were residents of the Judengasse. Moses Kann was a court Jew and belonged to one of the most influential Jewish families in Frankfurt. At their zenith, the Kanns were by far the wealthiest Jews in Frankfurt. Moses was not only a money lender, but also an expert of the Talmud. We can presume that these influential Jewish banking families of the 18th century were deeply influenced by the Frankfort-on-the-Main Talmud edition. This precipitates a closer examination of the possible Talmudic underpinnings within the burgeoning European banking houses.

Talmudic View of Gentiles (and Christians)

Of utmost importance is to first understand what the Talmud teaches with regard to the Gentiles or 'goyim.' As we have discussed, the core issue of the conflict between the Palestinians and the Israelis is the question of who does the land belong to? The Talmud has shaped Zionism by instructing the Jews that the property of the heathen, Akum, Gentile, or goy (synonyms for any non-Jewish person including Christians) is up for grabs.

Baba Bathra 54b "Rab Judah said in the name of Samuel: The property of a heathen is on the same footing as desert land; whoever first occupies it acquires ownership."[388]

Baba Kamma 113b "R. Ashi was once walking on the road when he noticed branches of vines outside a vineyard upon which ripe clusters of grapes were hanging. He said to his attendant: 'Go and see, if they belong to a heathen bring them to me, but if to an Israelite do not bring them to me.'"[389]

Coschen Hamm (266, 1) "A Jew may keep anything he finds which belongs to the Akum, for it is written: Return to thy brethren what is lost (Deuter. XXII, 3). For he who returns lost property [to Christians] sins against the Law by increasing the power of the transgressors of the Law. It is praiseworthy, however, to return lost property if it is done to honor the name of God, namely, if by so doing Christians will praise the Jews and look upon them as honorable people."[390]

To be fair to the Talmud, these are but a few examples within 63 volumes of text. Just as with the Torah or the Bible, the reader can interpret the text to condone nefarious acts or the reader can interpret the text with a desire to honor the Lord with their actions. Given what we know of the character of the Rothschilds, it isn't too big of a stretch to consider that the Talmud may have provided justification for their sense of entitlement to become oppressors.

Jewish critics of Talmudic preeminence are few and far between, but there are at least two Jewish religious movements who assert the Torah's authority over the Oral Law, they are Karaite Jews and Talmidis. Aside from these groups, mainline Judaism reveres the Talmud above the Torah. In essence, this elevates the word of rabbis above the Word of God, a dangerous position to take. We are reminded that the Talmud is a collection of Pharisaical teachings and we know how Jesus felt about the Pharisees.

Matthew 23:27 (TPT) *"Great sorrow awaits you religious scholars and Pharisees-frauds and imposters! You are nothing more than tombs painted with fresh coats of white paint – tombs that look shining and beautiful on the outside, but within are found decaying corpses full of nothing but corruption. Outwardly you masquerade as righteous people, but inside your hearts you are full of hypocrisy and lawlessness."*

The Pharisees and the religious scholars led many astray, but Jesus was able to see through their façade and called a spade, a spade. But how do we avoid being hoodwinked by the Talmud, if it's nearly impossible for a lay person to read and understand? There are countless Jews in Israel that haven't studied the Talmud, and yet it shapes their ideologies. I believe we have to rely on reputable people who were once insiders; those who extracted themselves after being greatly repulsed by what they saw. Just like with any secret society, we learn about the inner workings from those who have been on the inside and chose to escape. Once again, we look to the words of Benjamin Freedman, an insider who walked away from both Judaism and Zionism. He had this to say about the Talmud: "From the Birth of Jesus until this day there have never been recorded more vicious and vile libelous blasphemies of Jesus, or Christians and the Christian faith by anyone, anywhere or anytime than you will find between the covers of the infamous '63 books' which are 'the legal code which forms the basis of Jewish religious law' as well as the 'textbook used in the training of rabbis.' The explicit and implicit irreligious character and implications of the contents of the Talmud will open your eyes as they have never been opened before."[391]

Wow! That is a strong statement. What is he referring to? In order to find out, we have to follow the trail that Benjamin leaves us in his letter to Dr. David Goldstein. Freedman says that Reverend Pranaitis, one of the greatest students of the Talmud due to his proficiency in the Hebrew language, scrutinized the Talmud (Amsterdam Edition, 1644-48) for its caricature of Jesus and His followers. Let's look at what Rev. Pranaitis wrote in *The Talmud Unmasked, The Secret Rabbinical Teachings Concerning Christians*,

"The Talmud teaches that Jesus Christ was illegitimate and was conceived during menstruation; that he had the soul of **Esau**; that he was a fool, a conjurer, a seducer; that he was crucified, buried in hell and set up as an idol ever since by his followers."[392] (emphasis mine)

I find it very suspect that the Talmud teaches that Jesus had the soul of Esau. Is there an Edomite agenda underlying the Talmud, one that reverses the truth, whereby Edomites pose as a Judeans? Is this what the angel was referring to when he wrote to the church in Smyrna?

Revelation 2:9 (NIV) "*...I know about the slander of those who say they are Jews and are not, but are a synagogue of Satan.*"

History demonstrates that the Edomites were opportunistic and posed as Judeans when it was in their benefit to do so, i.e. Herod an Idumean, king of Judea. Were Edomites involved in writing the Talmud? It makes me wonder, but it is not a question we will resolve in this investigation. We turn back to the words of Reverend Pranaitis; he points out the disdain Talmudic Jews have for Christians (Akum),

Midrasch Talpioth (fol. 225d) "God created them in the form of men for the glory of Israel. But Akum were created for the sole end of ministering unto them [the Jews] day and night. Nor can they ever be relieved from this service. It is becoming to the son of a king [an Israelite] that animals in their natural form, and animals in the form of human beings should minister unto him."[393]

According to the Talmud, Jesus was an idol and Akum are idol worshipers. So not only does the Talmud view Christians as idol worshipers, but here we see that Christians are considered as animals with the sole purpose of serving Jews!

Are you beginning to see how the Talmud has shaped Zionism? There are underlying precepts within the Talmud that elevate Jews above other human beings, therefore non-Jews do not enjoy the same basic rights to property, fair wages, liberty, life and the pursuit of happiness. The Jewish Voice for Peace aptly describes how this has influenced Zionism and subsequently, the State of Israel.

"We represent a growing portion of Jewish Americans. Israel claims to be acting in the name of the Jewish people, so we are compelled to make sure the world knows that many Jews are opposed to their actions. There are often attempts to silence critics of Israel by conflating legitimate criticism with anti-Semitism. Israel is a state, not a person. Everyone has the right to criticize the unjust actions of a state.

Through the study and action, through deep relationship with Palestinians fighting for their own liberation, and through our own understanding of Jewish safety and self-determination, we have come to see that Zionism was a false and failed answer to the desperately real question many of our ancestors faced of how to protect Jewish lives from murderous anti-Semitism in Europe. While it had many strains historically, the Zionism that took hold and stands today is a settler-colonial movement establishing an apartheid state where **Jews have more rights than others**."[394] (emphasis mine)

From the few Talmudic passages we have looked at, we can see a theme emerge of the supremacy of Jewish rights. And as we have discovered, the Talmud is the preeminent text in which Judaism draws upon to guide cultural, economic, social, religious and political ideologies. As with the Khazar kingdom, the Talmud has shaped Zionism and subsequently, the State of Israel.

Talmudic View of Money Lending

The Talmud influences how Jewish people conduct business with Gentiles. I wish to highlight a principle within the Talmud that is especially pertinent to our investigation; it is the principle of money lending. This principle not only addresses the practice of money lending, but it also addresses usury. Before examining the Talmudic precepts on these issues, let's first look at the money lending principles in the Torah and the Bible as a means to compare and contrast with what the Talmud teaches.

The Torah says it is unlawful to provide an interest-bearing loan to a Jew, but to a non-Jew, it's permissible.

Deuteronomy 23:19-20 (NKJV) *"You shall not charge interest to your brother — interest on money or food or anything that is lent out at interest. To a foreigner you may charge interest, but to your brother you shall not charge interest, that the Lord your God may bless you in all to which you set your hand in the land which you are entering to possess."*

Given the Jews gravitation toward money lending as a primary means of income, it was critical for them to understand the parameters for what constitutes a non-Jewish person. Rashi, the 11th century French rabbi, provided commentary answering the question, who is considered a Jew and who is a non-Jew. Michael L. Brown summarizes Rashi's interpretation on this principle,

"…Rashi, the foremost biblical and Talmudic commentator of that era…ruled that the apostate Jew remained a Jew. It was in this connexion (sic) that Rashi quoted the maxim 'although he has sinned remains a Jew'…Behind this clear-cut statement lies an emphasis on the unchangeable character of the Jew…Rashi even applied this ruling when it touched on the very livelihood of the Jewish community, since Jewish law forbade the charging of interest on loans to fellow-Jews but permitted charging interest on loans to Gentiles…Rashi's ruling was the same: Even an apostate Jew is still a Jew and must be legally authorized as a Jew; therefore he could not be charged interest on loans." [395]

If we dig further into understanding the prohibition of lending on interest to a fellow Jew, we discover that it is not as clear cut as some make it out to be. For example, providing interest free loans is not just afforded to the fellow Jew, but also extends to the resident alien living among them (Leviticus 25:35-37). A permanent non-Jewish resident was to be treated like a brother according to the Torah. Rabbinic commentary explains that it is similar to sibling relationships. A sibling would not charge interest on a loan given to a brother or sister, similarly, Jews aren't to charge interest on a loan to a fellow brother or sister in the community. Gary North's economic biblical commentary provides more clarity regarding the resident alien.

"But as a man voluntarily living permanently under biblical civil law, he was entitled to the civil law's protection, including the prohibition against interest-bearing charitable loans. Permanently residing voluntarily under the law's authority, he was under its protection."[396]

The heart of the Torah on matters involving charitable loans is one of graciousness, generosity, and consideration of the plight of others. There were other circumstances in which lending on interest was permissible and even understandable, it was in business transactions and/or lending to foreigners.

The New Testament expands the recipients of charitable loans to include foreigners, as well as those we consider to be enemies (Luke 6:34-36). So, does this mean interest-bearing loans are unbiblical? The answer to this question lies within the parable of the talents found in Matthew 25:14-30. Three servants were given talents commensurate with their performance record. The servant who received one talent, buried it in the ground instead of investing it, whereas the other two servants invested their talents. When the master returned to collect the profit on his assets, he tells the servant who buried the one talent,

Matthew 25:27 (ESV) *"Then you ought to have invested my money with the bankers, and at my coming I should have received what was my own with interest."*

This parable illustrates that collecting interest is permissible and in fact, expected as the minimum in a business transaction. It also demonstrates that banking was part of Jewish culture in the first century. In *Daily Life in the Time of Jesus*, Henri Daniel-Rops writes,

"...it was essential that there should be men who could dispose of and manage large sums of money. These were the bankers. They were first of all moneychangers, an indispensable function in that confusion of currencies in a country traversed by so many nations...The parable of the talents in the Gospel... proves that wealthy peasants deposited their money in a bank. The system of letters of credit drawn by a banker upon a correspondent in a distant country, which was known in ancient Egypt and practiced throughout the empire, was certainly employed by the Jews."[397]

But what do we make of those money changers that incurred the wrath of Jesus? If the practice of money changing and banking was commonplace in those days, why did Jesus vehemently oppose the money changers in the temple? As you might expect, the reasons are numerous for Jesus' violent response, but the one pertinent to our investigation is that the money changers were taking advantage of worshipers through price gouging for the service of changing money. The money changers most likely were in cahoots with the priests to create a monopoly at the Temple. Gary North points out,

"The temple coins could have been sold at a premium beyond the weight and fineness of the coins' metals...Moneychangers inside the walls of the temple would not have faced competition from rivals who were not authorized by temple authorities... Higher prices charged by the temple's moneychangers would have raised suspicion about the priests' collusion...Jesus identified their practices as theft. They were stealing from the faithful who came to offer sacrifice…False weights and measures are an abomination to God."[398]

Monopolistic pricing is an abomination to the Lord. The story of the money changers in the Temple was not the first, nor the last time price gouging was carried out by Jewish bankers. Even though Jesus clearly opposed these deceptive monetary practices, the Talmud actually encourages it.

Coschen Hamm (156, 5 Hagah) "where another Jews [sic] is allowed to go to the same Akum, lead him on, do business with him and to deceive him and take his money. For the wealth of the Akum is to be regarded as common property and belongs to the first who can get it."[399]

Coschen Hamm (183, 7 Hagah) "If a Jew is doing business with an Akum and a fellow Israelite comes along and defrauds the Akum, either by false measures, weight or number, he must divide his profit with his fellow Israelite, since both had a part in the deal, and also in order to help him along."[400]

Abhodah Zarah (54a) "It is allowed to take usury from Apostates who fall into idolatry."[401]

Iore Dea (159, 1) "It is permitted, according to the Torah, to lend money to an Akum with usury. Some of the Elders, however, deny this except in a case of life and death. Nowadays it is permitted for any reason."[402]

A discrepancy emerges between the principles found in the Word of God versus the precepts found in the Talmud (the word of the rabbis). The Bible promotes integrity in money lending and graciousness in charitable cases. Whereas, the Talmud condones the practice of defrauding others, through the use of false weights and measures; usury of those who are idol worshipers (i.e. Christians); and the usage of deceptive schemes in order to confiscate money.

We have seen these Talmudic endorsed money lending practices at work within the House of Rothschild. This revelation requires us to pause for a moment and lay out some of the clues we have gathered along our journey. I can sense that the big picture is starting to come into focus.

- Esau became Edom by choosing "to be red," which opened the door to Nephilim traits within his genealogy.

- Edomites intermingled with the giants further propagating the Nephilim DNA within their genome.
- Edomites were opportunistic with Israel's misfortunes; they assisted Babylon in capturing Jerusalem and then took up residence in the southern part of Judah.
- Hyrcanus forced mass conversion upon the Idumeans (Edomites), resulting in admixture with the Judeans.
- Edomites migrated into Khazaria and Rome before and after the fall of Jerusalem in 70 A.D.
- Khazarians were converted to Judaism and instructed in the Babylonian Talmud.
- Khazarians migrated into Eastern Europe and became known as the Ashkenazi Jews.
- Rothschilds are Ashkenazi Jews, as were most of the influential Zionists.

Deceptive monopolistic monetary rule has been a hallmark of the banking dynasty birthed by Mayer Amschel Rothschild and tragically, it has continued into the 21st century. While Rothschild fingerprints may not have been found within the halls of the Jekyll Island Club in November 1910, we must examine whether their blood was flowing through the veins of the "six men" present for the infamous meetings.

Guess where we are headed next? I think you can sense it. Your investigative skills have vastly improved since we started our journey. Yep, that's right, we are headed to Jekyll Island. But not for the meetings that took place in 1910 under the cover of secrecy, at least not yet. We have to set our clocks further back in time.

Key Points
- Zionism refers to a national movement of Jewish people returning to the Land of Israel for the creation of a sovereign Jewish state.
- Not all Jews are Zionists and many Jews are opposed to Zionism. Most Zionists are Jews.
- The Star of David has its origins in Nimrod and has been an occult symbol throughout the ages. It is a symbol used in the Rothschild's family crest.
- Edmond de Rothschild established Jewish colonies within Palestine. He was an oppressive, authoritarian overlord.
- Dorothea de Rothschild introduced Chaim Weizmann to Lord Balfour, which later proved pivotal in the establishment of the State of Israel.

- The Balfour Declaration, addressed to Lord Lionel Walter Rothschild, changed the course of history for the Jewish people. It paved the way for Edmond de Rothschild to purchase mass amounts of land in Palestine.
- The Rothschild land grab of the most fertile area in Palestine led to nearly a century of displacement for the Palestinians.
- Not all Zionists understand the hidden agenda of Zionism. It operates similar to a secret society in that only the elite Zionist's in the inner circle are aware of the agenda for global domination.
- Babylonian Talmud has shaped Zionism.
- Talmud elevates Jews above other human beings, therefore non-Jews do not enjoy the same basic rights to property, fair wages, liberty, life and the pursuit of happiness.
- Talmud condones the practice of defrauding others, through the use of false weights and measures; usury of those who are idol worshipers (i.e. Christians); and the usage of deceptive schemes in order to confiscate money.

Chapter 20

A Mysterious People

Inhabitants of Jekyll Island

In our long-awaited return to Jekyll Island, we need to explore the early inhabitants of the land. This will allow us to identify the blessings and curses within the land itself. At this point in our investigation, we are well trained in identifying Nephilim traits, so we must detect whether Jekyll Island has been a breeding ground for Nephilim Hosts.

There are two primary theories among archaeologists explaining the existence of the native inhabitants. One theory is that the Paleo-Indians made their way to North America from the land bridge across the Bering Strait during the Pleistocene era, eventually making their way to the Atlantic Ocean. The second theory is that the early inhabitants arrived by ship from a southern route.[403] While it's hard to test these theories, archaeologists have uncovered artifacts that date as early as 2500 B.C. which provide information about Jekyll Island's later inhabitants. The artifacts demonstrate that there was human activity on Jekyll Island, but it appears that no one people group laid claim to the island; it was more of a cultural crossroads. This is true of the inhabitants of recent history; there was not any one people group with a long-standing occupation of Jekyll Island.

From approximately 1150 AD through the 1500's, the island was inhabited by several Native American tribes, the most notable were the Timucua. The Europeans began arriving on the shores of Jekyll Island in 1562 to encounter the Timucua people. The Timucua were a unique and mysterious indigenous people group that inhabited the territory from north central and northeast Florida to southeastern Georgia. Ironically, the European explorers who preserved a rich historical record of the Timucua people were the same ones, with their expansionist policies, that extinguished the Timucua culture. Despite the atrocities the Europeans committed against the Timucua, we can be thankful for their contribution to history. We can glean much from the Europeans documentation.

Governmental Structure

The Timucua were not a single tribe, but rather a vast people group divided by clans differentiated by animal names. The various animal names signified the cast to which a clan belonged. For example, the White Deer line constituted those belonging to the family line of the upper chief. The Fish and Earth lines were those from lower pedigrees and were considered common people. Additionally, there were Buzzard, Bear, Partridge, and Lion lines.[404] In total, there were about 35 chiefdoms among the Timucua territory. The Timucuans were not politically unified. Their territory was governed by several kings, but the local villages were governed by chiefs who paid tribute to the regional Timucua king. The most well-known Timucua kings were Saturiwa, Outina and Potano. The chiefs were generally male, although women also held positions as tribal leaders. It was a matrilineal society in which the chiefs were selected from the female lineage. The son of a male chief would not inherit tribal leadership as was common with most tribal groups, but rather the chief's sister's offspring would be the successor.

Physical Appearance

The appearance of the Timucua was noteworthy. They were tall in stature and muscular. Reports as to their actual height vary and myths abound. J. Michael Francis, a history professor from the University of South Florida, St. Petersburg who specializes in Spanish Colonial Florida, stated,

"Ponce de Leon has been said to be anywhere from 2½ feet tall to 6½ feet tall. The Timucuan Indians were 7 or 8 feet tall, like they were out of a space-age film or something."[405]

The work of Theodor de Bry, a German engraver, preserved the drawings of a French explorer name Le Moyne. Le Moyne's drawings give us an invaluable window into Timucuan life. Through these drawings, we have record of their physical appearance, culture, governing structure, village architecture, and religious ceremonies and beliefs.

One of the Timucuan king's sons, Athore, was said to be "a handsome man, wise, honorable and strong, more than half a foot taller than even the tallest of our men."[406] Interestingly, while the physical appearance of the Timucuans was noteworthy and well documented, the physical appearance of their neighboring tribes' seem inconsequential in comparison. In scouring historical records, it seems there is only one documented statement about the Guale's appearance; "physically the Guale were tall and quite agile."[407] But there are a great many resources that emphasize the height of the Timucua. This is our first piece of evidence of the possibility of Nephilim genes within the Timucua.

Timucuan Language

One of the most puzzling aspects of the Timucua is the origin of their language. Many historians believe they spoke a Muskogean language, similar to their coastal neighbors, the Guale (Muskogean was the most widely spoken language in Georgia). This proved to be incorrect. The coastal Timucuans spoke a Mocama dialect, which has no clear linguistic origins in North America.[408] Julian Granberry, a linguist, describes the vocabulary of Timucua as "very unusual, especially compared to the Muskhogean languages spoken in Apalachee, Guale, and other portions of the Southeast, because it resembles none of those languages."[409] If the language of the Timucua did not resemble any of the indigenous tribes of the Southeast, where did it originate?

Granberry's research has found some similarities to the Warao language once spoken along the Caribbean coast of South America. There are also aspects of the Timucua language that bare resemblance to the languages spoken in what are now Venezuela, Colombia and Panama. However, archaeological evidence does not support a connection between the people of the Caribbean and South America with the Timucua. Jerald Melanich writes in his book *The Timucua*:

"The discrepancy between the archaeological evidence and the linguistic evidence remains a puzzle that cannot be explained at this time."[410]

Marriage Customs

The marriage practice of the Timucua varied depending on rank and status. Generally, the Timucua were monogamous with each man having just one wife, but Laudonniere recounted that the kings were allowed to have multiple wives. The primary wife was the king's first wife and it was her children that would inherit the father's possessions. This polygamous practice was not the only aberrant marriage practice. Records indicate at least one account of incestual marriage. Le Moyne describes Saturiwa's son Athore, married his mother and had children by her.

"The king, Athore, is a handsome man, wise, honorable and strong, more than half a foot taller than even the tallest of our men. His modest gravity lends majesty to his already noble bearing. He married his mother and had by her several children of both sexes whom he proudly introduced to us, striking his thigh as he did so. It might be added that after he married his mother, his father, Saturiwa ceased to live with her. "[411]

Village Architecture

The Timucua lived in circular walled villages with the council house in the center of the village. The council house was said to be a round building not the rectangular building depicted in Le Moyne's drawing and it could hold approximately 300 people. It was a place for ceremonies, dances, and community celebrations. Some historical descriptions of the Timucua villages describe the chief's house located in the center of the village. It's not clear whether the king resided in the council house or if some villages were constructed with the council house in the center and some with the chief's house in the center. Either way, a prominent house was located in the center of the village. The individual homes of the Timucua were circular with thatched roofs of palmetto leaves; the villagers' homes encircled the council or chief's house. Generally, the elders or nobles of the village lived in the houses in closest proximity to the prominent central house. Le Moyne sketched a depiction of the Timucua village (see Figure 44). The following is a transcription that accompanied the drawing:

"This is how the Indians construct their towns: they choose a place near a swift stream and level it as much as possible. Next they make a circular ditch and fix in the ground, very close together, thick round palings the height of two men… The king's dwelling is in the middle and has been a little sunk into the ground to avoid the sun's heat. All around it are grouped the nobles' houses, lightly constructed and roofed with palm branches."[412]

This description and subsequent drawing from Le Moyne, reveal the familiar circumpunct symbol. Could this evidence potentially link the Timucua to the more ancient people of the Sapelo Shell Complex? Let's explore more about the Timucua's spiritual beliefs to see if we can gather more clues.

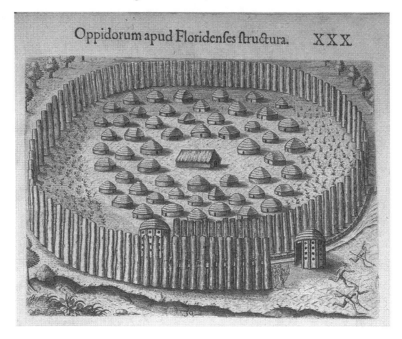

Figure 44. *Plate XXX Le Moyne Engravings.* Special Collections, Tampa Library, University of South Florida. https://digital.lib.usf.edu/?l11.30

Spiritual Beliefs

The discovery that the Timucua built their villages in circular patterns that resemble the ancient circumpunct symbol, necessitates further investigation into their spiritual beliefs. Are there other areas within their culture where the circumpunct is evident? If so, why would this ancient symbol linked to occult and pagan practices, originating from Egypt, be part of this Native American culture? The literature is void of answers to these questions because ethnographers, archaeologists, and historians have not asked these questions, our answers lie within the drawings of Le Moyne.

Battle Armor

First, let's take a look at the breastplate worn by the Timucua warriors (see Figures 45-46). It's not clear what these breastplates were used for, but some historians suggest they were used for protection in battle. This is a natural conclusion given the historical use of breastplates as a means of protection. But if this were true, it raises the question as to why every warrior was not equipped with this form of protection? It doesn't seem that protection was the primary purpose for these breastplates. Le Moyne described them as being made of copper, silver and gold. He observed that they were worn by the primary men, that is, the men of higher status.[413]

Figure 45. *Plate XII. Le Moyne Engravings: Detailed View of Warriors.* Special Collections, Tampa Library, University of South Florida. https://digital.lib.usf.edu/?l11.12

In Figure 46, we see that Chief Outina has a breastplate with multiple circumpuncts on it. This suggests that the ornamental breastplates signified a social status among the Timucua, which explains why Chief Outina adorned two circumpunct breastplates. In addition to signifying a warrior of importance, they may have been worn for spiritual protection. The Timucua worshiped the sun and prayed to the sun for protection before going out to battle, the breastplates may have been an outward sign of their allegiance to the sun god. As mentioned in Section I, the circumpunct is the ancient phallic symbol for the Egyptian sun god, Ra.

Figure 46. *Plate XIV. Le Moyne Engravings: Detailed View of Chief Outina.* Photo Credit: The Florida Center for Instructional Technology, University of South Florida

Sun Worship

The French explorers observed the Timucua engaging in ritualistic worship of the sun. Le Moyne provided evidence of idol worship. His detailed account brings further understanding to this mysterious people group (see Figure 47).

"The subject of the Chief Outina were accustomed every year, a little before their spring—that is, in the end of February—to take the skin of the largest stag they could get, keeping the horns on it; to stuff it full of all the choicest sorts of roots that grow among them, and to hang long wreaths or garlands of the best fruits on the horns, neck, and other parts of the body. Thus decorated, they carried it, with music and songs, to a very large and splendid level space, where they set it up on a very high tree, with the head and breast toward the sunrise. They then offered prayers to the sun, that he would cause to grow on their lands good things such as those offered him. The chief, with his sorcerer, stands nearest the tree and offers the prayer; the common people, placed at a distance, make responses. Then the chief and all the rest, saluting the sun, depart, leaving the deer's hide there until the next year. This ceremony they repeat annually. "[414]

In cerui exuvio Soli confecrando fo-　XXXV.
lennes ritus.

Figure 47. *Plate XXXV Le Moyne Engravings*. Photo Credit: The Florida Center for Instructional Technology, University of South Florida

This ceremony incorporated prayer and dance as an act of worship to the sun. This was but one of the Timucuan ceremonies honoring the sun. Before going into battle, Chief Saturiwa would gather the warriors who would sit in a circle with the chief in the middle of the circle (a circumpunct, see Figure 48). To the right of the chief were two containers of water and to the left, a fire. Fire was a symbol of the sun and was an important component of many of the Timucua sacred ceremonies to harness the power of the sun god. Le Moyne gives the following account of this ceremony: "Then, the chief, after rolling his eyes as if excited by anger, uttering some sounds deep down in his throat, and making various gestures, all at once raised a horrid yell; and all his soldiers repeated this yell, striking their hips and rattling their weapons. Then the chief, taking a wooden platter of water, turned toward the sun and worshiped it, praying to it for victory over the enemy, and that, as he should now scatter the water that he had dipped up in the wooden platter, so might their blood be poured out. Then he flung the water with a great cast up into the air, and as it fell down upon his men he added, "As I have done with this water, so I pray that you may do with the blood of your enemies." Then he poured the water in the other vase upon the fire and said, 'So may you be able to extinguish your enemies and bring back their scalps.'"[415]

Figure 48. *Plate XI Le Moyne Engravings*. Special Collections, Tampa Library, University of South Florida. https://digital.lib.usf.edu/?l11.11

The Timucuans looked to the sun for protection, victory, harvest, and prosperity. Consistent with the worship of the sun, we continue to see instances of the circumpunct displayed within Timucua rituals, ceremonies, and village life. When Chief Outina and his mighty warriors were marching out to battle, if they needed to camp for the night before reaching the place of battle, ten squads of the bravest men encamped in a circle around the chief. Then approximately ten paces outside this circle was another circle of twenty squads, then about twenty yards further, another circle of forty squads. This formation is a circumpunct with concentric circles.

Mourning Rituals

Additionally, the burial of the chief involves a ritual that incorporates a circumpunct (see Figure 49). The chief's grave is encircled by arrows with his drinking cup in the center of the burial mound. The people gather in a circle around the burial mound to mourn, forming an even larger circumpunct. Some of his possessions are buried with him but his house and the rest of his possessions are burned. The villagers hold a three day fast as part of the mourning process. The following is the burial customs as recorded by Laudonniere: "When a king dieth, they bury him very solemnly, and, upon his grave they set the cup wherein he was wont to drink; and round about the said grave, they stick many arrows, and weep and fast three days together, without ceasing. All the kings which were his friends make the like mourning; and, in token of the love which they bear him, they cut off more than the one-half of their hair, as well as men as women. During the space of six moons (so they reckon their months), there are certain women appointed which bewail the death of this king, crying, with a loud voice, thrice a day—to wit, in the morning, at noon, and at evening. All the goods of this king are put into his house, and, afterwards, they set it on fire, so that nothing is ever more after to be seen. The like is done with the goods of the priests; and, besides, they bury the bodies of their priests in their houses, and then set them on fire."[416]

Figure 49. *Plate XL Le Moyne Engravings*. Special Collections, Tampa Library, University of South Florida. https://digital.lib.usf.edu/?l11.40

Sorcery

Sorcery was the cornerstone of the Timucuans spiritual beliefs. The sorceror known as "Yaba," played a prominent role in the spiritual ceremonies and rituals. Sorcerers would engage in witchcraft to induce spells on people they wished to harm. The yaba would use the skin of a viper, a black snack, a portion of a palm tree, and other herbs during his incantation to cast a death curse on someone. If the person did not die as a result of this incantation, it was thought that the spell would reverberate back to the sorcerer and kill him. Witchcraft was used in many aspects of village life; it was used to manipulate people into marriage and to bribe the villagers to pay the sorcerer so they could avoid calamity. The yaba had tremendous power among the Timucua. The Timucuan kings would surround themselves with two primary men, the sorcerer and the counsel. One particular ceremony Le Moyne observed, provides us with further evidence that the circumpunct was of great significance (see Figure 50).

"The sorcerer made ready a place in the middle of the army, and, seeing the shield which D'Ottigny's page was carrying, asked to take it. On receiving it, he laid it on the ground, and drew around it a circle, upon which he inscribed various characters and signs. Then he knelt down on the shield, and sat on his heels, so that no part of him touched the earth, and began to recite some unknown words in a low tone, and to make various gestures, as if engaged in a vehement discourse. This lasted for a quarter of an hour, when he began to assume an appearance so frightful that he was hardly like a human being; for he twisted his limbs so that the bones could be heard to snap out of place and did many other unnatural things. After going through with all this he came back all at once to his ordinary condition, but in a very fatigued state, and with an air as if astonished; and then, stepping out of his circle, he saluted the chief, and told him the number of the enemy, and where they were intending to meet him."[417]

There are several aspects to this ceremony that I want to highlight. The sorcerer began the ceremony by grabbing the shield of D'Ottigny's page (D'Ottigny was second in command on Laudonniere's expedition from France). There was nothing sacred about this shield, it had not previously been used in a Timucua ceremony, nor had it been consecrated to the sun god. It was simply a shield used for protection in battle and it happened to be larger than the circumpunct breastplates worn by the Timucua warriors. The size of the shield allowed the sorcerer to kneel within its borders, so as to not touch the ground. The sorcerer drew a circle around the shield introducing sacred symbolism into the ceremony. He created a circumpunct and inserted himself within the circumpunct. The sorcerer drew symbols within the circle surrounding the shield. Figure 51 gives us a closer look at these symbols. Notice there are eight symbols repeated in a different order within the circle. The circumpunct is clearly visible as one of the symbols used. The use of circles in sorcery and paganism finds its origin within the Egyptian practices of magic. The circle represents a sacred space, a boundary.

Figure 48. *Plate XII. Le Moyne Engravings*. Photo Credit: The Florida Center for Instructional Technology, University of South Florida

"Some magical action was necessary to transform the ordinary to the sacred and casting a circle is a quick and effective way of doing that."[418]

It was also a common practice to write words of power and sacred names between the rings of the circle. This was thought to increase the power of the magic circle. The sorcerer became possessed by a demonic spirit during this ceremony and it was from this power source that he was able to foretell the outcome of the battle. Figure 52 provides a detailed look at the unnatural position of his extremities during this demonic encounter. This ceremony demonstrates the prominence of sorcery within the Timucua culture. To receive the strategy for battle, the kings relied on foretelling by the sorcerer rather than sending spies to engage in reconnaissance.

Figure 51. *Close-up of Plate XII. Le Moyne Engravings*. Special Collections, Tampa Library, University of South Florida. https://digital.lib.usf.edu/?l11.12

Figure 52. *Close-up of Plate XII. Le Moyne Engravings*. Special Collections, Tampa Library, University of South Florida. https://digital.lib.usf.edu/?l11.12

Child Sacrifice

Yet another example of a circumpunct being utilized in a Timucua sacred ceremony is the custom of sacrificing the firstborn son to the tribal chief (see Figure 53). As can be seen in this drawing, the women dance in a circle, while a female relative of the child stands in the center of the circle. Le Moyne described this ceremony: "Their custom is to offer up the first-born son to the chief. When the day for the sacrifice is notified to the chief, he proceeds to a place set apart for the purpose, where there is a bench for him, on which he takes a seat. In the middle of the area before him is a wooden stump two feet high, and as many thick, before which the mother sits on her heels, with her face covered in her hands lamenting the loss of her child. The principal one of her female relatives or friends now offers the child to the chief in worship, after which the women who have accompanied the mother, form a circle, and dance around with demonstrations of joy, but without joining hands. She who holds the child goes and dances in the middle, singing some praises of the chief. Meanwhile, six Indians, chosen for the purpose, take their stand apart in a certain place in the open area; and midway among them the sacrificing officer, who is decorated with a sort of magnificence, and holds a club. The ceremonies being through, the sacrificer takes the child, and slays it in honor of the chief, before them all, upon the wooden stump. The offering was on one occasion performed in our presence. "[419]

This is an unusual custom for Native American tribes. MacLeod William Christie documents in a 1931 journal article that there have been 10 Native American tribes that have engaged in child sacrifice. Most commonly, the sacrifices were made for propitiation of offended spirits. A few tribes sacrificed children to their gods as a form of worship.[420] Unique to the Timucuans was that they sacrificed the first-born son and this sacrifice was made to the tribal chief. The Encyclopedia of Religion and Ethics states, "the Indians of Florida sacrificed their first-born children to the sun or to the chief as child of the sun."[421]

Child sacrifice has its origins in Canaanite religious cults, such as the worship of Molech/Baal. We know from our investigation, that Canaan was inhabited by the offspring of the Nephilim. The first biblical mention of Molech is found in Leviticus.

Leviticus 18:21(NIV) *"Do not give any of your children to be sacrificed to Molech, for you must not profane the name of your God. I am the Lord."*

Figure 53. *Plate XXXIIII. Le Moyne Engravings*. Special Collections, Tampa Library, University of South Florida. https://digital.lib.usf.edu/?l11.34

This was written between 1500–1200 BC, but it's clear from the text that the worship of Molech was already established among other nations. King Solomon was the first of Israel's kings to offer up worship to Molech (I Kings 11:4-5). He married an Ammonite princess named Naamah. As his primary wife and the mother of his heir to the throne, he built an altar to the Ammonite god Molech to honor her. About 300 years later, King Josiah tore down this altar (II Kings 23:10). The center of worship for Molech was in Topheth, which means "place of fire." It was the place where children were sacrificed to Molech. The primitive root word for Topheth is '*taphaph*' which means "playing or beating a percussion instrument such as a timbrel, tambourine, or drum."[422] It is thought that percussion instruments were used to drown out the sound of the infants screaming as they were burned alive.

The word Molech comes from the root word '*malak*' which means "king or queen, to ascend the throne, or to be made king in order to reign."[423] Some biblical scholars postulate that the majority of scriptural references of Molech are not specifically referring to the Ammonite god, but rather any false god that people have established as a king with spiritual authority over them. In essence, the Timucuans were sacrificing their children to '*malak*,' their king/chief, who was seen as a personification of the sun god. But why was the sacrifice made of the first-born son?

In many cultures, including those in the Middle East, the first-born son holds a sacred place within the family. The first-born son is often seen as the most valuable of offerings. In Egyptian, Hebraic, and Canaanite cultures, the first-born son was the one to receive the inheritance of generational blessing. The fact that rituals involving child sacrifice were practiced among the Timucuans is strong evidentiary criteria of the Nephilim agenda at work (one of the criteria for classification as a Nephilim Host in Chapter 13).

Victory Ceremony

Of further note, is a ceremony that the Timucuans engaged in following a victory in battle. In the midst of battle, as soon as one of their enemy was slain, the Timucua would drag them off to the outskirts of the battle and dismember them (see Figure 54). Here is the description from Le Moyne: "In these skirmishes those who fall are immediately dragged off by men especially charged with this duty. With a sliver of reed, sharper than any steel blade, they cut the skin with the hair from the skull all the way round, the longest hairs being twisted into a plait, the hair from the forehead being rolled up for the length of two fingers with that of the back of the head in the manner of the ribbon of a bonnet. Immediately afterwards (if they have time), they dig a hole where they make a fire of smoldering moss which they carry around in their leather breechcloths. The fire lit, they dry the scalp until it becomes hard like parchment. At the end of the battle, they are accustomed to cut the arms of their victims off at the shoulder and their legs at the thighs. The bones laid bare are crushed and the pieces, still dripping with blood, are dried on the same fire. Then they return home triumphantly with the skin of the heads at the ends of their spears. What astonished me (for I was one of the men sent by Laudonniere under Ottigny's command), was that they never left the place of battle without piercing the mutilated corpses of their enemies right through the anus with an arrow. During this task a protective force always surrounded them."[424]

Figure 54 *Plate XV. Le Moyne Engravings.* Special Collections, Tampa Library, University of South Florida. https://digital.lib.usf.edu/?l11.15

Dismembering the enemy may seem especially gruesome, but it carried deep spiritual significance for the Timucua. It was an important preparation for the victory ceremony that took place following battle. Figure 55 depicts the solemn ceremony of which Le Moyne was privy to. "After returning from a military expedition they assembled in a place set apart for the purpose, to which they bring the legs, arms, and scalps which they have taken from the enemy, and with solemn formalities fix them upon tall poles set in the ground in a row. Then they all, men and women, sit down on the ground in a circle before these members; while the sorcerer, holding a small image in his hand, goes through a form of cursing the enemy, uttering in a low voice, according to their manner, a thousand imprecations. At the side of the circle opposite to him there are placed three men kneeling down, one of whom holds in both hands a club, with which he pounds on a flat stone, marking time to every word of the sorcerer. At each side of him the other two hold in each hand the fruit of a certain plant, something like a gourd or a pumpkin, which has been dried, opened at each end, its marrow and seeds taken out, and then mounted on a stick, and charged with small stones or seeds of some kind. These they rattle after the fashion of a bell, accompanying the words of the sorcerer with a kind of song after their manner. They have such a celebration as this every time they take any of the enemy."[425]

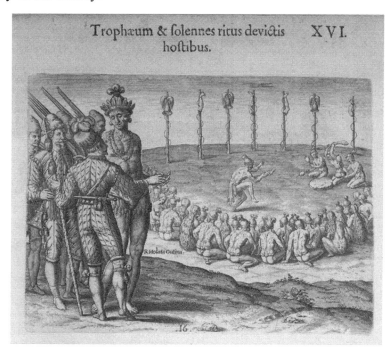

Figure 55. *Plate XVI. Le Moyne Engravings*. Special Collections, Tampa Library, University of South Florida. https://digital.lib.usf.edu/?l11.16

There are several aspects of this ceremony that are noteworthy. This victory celebration was rich in symbolism. It was a ceremony involving praise and worship to the sun god for providing protection and victory in the midst of battle. The Timucua sat in a semi-circle across from seven poles also positioned in a semi-circle. The dead and the living formed a circle with the sorcerer in the middle (yet another circumpunct). Casting the circle for the ceremony was part of the ritual of creating a sacred space as a conduit for the release of supernatural powers. The body parts or "trophies" of the enemy were mounted on the poles. As you can see in Figure 55, each pole had a vine draped around the pole connecting the "trophies" to the earth. This formed what is known as a "kapemni" symbol.

Kapemni is a whirling set of vortices by which it is believed the upper and lower worlds communicate with one another. Kapemni is a Lakhota term that means "what is above is like what is below and what is below is like what is above."[426] Remember this phrase? We discovered in Chapter 2 that this is alchemy's Hermetic Law. The Kapemni evolved from the concept of a "power line," which is a supernatural power source that radiates outward from a sacred central point. We see this illustrated in Figure 56, the center pole was one of prominence because it alone was draped with two vines forming a double helix. It represented the center of a sacred communication between that which is from above and that which is from below. Perhaps it symbolized a strand of DNA? Could it have represented the defiled genome of the Timucua? The sorcerer conducting the ceremony would release curses over the enemy while holding a fetish akin to a voodoo doll (see Figure 56). A fetish is an object that is believed to have special powers because it embodies a spirit that connects the human world to the supernatural world. A fetish can be a doll, a carved image, a stone, animal bones, etc. It is likely that the use of a fetish in this ceremony served two purposes; to bring down curses on their enemies, and to deepen the connection with the spirit world.

Figure 56. *Close-up Plate XVI. Le Moyne Engravings.* Special Collections, Tampa Library, University of South Florida. https://digital.lib.usf.edu/?l11.16

Putting the Pieces Together

If we put all these clues together, we find a mysterious people group, similar in some ways to their neighboring Native American tribes, but strikingly unique in a multitude of ways. The Timucua meet the classification of Nephilim Hosts: tall stature, extraordinary strength, sexual perverse incestual relations, child sacrifices, idol worship, occult blood rituals, sacred rituals worshiping the sun, practice of sorcery, and heinous acts against other living beings. Additionally, their unique language leads us to wonder whether this people group may have links to ancient cultures from far off lands. These puzzling aspects present a different picture of the Timucua than what historians have considered.

Timothy Bence has an interesting perspective on the early inhabitants of Jekyll Island. He is not a historian, he is not an anthropologist, nor is he an archaeologist; he is a prophetic intercessor with a specific call on his life to tear down ancient Canaanite altars. His assessment, after spending time on Jekyll Island, is that the altars built by the Timucua are unnervingly similar to the Canaanite altars he has dealt with in other parts of the world. Some may find it curious that Canaanite altars are located such a great distance from Canaan, but Bence suggests the Canaanites migrated to other parts of the world, including Europe and the Americas, after they were driven from their land. If this is accurate, it opens the door to the possibility that this mysterious tribe, the Timucua, may have originated from Canaan. Regardless, we know from our research that the Nephilim bloodline has been found on every continent but Antarctica. In fact, as we pointed out in Chapter 14, skeletal remains of giants have been found within 6 miles of Jekyll Island.

Spiritual DNA

Thanks to the detailed drawings of the early European explorers, we have discovered Nephilim traits among the Timucua. Bence offers the most intriguing theory, he suggests that Canaanite altars "release DNA" into the land; he describes DNA like an "information packet."[427] If this is accurate, then defiled DNA is released through altars of false worship, also known as, altars of offense. Let's dig a little here to see if there is some validity to this concept. I can sense breakthrough... something is about to unlock for us.

So, if DNA is released from altars of offense and we know that DNA emits different frequencies, then it stands to reason that the frequencies of defiled DNA have curses attached to them which then get absorbed by the land. Let's vet this hypothesis.

George Otis, Jr. and Alistair Petrie explain that we have "spiritual DNA" which is transferred to the land through our stewardship of it, whether good or bad.

"Such is the power of our spiritual DNA, the past still affecting the present. Tracing the transfer of cultures and the movement of people groups over the generations, Otis has found that, as ancient people began to migrate from Babylon into other lands, their inherited roots – and resultant strongholds- went with them. These roots incorporated the genetic, hereditary, social, psychic, and occult inheritance of their respective backgrounds... human stewardship would have a bearing on the land itself and, once established, would remain embedded until a concerted effort was taken to change it."[428]

The early inhabitants of Jekyll Island most likely established altars of offense and engaged in false worship, thus infusing the land with their spiritual DNA. Remember the Sapelo Shell Complex? It was our first discovery of a circumpunct. Throughout history, this symbol has been associated with false worship and occult practices, so the fact that it's still detectable on Sapelo Island may be evidence that there are still strongholds in the land. Essentially, it's a fossil record of the spiritual DNA deposited ages ago. The iniquity of the early inhabitants attached a curse to the land and these curses have impacted subsequent generations.

Deuteronomy 29: 26-27 (NKJV) *"for they went and served other gods and worshiped them, gods that they did not know and that He had not given to them. Then the anger of the Lord was aroused against this land, to bring on it every curse that is written in this book."*

String Theory

Blessings and curses emit a certain frequency. String theory provides a basis for understanding this concept. String theory proposes that at the sub-atomic core of all matter is a vibrating string and each elementary particle has a different vibration.[429] Therefore, all matter exerts energy through vibration, which is measured by frequency, meaning that all matter creates a sound. There is a grand symphony of creation from the smallest of particles to the largest of stars that has been discovered in recent years. This means that all creation resounds the character of the Creator. When the land releases a harmonious melody, it resonates with the character of God. But when curses have been released, there is a dissonant sound emitted that can alter matter even to the sub-atomic level. We need only look to the research of Masaru Emoto to grasp the spectacular impact dissonant frequencies have on matter, in particular, water molecules.

Emoto measured the impact of negative words and positive words spoken to water molecules. He examined the crystallized forms of these water molecules under a microscope and found that the structure of the water molecule changes based on the message it receives.[430] For example, words like "love and gratitude" form a perfect water crystal, whereas words like "you fool" form a chaotic crystal.

The land is influenced by the choices we make. Alistair Petrie has identified four major sins that bear consequences for the land: sexual immorality, idolatrous worship, bloodshed, and broken covenants.[431] When these sins are committed on the land, strongholds and curses are sown into the land. As we have discussed before, adaptive deceptions are methods of false worship which adapt over time and culture. The dissonant sounds released by strongholds and curses attract like-minded people, who further empower dark forces through false worship. It can be a vicious cycle entrapping the inhabitants of the land in sexual immorality, idolatrous worship, bloodshed, and/or broken covenants. This is what we are dealing with on Jekyll Island. What more will be revealed as we look at the Europeans' encounter with Jekyll Island?

Key Points
- Timucuans had aberrant marriage practices including polygamy and one occasion when Athore married his mother and had children with her.
- Village architecture of Timucuan is a circumpunct.
- Breastplates of Timucuan warriors and chiefs were circumpuncts.
- Timucua worshiped the sun; they sacrificed their first-born sons to the tribal chief as a representation of the sun god.
- Sacred ceremonies including sorcery involved circumpuncts.
- Timucuans met criteria for classification as Nephilim Hosts: tall stature, extraordinary strength, sexual perverse incestual relations, child sacrifices, idol worship, occult blood rituals, sacred rituals worshiping the sun, practice of sorcery, and heinous acts against other living beings.

- The land on Jekyll Island was defiled by sexual immorality, idolatrous worship, and bloodshed. An altar of offense was established through false worship.
- The spiritual DNA released upon Jekyll Island releases a sound of dissonance that attracts spiritual darkness.
- The Nephilim agenda was deposited into the soil of Jekyll Island.

Chapter 21

European Footprint on Jekyll Island

There are a thousand hacking at the branches of evil
to one who is striking at the root.
~ Henry David Thoreau

The Europeans began arriving on the shores of Jekyll Island in 1562. A Frenchmen by the name of Jean Ribault led a group of Huguenots to the New World in search of religious freedom. The French were the first Europeans to set foot on Jekyll Island. The Huguenots were Protestants who had found new passion in their faith during the Reformation. They were upstanding French citizens; comprised of nobility, the intellectual elite, and professionals in trade, medicine, and crafts.[432] For a time, the Huguenots enjoyed preferential treatment in France, but the tide changed in the mid-1500s when the Roman Catholic Church exerted its control of religious expression upon the French. Brutal persecution ensued, and the Huguenots became the primary target of the religious cleansing. Those that sailed the seas with Jean Ribault in 1562, were escaping religious persecution in hopes of finding a land of religious freedom. When the French landed on Jekyll Island, they were inspired by the fertile land and the rivers teaming with fish. Ribault's description of Jekyll Island, "a country full of havens, rivers and islands of such fruitfulness as cannot be expressed, and where in a short time great and precious commodity might be found."[433]

The French aptly named the island, "Ile de la Somme," which means "island of the sum or fullness." The Huguenots were Spirit led believers who identified the redemptive purposes of this island and declared it as such through its namesake. They were able to recognize the many blessings contained within the land of Jekyll Island; it is a land of abundant harvest; it is a land in which a fountain of prosperity flows for the enrichment of not only its inhabitants, but for people beyond its borders. This is the first time in recorded history that people carrying the Spirit of God within them set foot on Jekyll Island.

The Huguenots arrival on Jekyll Island led to decades of French exploration into the New World. Their copious notes and drawings provide us with the earliest documentation of the life and culture of the indigenous people prior to the significant alterations the Europeans imposed. The Huguenots were able to establish friendly relations with the Timucuans, but they did not tarry long on Jekyll Island. They were particularly disturbed by some of the rituals they witnessed of these native people. Unfortunately, the defilement of the land at the hands of the Timucuan rituals, empowered the curses. Instead of abundance and prosperity, it became a land of enslavement and captivity. What would have happened if the Huguenots choose to stay and redeem the land? What if they would have broken the curses off the land and released the full measure of blessings instead? How might the course of history have been changed? Would the Federal Reserve have been thwarted at the moment of incubation?

In 1510, the Spanish explorers staked a claim to the island. They were followed by the French in 1562. Conflicts ensued between the French and Spanish over the rights to the island. The Spanish overtook the French and established missions among the coastal islands with the purpose of converting the Native Americans to Christianity. The Native Americans were not open to the gospel because their cultural ways were suppressed by the Spanish priests. There was an uprising and many of the Spanish priests were executed along the Sea Islands. The Spanish priest from Jekyll Island was taken captive and later exchanged for a Native American captive.

In the mid 1600's, the English were rapidly establishing settlements up and down the Atlantic seaboard. They partnered with Creek tribes to drive the Spanish out of the Sea Islands. By 1702, the Spanish were completely driven out of the area and the English began to establish colonies. In 1733, General James Oglethorpe established Georgia as a colony. He named Jekyll Island after his friend, Sir Joseph Jekyll, a financier from England. Fitting isn't it? He appointed William Horton to set up a military post to protect Fort Frederica located on a nearby island. Horton built a home and established a plantation. The plantation was so prosperous that it provided beef and corn to everyone stationed at Fort Frederica. The Spanish attacked Horton several times, burning down his home and plantation.[434]

Following the death of William Horton, the entire island became the property of Christophe du Bignon in 1792. The du Bignon family fled to the United States to escape the French Revolution. Du Bignon established plantations that became extremely prosperous, a blessing from the fertile land. However, Christophe du Bignon released a curse upon the land by opening the door to a spirit of slavery on the island. The practice of slavery was carried on by his son, Henri Charles du Bignon. With a total disregard for an American law passed 50 years earlier, rendering the importation of slaves illegal, in November 1858, Henri Charles du Bignon managed to orchestrate the arrival of *The Wanderer*, a ship carrying 465 African slaves. This was the second to last ship of slaves that arrived on American shores.[435]

Ownership of Jekyll Island was passed down three generations in the du Bignon family until John Eugene du Bignon, a grandson of Christophe du Bignon, purchased the whole island from the remaining heirs. He, along with his brother-in-law, Newton Finney, established a business plan to sell the island to a group of investors for the purpose of establishing a prestigious hunting club for the world's elite. Their dream become a reality in February 1886, when the Jekyll Island Club purchased the island. What followed was the development of a winter retreat for the wealthiest elite. Membership of this club was limited and among the list of prestigious members were the Rockefeller, Morgan, and Vanderbilt "titans."[436] It was under the guise of a hunting retreat that "six men" devised a devious scheme of enslaving the American people.

Before we investigate the "six men," I want to draw your attention to a few of the investigative questions we identified at the start of our journey:

- Were the seeds of the Federal Reserve planted in the soil of Jekyll Island long before the birth of our nation?
- What are the ancient roots of defilement and deception buried deep in the land that nourished the incubation of the Federal Reserve?

We are able to answer these questions based on the evidence we have collected thus far. Assuredly, the Nephilim agenda was deposited within the soil of Jekyll Island through the spiritual DNA released from the altars of offense. The Timucua exhibited the phenotype of the Nephilim by meeting the criteria for classification as Nephilim Hosts.

In the case of the Roots of the Federal Reserve, the seeds of '*nachash*' (divination, enchantment, the whisper of a magic spell) were planted in the soil ages ago. The fruit of this has been a pervasive pattern of false worship, idolatry, enslavement, and bloodshed on the land. Furthermore, a spirit of slavery operated uninhibited on Jekyll Island and was strengthened by centuries of false worship. Subsequently, the defilement of the land created the perfect breeding ground for the incubation of the Federal Reserve. We will soon discover that the Federal Reserve Act was a secret pact to enslave billions of people through the art of deception, that is, '*nasha*,' the language of the Nephilim, the seed of Satan! At the heart of '*nasha*' is the fruit to deceive, beguile, mentally delude, and morally seduce in order to impose usury on others. It's utterly reprehensible!

We must not turn away as the Huguenots did. We must press on to the call for freedom. The land is groaning in anticipation of its redemption. We have the Spirit of God within us. We are carriers of divine DNA. We have been given a dominion mandate to tear down strongholds, break curses, and release blessings. Remember, Jesus reclaimed the Kingdom of God on earth and then gave us the keys to operate with dominion authority (Matthew 16:19).

Are you ready? The moment we have been waiting for has arrived. Next stop, Jekyll Island... 1910.

Key Points
- First Europeans on Jekyll Island were the Huguenots in 1562. They were Spirit led believers who fled France because of religious persecution.
- Huguenots identified the redemptive blessings of abundance and prosperity on Jekyll Island, but they did not break the curses.
- Jekyll Island was a land of enslavement and captivity.
- Christopher Du Bignon empowered the curse upon the land by bringing a slave ship upon the shores of Jekyll Island 50 years after slavery was outlawed.
- Seeds of the 'nachash' was planted in the soil of Jekyll Island ages ago, the fruit of which has been a pervasive pattern of false worship, idolatry, enslavement, and bloodshed on the land.

Chapter 22

A Shrouded Foundation

No matter how many centuries go by, no matter how much the world changes, the central drama of human history remains the same. On one side are those who seek power, control and domination and on the other side are patriots... who stand upright and plant their feet in eternal defense of our liberty. And with God as our witness, we swear today that we will defend our rights, we will safeguard our freedoms, we will uphold our heritage, we will protect our constitution and we will make America stronger, prouder, safer and greater than ever, ever, ever before.
~ President Donald Trump

If the American people only understood the rank injustice of our banking and money system – there would be a revolution before morning.
~ Andrew Jackson

It's time to return to the clandestine meeting…On November 22, 1910, under the cover of night, "six men" boarded a train in New Jersey bound for Jekyll Island. Secrecy was thick in the air like a heavy fog. These men were instructed to arrive separately at the New Jersey Station, to avoid curious onlookers and reporters, to pretend they did not know each other, and to use first names only to maintain anonymity. The curious residents of Jekyll Island were told that these men had gathered for a duck hunt. This was partially true; they were in fact assembled to kill something… but it wasn't ducks!

Senator Nelson Aldrich was responsible for assembling these financiers. In total, these "six men" (seven if you count Aldrich's secretary) were estimated to represent one-fourth of the world's wealth. Their secret meetings established the foundation of a clandestine banking cartel which would change the course of our nation and set us on a path toward destruction. The "six men" responsible for this, as recorded by G. Edward Griffin in his book *The Creature from Jekyll Island*, were Nelson W. Aldrich, Abraham Piatt Andrew, Frank A. Vanderlip, Henry P. Davison, Benjamin Strong, Paul M. Warburg. [437]

The six "duck hunters" that holed up at Jekyll Island were not just brilliantly, influential men in their own right, but more consequentially, they were intertwined with the powerful "titans" of the Gilded Age.

Nelson Aldrich → John D. Rockefeller

Abraham Piatt Andrew → George Cortelyou → J.P. Morgan

Frank Vanderlip → William Rockefeller → Jacob Schiff → Rothschild

Henry Davison → J.P. Morgan

Benjamin Strong → J.P. Morgan

Paul Warburg → Jacob Schiff → Rothschild

As you might imagine, this group did not gather by happenstance for an adventurous hunting retreat at Jekyll Island. Not at all, this was several years in the making…

The Age of Monopolies

In order to assess the motives of the "six men," we first need to understand the societal, political, and economic landscape at the turn of the 19th century. This era was marked by a central control of wealth by the Gilded Age monopolies. There were two primary groups in control of the wealth in America: the Morgan group and the Rockefeller group. In Europe, the same dynamic had occurred; the two groups controlling the wealth of Europe were the Rothschild group and the Warburg group. As you can see from the above diagram, the financiers that Senator Aldrich assembled, represented these four "titans."

The Gilded Age titans dominated industry and banking in America; Rockefeller controlled the oil industry, Carnegie was king of steel, Vanderbilt and Gould were railroad magnates, and the baron of banking was unquestionably, J.P. Morgan. It was an unusual time in American history. The cutthroat competition of these titans knew no bounds and predatory business practices were left unrestrained by lawmakers. Numerous corporate mergers thrust American industries into "giant" holding companies called trusts. The titans of these industries scraped their way to the top using opportunism combined with exploitation of human labor, which fostered "sweatshop" conditions for workers. The titans had little regard for social justice. They demanded long, grueling work hours of their employees in unsafe conditions. It was not uncommon for men to die from work-related accidents. Labor strikes ensued, riots broke out, and men died, all while the titans amassed enormous wealth and power. The monopolists were concerned with beating out their competitors, even if that meant sacrificing the lives of their employees to do so. In their minds, the ends justified the means. Allan Nevins, biographer and author of *John D. Rockefeller* wrote, "the United States more than any other nation produced genuine captains of industry, men who thought and operated on the grand scale, and were content with nothing less than absolute sway…The pioneer in the American movement toward industrial consolidation was the Standard, and its Augustan leader was Rockefeller."[438]

John D. Rockefeller was an innovative pioneer but also, unmistakably, a ravenous predator. At breakneck speed, he not only developed all facets of the oil industry, but he also consolidated extracting, refining, storing, shipping and sales of "black gold" into a trust named Standard Oil. He combined creative management strategies with ruthlessly aggressive tactics to form the behemoth trust. By the turn of the century, Standard Oil employed 100,000 people, utilized 4,000 miles of pipeline, and ran 5,000 oil tank railcars.[439] He drove his competitors to despair with his strangle hold on all aspects of the industry. He was their worst nightmare. He hoarded critical industry supplies, but that was child's play compared to his manipulation of the railroads. He became most notorious for choking out the transportation of his competitors' oil products. Railroads were the life blood of the economy and shaped the distribution of wealth. Small business owners were dependent upon shipments of supplies and the transportation of their goods. When Rockefeller negotiated advantageous backroom deals for Standard Oil, in the form of rebates, he turned the railroad magnates into "conspiratorial allies of his budding monopoly."[440] It's certainly not surprising that when Teddy Roosevelt ran on the platform of being a "trust buster," he first went after Standard Oil.

Equivalent to the largeness of John D. Rockefeller was a peculiar man, John Pierpont Morgan. He was groomed at a young age in the banking industry by his father, Junius Morgan. In the 1800's, merchant-banking families relied entirely on their male offspring to continue the banking dynasty. Their capital depended upon the reputation of the family name. Pierpont was the only son of Junius Morgan, so it was an enormous weight to carry. Pierpont felt suppressed under his exacting father; but a shackle was lifted off his spirit when Junius died. It was then that Pierpont became J.P. Morgan. He stepped into the role of the baron of banking with grandeur. Ron Chernow describes J.P. Morgan's peculiar persona,

"Pierpont's metamorphosis from a dashing, muscular young man into a portly tycoon with fierce visage and blown-up nose…The acne rosacea…took root in his nose, enlarging and inflaming it until it became Wall Street's most talked about protuberance…it would take on a cauliflower texture. Many people would notice a link between the nose and Pierpont's fiery temper."[441]

J.P. Morgan was a gruff individual who remained aloof, even to his closest confidants, who described conversations with the titan as having a paucity of words, but an abundance of grunts. Morgan quickly ascended to become the most powerful private banker in America. He did not limit his dominance to the realm of finance; he dabbled in the steel industry as well. Consistent with his titan mentality, he did not enjoy competition with Carnegie. The two battled head to head on numerous occasions, trying to squeeze the other out of business. Finally, Morgan got the best of Carnegie by getting into his psyche. Morgan understood that Carnegie and Rockefeller prided themselves in besting the other for title of "richest man in America." Charles Schwab, a "faithful lieutenant" of Carnegie proposed a merger of steel companies into a trust. Morgan saw this as the opportune time to buy Carnegie out of his steel company. Pierpont knew that he could tempt Carnegie with a purchase price that would secure Carnegie with the title of "richest man in America." When the two sat down to negotiate, Carnegie drew up a figure on a piece of paper of $480 million. Morgan accepted it without hesitation and in parting said, "Mr, Carnegie, I want to congratulate you on being the richest man in the world."[442] Later Carnegie would realize he sold out to cheap, Morgan agreed. U.S. Steel would become America's first billion-dollar company.

In 1901, with Morgan at the helm of the U.S. Steel trust, he became larger than life, a true giant in the American economy. His indispensability was a proven fact, especially during times of panic, within America's banking system.

"He filled the vacuum of central banker like a Medici prince, holding council in the evenings in his library…Morgan's centrality was so critical that the *Times* reported, worryingly, when he caught a mild cold…Jacob Schiff bluntly declared, 'You stand between us and financial chaos.'"[443]

This proved to be true, as he single-handedly orchestrated the rescue of the country from absolute ruin during the Panic of 1907.

Key Players

Equipped with a character sketch of the two great titans, John D, Rockefeller and J.P. Morgan, we now turn to investigate some of the key players in the creation of the Federal Reserve. Paul Warburg is a central figure, a name you undoubtedly recognize from Chapter 18; a man who, later, would become known as "the Father of the Federal Reserve."

Warburg immigrated from Germany in 1902 and within a few years, he jettisoned to the forefront of American banking. Warburg was astounded by the primitiveness of the American banking system; he likened it to the 15th century Medici banking of Italy. Warburg had this to say about the system, "I was not here for three weeks, before I was trying to explain myself the roots of the evil."[444]

At the behest of Jacob Schiff, Warburg began lobbying his colleagues on the necessity of banking reform. He penned an essay entitled "Defects and Needs of Our Banking System." Warburg astutely and presciently detected the problems within the system, most notably, the failure of the currency to respond to increases in demand. The inelasticity of the currency could trigger unimaginable devastation due to its inability to respond to demands tied to cycles of agriculture. Warburg assessed that the key problem was a lack of central reserves. In 1906, Warburg warned the Chamber of Commerce by stating,

"I do not like to play the role of Cassandra, but mark what I say. If this condition of affairs is not changed, and changed soon, we will get a panic in this country compared with which those which have preceded it will look like child's play."[445]

Though Warburg persisted in sounding the alarm, it was difficult to convince financiers of the need for a central bank. Many bankers wanted reform, but reform that would implement decentralized strategies. It wasn't until Warburg coalesced with Nelson Aldrich that his message gained traction.

Nelson Aldrich was arguably the most influential Senator at the turn of the 19th century. He was head of the Senate Finance Committee and wielded enormous power. Newspapers referred to him as the "general manager of the United States" and "the power behind the throne."[446] One of his responsibilities was to manage the federal tariff system. He mastered this role and became nimble at suiting the needs of the industrialists. Aldrich amassed a great fortune through backroom deals with monopolists. He genuinely believed it was in the best interest of the American people, when politicians were in lockstep with the titans of the Gilded Age. Naturally, he followed suit. He was a card playing companion and confidant of J.P. Morgan and he became father-in-law to John D. Rockefeller, Jr. Years later, Aldrich's great-grandson, Michael Rockefeller wrote, "it became easy for Aldrich to conceive of legislation as being primarily a problem of consultation with the economic aristocracy followed by the application of personal authority."[447]

During this time in America's history, the nation had already experienced multiple banking panics, but nothing rivaled what was about to happen in the Panic of 1907. Heavy speculation occurred in the copper market and with the banking system ripe for implosion, the panic ensued. Trusts, which initially had begun as repositories for estates and trust funds, ballooned to enormous entities thanks to greed and an insatiable appetite for power. Trusts became leveraged in risky assets because they operated outside regulatory oversight, sounds eerily similar to the off-balance-sheet instruments a century later, called derivatives. In 1907, roughly 40% of all deposits within New York were placed in trusts and for every dollar deposited in a trust, only 6 cents were kept in reserve![448] Virtually overnight, banks were stripped of their reserves as panicked depositors rushed to withdraw their cash.

The Knickerbocker Trust was the first banking institution to fall, it happened the afternoon of October 22nd, 1907. Upon hearing the news, George Cortelyou, the Secretary of the Treasury, raced by train to New York to meet that evening with J.P. Morgan and other bankers. By the following day, Cortelyou had relinquished $25 million of U.S. funds to Morgan, a private banker, to orchestrate the rescue of the nation. This was an astonishing transfer of power but was representative of the confidence Teddy Roosevelt had in the titan. The panic worsened when news spread that Charles Barney, the president of Knickerbocker, shot himself. The bank had 18,000 depositors who stormed the doors during the panic, only to be shut out. The ensuing chaos and news of his suicide tragically prompted a wave of suicides among Knicker-bocker's depositors.

The panic seemed like a typhon on the heels of a tsunami. On October 24th, the stock market was on the verge of seeing 50 brokerage houses fall, unless $25 million was raised immediately. Within 15 minutes, Morgan was able to convince the bank presidents to front the money, a herculean feat for sure. The waves of catastrophe kept rolling in though. The finale to J. P. Morgan's heroic efforts to save the U.S. economy from the edge of the abyss was to rescue three institutions that were on shaky ground: the Trust Company of America, the Lincoln Trust, and Moore and Schley, a speculative brokerage house. If either one of these institutions failed, it would have led to the total collapse of the stock market, something Pierpont was valiantly trying to avoid at all cost. But another $25 million was needed for the rescue. Ron Chernow describes the scene on November 2nd, 1907 in *The House of Morgan,*

"Pierpont gathered the city's bankers at his library. He settled commercial bankers in the East Room…while in the West Room trust-company presidents…Pierpont played solitaire in Belle Greene's office…To save Moore and Schely, Pierpont wanted some payoff for himself…some *quid pro quo*…Ben Strong noticed that Pierpont had locked the enormous bronze doors and pocketed the key. He was up to his old tricks – confinement of adversaries, a deadline, the abrupt appearance of the menacing host after long hours of bargaining…Beaten down by all-night bargaining, King and the other trust company presidents agreed to contribute to the $25-million pool."[449]

The 70-year-old titan had single handedly orchestrated the rescue of the U.S. economy, but not before innumerable causalities; the Panic of 1907 caused New York trusts to lose 48% of their deposits.[450] The shockwaves of the crisis altered the American psyche. Depositors lost confidence in their banking institutions. In response to the panic, Congress passed the Aldrich-Vreeland Act on May 30, 1908, which called for a National Monetary Commission to investigate what went awry in America's banking system. Nelson Aldrich was chairman of the commission; he along with other commission members traveled to Europe during the summer of 1908 to examine the inner workings of the European central banks, all of which were heavily influenced by the House of Rothschild, if not completely controlled by it. The European central bankers and diplomats described a system of banking that was integrated and able to withstand drastic fluctuations in monetary demand. Aldrich was convinced a central bank patterned after the European model was the solution to eradicate the defects of the American banking system. He was sold on the idea of banking reform and realized that Warburg's proposal called for a central bank.

When Jacob Schiff first introduced Nelson Aldrich to Paul Warburg in December of 1907, it was before Nelson's "conversion." Warburg was greatly encouraged by their first encounter though; he could see Aldrich had the potential for altering his views on banking reform. When Aldrich returned from Europe a changed man, he met with Warburg right away to discuss his support of Warburg's banking reform. From that moment on, the two developed a powerful alliance that would alter the course of our nation. The nation seemed ripe for a change but the two had their work cut out for them. Despite the devastation brought on by the Panic of 1907, the predominant sentiment among politicians and financiers was still one of strong disdain for the "Big-Brother" style of central banking. It was as if Warburg and Aldrich were fighting against the ghost of Andrew Jackson.

Warburg's banking reform ideas called for a central bank that could issue uniform, asset backed national currency backed by both gold and commercial paper. He favored an elastic currency that was not tied to government bonds. He proposed a central bank that could rediscount commercial paper to provide banks with liquid assets to pay depositors in times of need. His proposed central bank would also serve as "lender of last resort" in times of financial crisis.[451] Essentially, he had to convince politicians, bankers, and the American public that he was proposing a banking system with currency based to some degree on "commercial paper," which is bankers' language to obfuscate that currency would be based on corporate IOUs.[452] This would take some finagling!

The Furtive "Duck Hunt"

It turns out the "six men" were masters at finagling. One of the participants of the "duck hunt" revealed decades later, the nature of what transpired on Jekyll Island during those fateful days of sworn secrecy. Frank Vanderlip provided a retelling of the expedition in *The Saturday Evening post*, February 9, 1935: "There was an occasion, near the close of 1910, when I was as secretive, indeed, as furtive, as any conspirator. I do not feel it is any exaggeration to speak of our secret expedition to Jekyll Island as the occasion of the actual conception of what eventually became the Federal Reserve System. We were told to leave our last names behind us…We were instructed to come one at a time and as unobtrusively as possible to the railroad terminal on the New Jersey littoral of the Hudson, where Senator Aldrich's private car would be in readiness… The servants and train crew may have known the identities of one or two of us, but they did not know all, and it was the names of all printed together that would have made our mysterious journey significant in Washington, in Wall Street, even in London. Discovery, we knew, simply must not happen, or else all our time and effort would be wasted. If it were to be exposed publicly that our particular group had got together and written a banking bill, that bill would have no chance whatever of passage by Congress."[453]

Vanderlip provided a telling confession of the covert nature of their expedition. He acknowledged that if they had been transparent with what they devised on Jekyll Island, the "bill would have no chance" in passing the Congress. And I would add, for good reason!! Here is our first glimpse at motive… **the "six men" had an intent to deceive.**

It would be six years after the "duck hunt," before the American public had any hint of what actually took place on Jekyll Island. Forbes magazine founder, Bertie Charles Forbes, was the first to expose the clandestine gathering in 1916:

"Picture a party of the nation's greatest bankers stealing out of New York on a private railroad car under cover of darkness, stealthily riding hundred[s] of miles South, embarking on a mysterious launch, sneaking onto an island deserted by all but a few servants, living there a full week under such rigid secrecy that the names of not one of them was once mentioned, lest the servants learn the identity and disclose to the world this strangest, most secret expedition in the history of American finance. I am not romancing; I am giving to the world, for the first time, the real story of how the famous Aldrich currency report, the foundation of our new currency system, was written... The utmost secrecy was enjoined upon all. The public must not glean a hint of what was to be done. Senator Aldrich notified each one to go quietly into a private car of which the railroad had received orders to draw up on an unfrequented platform. Off the party set. New York's ubiquitous reporters had been foiled... Nelson (Aldrich) had confided to Henry, Frank, Paul, and Piatt that he was to keep them locked up at Jekyll Island, out of the rest of the world, until they had evolved and compiled a scientific currency system for the United States, the real birth of the present Federal Reserve System, the plan done on Jekyll Island in the conference with Paul, Frank, and Henry... Warburg is the link that binds the Aldrich system and the present system together. He more than any one man has made the system possible as a working reality."[454]

To get a sense of the immense influence Paul Warburg yielded upon the framework of the Federal Reserve System, we look to an article written in 1915 in *The Century Magazine* by journalist Harold Kellock, "Paul M. Warburg is probably the mildest mannered man that ever personally conducted a revolution. It was a bloodless revolution; he did not attempt to rouse the populace to arms. He stepped forth armed simply with an idea. And he conquered. That is the amazing thing. A shy, sensitive man, he imposed his idea on a nation of a hundred million people… Having perceived that our national banking laws were barbaric and obsolete, single-handed, he set out to bring about a radical constructive change… There is no doubt that without Mr. Warburg there would have been no Federal Reserve Act."[455]

While this is a flattering description of Paul Warburg, it also reveals that a German from a powerful European banking dynasty, "imposed" his banking strategies upon the American people. He had only become a naturalized citizen a few years prior. We need to dig deeper to understand his potential motives. What were his views on banking? We find within Warburg's 1914 writings (as cited in Naclerio, 2013), a glimpse of the god-like, omnipotent qualities he attributed to a central bank system,

"We need some centralized power to protect us against others and to protect us against ourselves, some power able to provide for the legitimate needs of the country and able at the same time to apply the brakes when the car is moving too fast. Whatever causes that may have precipitated the present crisis, it is certain that they never could have brought about the existing outrageous conditions, which fill us with horror and shame, if we had had a modern banking and currency system."[456]

What were some of the potential motivations behind such a "bloodless revolution"? This revolution happened during a time when there were 22,000 competing banks in America, and 6,500 of these banks could issue notes. When crisis lurked, these banks held on to their gold as a protective measure. In the age of monopolies, free competition was frowned upon. Kellock captured the sentiment of the monopolists,

"Free competition, which in industry has given us the sweatshop, child labor, underpaid workers, and scamped products, in finance made for over speculation and panics and periods of general insolvency."[457]

We have learned from our investigation that the Warburgs and the Rothschilds have enjoyed an air of hegemony. In particular, the Rothschilds expect that their banking prowess entitles them to wield control in the nations of the world. Why should the United States of America be any different?

The motivation to gather under such secrecy was to devise a scheme that would eliminate competition within the banking world and consequently maximize profit for these financiers. **Make no mistake, Jekyll Island became the birthplace of America's banking cartel.** The labor lasted nine days; this tiny creature that was birthed to the titans in 1910 would soon become such a ravenous beast that it would destroy the foundations of freedom that formed this nation.

But how did the "six men" intend to feed this creature once it was born and how would it grow without the masses recognizing it?

The skeletal of this creature was the structure of a cartel. Investopedia defines a cartel as follows: "A cartel is a collection of businesses or countries that act together as a single producer and agree to influence prices for certain goods and services by controlling production and marketing."[458]

Surely, if Americans recognized this creature for what it was, it would have been shot dead by public outcry. Afterall, Americans were leery of central banks because of the previous failed attempts at central banking. The pain of these failures was still fresh in the minds of the citizens. So, these financiers were faced with several challenges as explained by G. Edward Griffin:

1. How to stop the growing influence of small, rival banks and to ensure that control over the nation's financial resources would remain in the hands of those present;
2. How to make the money supply more elastic in order to reverse the trend of private capital formation and to recapture the industrial loan market;
3. How to pool the meager reserves of the nation's banks into one large reserve so that all banks will be motivated to follow the same loan-to-deposit ratios. This would protect at least some of them from currency drains and bank runs;
4. Should this lead eventually to the collapse of the whole banking system, then how to shift the losses from the owners of the banks to the taxpayers;
5. How to convince Congress that the scheme was a measure to protect the public.[459]

These challenges were a tall order. Somehow, they needed to convince a free-enterprising society to accept the controlling spirit of a cartel which would enslave humanity in debt. Their strategy to accomplish this great feat… was to shroud the truth in a cloak of deception.

A Sleight of Tongue, A Sleight of Hand

With the prevailing societal attitude toward central banking being one of animosity, it was clear to the "six men" on Jekyll Island, that they must not use the words "central bank" or "cartel" when selecting a name for this creature. Instead they drew upon the well of wordsmiths among them to create a name that was neutral or perhaps even endearing. It was important to avoid even the word "bank" in the name, if their scheme were to get past legislators and the public eye. What would allure the voters and legislators to allow the operation of a banking cartel?

First, if they could create the illusion that the government had oversight of the creature, it would eliminate all suspicion that this was a cartel. Thus, the word "Federal" was chosen. Next, if they could create the illusion that the cartel was not enslaving American citizens with the responsibility of paying the debt created by this creature, they just might secure long life for this beast. They chose the word "Reserve," as a slight of tongue, to imply that this banking cartel had capital built up to provide stability to the banking world and the US economy. The name given to this banking cartel, **The Federal Reserve**, was intended to deceive and confuse. Their intentions hit the mark because the masterminds have been successful for over a century in pulling the wool over the eyes of the American public. Our second glimpse at motive… **the "six men" intended to connive Americans by the use of trickery and obfuscation.**

Not only was selecting the right name of utmost importance to their scheme, but implementing the right structure was important to create the illusion that power was decentralized. To throw off the scent from the hounds, it was conceived that several branches of the Federal Reserve would open in different regions of the country.

The predominant obstacle in letting this creature loose on the mainland was the passing of legislation legalizing this newly formed banking cartel. The architects on Jekyll Island drafted a bill called, the Aldrich Plan, in which they proposed a private central bank, they and the titans would own. Heated debates ensued when the Aldrich Plan was presented to Congress. Congressman Charles Lindbergh was one of the staunchest opponents of the Federal Reserve. He saw right through the veil of deception and called it as such, on the floor of the House of Representatives on December 15, 1911.

"The Aldrich Plan is the Wall Street Plan. It is a broad challenge to the Government by the champion of the Money Trust. It means another panic, if necessary, to intimidate the people. Aldrich, paid by the Government to represent the people, proposes a plan for the trusts instead. It was by a very clever move that the National Monetary Commission was created. In 1907 nature responded most beautifully and gave this country the most bountiful crop it had ever had. Other industries were busy too, and from a natural standpoint all the conditions were right for a most prosperous year. Instead, a panic entailed enormous losses upon us. Wall Street knew the American people demanding a remedy against the recurrence of such a ridiculously unnatural condition. Most Senators and Representatives fell into the Wall Street trap and passed the Aldrich-Vreeland Emergency Currency Bill…Wall Street speculation brought on the Panic of 1907. The depositors' funds were loaned to gamblers and anybody the Money Trust wanted to favor. Then when the depositors wanted their money, the banks did not have it. That made the panic."[460]

The Aldrich Plan never reached the floor for a vote because it was a Republican backed bill and the Republicans lost control of the House in 1910, and the Senate in 1912. The cartel members were not ready to give up the fight. They changed a few details and repackaged the bill under the name The Federal Reserve Act and presented it before Congress. A handful of Congressmen recognized that it was just a prettier package of the Aldrich Plan. Despite the debates, on December 22, 1913, Congress passed the Federal Reserve Act and the following day, on December 23, Woodrow Wilson signed it into law. The timing of this cannot go unnoticed. An article in *The Nation* on January 1st, 1914 sums up the significance,

"When the historian who leaves nothing out comes to write the full account of the passage of the currency bill, he will not emit reference to the influence of the **Christmas spirit.** Congress was so eager as a small boy to get off for the holidays; and there stood the cruel resolution of the Democratic majority not to adjourn unless the bill was passed. This undoubtedly had the effect of hastening final action. The drawing near of the gracious Christmastide seemed to calm the savage beast of the filibuster, and to still the passions of the makers of long speeches…he could hardly have faced the universal rage that would have fallen upon him if he had ruined the Congressional vacation over the holidays. **The whole thing was a wonderful demonstration of what Christmas can do in the sphere of legislation. Senatorial eloquence dried up,**

obstruction laid down its weapons and Congress and country seized their Milton and echoed – at last our bliss full and perfect is."[461] (emphasis mine)

Within this article lies a clue that most people would miss, but not us! If you remember from our deep dive into the life of Nimrod, the '*gibbowr*,' we discovered that the "spirit" behind Christmas, is in fact Nimrod, and within the spirit of Nimrod lies the root of all paganism and occult worship. Consider the gravity of this… The timing of the birth of this beastly bill was orchestrated to pay homage to the spirit of Nimrod. Senators that would have normally given an ardent fight against this beast, instead, rolled over and placated it for sake of "Christmastide."

I am getting a whiff of a stench that is generally unmistakable; a stench produced from a rotten core. Could it be that at the very core of the Federal Reserve Act is a pact that was made with the Nephilim? As we move toward the final stages of our investigation, we will need to answer this question.

Key Points
- The "six men" who designed the Federal Reserve represented 1/4th of the world's wealth. They were intertwined with the powerful "titans" of the Gilded Age.
- Paul Warburg and Nelson Aldrich were powerful influencers of the central bank system.
- Panic of 1907 set the stage for banking reform. Trusts were leveraged in risky assets.
- Clandestine meetings on Jekyll Island led to the formation of America's banking cartel.
- The motives of the "six men" were an intent to deceive and connive Americans by the use of trickery and obfuscation.
- "Federal Reserve" is not an accurate depiction. It's not a government agency nor does it have reserves.
- Federal Reserve Act passed due to "Christmas spirit" (Nimrod) that came over Congress.

Chapter 23

What Have You Done for Me Lately?

*A country which expects to remain ignorant and free…expects that
which has never been and that which will never be. There is
scarcely a King in a hundred who would not, if he could, follow the
example of Pharaoh – get first all the people's money, then all their
lands and then make them and their children servants
forever…banking establishments are more dangerous than standing
armies. Already they have raised up a money aristocracy.*
~ Thomas Jefferson

*It is well enough that people of the nation do not understand our
banking and monetary system, for if they did, I believe there would
be a revolution before tomorrow morning.*
~ Henry Ford

During the final days of Christmas, 1913, while most people were nestled in bed for a long winter's nap, what should occur in the halls of government, but the most egregious act of cowardice from so-called patriots, and the most sinister act of subversion from legislators who were bought by the international banksters. In essence, Congress relinquished its Constitutional right to coin money and to regulate its value.

U.S. Constitution Article 1, Section 8, Clause 5 – "Congress shall have the power to coin money, regulate the value thereof…and fix the Standard of Weights and Measures"[462]

Instead, this right was passed on to a private corporation.[463] America's third central bank was birthed.

Three years after the Federal Reserve Act was signed into law by President Woodrow Wilson, he made this astounding confession,

"A great industrial nation is controlled by its system of credit. Our system of credit is concentrated. The growth of the Nation, therefore, and all our activities are in the hands of a few men… We have come to be one of the worst ruled, one of the most completely controlled and dominated Governments in the civilized world—no longer a Government by free opinion, no longer a Government by conviction and the vote of the majority, but a Government by the opinion and duress of a small group of dominant men."[464]

A vast majority of Americans don't understand that there is a connection between the Federal Reserve and the federal income tax. The Revenue Act was enacted in 1913, which was not a coincidence.

"Does it not seem just a bit odd that a "heavy progressive or graduated income tax" was enacted in 1913, coinciding with the Federal Reserve Act, and the debauching of our money by the Fed's 'elastic currency' policies? Both ideas are straight out of the Communist Manifesto, and one is imperative in order to ensure the survival of the other…The purpose of the income tax is <u>not</u> to finance the necessary operation of the government. Congress had done an admirable job of that for some 137 years, without an income tax, and for the most part, operated on a balanced budget without incurring a national debt. The chief purpose of the income tax was to enrich the Fed. How else would they ensure payment of the usury they charge our government for the fiat currency!"[465]

The Federal Reserve System

The structure of the Federal Reserve is a bit of an enigma and, by design, was intended to masquerade the central power it wields. The architects of the Federal Reserve Act wanted to create the impression that the Federal Reserve is a decentralized banking system with 12 regional Federal Reserve Banks dispersed throughout the country. But make no mistake, the Federal Reserve Bank of New York (FRBNY) holds the lion share of the power because of the Wall Street interests it serves.

The Federal Reserve is run by a Board of Governors, 12 regional banks, and the Federal Open Market Committee (FOMC). The President of the United States appoints the seven members of the Board of Governors and the U.S. Senate confirms them. The members of the Board of Governors have terms that span multiple presidential and congressional terms. The Federal Reserve Board is headquartered in Washington D.C., but it is not a government agency. **The Federal Reserve is an independent agency made up of privately-owned banks.** The Federal Reserve explains on their website:

"...though the Congress sets the goals for monetary policy, decisions of the Board— and the Fed's monetary policy-setting body, the Federal Open Market Committee— about how to reach those goals do not require approval by the President or anyone else in the executive or legislative branches of government."[466]

This sounds like dangerous autonomy. The stark reality is that the governors cannot be removed on the basis of policy; they have total immunity. The President nor Congress has the authority to remove them from the Board of Governors. Alan Greenspan, former Chair of the Federal Reserve, was asked in an interview about the proper relationship between the President of the United States and the Chair of the Fed. Greenspan said the following, "well first of all, the Federal Reserve is an independent agency and that means, basically, that there is no other agency of government which can overrule actions that we take."[467]

Senior counsel for the Federal Reserve, Yvonne Mizusawa, reiterated the independent nature of the Fed in her testimony given in a Freedom of Information case. She testified that the Federal Reserve Banks are 100% privately owned by banks in their district.[468] Charles A. Lindbergh spelled it out plainly in his book *The Economic Pinch*.

"The system is private, conducted for the sole purpose of obtaining the greatest possible profits from the use of other people's money, and in the interest of the stockholders and those allied with them. It is inconsistent with free government to subject every industry and enterprise in the country to the domination of the big banks which have been granted the exclusive privilege to control our finances."[469]

In essence, the Federal Reserve Act handed an independent agency, called the Federal Reserve, complete autonomy to act with supreme authority in determining the monetary policy for our nation. The Federal Reserve Act was amended in 1977 to give the FOMC two mandates 1) "maximum employment, which means all Americans that want to work are gainfully employed, and 2) stable prices for the goods and services we all purchase. **In this way, the Fed's monetary policy decisions truly affect the**

financial lives of all Americans." (emphasis mine)[470] The tools the Fed uses to reach these objectives are adjusting both, short-term interest rates and the money supply.

Not only did Congress relinquish its responsibility to govern monetary policy, but it forfeited its Constitutional responsibility to coin the nation's currency and regulate its value. To understand the magnitude of this, we first need to understand the difference between currency and money. Michael Maloney in his book *Guide to Investing in Gold and Silver* defines currency as a "medium whereby you can transfer value from one asset to another."[471] The root word is 'current' and just as with electricity, it needs to keep moving or else it ceases to exist. Currency by itself, does not store value, but money does. Money is something that always has value, such as gold. Money is always considered currency because it has purchasing power, but the reverse is not true. Currency is not always money. During times of hyperinflation, currency is just paper with nothing of value attached to it.

The Federal Reserve issues America's currency called the U.S. dollar, but technically, it is a Federal Reserve Note. What is a note, you say? A note is an I.O.U. Yes, that's right, an I.O.U.; **the product of the Federal Reserve is a debt note**. The Federal Reserve peddles debt. The Fed produces this debt note by using money magic.

Picture yourself at a magic show and the magician pulls out of thin air, the first ever, one-dollar bill. The magician gives you the one-dollar bill and says that you can have it, but you will have to pay him back one dollar plus interest. Now you might be thinking, if it's the first ever minted dollar bill and there is no other currency yet created, what currency will you use to pay the interest? Well, have no fear, the magician creates a second dollar bill out of thin air and gives it to you. Now you have the money to pay the magician back, right? Not really. He tells you that you now owe him $2 plus interest. Once again, there is no other currency to pay for the interest. He goes back to his magic act and creates a third dollar bill. But by now you have caught on and can see that this is an endless cycle with no possible way to pay the I.O.U. off. Welcome to the debt enslavement trick! The Federal Reserve creates Federal Reserve Notes out of thin air; they are just paper or in most cases, just digital numbers on a computer screen. The Boston Federal Reserve Bank admitted to this as well.

"When you or I write a check there must be sufficient funds in our account to cover the check, but when the Federal Reserve writes a check there is no bank deposit on which that check is drawn. When the Federal Reserve writes a check, it is creating money."[472]

Are you beginning to see the madness of this system? Well unfortunately, there is more to it. Our entire banking system is built on a house of cards called fractional reserve banking. Fractional reserve banking is the practice of holding only a portion of deposits within reserves. It's based on the likelihood that depositors will stagger their withdrawals, rather than withdraw their deposits all at once. The Fed set the reserve requirement for banks with deposits greater than $122.3 million at 10% and banks with less than $122.3 million at 3%. What does this mean? If I deposit $100 in my bank account (with a bank reserve of 10%), the bank keeps $10 of my deposit in their reserves and then lends out the rest. The $90 in new loans generates interest for the bank. The bank may charge, let's say, 12% in interest on the loans they created with my money, but yet they only give me 1% (or less) in interest for providing them with access to my money. Shouldn't this be illegal? Just another example of the exploitation of the banking system.

The FOMC determines monetary policy for the country by setting interest rates based on the current state of the markets. For example, they will adjust short-term interest rates as a means to ensure liquidity and stability in the economy. Herein lies one of the most direct ways the Fed impacts all Americans. In the current debt system, we call monetary policy, the majority of Americans have outstanding debt from a mortgage, car loan, school loan, credit cards, etc. When interest rates rise, our debt costs more; when interest rates drop, our debt is more affordable. The decisions the FOMC make have a tremendous impact on our daily lives. So, who are these decision makers?

The FOMC consists of the seven members of the Board of Governors, the president of the Federal Reserve Bank of New York and four other Federal Reserve Bank presidents, who serve on a rotating basis. Given that the Federal Reserve banks are privately owned, it is natural to wonder how much the decision to raise or lower interest rates is weighted in favor of these privately-owned banks. It would be naïve to assume that the FOMC acts strictly in the public's best interest, especially given that deception is part of the bedrock of the Federal Reserve. We will investigate whether there are conflicts of interest shortly.

The Federal Reserve holds closely to the tenet that the central bank must remain independent of government. The mainstream media repeatedly echoes this same mantra. But we need to recognize that the independent nature of the Federal Reserve is a double-edged sword. Yes, it's true that the American economy benefits when the institution that drives our monetary policy is outside the political fray, but the temptation for this independent institution to abuse its power by lining the pockets of its members is all too real. The lust for power among the elite banksters heavily influences their decisions. Is the argument to maintain the Fed's independence just a firewall of protection to keep the public from understanding the workings of this banking cartel? Why would we want a banking cartel, made up of private banks, determining our monetary policy anyway? It's time we wake up! Who are these private banks that own the regional Federal Reserve banks? That is a closely guarded secret that Peter Kershaw, author of *Economic Solutions*, has exposed.

"The major shareholders (Class "A" stock) of the Federal Reserve Bank Systems are identified as:

- Rothschild: London and Berlin
- Lazard Bros: Paris
- Israel Seiff: Italy
- Kuhn-Loeb Company: Germany
- Warburg: Hamburg, Amsterdam, The Netherlands
- Lehman Bros: NY
- Goldman and Sachs: NY
- Rockefeller: NY

The balance of stock is owned by the major commercial member banks."[473]

A handful of Congressmen over the past decade have been strong advocates for auditing the Federal Reserve, but anytime this issue has been raised, the Fed Chair doggedly repudiates Congressional accountability. Representative John Duncan asked Ben Bernanke in a Congressional hearing if he thought "it would cause problems for the Fed or for the economy if that legislation were to pass" (legislation that would audit the Fed). Bernanke's response was, "My concern about the legislation is that if the GAO [Government Accountability Office] is auditing not only the operational aspects of our programs and the details of the programs but is making judgements about our policy decisions that would effectively be a takeover of monetary policy by the Congress, a repudiation of the independence of the Federal Reserve which would be highly destructive to the stability of the financial system, the dollar, and our national economy situation."[474]

It's clear that the Federal Reserve Chair shudders at the thought of being held accountable for their actions. The omnipotent, god-like power that Warburg infused within the DNA of the Federal Reserve still manifests with great vigor. Bernanke intimates that the sky will fall if the Fed is audited. Hmmm… Thou doth protest too much!

The Federal Reserve admits to having the power to affect the lives of all Americans. So how have they stewarded this power? To be blunt, they have created a century of debt enslavement for all of humanity. Unfortunately, this is not hyperbole. The U.S. Dollar has held the position of being the global reserve currency which means the monetary policies of the Federal Reserve effect all other nations, not just America.

Debt Enslavement

In 1912, Alfred Crozier provided a prescient warning of the impending monster he saw coming down the birth canal. He both illustrated it (see Figure 57) and aptly described it in *U.S. Money vs. Corporate Currency,*

"It will have the power to abolish prosperity and inflict panic, plunging the entire nation into the horrors of a financial catastrophe that would paralyze industry and commerce, close the factories and turn millions of workmen out to tramp the streets without means to provide food and shelter for their helpless wives and children…That is the **omnipotent and deadly octopus** Congress is urged to legally set loose and install as the master of American banks, business, finance, industry, commerce and politics. Its **poisonous and itching tentacles** will gradually reach out and bind themselves about every home, farm, industry, bank, the public treasury, courts, Congress and the White House, gathering to itself supreme political power, sucking the wealth and substance of the people into Wall Street and dumping it into the Stock Exchange or the eager laps of the handful of men who will seek by moral if not by legal treason to rob the people of their God-given liberty, destroy the republic as a living reality and in its place erect an empire disguised as a democracy with incorporated wealth crowned as the ruling sovereign and all the people its subjects."[475] (emphasis mine)

Crozier was an attorney from the Midwest, but he could have been a prophet given his accurate depiction of the Great Depression caused by this unleashed octopus. It's particularly curious that an attorney could see the handwriting on the wall so clearly, but the architect of the Aldrich Plan, Paul Warburg himself, could not. In fact, Warburg vowed that a central bank would create stability by removing the uncertainty of panics. Warburg was a very intelligent man; we would be remiss to consider him naïve. The Rothschilds and the Warburgs are master strategists in the art of deception. They know how to play their hand just right to entrap their prey.

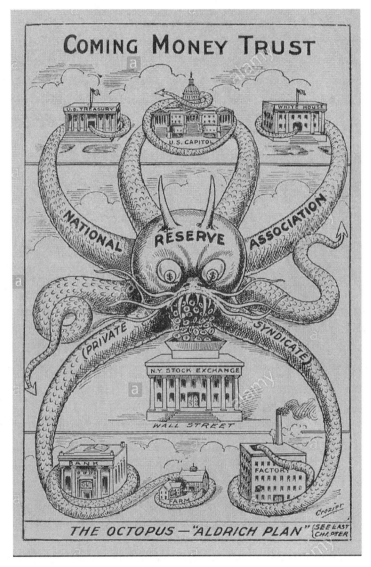

Figure 57. The Frontispiece–The Octopus–"Aldrich Plan". Illustration by Alfred Owen Crozier (1912). Retrieved from https://www.scribd.com/document/393454918/BOOK-USMoneyVSCorporateCurrency-Crozier-AlfredOwen-c1912

The Great Depression began in 1929 and ended in 1941. It was the longest protracted economic downturn in America's history. Ben Bernanke admitted in a 2002 speech, that the Federal Reserve was to blame for the Great Depression. Bernanke confessed, "regarding the Great Depression, … we did it. We're very sorry. … We won't do it again."[476]

Allow this trite confession from Bernanke to sink in for a moment. The beast was only a teenager; 15 years into the Fed's inception, it unleashed a diabolical plan to destroy the lifeblood of America. The plan was debt slavery on steroids. It was an attack on the economy from numerous fronts, all within the purview of the Federal Reserve to defend against, but instead, the beast triggered the meltdown by raising interest rates in 1928 and in 1929. The dominoes of destruction began falling; the contraction in the system caused by increased interest rates, triggered the stock market crash, which in turn, triggered numerous regional banking panics and finally led to national and international financial meltdowns.[477] When the dust settled, unemployment had reached 25%, over half of the banks in the nation had failed, real gross domestic product (GDP) fell 30%, and deflation hit the country.[478]

While in the throes of the Great Depression, Congressmen Louis T. McFadden, Chairman of the House Banking and Currency Committee, clearly delineated the nature of the Federal Reserve when he gave a speech on the floor of the House of Representatives on June 10, 1932. Keep in mind that he witnessed first-hand the devastation a predatory lending institution controlled by "moneyed vultures" can have on the people. In one state alone, "60,000 dwelling homes and farms were brought under the hammer in a single day."[479]

"We have in this country one of the most corrupt institutions the world has ever known. I refer to the Federal Reserve Board and the Federal Reserve Banks…This **evil institution** has impoverished and ruined the people of the United States…It has done this through the defects of the law under which it operates, through maladministration of that law by the Federal Reserve Board, and through the corrupt practices of the **moneyed vultures who control it.** Some people think the Federal Reserve Banks are U.S. Government institutions. They are not government institutions. They are private credit monopolies which **prey upon the people** of the United States for the benefit of themselves and their foreign customers; foreign and domestic speculators and swindlers; and rich and **predatory money lenders**. In that dark crew of **financial pirates** there are those who would cut a man's throat to get a dollar out of his pocket…At no time in our history has the general welfare of the people of the United States been at a lower level or the mind of the people so filled with despair…They are the victims of the dishonest and unscrupulous Federal Reserve Board and the Federal reserve banks. **Their children are the new slaves** of the auction block in the revival here of the **institution of human slavery.**" [480] (emphasis mine)

I have highlighted several key phrases within McFadden's speech that provide us with a greater understanding of the motive of the "six men" and their puppet masters. Some might say that McFadden was exaggerating when he delivered this passionate speech on the House Floor, but frighteningly, there is not one use of overemphasis in the above quote. Nothing that he stated was inflated. Instead, McFadden was spot on with his assessment of the devastation the Federal Reserve has brought to our nation. He also was accurate with his discernment of the spiritual underpinnings of the beast.

McFadden provides us with our third glimpse at motive… **the "six men" intended to create an institution of human slavery.** At the core of these "six men" was an **evil desire to carry out predatory money lending.** At the heart of the puppet masters that controlled these "six men" was a **lack of remorse for heinous acts against other living beings.**

Once again, with amazing foresight, Crozier described the destructive force of debt slavery. "This is human slavery; slavery of the toiling millions to the usurers, their masters. The interest burden is the lash that forever goads and drives. It is worse than the "blacksnake" because it is constantly plyed [sic] night as well as daytime. It never stops. It is constant as the flight of time. It is as merciless as fate. The one object of ordinary involuntary servitude is to get the fruit of other's toil without paying for it. That is the object of interest slavery. In ordinary slavery the master is obligated to feed, clothe and preserve the life and health of his human asset. It pays him to do so. The invisible foreign masters who profit from the grinding system of slavery through debt acknowledge no responsibility for the welfare, health or even the lives of their victims. As time goes on and the human burden is steadily increased by multiplication of…debts, and interest rates are compounded and advanced throughout the world, humanity can only feel the pinch as it groans and staggers under the cumulating load. It can never know just how the mysterious game is worked or just who tightens down the screws…The pressure is applied on every living soul at the cradle and ends only at the grave. Every child is born with a mortgage on its back that dooms it to life-long toil. Unborn generations are mortgaged into involuntary, life-long toil, helpless debt slavery years before the Almighty breathes into them the breath of life. Their immortal souls are predestined by the universal debt system to be coined into additional dollars to gratify the insatiable greed and avarice and profit-lust of the usurers."[481]

The gravity of debt slavery cannot be understated and thankfully, Crozier did not shy away from exposing the truth of what it is! It's heavy! It's unbearable! It's punishing! It's suffocating! Take a moment right now to go to https://usdebtclock.org/ and watch the U.S. Debt escalate by the millisecond. Notice to the right of the U.S. Debt, there are two numbers, one that lists the debt for every U.S. Citizen and the debt for every taxpayer. As I write this sentence, every U.S. Citizen owes $70,722 and every taxpayer owes $188,167! No wonder one of the leading causes of divorce is financial strain.

Crozier aptly described our reality under the Federal Reserve System; every child is born with a life-long toil of financial debt. The usurers are the masters. Humanity are their slaves. We all are in chains to debt from cradle to grave, unless we rise up and take back our freedom!

The Root of Usury

We have discovered that the root of usury is found in the heart of the serpent, the enemy of our soul. Let's review the evidence we have collected along our journey, starting with the deception of Eve.

Genesis 3:13 (NKJV) *"And the Lord God said to the woman 'What is this you have done?' The woman said, 'The serpent deceived me, and I ate."*

We discovered that the Hebrew word for deceived in this passage is '*nasha*' which means "to deceive, beguile, mentally delude, morally seduce, to impose, to cause to go astray."[482] But the Hebrew and English lexicon known as Brown-Driver-Briggs (BDB) defines '*nasha*' as "to lend on interest, or usury, to become a creditor."[483] Therefore, the root of usury is '*nasha*' and we have found this to be a hallmark characteristic of the seed of Satan. Satan is the father of lies. Truth does not exist within him. He has a Master of Arts in Deception.

We have been beguiled by elite banksters who have been led by the great deceiver, Satan himself. The entire Federal Reserve system is rooted in '*nasha.*' The players involved in the creation of the Federal Reserve, exuded Nephilim traits. They were master deceivers, skilled at lying to the American people, pretending to have the nation's best interest in mind, while crafting an insidious system of enslavement.

Our investigation into the roots of the Federal Reserve has required us to uncover the ancient layers of deception that began at the dawn of humanity. We have followed the trail of the Nephilim (see Figure 58), albeit it hasn't been easy, especially because of the Nephilim's adaptive deceptions spanning time and cultures. Just as we think we are about to trap the serpent; it slithers away and morphs into a different creature. The Nephilim have tried to cover their scent, but as we honed our senses to the stench of their presence, we have been able to trace them all the way from the days of Noah to the dollar bill in our pocket.

The Nephilim were born with treason, lust, deceit, usury, greed, rebellion and pride in their spiritual DNA. We have found these same characteristics filter down from the Nephilim to the Edomites, to the Khazarians, to the Rothschilds, and to the "six men" that stole away in the dark of night under a cloak of deception to give birth to the Federal Reserve.

The fruit exposes the roots. So how has our economy fared since 1913 when this beast was unleashed upon us?

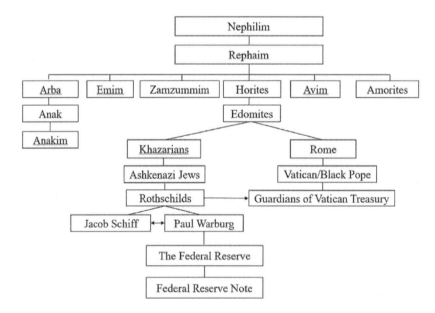

Figure 58. Chart of Nephilim Connection to Federal Reserve. Created by Laura Sanger

U.S. Economy Under the Federal Reserve System

*The best way to destroy the capitalist system is to
debauch the currency
~Vladimir Lenin*

Since the inception of the Federal Reserve, it's been a rollercoaster ride with exhilarating highs and death-defying plunges! The boom and bust cycle was not eradicated by the "stability" promised by Warburg's central bank system. Instead, booms and busts have become the new normal. It is the fruit of a central banking system. A century of the boom and bust cycle has led to the wholesale redistribution of wealth from the masses to the top 1%.

The debasement of the dollar over the past century tells the grim story of how our economy has fared under the Federal Reserve System. When the Federal Reserve first started printing dollars, the currency was backed by gold, but now it is simply a fiat currency. A fiat currency is not backed by anything of value, but instead, only has value because the U.S. government decrees it so. The value only lasts as long as the public has confidence in the ability of the government to back its value. When this confidence is eroded, bank runs ensue, inflation rises, and in the worst-case scenarios, hyperinflation sets in. As Maloney puts it, "fiat currency is designed to lose value. Its very purpose is to confiscate your wealth and transfer it to the government. As each new dollar enters circulation it devalues all the other dollars in existence because there are now more dollars chasing the same amount of goods and services. This causes prices to rise. It is the insidious stealth tax known as inflation, robbing you of your wealth like a thief in the night."[484]

The classical gold standard was in operation from approximately 1871 to 1914 when the majority of the world's currencies were pegged to gold. During that time, U.S. currency was actually real money because it served as a receipt for gold held in the Treasury. But since the inception of the Federal Reserve's money magic, we have borrowed every dollar into existence with interest attached. It's important to note that the same year the Federal Reserve Act was passed in 1913, the Sixteenth Amendment to the Constitution was ratified which allowed Congress to impose a federal income tax for the purpose of paying off the interest from the dollars borrowed from the Federal Reserve.

The Federal Reserve Act factored the gold standard into the framework of the central bank. The law required the Federal Reserve to keep gold within its reserve that equaled 40% of the value of the currency it issued. The conversion rate for dollars into gold was fixed at $20.67 per ounce of gold.[485] During the Great Depression, large amounts of gold were withdrawn from the Federal Reserve vaults because corporations, individuals and foreign investors feared the devaluation of the dollar. President Franklin Roosevelt implemented several draconian measures to stop the draining of the Federal Reserve's gold. He weakened the link between gold and the dollar. In 1933, he outlawed the constitutional right for Americans to own gold, and he cancelled the "gold clause" which had been in place since the end of the Civil War. Most contracts required payment in gold or currency equal to its value in gold, as a way to protect against currency devaluation. This egregious act allowed the government to default on payments owed to Americans. In 1934, Roosevelt continued to devalue the dollar by raising the price of gold to $35 per ounce. In essence, this measure stole roughly 40% of the dollar's purchasing power. So not only was it illegal for Americans to own gold (true money), but the government then confiscated 40% of the wealth of its citizens. The gold standard took a beating.

We have to wonder if this was part of the strategy of the Federal Reserve in creating the Great Depression. Weakening the link between gold and the dollar effectively loosened the natural accountability the Federal Reserve experienced under the gold standard. Roosevelt was certainly influenced by the big bankers and during his presidency, the government served the interests of the banking cartel at the detriment of American citizens.

The next major shift in the monetary system occurred in 1944 at Brenton Woods, New Hampshire. Representatives from 44 countries gathered to discuss international trade and the establishment of a global monetary system. The Brenton Woods agreement was a pact with foreign central banks to fix their currency to the U.S. dollar, rather than to gold. The U.S. held the majority of the world's gold after WWII. The Brenton Woods agreement crowned the dollar as the world's reserve currency. In turn, the U.S. agreed that foreign central banks could redeem the dollar in gold at a price of $35 per ounce. In a nutshell, the Brenton Woods agreement resulted in foreign currencies being pegged to the dollar instead of gold, and the dollar was pegged to gold. This effectively expanded the reach of the Federal Reserve's tentacles, exponentially increasing its power.

A major flaw in the Brenton Woods System is that there were no limits placed on the Federal Reserve with regard to currency creation. At that time, there was a growing demand for the dollar by foreign banks. The Federal Reserve obliged by creating more currency, but this outpaced the growth of gold held in reserves. By 1971, the United States economy was in stagflation, a condition of slow growth and inflation, and countries were losing their confidence in gold convertibility. President Nixon met with 15 top financial advisers including Federal Reserve Chair, Arthur Burns, at Camp David in August, 1971.[486] Together, they devised a new economic policy that would end the dollar's convertibility to gold in order to stave off a looming gold run. By 1973, the Brenton Woods System had come to an end, the dollar became entirely a fiat currency backed by nothing other than the "good faith" of the U.S. government. Yes, the same government that confiscated the gold of American citizens a generation earlier and failed to make good on gold bonds that Americans had purchased. This shift in monetary policy not only effected the United States, but it effectively forced the entire world onto a fiat currency because the U.S. dollar still remained the world's reserve currency. The Federal Reserve had finally managed to free itself from the natural accountability of the gold standard.

With the monster freed from constraints, it could wreak unimaginable havoc. The Minneapolis Federal Reserve reported that total inflation as measured by the Consumer Price Index (CPI) was approximately 22 percent between the years 2000 and 2008. The problem with this measure is that the CPI has been manipulated by the money magicians over the years. The Bureau of Labor Statistics (BLS) used to track the price of the same basket of goods and services year after year, but when the numbers began looking unfavorable, they changed their practices.

"For example, if the price of an item has changed dramatically from one year to the next…the item can be dropped from the basket of goods (deletion), substituted with another item (substitution), or simply assigned a new price (hedonic adjustment)."[487]

The BLS has created a measure of inflation that is virtually irrelevant to the consumer. It's called the Core CPI but it excludes the prices of necessary items, such as food and energy. A more accurate picture of price inflation is provided by John Williams of Shadow Government Statistics (see Figure 59). The blue line indicates the CPI before the BLS began manipulating the numbers and the red line indicates the broadest measure of the CPI currently published by the BLS.

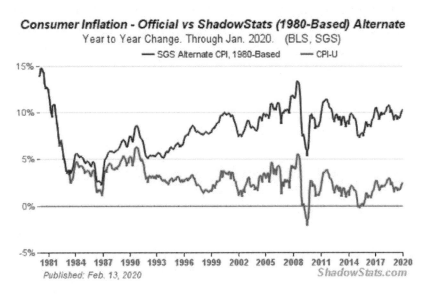

Figure 59. Consumer Inflation. Courtesy of ShadowStats.com.

The Federal Reserve certainly benefits from the manipulation of the inflation numbers because it allows them to claim an inflation rate around two percent, their targeted goal. But for those of us who grocery shop and pay bills, which is the majority of Americans, we recognize that the CPI-U is not accurate. Inflation is actually hovering around 10%. This is an invisible tax on the American people caused by deficit spending from the government, and the eagerness of the Fed to oblige. From 2000 to 2008, the Federal Reserve increased the currency supply by 112%.[488] I encourage you to run the other direction whenever a politician promises free healthcare or free college education because nothing is ever really free. They are just engaging in money magic. The government will engage in astronomical deficit spending and the Fed will skyrocket the currency supply and you know what that means… you and I, the average American will pay for it in inflation or worse yet, the collapse of our economy.

The Great Recession of 2007-2010, was the largest bust since the Great Depression. It is yet another example of the failure on the part of the Federal Reserve to fortify the economy, instead they have repeatedly made it more vulnerable. Greenspan is the culprit of the massive housing bubble that burst in 2007/2008. He aggressively cut interest rates numerous times during his tenure as Fed Chair which led to the inflation of multiple bubbles. His response after the dot.com bubble burst in 2001 was to cut interest rates, this set the stage for the economic meltdown in 2008. Although as far back as 1993, the Federal Reserve's fingerprints can be found on the origins of the housing boom. During the Clinton administration, an emphasis was made to provide affordable housing for minorities and low-income citizens The Boston Fed wrote a paper entitled "Closing the Gap: A Guide to Equal Opportunity Lending," in which they encouraged lowering traditionally sanctioned mortgage-lending standards.[489] This practice took root in the mortgage lending industry and Wall Street investment banks creating a feeding frenzy for greed.

Greed is a powerful driving force that compelled investors and bankers to engage in "moral hazards." The dollar signs attached to risky investments were more enticing than sound financial investments. The Too Big To Fail (TBTF) banks understood that the Federal Reserve would rescue them if they teetered on the edge of insolvency. The checks and balances of accounting practices were manipulated into shadow banking practices called off-balance-sheet (OBS) accounting. Hot shot Wall Street investors created new streams of cash that exploited the lower standards within the mortgage lending industry. The use of "credit risk transfer instruments," such as mortgage backed securities (MBS), collateralized debt obligations (CDO), and asset backed securities (ABS) were invented to hide the credit risk within the mortgage industry. The shadow banking system created the derivatives market, yet another tool of obfuscation. Who became king of the derivatives market? None other than JP Morgan Chase.

According to the Fourth Quarter 2007 report from the Office of the Comptroller of Currency (OCC), JP Morgan Chase was leveraged 64:1 in the derivatives market.[490] For every dollar the bank had in assets, they carried $64 in debt tied to purchases in derivatives. The derivatives market is fractional reserve banking on crack! It's endemic within the banking system. When the massive bubble burst in 2008, it triggered the worst financial crisis since the Great Depression. The Federal Reserve stepped in as the lender of *first* resort awarding massive bailouts at near zero interest rates to banking institutions that engaged in "moral hazards." The Federal Reserve's willingness to lend freely and buy up the junk investment instruments that were rejected on Wall Street, communicated to the TBTF banks that they can continue with their reckless investment strategies and not face the consequences. Is it any wonder the TBTF banks haven't changed their practices?

The OCC Third Quarter Report for 2019 reveals that TBTF banks are engaged in outrageously dangerous behavior. It shows that Goldman Sachs' derivatives activities are leveraged 231:1![491] Yes that's right, **231:1.** When Lehman Brothers was deemed insolvent and forced to close their doors in 2008, causing 25,000 employees to lose their jobs, they were only leveraged 5:1. The irresponsible behavior of Goldman Sachs could trigger a collapse in the global economy at any moment.

Lack of Transparency

In 2015, Jerome Powell wrote a paper prior to his appointment as current Chair of the Federal Reserve, entitled *"Audit the Fed" and Other Proposals.* His remarks were a response to The Federal Reserve Transparency Act of 2015, a bill introduced in the House of Representatives by Thomas Massie and introduced in the Senate by Rand Paul; it has not been passed into law yet. It is a reformed bill that was originally proposed by Representative Ron Paul and amended by Senator Bernie Sanders. In his response, Powell makes the following assertions:

"'Audit the Fed'…would subject the Federal Reserve's conduct of monetary policy to unlimited congressional policy audits…these proposals are based on the assertion that the Federal Reserve operates in secrecy and was not accountable for its actions during the crisis, a perspective that is in violent conflict with the facts…The Federal Reserve is highly transparent and accountable to the public and to the Congress…monetary policy decisions were debated and voted on by the FOMC and announced immediately, with detailed explanations provided in the minutes of these deliberations. The Fed provided public guidance on its plans to purchase assets and made those purchases in open, competitive transactions that were disclosed as soon as they occurred…It is important to note that GAO investigations are not the financial audits that many assume them to be. They extend beyond mere accounting to examine strategy, judgments and day-to-day decisionmaking."[492]

Let's dissect Jerome Powell's remarks to see if he is accurately representing the facts. First, is the Federal Reserve highly transparent? "Highly transparent" would suggest the public has access to pertinent information regarding the Federal Reserve, and given that there are no public records available listing the member banks that own stock in the 12 regional Federal Reserve Banks, the Fed falls short of being "highly transparent." Second, does the FOMC provide detailed explanations of their deliberations of monetary policy decisions? It is true that the FOMC provides minutes within three weeks of their meetings, but these cannot be considered detailed explanations. Detailed explanations of FOMC deliberations would be contained in the transcripts and these are not made available until five years after each FOMC meeting.[493] Their delay in releasing transcripts seems suspect.

Robert Auerbach, an economist who served at the U.S. Treasury and the Federal Reserve, testified October 4, 2011 before the U.S. House of Representatives Subcommittee on Domestic Monetary Policy and Technology. He provided evidence that the Federal Reserve lacks transparency.

"...the 'Government in the Sunshine Act' that was signed into law September 13, 1976. That law required that: 'The agency shall make promptly available to the public, in a place easily accessible to the public, the transcript, electronic recording or minutes of the meeting.' The Fed frantically tried to protect itself from such transparency and individual accountability. Fearing the new legislation and the pending legal action for the disclosure of their records, Federal Reserve Chairman Arthur Burns led the Federal Reserve Open Market Committee in a 10 to 1 vote to discontinue transcripts of its meeting in 1976. That vote began the official 17-year Fed lie asserting that no transcripts were being maintained of FOMC meetings. On October 19, 1993, Chairman Gonzalez [Chairman of U.S. House of Representatives Committee on Financial Services] convened a Fed oversight hearing focusing on transcripts...witnesses were given specific instructions that they reveal details of what records are kept by the Fed of their meetings...Greenspan clearly intended to mislead Congress about the written records of the FOMC...Mr. Greenspan avoided drawing attention to the existence of transcripts...the Cleveland Fed...informed the Congress of the deception. Chairman Greenspan then sent a letter admitting that transcripts existed. He claimed to have had memory problems...the Fed staff showed us 17 years of neatly typed transcripts around the corner from Chairman Greenspan's office."[494]

This further validates the deceptive practices of the Federal Reserve.

The third assertion that Jerome Powell made in his 2015 response was that the "Fed provided public guidance on its plans to purchase assets and made those purchases in open, competitive transactions that were disclosed as soon as they occurred." He is speaking of the transactions that occurred during the financial crisis of 2007-2010; he claims their transactions were competitive. Were they competitive? We need to examine the 2011 GAO report to answer this question.

Congressmen Ron Paul and Bernie Sanders were strong advocates for auditing the Fed and deserve recognition for their tireless pursuit of demanding accountability from them. They were successful in inserting the GAO audit of the Federal Reserve into the Dodd-Frank Act. The GAO audit was the first ever, top to bottom audit in nearly a century of the Fed's existence. The scope of the audit was to examine the emergency actions taken by the Federal Reserve Board from December 1, 2007 to July 21, 2010.[495] The findings of this audit reveal astonishing decisions and transactions that the Federal Reserve engaged in during the financial crisis.

One finding disproves Powell's assertion that the Federal Reserve engaged in open, competitive transactions. The GAO report states, "vendors have been a critical component of helping create and operate the emergency programs, with most of the fees concentrated among a few contracts that were awarded **without competition**."[496] (emphasis mine) These vendors included JP Morgan Chase, Morgan Stanley and Wells Fargo. The report found that approximately two-thirds of the contracts awarded were no-bid, non-competitive contracts.

The primary reason every Fed Chair engages in fear mongering when it comes to the notion that the Federal Reserve should be audited is because they don't want their strategy, judgments and day-to-day decision making examined for fear of being exposed. The GAO report exposed conflicts of interest during the financial crisis by showing that emergency assistance, otherwise known as bailouts, were awarded to institutions that Federal Reserve staff held interests in. For example, Jaime Dimon, the CEO of JP Morgan Chase also served on the Board of the FRBNY when the FRBNY decided to award $391 billion in bailouts to JP Morgan Chase bank.[497] Jaime Dimon earned himself a stock bonus valued at $16 million as a result of the bailout.[498] As I pointed out earlier, JP Morgan Chase was the worst offender in leveraging within the derivatives market. Another example is that William Dudley, a board member of the FRBNY, was granted a waiver for his conflict of interest, so that he could maintain his investments in AIG and GE, while the FRBNY awarded bailout funds to these institutions. I guess it pays to be part of the board of the FRBNY, literally. The GAO report found that as of 2011, the FRBNY had not yet established policy to mitigate conflict of interests. In response to these findings, Senator Bernie Sanders remarked, "no one who works for a firm receiving direct financial assistance from the Fed should be allowed to sit on the Fed's board of directors or be employed by the Fed."[499]

Another disturbing finding from the GAO report is that the Federal Reserve gave $3.1 trillion to bailout foreign banks from France, Switzerland, Germany, Belgium, New Zealand and the United Kingdom. Sanders stated, "no agency of the United States government should be allowed to bailout a foreign bank or corporation without the direct approval of Congress and the president."[500]

When Ben Bernanke was testifying before the Congress regarding the state of the economy and monetary policy in 2009, Representative Alan Grayson called him to task regarding the FOMC deciding to give a half-trillion dollars to foreign central banks. One arrangement included $9 billion to New Zealand, which works out to about $3000 for every New Zealander. Rep. Grayson asked Bernanke if he thought it would have been better to extend that type of credit to Americans? Bernanke seemed to think that Americans were not impacted by the FOMC's decision to lend a half-trillion dollars to foreign banks. But Grayson pointed out that the USD nominal exchange rate increased 20% at the same time the Fed doled out half a trillion dollars. Bernanke stated that this was just coincidence, but Grayson disagreed. The point Grayson was making is that a small group of unelected people, the 12 member FOMC, decides the fate of American's financial stability. He told the Huffington Post in 2009,

"It's speculation. It's exactly the thing that hedge funds do all the time and hedge funds do blow up. Look at the Fed balance sheet right now. It has 40 times as much in liabilities as it does in capital. Historically that's a dangerous place to be."[501]

The Federal Reserve is slippery because they are not an agency of the United States government. So, they can bailout foreign banks, while strapping Americans with an invisible tax called inflation and get away with it. The Fed knows that they can dance around questions from Congress and they won't have to answer to the President of the United States, well unless that President is Donald J. Trump!

President Trump is gradually educating the public by exposing the madness of the Federal Reserve system. We have reached the end of the fiat currency's viability. Our monetary system needs to return to a sound money system tied to gold or a basket of assets. The Federal Reserve needs to be restructured or entirely removed from the system. President Trump has Andrew Jackson's portrait hanging in the Oval Office. My guess is that he draws inspiration from Jackson's fortitude to dismantle America's central bank.

Key Points

- Congress relinquished its Constitutional right to coin money in 1913 by passing the Federal Reserve Act.
- Fed has the appearance of a decentralized system with 12 regional banks, but FRBNY holds the majority of the power.
- Fed is an independent agency made up of privately-owned banks that benefit themselves and their foreign customers.
- The Fed's monetary policy decisions truly affect the financial lives of all Americans.
- The Federal Reserve Note is an I.O.U. The product of the Federal Reserve is DEBT.
- The motive of the "six men" was to create an institution of human slavery to carry out predatory money lending practices.
- Usury is a hallmark trait of the seed of '*nasha*' (Satan).
- Since 1913, the U.S. monetary policy gradually moved away from sound money backed by gold. In 1944, the U.S. dollar became the world's reserve currency. In 1971, Nixon severed the tie between the U.S. dollar and gold. U.S. dollar has been a fiat currency ever since.
- Greed is a powerful force that entices bankers/investors to engage in "moral hazards."
- The Fed tries to skirt transparency and accountability.
- Great Recession exposed the Federal Reserve's priority of benefiting its own interests and foreign interests before the interests of the American people.

Chapter 24

Unveiling the Masterminds

How often have I said that when you have excluded the impossible,
whatever remains, however improbable, must be the truth.
~Sherlock Holmes

We have arrived at our final investigative destination! You have done well to stay the course. It is time that we go behind the veil of secrecy that has shrouded the Federal Reserve for over a century. We have discovered the identity of the "six men" and their motives, but now it's time to decipher the clues that uncover the masterminds behind it all. Has there been a geopolitical blueprint established long ago by sinister figures for the purpose of gaining power and control over humanity? To answer these questions, we need to lean upon the Lord to bring revelation of what has been lingering in the dark recesses of history.

Daniel 2:22 (NIV) *"He reveals deep and hidden things; he knows what lies in darkness, and light dwells with him."*

Heed the Warnings

There are three Presidents that have warned the American people about the dangers of the geopolitical blueprint of a one world government. I would surmise that the majority of Americans are unaware of the dire warning our presidents have given us. As we lay out the transcript from these speeches, the message becomes clear. Presidents Eisenhower, Kennedy and Reagan express grave concern for future generations should our country be unsuccessful in thwarting a one world government. The gravity in their words can be felt even now, decades later. My hairs stand on end when I read their warnings.

On January 17, 1961 in the final days of his presidency, President Dwight D. Eisenhower gave this warning in his farewell speech, "Throughout America's adventure in free government, our basic purposes have been to keep the peace, to foster progress in human achievement, and enhance liberty, dignity and integrity among people and among nations. To strive for less would be unworthy of a free and religious people. Any failure traceable to arrogance, or our lack of comprehension or readiness to sacrifice would inflict upon us grievous hurt both at home and abroad.

Progress toward these noble goals is persistently threatened by the conflict now engulfing the world, it commands our whole attention, absorbs our very beings. **We face a hostile ideology – global in scope, atheistic in character, ruthless in purpose, and insidious in method. Unhappily the danger it poses promises to be of indefinite duration**."[502] (emphasis mine)

Just a few months later, on April 27, 1961, President John F. Kennedy gives a speech entitled The President and the Press, "The very word 'secrecy' is repugnant in a free and open society; and we are as a people inherently and historically opposed to secret societies, to secret oaths and to secret proceedings. We decided long ago that the dangers of excessive and unwarranted concealment of pertinent facts far outweighed the dangers which are cited to justify it. Even today, there is little value in opposing the threat of a closed society by imitating its arbitrary restrictions. Even today, there is little value in ensuring the survival of our nation if our traditions do not survive with it. And there is very grave danger that an announced need for increased security will be seized upon by those anxious to expand its meaning to the very limits of official censorship and concealment…Today no war has been declared – and however fierce the struggle may be, it may never be declared in the traditional fashion. Our way of life is under attack…**For we are opposed around the world by a monolithic and ruthless conspiracy that relies primarily on covert means for expanding its sphere of influence** – on infiltration instead of invasion, on subversion instead of elections, on intimidation instead of free choice, on guerrillas by night instead of armies by day. It is a system which has conscripted vast human and material resources into the building of a tightly knit, highly efficient machine that combines military, diplomatic, intelligence, economic, scientific, and political operations…**Its preparations are concealed, not published. Its mistakes are buried, not headlined. Its dissenters are**

silenced, not praised. No expenditure is questioned, no rumor is printed, no secret is revealed."[503] (emphasis mine)

JFK was so deeply disturbed by the geopolitical blueprint that he alerted the American public at the outset of his presidency. The subversive monolithic conspiracy was so troubling that JFK created the Special Forces within the military for the purposes of defending against the globalists. Tragically, President Kennedy was a dissenter that was "silenced."

On October 27, 1964, Ronald Reagan delivered a speech entitled A Time for Choosing. "And this idea that government is beholden to the people, that it has no other source of power except the sovereign people, is still the newest and the most unique idea in all the long history of man's relation to man. This is the issue… whether we believe in our capacity of self-government or whether we abandon the American revolution and confess that **a little intellectual elite in a far-distant capitol can plan our lives for us better than we can plan them ourselves…'the full power of centralized government'** this was the very thing the Founding Fathers sought to minimize. They knew that governments don't control things. A government can't control the economy without controlling people. And they know when a government sets out to do that, it must use force and coercion to achieve its purpose. They also knew, those Founding Fathers, that outside of its legitimate functions, government does nothing as well or as economically as the private sector of the economy…You and I know and do not believe that life is so dear and peace so sweet as to be purchased at the price of chains and slavery…You and I have the courage to say to our enemies, 'There is a price we will not pay.' 'There is a point beyond which they must not advance.' And this is the meaning in the phrase…'peace through strength.' You and I have a rendezvous with destiny. We'll preserve for our children this, the last best hope of man on earth, or we'll sentence them to take the last step into a thousand years of darkness."[504] (emphasis mine)

While Eisenhower, Kennedy and Reagan warned the American people of the evils of a one world government and secret societies, President George H. W. Bush, the quintessential globalist, beguiled the American people by praising the New World Order (NWO). He introduced the concept for the first time in his 1991 State of the Union Address, "What is at stake is more than one small country; it is a big idea: a **new world order**, where diverse nations are drawn together in common cause to achieve the universal aspirations of mankind – peace and security, freedom and the rule of law.

391

Such is a world worthy of our struggle and worthy of our children's future...We have within our reach the promise of a renewed America. We can find meaning and reward by serving some higher purpose than ourselves, a shining purpose, **the illumination of a Thousand Points of Light**."[506] (emphasis mine)

The juxtaposition of Reagan speaking of a one world government as a "thousand years of darkness," and his successor speaking of it as a "thousand points of light" is astounding. We are, in fact, in a battle between light and darkness, between Yahweh and Lucifer. As JFK revealed, the agenda of secret societies is to dictate the course of nations and manipulate others for the benefit of their schemes. It's imperative that we shine a light upon the darkness to expose the spiritual forces at work within these secret societies. Time is of the essence!

We are on the verge of a global transformation. All we need is the right major crisis and the nations will accept the New World Order.
~ David Rockefeller

Uncovering Secret Societies

At the core of every secret society is the belief that a select few individuals can attain a superior level of wisdom, knowledge, understanding and intellect by which to rule the masses. The father of lies beguiles his initiates by promising a god-like transmutation. It is the same temptation that Eve faced, the same trap the 'sons of God' laid out. It is the promise of divine knowledge to entice humanity away from relationship with God. The central doctrine of secret societies is that Lucifer is the light bearer, the illuminator, and therefore, is superior to Yahweh. Most secret societies are structured to be "circles within circles" (a circumpunct), meaning that initiates in the outer circles are often unaware of the true nature of the organization in which they belong, and only those in the inner circle understand the true agenda. For this reason, it is difficult to investigate secret societies because disinformation and obfuscation keep them shrouded in mystery.

Secret societies are cogs in the wheels of the machination working to form the New World Order. Make no mistake, a one world government is an antichrist agenda. A central tenet of globalism is to dismantle sovereign nations by disregarding borders and forcing mass migration to upend the cultural fabric of sovereign nations; the end goal is the establishment of a one world government.

As we discussed in Section II of our investigation, this is not a new strategy, in fact, this strategy has been employed since shortly after the Seed War began. Two hundred 'Watchers' left their place of habitation, crossed the boundaries of their authority in heaven to invade the earth realm for the purpose of staging a coup d'état. The 'Watchers' sexual defilement of the daughters of men created the hybrid race of Nephilim. The Nephilim brought a frontal assault on the survival of humanity. This admixture of the human genome was the enemy's best attempt at thwarting the birth of the Messiah, but it was an abject failure. Globalism has since become the preeminent war tactic of the enemy. We see this strategy used over and over again throughout scripture.

In the narrative of Genesis 10, we learned that Nimrod was the first "globalist" in human history. He amassed great power and control in hopes of leading a coup d'état. The Tower of Babel was a display of man's blatant defiance of the Lord. The people coalesced to worship their own greatness and open a portal of unimaginable destruction. Nimrod operated under an antichrist spirit and became a '*gibbowr*' manifesting the phenotype of the Nephilim. Yahweh's response to globalism was to scatter the people across the face of the earth and give them distinct languages, which effectively birthed sovereign nations.

In Psalm 2, we see that the power brokers of the world were at it again, trying to carry out the antichrist agenda of globalism.

Psalm 2: 1-3 (TPT) "*How dare the nations plan a rebellion. Their foolish plots are futile! Look at how the power brokers of the world rise up to hold their summit as the rulers scheme and confer together against Yahweh and his Anointed King, saying: 'Let's come together and break away from the Creator. Once and for all let's cast off these controlling chains of God and his Christ!'*"

Finally, we see in the Book of Revelation that the Antichrist will govern a one world government at the end of the ages.

Revelation 13:7-8 (NIV) "*It was given power to wage war against God's holy people and to conquer them. And it was given authority over every tribe, people, language and nation. All inhabitants of the earth will worship the beast – all whose names have not been written in the Lamb's book of life, the Lamb who was slain from the creation of the world.*"

Now that we understand that this is the strategy of the enemy, the most effective way to thwart his schemes is to expose them. Rats scatter when the lights are turned on! We will shine an investigative light on the secret societies that are most closely intertwined with the Federal Reserve, but keep in mind this is not an exhaustive study. The web of interconnectedness between secret societies runs deep and wide. It's important we return to the hidden agenda of Zionism that we discussed in Chapter 19. We have some loose ends to tie up.

Sabbatean-Frankists

Sabbatean-Frankists form the inner core of Zionism and exploit Judaism and Jews for the advancement of a NWO. Like most secret societies, it's members worship Lucifer, but it is not as visible as Freemasonry or the Illuminati. It is one of the least known secret societies because it has hidden itself deep within Zionism. It has created a barricade known as anti-Semitism that keeps intruders out. Its origins are in the person of Sabbatai Zevi.

Sabbatai Zevi was born in 1626 to a wealthy merchant family in Smyrna, modern day Turkey. He was trained in the Talmud, but in his adolescence, he became interested in Jewish mysticism and studied the kabbalah. He was an eccentric person with, what now would be considered, bipolar disorder. Sabbatai was charismatic during times of mania and claimed he had episodes of "illumination." He attracted a group of followers whom he initiated into the secrets of kabbalism. In 1648, during an "illumined" episode, he declared himself to be the long-awaited Messiah, and subsequently engaged in strange acts that contravened Jewish law. This is what I would diagnose as Bipolar Disorder with psychotic features. But nonetheless, over the span of a few decades, he amassed a large following of Jewish people.

Sabbateanism erupted during a time when traditional Judaism was weakening, and hopelessness had begun to set in for the long-awaited Messiah. When Sabbatai claimed to be the Messiah, word spread within a few months across Europe, Africa, the Arabian desert and into Babylonia. Sabbatai preached a new law which freed the Jewish people from keeping 613 laws. As you can imagine, this movement gained momentum especially when the "new law" was really no law at all. Sabbateans were taught they could engage in whatever behavior they desired, including licentiousness and orgies.[505] Sabbatai led a million followers away from Judaism. In 1666, Shabbatai was captured by the Sultan, who forced him to convert to Islam or die. His conversion disillusioned many of his followers, but those who remained went further underground and became even more radical. Gershom Scholem, a Jewish mysticism historian, argues that Sabbatai created a split within Judaism between "outward orthodoxy and secret heresy."[507]

Following the death of Sabbatai, a radical sect within the Sabbateans continued. They believed in the doctrine of the "nullification of the Torah and its true fulfillment."[508] In the 18th century, this radical wing of the Sabbateans would be revived under Jacob Frank, who declared himself to be the reincarnation of Shabbetai Zevi. Jacob Frank (1726-1791) was introduced to Sabbateans during his youth when he was studying the Zohar. He developed a reputation among the Sabbateans as a "man possessed of special powers and inspiration," "a man of unbridled ambition, domineering to the point of despotism."[509] He established a reformed Sabbatean sect, and his followers became known as Frankists.

Jacob Frank revealed his teachings to his followers in short statements and parables promoting that all religions were merely stages which "believers" pass through. Religion was like a garment you wear for a time and then discard because ultimately it is of no worth. He proclaimed that true worth is in the hidden faith of the Frankists. Frank advocated taking on the cloak of Christianity outwardly to conceal the secrets of their faith. Interestingly, a central doctrine of Frankists was called the "way to Esau." Edom symbolized liberty in all areas of life, a road to religious anarchy. In order for the Frankists to "achieve this goal, it was necessary to abolish and destroy the laws, teachings and practices which constrict the power of life, but this must be done in secret."[510] Frank led his sect to embrace licentiousness, as evidenced by the practice of ritualistic sexual orgies. The core belief of the Sabbatean-Frankists is that the Godhead takes on human form through the leaders of the sect, first Sabbatai and then Frank. Members of the sect were supposed to blend in with the predominant religion whether it be Judaism, Christianity, or Islam. They were forbidden to reveal their beliefs that Sabbatai and Frank were the Messiah. Frank led 60,000 European Jews in baptism into the Catholic Church.

Many are unaware of the influence the Sabbatean-Frankists have had upon the world, which is precisely the point of secret societies, to go undetected. Gershom Scholem in his book *Kabbalah and Its Symbolism* writes, "For Frank, anarchic destruction represented all the Luciferian radiance, all the positive tones and overtones, of the word 'Life.' The nihilistic mystic descends into the abyss in which the freedom of living things is born: he passes through all the embodiments and forms that come his way, committing himself to none; and not content with rejecting and abrogating all values and laws, he tramples them underfoot and desecrates them, in order to attain the elixir of Life...It goes without saying that from the standpoint of the community and its institutions, such mysticism should have regarded as demonic possession."[511]

The Illuminati

In the 1770s, Jacob Frank made a pact with Adam Weishaupt to join the Sabbatean-Frankists with the Illuminati. It was at this juncture in history that the Rothschilds became intertwined in these Luciferian secret societies. All three converged in Frankfurt. The Rothschilds provided much needed funding for Frank which solidified the triad union.[512] Barry Chamish, a Canadian born Israeli author writes,

"The initial financiers of Labor Zionism and Theodore Herzl were barons of the Rothschild clan. Their goal was the creation of a state in the image of their Sabbataian beliefs; that is, anti-Torah, anti-Talmudic, anti-religious and anti-Jewish. To the Sabbataians, any Jew who does not accept anti-Judaism is fit for execution. Israel has chosen morality and God, and that means execution is the correct punishment. Rabbi Antelman is not alone in tracing the Rothschild path to an American financial takeover. Hundreds, if not thousands of researchers have proved that the European Rothschilds sent their German agents of the Schiff, Astor and Warburg families to serve the interests of the cabal formed by the Jesuit illuminati, British Freemasonry and Sabbataianism."[513]

In 1770, Mayer Amschel Rothschild commissioned Adam Weishaupt to establish a secret society called the Order of the Illuminati. Amschel, along with a handful of influential cohorts, had been working on plans for global domination. Adam Weishaupt caught the attention of Amschel because of his intelligence and repugnant, narcissistic personality (Weishaupt impregnated his sister-in-law and tried to abort the baby because he didn't want his reputation tarnished).[514]

Adam Weishaupt was born in Ingolstadt, Bavaria in 1748. He was born to Jewish parents who converted to Catholicism. Accordingly, Weishaupt attended Jesuits schools and learned five languages including Latin, Greek and Hebrew. He became a Professor of Canon Law at the University of Ingolstadt. In his early 20's, he began collecting and reading every ancient text he could get a hold of. He was particularly drawn to the mysteries of the Great Pyramid. In 1771, he met a merchant who had lived in Egypt and taught him some of the mysteries of the ancient Illuminees.[515]

Weishaupt enjoyed his influence as a professor in shaping the minds of his students, but this small group of adepts was not enough to satisfy him. Instead, he envisioned impacting all of humanity by forming a secret society with laws patterned after the Jesuits, but diametrically opposite. Weishaupt stated,

"What these men [Jesuits] have done for the Altar and the Throne (said he to himself) why would not I do in opposition to the Altar and the Throne? With legions of adepts subject to my laws, and by the lure of mysteries, why may not I destroy under the cover of darkness, what they edified in broad day? What Christ even did for God and for Caesar, why shall I not do against God and Caesar, by means of adepts now become my apostles?"[516]

Weishaupt was just twenty-eight years of age when he formally instituted the Order of the Illuminati on May 1, 1776. He, along with two of his brightest and most devious followers, formed the highest echelon of the secret society. They took on secret names, Weishaupt became 'Spartacus.' The name chosen for their order, the Illuminati, was in honor of Lucifer, the 'bearer of light.' It was founded to establish a Novus Ordo Seclorum or a New World Order. A prominent symbol of the Illuminati is the Great Pyramid and the "all seeing eye." Weishaupt stated, "Do you realize sufficiently what it means to rule – to rule in a secret society? Not only over the lesser or more important of the populace, but over the best men, over men of all ranks, nations, and religions, to rule without external force, to unite them indissolubly, to breathe one spirit and soul into them, men distributed over all parts of the world. [We] are convinced that The Order will rule the world. Every member therefore becomes a ruler. We all think of ourselves as qualified to rule. It is therefore an alluring thought both to good and bad men. Therefore the Order will spread."[517]

Weishaupt's plan for world domination can be summarized as follows:

1. Abolish all national governments
2. Abolish private property
3. Abolish inheritance
4. Destroy patriotism
5. Destroy Christianity
6. Destroy the family unit

7.   Create a New World Order/One World Government

Abbé Augustin Barruel, a French Jesuit Priest from the late 18th century studied the life and character of Adam Weishaupt. He described him in this way, "An odious phenomenon in nature, an Atheist void of remorse, a profound hypocrite, destitute of those superior talents which lead to the vindication of truth, he is possessed of all that energy and ardour in vice which generates conspirators for impiety and anarchy. Shunning, like the ill-boding owl, the genial rays of the sun, he wraps around him the mantle of darkness; and history shall record of him, as of the evil spirit, only the black deeds which he planned or executed."[518]

Reverend Seth Payson, who wrote *Proofs of the Real Existence, and Dangerous Tendency of Illuminism* in 1802, provided a thorough examination of the secret society. Payson wrote, "His [Weishaupt's] scheme appears to be calculated, not so much for uniting persons of similar sentiments in one society, as for seducing those of opposite inclinations, and by a most artful and detestable process, gradually obliterating from their minds every moral and religious sentiment."[519]

To spread this parasitic secret society, the Rothschilds directed Weishaupt to infiltrate the Continental Order of Freemasons with the doctrines of the Illuminati. The Rothschilds were Freemasons and this conjoining of forces was seamless. Weishaupt established the lodges of the Grand Orient as the headquarters for the Illuminati. He also hired 2,000 recruits which were among the most intelligent men in industries such as, arts, writing, education, science, finance, and business. These recruits were tasked with utilizing four methods of social engineering to control people: 1) use monetary and sex bribery to control high level officials in government and other industries, once these influential men were entrapped in the snares of sex scandals and/or financial impieties, blackmail them with threats of harm to their families or themselves; 2) cull the student body from colleges and universities for those with exceptional mental acuity from well-bred families and award them scholarships (i.e. Rhodes Scholar) to study international/globalists affairs; 3) place these agents of the Illuminati, who have been trapped by blackmail or indebted from scholarship, into positions of government to serve as experts/advisers in order to steer policies to align with Illuminati plans of one world government; 4) obtain absolute control of the press (media) to sway the narrative in support of Illuminati agendas.[520]

It's a bit eerie to read these social engineering methods that were drafted in the 18th century and realize that these same methods are being used today with great effectiveness. The Council on Foreign Relations (CFR) is essentially the Illuminati in the United States. There are currently 5,084 members who comprise the most prominent leaders in foreign policy. It was first established by "Colonel" Edward Mandell House, Woodrow Wilson's "alter ego," at the direction of Jacob Schiff. Some say that House was the most politically powerful person in the country during President Wilson's administration. He essentially ran the presidency. House was a Marxist committed to seeing the United States become a socialistic nation. Both House and Karl Marx were members of the Illuminati. House wielded the power he was given to steer the government to create the framework for socialism. He called for the passage of a "graduated income tax and for the establishment of a state-controlled central bank,"[521] which is exactly what happened within his first year "in office."

As you can see from the character sketch we have developed based on testimonies from others, the founder of the Bavarian Illuminati, Weishaupt, was a narcissist of the highest order. He had a grandiose sense of self-importance, a preoccupation with fantasies of unlimited power, a belief that he functioned at a higher level of intellect that entitled him to exploit others, and a persistent arrogant attitude. He was without remorse for heinous crimes and replete with sinister motives to enslave humanity under his system of domination. He was acutely aware that success of the Illuminati's New World Order rested in its members ability to connive, deceive, beguile, and subjugate humanity by any and all means. These characteristics most definitely meet the criteria for a Nephilim Host.

The triad that formed in Frankfort-on-the-Main in the late 18th century between the Sabbatean-Frankists, the Illuminati, and the Rothschilds has been a formidable breeding ground for Nephilim Hosts. There have been points in history when their Nephilim agendas designed in darkness have been exposed. But the masters of deception have recoiled further underground to become largely undetected as the masterminds behind every war since the French Revolution.

In 1784, an Illuminati agent carrying documents that detailed the order of the French Revolution as plotted by the Illuminati, was struck by lightning and killed while riding on horseback. The Bavarian officials examined the documents found within the saddle bags and discovered the sinister scheme. The Bavarian government raided the homes and the masonic lodges of the Grand Orient to arrest as many members of the Illuminati they were able to locate, but Weishaupt escaped. Additionally, the Bavarian government alerted France of the impending disaster, but unfortunately the French government did not take the warning seriously. Wieshaupt and his cohorts were banished from Bavaria but regrouped and became even more potent in their practices. They burrowed deep within the structure of Freemasonry which became a front organization for the Illuminati, essentially a secret society within a secret society…a circle within a circle.

Freemasonry

The origins of Freemasonry pre-date the Illuminati. During the Middle Ages, the term "freemasons" was used for skilled stonemasons that bid jobs building cathedrals and castles. Inherent with the job was risk of injury, so the "freemasons" formed organizations to care for one another and the place where they met was called a "lodge." In 1648, there is record of a gentleman enrolled in membership at the Lodge in Warrington who is thought to be the first non-mason member. The first Grand Lodge of Free and Accepted Masons was established in London in 1717.[522]

In 1789, John Robison, Professor of Natural Philosophy and Secretary to Royal Society of Edinburgh wrote *Proofs of a Conspiracy Against All Religions and Governments of Europe, Carried on in the Secret Meetings of Free Masons, Illuminati, and Reading Societies*. Robison was once employed as a mason and participated in activities in the masonic lodges for which he described as "decent conviviality." He gradually disengaged from his participation in the lodge due to his advancing career in academia, but he still cultivated the connections he had made. It was through these relationships that he became aware of the growing secrecy and subversive doctrines. He attributed the changes in the direction of Freemasonry to the influence of the Jesuits and the Illuminati.[523] This was during an era when an influx of influential men who were not masons by trade became Freemasons. Three of the five Rothschild brothers were Freemasons. James de Rothschild was a 33rd degree Scottish Rite Freemason in Paris; Nathan Mayer Rothschild was a member of the Masonic Lodge of Emulation in London; and Solomon Mayer Rothschild was initiated into an Austrian masonic lodge in 1809.

As with most secret societies, Masons who are in the lower degrees are unaware of the inner workings of Freemasonry. Many professing Christians are Freemasons and firmly believe they are part of a fraternal order providing good deeds for humanity. It's not until Masons reach the 33rd degree that they are "illuminated" to the sacred teachings. This is the familiar structure of a circle within a circle. Only those within the inner circle are illuminated by the doctrines of Freemasonry. Manly P. Hall, a 33rd degree Mason stated, "Freemasonry is a fraternity within a fraternity – an outer organization concealing an inner brotherhood of the elect…the one visible and the other invisible…The visible society is a splendid camaraderie of 'free and accepted' men enjoined to devote themselves to ethical, educational, fraternal, patriotic and humanitarian concerns. The invisible society is a secret and most august fraternity whose members are dedicated to the service of a mysterious arcanum arcanorum [sacred secret]."[524]

The writings of Albert Pike will give us a window into these doctrines. Albert Pike was a Brigadier General in the Confederate Army and the Grand Commander of North American Freemasonry from 1859 through his death in 1891. In 1871, he was recruited into the Illuminati by an Italian revolutionary named Guissepe Mazzini who was head of the Illuminati after Weishaupt's death. Pike was easily lured into the Illuminati because of his desire to see a one world government. He crafted a blueprint envisioning three global wars that would lead to the establishment of the NWO. Pike called for communism, Nazism and Zionism to be used to create three world wars. The first world war would usher in communism to destroy the reign of the Russian Czars because of their opposition to Rothschild plans at the Congress in Vienna. The second world war would create conflict between Fascism and Zionism. Hitler was financed by the Jewish international bankers (i.e. Warburg and Rothschild) to foment hatred from other nations toward Germany for the extermination of millions of Jews. Nazism would be defeated so that Zionism could rise to pave the way for the creation of the State of Israel. The third world war would be a conflict between Israel and the Muslim world to draw other nations in.[525]

Perhaps David Ben-Gurion, the first Prime Minister of Israel, gave the world a glimpse of the end goal of the Illuminati blueprint, essentially what life would be like after WWIII. Ben-Gurion was asked by Look Magazine, to give a prediction of the future. "With the exception of U.S.S.R. as a federated Eurasian state, all other continents will become united in a world alliance, at whose disposal will be an International police force. All armies will be abolished, and there will be no more wars. In Jerusalem, the United Nations…will build a Shrine of the Prophets to serve the federated union of all continents; this will be the seat of the Supreme Court of Mankind, to settle all controversies among the federated continents."[526]

Jesuits

The Society of Jesus, founded by Ignatius of Loyola, began with six young men and their fervent leader. Ignatius taught his young followers "Spiritual Exercises" he had developed which included austerity, prayer, secret penances, and scourging. When they had proved themselves committed to the new order, the band of disciples took their vows in a vault-like room below a small chapel in Montmartre, Paris. It was the morning of August 15th, 1534 when arguably one of the most "formidable forces in the religious life of Europe" was birthed; the Parisians were none the wiser.[527] These men vowed to live a life of poverty, chastity, obedience to the Church, and special obedience to the Pope. Distinctly different from monks, the Jesuits blend in to whatever culture they are a part of. Many of them are doctors, lawyers, writers, philosophers, financiers, businessmen or whatever the papacy requires of them.

Pope Paul III was the first to officially approve of Ignatius' plan to have a "minimal society that would do battle in the Lord God's service under the banner of the Cross." The initial plan involved a small militia, but it grew by the thousands. Ignatius was the Superior General of the Society of Jesus. The Superior General was to be "obeyed and reverenced at all times as the one who holds the place of Christ our Lord"[528] The Superior General holds an equal position to the Pope, although is essentially an invisible, commander-in-chief with the title *'Papa Nero'* or Black Pope.

F. Tupper Saussy, author of *Rulers of Evil*, included the Jesuit oath as translated by Edwin A. Sherman and on file at the Library of Congress. A Jesuit who is elevated to command level within the Order, takes this oath. I will only include a portion of the oath; it happens to be the most disturbing part in my opinion. "…I furthermore promise and declare that I will, when opportunity presents, make and wage relentless war, secretly or openly, against all heretics, Protestants and Liberals, as I am directed to do, to extirpate and exterminate them from the face of the whole earth; and that I will spare neither age, sex or condition; and that I will hang, burn, waste, boil, flay, strangle, and bury alive these infamous heretics, rip up the stomachs and wombs of their women and crush their infants' heads against the walls, in order to annihilate forever their execrable race."[529]

In response to Ignatius' plan, Pope Paul III said "this is the fingerstroke of God." Paul III gave the highest seal of papacy approval called a "bull" document. The Pope ordained the Society of Jesus with his bull as a decree that the Jesuits would secure the salvation of the Roman Empire through "arts of war." At the Council of Trent, the supremacy of the Jesuits was solidified within the Roman Catholic Church. It was recommended that the "Jesuits should be given pride of place over members of other orders as preachers and professors." [530] From this point in history, the Black Pope has been the Commander-in-Chief of the Catholic Church.

Our examination of the web of connectivity between Sabbatean-Frankists, Illuminati, Freemasonry, and Jesuits provides a framework in which to inspect a controversial document called the Protocols of the Learned Elders of Zion.

The Protocols

The Protocols of the Learned Elders of Zion is a collection of tenets that have created much debate over the years. Some say it's a fraud, some say it was written at the First Zionist Congress, some say it is an Illuminati blueprint for world domination, and some say that it is the minutes from a secret meeting of high-ranking Jesuits. Rather than split hairs to identify the original authors, it's safe to say that the Zionists, (or more specifically, the Sabbatean-Frankists), Illuminati, and the Jesuits are in alignment with the agenda mapped out in the Protocols. Given what we have learned about the structure of secret societies being like a circumpunct, a circle within a circle, we cannot take at face value that Jewish elders wrote these. On the surface, the Protocols are intended to have Jewish fingerprints on them, but this is just a firewall of protection so that the true architects of the blueprints are not detected.

The Protocols first surfaced when Professor Sergyei Nilus, a Russian Orthodox priest received them from a deceased friend. Nilus reported that the protocols were stolen from a woman who was connected to a 33rd degree Freemason.[531] He published the protocols in 1905 and they were translated, into English, by Victor E. Marsden in 1922. The content of the Protocols is consistent with Weishaupt's plan of world domination and is an antichrist agenda. Here is a sampling of excerpts:

Protocol 1: Seizure of our freedom by agents of their plan

"Our power...will be more invincible than any other, because it will remain invisible until the moment when it has gained such strength that no cunning can any longer undermine it. Out of the temporary evil we are now compelled to commit will emerge the good of an unshakeable rule... The result justifies the means...It is only with a despotic rule that plans can be elaborated extensively and clearly in such a way as to distribute the whole properly among the several parts of the machinery of the State...Violence must be the principle, and cunning and make-believe the rule for governments which do not want to lay down their crowns at the feet of agents of some new power."[532]

Protocol 4: Destroy faith in God

"This is the reason why it is so indispensable for us to undermine all faith, to tear out of the minds of the Goyim [non-Jews] the very principle of Godhead and the spirit, and to put in its place arithmetical calculations and material needs."[533]

Protocol 10: Manipulate elections

"...we shall arrange elections in favour of such presidents as have in their past some dark, undiscovered stain...then they will be trustworthy agents for the accomplishment of our plans out of fear of revelations."[534]

Protocol 12: Control of the media, propaganda arm

"We shall deal with the press in the following way: What is the part played by the press to-day? It serves to excite and influence those passions which are needed for our purpose...the public have not the slightest idea what ends the press really serves. I beg you to note that among those making attacks upon us will also be organs established by us, but they will attack exclusively points that we have pre-determined to alter. Not a single announcement will reach the public without our control. Even now this is already being attained by us inasmuch as all news items are received by a few agencies, in whose offices they are focused from all parts of the world. These agencies will then be already entirely ours and will give publicity only to what we dictate to them."[535]

Protocol 21: Usurp the monetary systems of sovereign nations through central banks

"But when the comedy is played out there emerges the fact that a debit and an exceedingly burdensome debit has been treated. For the payment of interest, it becomes necessary to have recourse to new loans, which do not swallow up but only add to the capital debt. And when this credit is exhausted it becomes necessary by new taxes to cover, not the loan, but only the interest on it. These taxes are a debit employed to cover a debit"[536]

Does your stomach turn as you read these excerpts? I strongly recommend you read the entire document, but it is not for the faint of heart, especially given that we are in the 21st century, living out this 19th century diabolical plan to strip us of all our freedoms.

Hegelian Dialectic

The globalists utilize the Hegelian dialectic to control and manipulate humanity so that the Protocols are achieved. In order for us to gain freedom from this oppressive tactic, we need to first understand what it is and how we have come under its spell.

George W. F. Hegel was a German philosopher from the early 19th century. He developed a method by which to arrive at a conclusion. A dialectic is a method of thinking, a basic brain function of differentiation. Hegel believed that the human mind comprehends better when two opposites exist, i.e. right and wrong, black and white, hot and cold. Throughout our investigation, we have been collecting evidence, examining documents and historical records, gathering testimonies, and using discernment for the purpose of drawing a conclusion based on the observed facts, this method aligns with Aristotelian logic. The Hegelian dialectic creates a different path of arriving at a conclusion; a thought occurs, which at first seems satisfactory, but upon reflection seems incomplete (thesis), the negation of the original thought then seems satisfactory, but upon reflection also seems inadequate (antithesis), and so it too is negated (synthesis).[537] Rather than the synthesis just supporting the original thesis as in traditional logic, the synthesis has "overcome and preserved" the movement of thought from thesis to antithesis. The synthesis forms a new thesis and the cycle continues. The progression of thought is like a spiral toward a higher rational unity when the totality of truth is discovered.

"Hegel describes it as a kind of ladder by means of which we can climb from our immediate, limited experience of the world, up to a truly philosophic vantage point. Once we have attained such a properly philosophical point of view, the ladder can be dropped or discarded. Hegel insists that the beginning of philosophy presupposes the point of view reached only at the end of the *Phenomenology*. But this ladder takes a very peculiar form. In fact, as Hegel himself notes, it is circular. Indeed, in this and later books, Hegel refers to '**circles within circles**.'"[538] (emphasis mine)

Circles within circles… yet another Nephilim calling card. I picture the Tower of Babel in this description of the Hegelian dialectic (see Figure 60). It is a spiraling ascension of gnosis that characterizes the structure of most secret societies. A desire to attain higher rational union and the totality of truth might describe Nimrod's motives just as much as Hegel's. It's no wonder the Illuminists gravitated toward this dialectic as a method for manipulating humanity.

Figure 60. By Lucas van Valckenborch - Tour_de_babel.jpeg, 2010-05-28 06:29 (UTC), Derivative work: Gordon P. Hemsley, Public Domain, https://commons.wikimedia.org/w/index.php?curid=10471408

The Illuminati symbol of the triangle with the all-seeing eye is another illustration of the Hegelian dialectic (see Figure 61). The thesis and antithesis form the base of the triangle with the final synthesis incapsulating the totality of truth as the all-seeing eye capstone. Social engineers have advanced the Hegelian dialectic into realms that perhaps Hegel himself did not foresee.

Figure 61. By de:Benutzer:Verwüstung—de:Bild:Dollarnote_siegel_hq.jpg, Public Domain, https://commons.wikimedia.org/w/index.php?curid=2140203

As we have discussed, the end goal for the cabal is the establishment of a NWO, but there are many obstacles in reaching this end goal. The biggest is **WE THE PEOPLE** who value life, liberty and the pursuit of happiness. Americans are not willing to give up the freedoms that form the bedrock of our great nation. So, how do the globalists overcome this obstacle? They fuel conflict between blacks and whites, Christians and Muslims, Jews and Arabs, Democrats and Republicans, liberals and conservatives, in order to foment crises. Once a crisis has emerged, the globalists offer a solution, one that Americans would not otherwise accept. However, given the intensity of the crisis (i.e. 9/11), the solution offered (i.e. The Patriot Act's expanded surveillance) to combat the new reality (foreign terrorism on American shores) moves the American people a step closer toward one world government by relinquishing our privacy. A telltale sign the Illuminati is using the Hegelian dialectic on the masses is when there is a pre-scribed solution before the crisis erupts. Consider the Chinese surveillance state.

"Chinese have long been aware that they are tracked by the world's most sophisticated system of electronic surveillance. The coronavirus emergency has brought some of that technology out of the shadows, providing the authorities with a justification for sweeping methods of high-tech social control...Although there has been some anonymous grumbling on social media, for now Chinese citizens seem to be accepting the extra intrusion, or even embracing it, as a means to combat the health engineering."[539]

Under normal circumstances, there would be more protest from the Chinese, but they are being socially engineered through the tragedy of the COVID-19 outbreak. Are the Chinese the only ones being socially engineered? Consider Henry Kissinger's statements from 1992, in light of the current global pandemic. "Today American's would be outraged if U.N. troops entered Los Angeles to restore order; tomorrow they will be grateful. This is especially true if they were told there was an outside threat from beyond, whether real or promulgated, that threatened our very existence. It is then that all peoples of the world will plead with world leaders to deliver them from this evil. **The one thing every man fears is the unknown. When presented with this scenario, individual rights will be willingly relinquished for the guarantee of their well-being granted to them by their world government.**"[540] (emphasis mine)

Another example of the Hegelian dialectic at work in our nation is when a mass shooting occurs, politicians are ready to move on a bill that would reduce our 2nd Amendment rights by limiting the sale of guns. The ultimate goal of gun control according to the blueprints of the globalists, is the confiscation of guns from American citizens. Without the opportunity to defend ourselves, the globalists have an easier path toward total domination.

Symbolism Will be Their Downfall

We began our investigation just off the shores of Jekyll Island as we examined the shell complex on Sapelo Island. Do you remember the shape of the shell complex? It was a circle with a dot, a circumpunct. This discovery launched us to investigate faraway lands in search of other ancient circumpuncts. We were not disappointed, but instead, rather surprised to find that the megalithic civilizations were prolific in their use of the circumpunct. For example, the countryside of England alone has approximately 1000 stone circle monuments. A question that consistently arose during the first phase of our investigation was how ancient civilizations were able to quarry, transport and construct with stone blocks weighing upwards of 800 tons. As we continued our journey across the continents, investigating different periods of history and diverse people groups, we kept finding circumpuncts. The circle within a circle is a universal symbol that represents the occult and adaptive deceptions spanning from ancient traditions to 21st century secret societies. For our final examination of the circumpunct, we will investigate the all-seeing-eye that appears on the Great Seal and on the reverse side of the one-dollar Federal Reserve Note.

The all-seeing-eye has its origins in the eye of Ra (see Figure 62). The Illuminati and Freemasonry use the all-seeing-eye as a central component in their symbolism, along with the pyramid. The Great Seal incorporates both of these symbols and not surprisingly, was chosen to be placed on the one-dollar Federal Reserve Note (see Figure 63). The Great Seal is the national coat of arms for the United States. The designing of it began on July 4th, 1776 when Thomas Jefferson, Benjamin Franklin, and John Adams were tasked with designing America's seal. It took six years and three different committees before the final design was presented and accepted by Congress on June 13th, 1782. The Great Seal first appeared on the Federal Reserve Note during FDR's administration in 1934. Henry Wallace, a Freemason and FDR's Secretary of Agriculture, was drawn to the symbolism of the Great Seal. He suggested that it be added to our nation's currency. FDR, also a Freemason, recognized the significance of the symbolism in the all-seeing-eye as the capstone of the unfinished pyramid, so he rendered the decision to place the Great Seal on the back of the one-dollar Federal Reserve Note.

The unfinished pyramid has 13 rows, symbolizing the 13 colonies, but 13 is also a significant number within the occult. It represents illumination and the ability to achieve perfection. The dollar bill has thirteen uses of the number 13, which signifies the magical numerology used in its design.[541] The all-seeing-eye was said to represent the Eye of Providence, but to Freemasons and the Illuminati, it represents the Great Architect of the Universe. In ancient lore, the all-seeing-eye represented Saturn with its ring and Saturn was an adaptive deception of the deified Nimrod, a '*gibbowr*.' The all-seeing-eye also represents the watchful eye of the 'sons of God,' a.k.a. 'Watchers,' who watched over humanity and began to lust after the daughters of men. We know how that story goes! The all-seeing-eye, a type of circle within a circle (circumpunct) is a calling card of the Nephilim.

Figure 62. Horus Eye Egypt by Miceking. https://www.shutterstock.com/image-vector/horus-eye-egypt-425351410

Figure 63. Reverse side one-dollar bill. https://www.shutterstock.com/image-photo/denomination-one-dollar-on-back-side-274686851

Embedded within the obverse side of the one-dollar Federal Reserve Note is a tribute to Lilith, the Queen of Heaven. As you may remember from Chapter 10, the owl is a symbol of this goddess and it can be found on the dollar bill. It takes a magnifying glass to detect it. Rather than give away where it is located, I thought I would let you do a little investigative work on your own to find it. Consider it like a scavenger hunt 😊

Spiritual Forces of Evil

We are about to get to the root of evil that is at the core of the Federal Reserve, but before we do, let's review what we have discovered about the nature of the spiritual battle. From the Enochian texts, we have identified the origin of demons as being the spirits of the deceased Nephilim. We have come to understand the Nephilim agenda, conceived at the genesis of the Seed war, to be intent on defiling the human genome in order to thwart the birth of the Messiah. But since that strategy was an utter failure and Jesus won the Seed war, the Nephilim were forced to alter their end goal. The Nephilim agenda, in the Common Era, has been to destroy those who follow Jesus, while enslaving the masses through control, manipulation and domination. Satan, the 'Watchers,' and the Nephilim are aware that a final battle will ensue at the end of the age; this battle will end in their eternal banishment to the lake of fire. While there is no way they can win this battle, they have set out to claim as many causalities as possible. The fulfillment of the Nephilim agenda has been entrusted to a subset of ruling families with a bloodline admixture with the Nephilim.

It's important we keep in mind that our struggles are not against flesh and blood, but rather against spiritual forces of evil (Ephesians 6:12). The masterminds behind the creation of the Federal Reserve operate in conjunction with spiritual forces of evil. To pinpoint these entities, we must revisit the significance of the Great Pyramid. As you recall, the mysteries of the Great Pyramid abound with respect to the precision in which it was built, its geodetic coordinates, its alignment with other pyramids around the globe, and the presence of a sarcophagus with absolutely no funerary evidence to be found. The mainstream narrative that the Great Pyramid was built by Khufu and used as a tomb, doesn't explain the endless mysteries.

I would like to draw our attention to the symbolism of the pyramid among occult practices and secret societies as I believe it ties back to the Nephilim. There are numerous theories (laid out in Chapter 4) that attempt to address why the pyramid was built. One theory that I think stands above the rest, especially given all that we have discovered in our investigation, is that the Great Pyramid was a temple for Isis/Osiris. The Inventory Stele confirms this conclusion. It is conceivable that the Great Pyramid was built by the offspring of the Nephilim for the purpose of populating the earth with the seed of the Nephilim. In other words, the agenda of the 'Watchers,' and subsequently the Nephilim, was to directly attack the family mandate to "be fruitful and increase in number." If this is true, then the sarcophagus was most likely a bed of iniquity used for ritualistic sex acts. We know from archaeological and historical evidence that this practice occurred in ancient Mesopotamia where Ziggurats functioned as temples housing the ritual beds for the gods.[542] The initiate would enter the sarcophagus, much like Freemasons lay in a coffin, to offer themselves in sexual union with a Nephilim spirit. Within Satanic cults, members enter into sexual union on high holy days to invite a demonic spirit to enter at the point of copulation to propagate Nephilim offspring. These perverse sex acts are common forms of worship to Baal and the Queen of Heaven.

Baal is the god with a "thousand faces." He morphs into different forms of adaptive deceptions. Baal is the quintessential shape shifter. Within Satan's camp, Baal is the principality in charge of two primary assignments: 1) to stop the promises of God, and 2) to control the earth and its resources.[543] Baal was assigned these tasks shortly after the Seed war began. Baal is the ruler of the Nephilim spirits (Mt 12:24). The principality Baal has a male form and a female form. The male form is Baal and the female form is the Queen of Heaven. The first male and female manifestations in flesh of this god, were Nimrod and Semiramis. In Chapter 10, we listed many of the names of Nimrod (Baal) and Semiramis (Queen of Heaven). If you look back, Columbia is one of the names of the Queen of Heaven. This is the deity the District of Columbia is named after. It's no surprise that Washington, D.C. is a critical center in Baal's power grid. It is well known that the architect and designer of the layout of Washington, D.C., Pierre L'Enfant, was a Freemason. His design intentionally incorporated Masonic symbols throughout the layout of the city.

As we discovered in Chapters 1 & 2, the enemy establishes ley-lines and spiritual power grids across the globe through pagan and occult worship. These ley-lines are reinforced through ritualistic blood sacrifices, broken covenants, idolatry, and fornication/sexual perversion. There are three city states that control the world and are ruled by Baal/Queen of Heaven: City of London Corporation (financial power center), Vatican City (religious power center), and District of Columbia (military power center) (see Figure 64). The triangle is a significant symbol within the occult, as you might remember from our jaunt to Torino, Italy when we discussed the triangles of white and black magic across the globe. A triangle represents a counterfeit system of the triune God. Baal/Queen of Heaven/Leviathan is the triune nature of the god Baal. Baal establishes triangular power grids across the globe to enslave people living within the boundaries of the triangle. Spiritual triangles are also used in the occult as doorways or gateways to other dimensions. The Federal Reserve Building in Washington D.C. houses the Board of the Federal Reserve and is part of this demonic power grid within Baal's triangle.

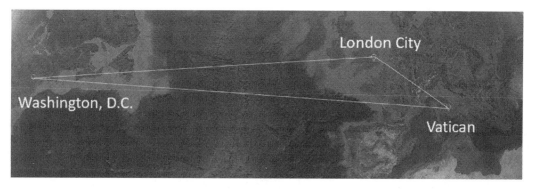

Figure 64. Three power centers. Created by Laura Sanger.

Baal is the principality controlling the masterminds behind the "six men." One of the names for Baal in scripture (Song of Solomon 8:11) is *'Ba`al Hamown'* and means "lord or possessor of abundance"[544] The Federal Reserve System is ruled by this principality. This is the principality that is holding back the great transfer of wealth that has been prophesied for more than a decade. It's a parasitic entity. It feeds off the usury of its captives. It feeds off the detriment of WE THE PEOPLE. The Nephilim Hosts that serve *'Ba`al Hamown'* engage in human trafficking, child sacrifices, sexual perversion, spirit cooking/cannibalism, money laundering, usury, dishonest trade/business practices, and enslavement of humanity. The Nephilim Hosts and global elites are one in the same. The globalists, who are driving toward one world government, have the same goal Nimrod had, which is to open up a stargate to unleash the hordes of hell. If they are able to accomplish their blueprint for the NWO, the global leader who will rule the world, will be empowered by the hordes of hell to incite every form of wickedness, just as in the days of Noah. Now is the time for WE THE PEOPLE to arise from our slumber. We were born for such a time as this!

Key Points

- Globalism has become the preeminent war tactic of the enemy. It strengthens the Nephilim agenda.
- Secret societies are cogs in the wheels of the machination working to form the NWO.
- Sabbatean-Frankists are a secret society within the inner core of Zionism who take on the appearance of religion to keep their beliefs hidden. They espouse anarchy as the elixir of life.

- Jacob Frank, Adam Weishaupt, and Mayer Amschel Rothschild formed a triad union to join the Sabbatean-Frankists with the Illuminati. Rothschild financed both Luciferian sects.
- Weishaupt, a Nephilim Host, developed the Illuminati's plan for world domination: abolish all national governments, abolish private property, abolish inheritance, destroy patriotism, destroy Christianity, destroy the family unit, and create a NWO.
- Social engineering methods drafted in the 18th century by the Illuminati are still at work in the 21st century throughout all aspects of our society.
- Edward Mandell House, who essentially ran Woodrow Wilson's presidency, was a Marxist and member of the Illuminati. He steered the government toward a framework of socialism by calling for the passage of a graduated income tax and a central bank.
- The Illuminati burrowed deep within the structure of Freemasonry. Freemasonry became a front organization for the Illuminati, essentially a secret society within a secret society…a circle within a circle.
- James de Rothschild, Nathan Rothschild, and Solomon Mayer Rothschild were all Freemasons.
- The Jesuits are the most powerful order within Catholicism. The Superior General of the Jesuits is the Black Pope who is considered the Commander-in-Chief of the Catholic Church.
- The inner circle of the Jesuit order are violent mercenaries.
- The Protocols document the Nephilim agenda for world domination.
- Hegelian dialectic is a framework to direct our thoughts and behaviors into a conflict which then leads to a pre-scribed solution.
- We began our investigation with the circumpunct on Sapelo Island and discovered this symbol spans culture, land mass, and time. The circumpunct was used by the inhabitants of Jekyll Island. We come full circle to find the circumpunct on the Federal Reserve Note.
- The Federal Reserve system is ruled by the principality called Baal. The Nephilim Hosts, or global elites, serve Baal and are attempting to establish a NWO.

Chapter 25

Freedom!

*The only thing necessary for the triumph of evil
is for good men to do nothing.*
~ Edmund Burke

I prefer dangerous freedom over peaceful slavery.
~ Thomas Jefferson

*Freedom is never more than one generation away from extinction.
We didn't pass it to our children in the bloodstream. It must be
fought for, protected, and handed on for them to do the same.*
~ Ronald Reagan

We must heed President Reagan's warning. We are a generation whose freedoms are on the verge of extinction. It's interesting to me that as I began writing the Introduction for this book, Janet Yellan had just announced the end of the Federal Reserve's Quantitative Easing (QE3). As I begin writing this last chapter, we are in the midst of the COVID-19 Global Pandemic. Everyday seems to bring unthinkable news. India issued a lockdown of 1.3 billion citizens for 21 days. In the United States, life is slowly grinding to a halt. Our borders are closed, schools are closed, restaurants are closed for dine-in customers, movie theaters are closed, sporting events canceled, travel restricted, an increasing number of states are under "Shelter in Place" or "Stay at Home" orders, unemployment is skyrocketing, and Congress passed a $2 trillion stimulus package.

President Trump says that we are at war with an invisible enemy. The enemy is invisible alright, but it's not COVID-19. The enemy we are fighting are the globalists, the Nephilim Hosts, the Deep State, the Illuminati, the agents of Baal. If we use critical thinking skills, it raises the question, is COVID-19 a cover for an underlying agenda at work? While it's tragic the number of Americans that have died from the virus, the response to it doesn't add up. The CDC COVID-19 Situation Report for 3/23/20 indicates that 33,404 Americans have been infected with the virus and 400 Americans have died. Consider that the H1N1 Swine Flu epidemic of 2009-2010 infected 60.8 million Americans, 274,304 Americans were hospitalized, and 12,480 Americans died.[545] Notice how there wasn't the level of societal shutdown then that we are experiencing during COVID-19. Something else is going on behind the scenes!

St. Louis Fed President, James Bullard proposed a system for universal COVID-19 testing. He suggested in order to get the economy jumpstarted following this pandemic, **every** American should be tested **every** day and wear a badge with their negative results. He thinks this universal testing system would allow people to be able to interact with one another with "confidence."[546] What if I don't want to be subjected to testing every single day? It sounds like under this system, I wouldn't receive a badge that permits me to interact with others. Bill Gates hosted a "AskMeAnything" session on Reddit. A question was asked of him "What changes are we going to have to make to how businesses operate to maintain our economy while providing social distancing?" Gates responded: "The question of which businesses should keep going is tricky. Certainly, food supply and the health system. We still need water, electricity and the internet. Supply chains for critical things need to be maintained. Countries are still figuring out what to keep running. **Eventually we will have some digital certificates to show who has recovered or been tested recently or when we have a vaccine who has received it.**"[547] (emphasis mine)

We are witnessing the unfolding of a global health surveillance system. Are we experiencing yet another cycle in a Hegelian dialectic, at the hands of the globalists, to strip us of our freedoms for the sake of "public safety"? Are the Patriots, those in both government and the military who are fighting to save our Republic, turning the tide by going after the Deep State during this global shutdown? My hunch is that both are at play.

There are currently over 156,000 sealed criminal cases in U.S. Federal Courts. Grand juries have been convened for some time now weighing evidence from federal prosecutors so arrests can be made. To give you an idea of what is typical, in 2006, there were 1,077 sealed criminal cases.[548] In the fall of 2019, the Drug Enforcement Administration (DEA) launched Project Python and within six months, 750 Mexican

416

drug cartel members have been arrested and $20 million in drugs have been confiscated. Assistant Attorney General Brian A. Benczkowski stated, "Project Python marks the most comprehensive action to date…to disrupt, dismantle, and ultimately destroy CJNG…one of the highest-priority, transnational organized crime threats we face."[549]

As recently as March 11, 2020, the day the World Health Organization declared COVID-19 to be a global pandemic, 250 drug cartel members from CJNG were arrested, but you won't hear about this on mainstream media (MSM). All we hear is sensational reporting by MSM to create fear and panic in the American people regarding COVID-19.

President Trump signed Executive Order (EO) 13818 on December 21, 2017 "blocking the property of persons involved in serious human rights abuse or corruption." This EO allowed the Treasury to seize the assets of people involved in human trafficking or any other form of human rights abuse.[550] This dried up the spicket of money laundering for the global elites. Subsequently, one month later, Rothschild heirs who live in the United States, Nancy Clarice Tilghman and Geoffrey R. Hoguet, sold the 5,412-hectare Austrian hunting estate known as Langau.[551] The Rothschilds owned this property for 143 years. Did they sell because they were directly impacted by EO 13818? Could it be that the walls are beginning to close in on the global elites?

We must join the fight! We cannot allow the globalists to enslave us any longer. This battle is not for us alone, but it is for our posterity. The opportune time is upon us. What the globalists fear the most are **American citizens awakened out of our slumber, aware of the Nephilim agenda and armed with the TRUTH!** The words of patriots who have gone before us are reverberating in our land. Listen closely, put your ear to the ground, can you feel the rumbling? Their warnings, their call to bravery, their encouragement to rise to greatness, their collective sound is breaking forth once again. The inaugural words of JFK in 1961 are even more true for our generation:

"In your hands, my fellow citizens…will rest the final success or failure of our course. Since this country was founded, each generation of Americans has been summoned to give testimony to its national loyalty…Now the trumpet summons again…In the long history of the world, only a few generations have been granted the role of defending freedom in its hour of maximum danger…The energy, the faith, the devotion which we bring to this endeavour will light our country and all who serve it – and the glow from that fire can truly light the world. And so, my fellow Americans, ask not what your country can do for you – ask what you can do for your country."[552]

The clarion call is being heralded from the mountaintops and echoed in the valleys. Let the blind see, let the deaf hear, it's time to break free from our shackles! Americans arise, shake off your slumber, take up your shield, and brandish your swords. It's time to engage in the spiritual battle that will return our Republic to us.

Daniel 2:21 (NIV) *"He changes times and seasons; he deposes kings and raises up others. He gives wisdom to the wise and knowledge to the discerning."*

His purposes will be accomplished in His perfect timing. The plans of the nations will be thwarted if they are not aligned with His kingdom purposes. As I write this last chapter, we have just begun the Hebrew month of Nissan, in the new decade of 5780. This is the decade of declaring His purposes with our spoken word.

Nissan is the month of Passover. I am reminded of the significance of the month of Nissan. It was the time the Israelites were delivered from Egyptian captivity. The story of their exodus included plagues. Pharaoh was unwilling to set the Israelites free to worship Yahweh. His stubbornness brought 10 plagues upon the Egyptians. I can't help but make the connection between the plagues of Egypt and our current global pandemic. May it be a signal of our coming freedom!

Yahweh Yireh (God as Provider) miraculously made a way for the Israelites when it seemed like there was no way. This is His nature. He is faithful to provide a path of deliverance. As the Israelites fled Egypt, the path to freedom seemed improbable, especially when they arrived at the Red Sea knowing the Egyptian army was pursuing them. Their situation seemed impossible, but our God is able to do the impossible, the unthinkable, and the unimaginable in order to lead us to freedom. When the **Red** Sea parted, each Israelite had to make a decision to step into the unknown by crossing the parted waters. I imagine with each step they took, their faith increased in measure.

The path of freedom set before us requires stepping into the unknown. In our lifetime, we have never known a monetary system free from the control of a central bank. Each step we take will require increasing measures of faith. Right now, the Federal Reserve may seem like an impenetrable system. The level of corruption within our monetary system may seem too immense. The US debt load may seem insurmountable, BUT WITH GOD NOTHING IS IMPOSSIBLE!! The Federal Reserve **IS** a giant in our land, but we are giant slayers! We have been given dominion authority to go into all the systems of this world to redeem and reestablish Kingdom order. There will come a day when all the kingdoms of this world will become the kingdoms of our Lord and Savior (Revelation 11:15).

In September 2019, Dutch Sheets prophesied regarding the importance of the Hebrew year 5780 that began sundown on September 30th, 2019. He said, "It will become one of the most strategic years of our life; history will write that this year was a hinge year. God will cause the enemy to move right into your trap. This Oct [2019] to next Oct [2020] we will lay out continual sieges. We will knock out the giants in this nation. This is the year we will break the back of the principalities that have ruled this nation for a longtime. This year we will dislodge them, uproot them, tear down their structures. We go on the offense to invade the land; we are the rising ecclesia of the Kingdom of God."[553]

Hallelujah!! As Christ's ambassadors, we have been given the assignment to exercise our God given authority to govern earth according to His purposes. Jesus delegated to us the dominion authority He restored through the Cross. When He ascended into heaven, the responsibility of governing was placed on our shoulders. This is why He declared that we have been given the keys of the kingdom of heaven (Matthew 16:19). We can loose that which has been bound. Our responsibility is to enforce the victory that Jesus secured at the Cross. The Great Commission, as recorded in Matthew, calls us to disciple nations. We must apprehend heaven's agenda over our nation and bring it down into the earth realm. How do we do this?

- We inquire of the King of kings regarding His purposes for our nation
- We render the King's decrees through spoken declarations
- We steward the land by cleansing it of defilement and uprooting altars of offense
- We change the atmosphere over cities, regions, and nations through informed intercession

James 5:16 (AMP) "…*The heartfelt and persistent prayer of a righteous man (believer) can accomplish much [when put into action and made effective by God – it is dynamic and can have tremendous power]*."

I cannot overstate the power that is released when the saints join together in intercession. We have been given the ministry of reconciliation, so as intercessors, we can release the redemptive work of Christ over a nation. George Otis Jr. says, "It has been said that history, although sometimes made up of the few acts of the great, is more often shaped by the many acts of the small. Nowhere is this truer than in the realm of spiritual intercession."[554]

As we join together in intercession, locking in on our target, the "omnipotent and deadly octopus" with its "poisonous and itching tentacles," we drive a stake in each tentacle with every prayer offered up. The spiritual forces of evil rooted in the Federal Reserve System are no match for the Body of Christ.

Luke 10:19 (TPT) *"Now you understand that I have imparted to you all my authority to trample over his kingdom. You will trample upon every demon before you and overcome every power Satan possesses. Absolutely nothing will be able to harm you as you walk in this authority."*

It's important we remember the lessons we learned from the giant slayers, Deborah, Joshua, Caleb and David. They were fashioned into giant slayers by cultivating intimacy with the Lord, which developed a fear of the Lord and in turn, led to the supernatural strength and courage to defeat the giants. If we cultivate an intimate relationship with the Lord, we can walk in the confidence of who we are and who He is. When we draw near to Him, we know the sound of His voice. He will direct our steps in this battle because we each have a role to fill. Some of us will be called into governmental positions for such a time as this. Some of us will be called to write books. Some of us will be called to broadcast through social media. Some of us will be called to fight this battle in the courts. Some of us will be called to travel to specific locations to cut ley-lines, uproot spiritual grids and cleanse defiled portals. Some of us will be called to strategic level warfare. One role that we all share as the Body of Christ is that we are all called to pray. Our investigation has exposed evil lurking in the darkness and has flooded it with the light of TRUTH. We are now equipped to strike the mark through intercession that is informed.

Just like with any military campaign, no matter what role we are given, whether it's on the front lines or behind the scenes, we carry it out with integrity and excellence. The battle for souls is on the line. Now that we understand the enemy's battle plan, we can strategically pray to thwart his schemes.

Saints, pick up your spiritual weapons and **FIRE**, continuously and unceasingly until the giant of the Federal Reserve falls. For God and country! WWG1WGA!

Informed Intercession

This grand adventure we embarked on to uncover the roots of the Federal Reserve was a spiritual mapping investigation. We conducted thorough research to expose the ancient roots of defilement within our nation's monetary system. As Christ's ambassadors, we have been given dominion authority to establish the Lord's purpose in our land. We are now equipped with knowledge and understanding, from the information we collected, to engage in intercession.

Intercession is like a meeting between two parties. Intercessors are mediators; we represent the Lord's purpose in our communities, regions, and nation. We apprehend heaven's decrees and release it over our nation through declarations made in prayer. Through intercession, we can uproot the Nephilim agenda from our monetary system and our land. Our directive is to come before the Lord on behalf of our nation's leaders (those in government, business, finance, etc.) and ask forgiveness for sexual perversion/immorality, idolatry, broken covenants, and bloodshed. This weakens the strongholds over our nation, so we can break curses and release blessings. The ultimate goal is to see America and WE THE PEOPLE transformed for the glory of the Lord.

Prayer for Protection and Covering

Yahweh, Creator of heaven and earth, we come to you in the name of Jesus. We come before your throne on behalf of ourselves, our families, our fellow Americans, and our land. We are thankful for Jesus' work on the cross, his blood that was shed, and his resurrection power that defeated death and the Nephilim agenda. Thank you, Jesus, that you have made a way for our salvation, provision and freedom. We come under your covering and protection as we intercede on behalf of our nation and its monetary system. We declare protection over our body, soul (mind, will, and emotions) and spirit. We ask for protection over our families, our assets and our land. We stand in authority as Christ's ambassadors to be ministers of reconciliation and restoration. We thank you Holy Spirt for releasing revelation, wisdom, knowledge, understanding and power as we confront the spiritual forces of evil in our land and contend for the Father's purposes to prevail.

Prayer Points

- Pray that all ancient and modern pathways of iniquity are cleansed. Close the gateways for drug, weapons and human trafficking in our land.
- Pronounce that our monetary system is no longer bound by Baal and his Nephilim Hosts.
- Bind up usury in our monetary system.
- Pray for the dismantling or restructuring of the Federal Reserve, uproot every form of wickedness in the system.
- Pray for the return to a sound monetary system with a currency backed by assets.
- Cut all ties to Baal and Queen of Heaven over your life as well as our nation. Declare your devotion to the Lord and call Americans into genuine relationship with the one true God.
- Pray for a great awakening among the American people.
- Declare Jubilee over your finances and over our nation, that debts are wiped clean.
- Loose prosperity over your personal finances and proclaim recompense, so everything that has been stolen from you will return to you seven-fold.
- Declare the rule of law has returned to our land and the two-tiered justice system is uprooted.
- Pray the Lord will raise up creative solutions for monetary policy in our nation.
- Pray that people in communities come together and the Holy Spirit releases a synergistic flow of divine creativity.
- Proclaim freedom, that we are no longer held in captivity by the globalists.
- Decree that the globalists/Nephilim Hosts/Illuminati/Deep State plans are thwarted. Pray they are caught in their own traps and brought to justice.
- Pray that those participating in pedophilia rings and child sacrifices are exposed and God's righteous judgments are issued.

About the Author

Laura Sanger, Ph.D.

Laura Sanger is a psychologist and a small business owner. She has lived in Illinois and California, but calls Utah home. She earned a B.A. in Psychology from the University of California, San Diego. She worked at the Veterans Administration Hospital in La Jolla, Los Angeles, Westwood, and Salt Lake City. She received a M.A. in Theology and a Ph.D. in Clinical Psychology from Fuller Theological Seminary. She practiced as a clinical psychologist for 15 years specializing in chronic mental illness, addictions, personality disorders, and adolescent treatment. She has been involved in youth ministry for 16 years and has been serving in leadership at The Fellowship church for over two decades. As a researcher and intercessor, Laura has been involved in city-wide and state-wide prayer initiatives. She and her husband have been married for 28 years and have three children. She is currently the managing partner of a real-estate investment business. She is an avid learner and believes an investment in knowledge yields the best return. Laura is passionate about helping people reach their full potential by breaking free from systems of enslavement.

About Relentlessly Creative Books LLC

If you would like to receive
notification of upcoming books
by Laura Sanger, Ph.D. or
Relentlessly Creative Books,
please join our email here.
We promise to use the utmost
respect in contacting you.

Relentlessly Creative Books™ offers an exciting new
publishing option for authors. Our "middle-path
publishing" approach includes many of the advantages of
both traditional publishing and self-publishing without the
drawbacks. For more information and a complete online
catalog of our books, please visit us at.

RelentlesslyCreativeBooks.com

books@relentlesslycreative.com

Sign up to join our Relentless Readers Group here http://eepurl.com/gipluH

References

1. conspiracy. (n.d.). In *Merriam-Webster's online dictionary*. (11th ed.).
2. Maloney, M. [GoldSilver]. (2013, August 13). *Seven Stages of Empire – Hidden Secrets of Money Episode 2* [Video File]. https://www.youtube.com/watch?v=EdSq5H7awi8&list=PLE88E9ICdipidHkTehs1VbFzgwrq1jkUJ&index=2
3. Missler, C. (2009, October 1). The shackles of our presupposition. *Koinonia House,* p. 1.
4. Ibid.
5. Griffin, Edward G. (2010). *The Creature from Jekyll Island.* 5th edition. Westlake Village: American Media.
6. McKinley, William (1872). *Mounds in Georgia.* Annual Report of the Board of Regents of the Smithsonian Institution, pgs. 422–424.
7. Thompson, Victor D., Reynolds, Matthew D., Haley, Bryan, Jeffries, Richard, Johnson, Jay K., and Humphries, Laura (2004). *The Sapello Shell Ring Complex: Shallow Geophysics on a Georgia Sea Island.* Southeastern Archaeology 23 (2), pgs. 192–201.
8. Daniels, Gary C. (2011, February 24). *Sapello Shell Rings.* [blog post]. Retrieved from www.frontiers-of-anthropology.blogspot.com.
9. Thompson, Victor (2005, December, 20). *Coastal Shell Rings.* New Georgia Encyclopedia, History and Archaeology. www.georgiaencyclopedia.org.
10. *Points in circle (solstices, circumpunct).* Symbol Dictionary: a Visual Glossary. www.symboldictionary.net.
11. Moe (2015, October 6). *The Meaning of the Circumpunct.* www.gnosticwarrior.com.
12. Beckett, John (2017). *The Path of Paganism: An Experience Based Guide to Modern Pagan Practice.* Llewellyn Worldwide: Woodbury, MN.
13. Brown, Dan (2009). *The Lost Symbol: Featuring Robert Langdon.* Knopf Doubleday Publishing Group: New York City, NY.
14. Cox, Simon (2009). *Decoding the Lost Symbol.* Simon & Schuster: New York.
15. Quayle, Stephen and Horn, Thomas R. (2017). *Unearthing the Lost World of the Cloudeaters.* Crane, MO: Defender Publishing.
16. Gannon, Megan (2014, September 10). *Hidden Monuments Reveal 'Stonehenge Is Not Alone.'* www.livescience.com/47766-hidden-monuments-reveal-stonehenge-is-not-alone
17. Kennedy, Maev (2014, July 3). *Prehistoric Circle Dated to Same Summer as Seahenge Neighbour.* The Guardian. www.theguardian.com/science/2014/jul/03/prehistoric-circle-dated-same-seahenge-2049-bc.
18. Whitcombe, Chris (2011). *Earth Mysteries: Alexander Thom (1894-1985).* Britannia. http://www.britannia.com/wonder/thom.html
19. Higginbottom, Gail (2016, August 9). *Origins of Standing Stone Astronomy in Britain: New quantitative techniques for the study of archaeoastronomy.* Journal of Archaeological Science: Reports.
20. Hogenboom, Melissa (2016, October 13). *The Strange Origin of Scotland's Stone Circles.* BBC Earth. www.bbc.com/earth/story/20161012-the-strange-origin-of-scotland-stone-circles.
21. Ibid.
22. Petrie, Alistair (2000). *Releasing Heaven on Earth.* Chosen: Grand Rapids, MI.
23. Watkins, Alfred (1921). *Early British Trackways, Moats, Mounds, Camps and Sites.* Lecture given to Woolhope Naturalists Field Club, Hereford, England.
24. Watkins, Alfred (1925). *The Old Straight Track.* London: Methuen.
25. Blue Letter Bible. "Dictionary and Word Search for *bamah (Strong's H1116)."* (1996-2020).

26. Ibid.
27. Petrie, Alistair (2000). *Releasing Heaven on Earth.* Chosen: Grand Rapids, MI.
28. Bedard, M. (n.d.) *White Magic v. Black Magic.* Retrieved from https://gnosticwarrior.com/white-magic-vs-black-magic.html
29. Zaccarelli, C. (2018). *Itinerary: Esoteric Turn.* Retrieved from http://www.whereitalia.com/itinerary-esoteric-turin/
30. Alvarez, B. (January 13, 2018). *What is the meaning of the pentagram?* Retrieved from https://www.bernardalvarez.com/post/2018/01/13/what-is-the-meaning-of-the-pentagram
31. Petrie, Alistair (2000). *Releasing Heaven on Earth.* Chosen: Grand Rapids, MI.
32. Perotti, E. (May 28, 2014). *Turin: City of Mystery.* World Association of Newspapers and News Publishers. Retrieved from http://www.wan-ifra.org/articles/2014/05/28/turin-city-of-mystery.
33. Ibid.
34. A Brief History of Alchemy. (n.d.) Retrieved from http://www.chm.bris.ac.uk/webprojects2002/crabb/history.html
35. Cox, Simon (2009). *Decoding the Lost Symbol.* Simon & Schuster: New York.
36. Dembach, G. (1995). *Torino città magica.* Ariete Mulitmedia.
37. Ibid.
38. Petrie, Alistair (2000). *Releasing Heaven on Earth.* Chosen: Grand Rapids, MI.
39. Otis, G. (1997). *The Twilight Labryinth.* Grand Rapids, MI: Chosen Books.
40. Hancock, Graham (2014). *Third Giant Megalith, Weighing 1,650 tons, Confirmed at Baalbek.* Graham Hancock. https://grahamhancock.com/third-megalith-baalbek-hancock/
41. Josephus, Flavius (1773-1775). *The Works of Josephus. Complete and Unabridged. New Updated Edition.* Translated into English by William Whiston. *I. The Life of Joshephus. Written by himself. II. The antiquities of the Jews. In twenty books. III. The wars of the Jews or the history of the destruction of Jerusalem. IV. Flavius Josephus against Apion or antiquity of the Jews.*
42. Aveni, A. and Mizrachi, Y. (1998). The geometry and astronomy of Rujm el-Hiri, a megalithic site in the Southern Levant. *Journal of Field Archaeology, 25*(4), 475-496.
43. Ibid.
44. Horn, T. and Putnam, C. (2015). *On the Path of the Immortals.* Crane, MO: Defender Publishing.
45. Clark, Lisel and Tyson, Peter (June 23, 2011). *Pyramids: The Inside Story.* NOVA Retrieved from http://www.pbs.org/wgbh/nova/pyramid/
46. Petrie, Flinders W. M. (1883). The Pyramids and Temples of Gizeh. London: Field & Tuer.
47. Hancock, Graham (2016, September 29). New Claims About the Great Pyramid, Citing the Oldest Papyrus Ever Found. Do the Claims Stand Up? Retrieved from https://grahamhancock.com/peetp1/
48. Pooyard, Patrice (Director) and Lecetre, Laurent (Producer). (2010). *The Revelation of the Pyramids.* [Online] Retrieved from https://www.youtube.com/watch?v=2fS9ixfQ_no.
49. Herodotus. *The History of Herodotus parallel English/Greek English translation*: G. C. Macaulay, Book 2, 123. Macmillan Publishing: London and NY 1890. http://www.sacred-texts.com/cla/hh/hh2120.htm
50. Ibid.
51. Vyse, Howard (1840). *Operations Carried on at the Pyramid in Gizeh in 1837, Volume 1.* London: Moves and Barclay.
52. Ibid.
53. Clark, Liesl and Tyson, Peter (June 23, 2011). *Pyramids: The Inside Story.* NOVA Retrieved from http://www.pbs.org/wgbh/nova/pyramid/
54. Creighton, Scott (2017). *The Great Pyramid Hoax.* Rochester, Vermont: Bear & Company.
55. Ibid.
56. Vyse, Howard (1840). *Operations Carried on at the Pyramid in Gizeh in 1837, Volume 2.* London: Moves and Barclay.
57. Ibid.
58. Ibid.
59. Creighton, Scott (2017). *The Great Pyramid Hoax.* Rochester, Vermont: Bear & Company.

60. Lawton, Ian and Ogilvie-Herald, Chris (1999). *Giza the Truth.* London: Virgin Publishing.
61. Schoch, Robert M. and Bauval, Robert (2017). *Origins of the Sphinx.* Rochester, New York: Inner Traditions.
62. Mark, Joshua J. (February 14, 2016). *The Step Pyramid of Djoser.* Retrieved from https://www.ancient.eu/article/862/the-step-pyramid-of-djoser/.
63. Schwaller de Lubiez, R. A. (1981). *The Temple In Man: Sacred Architecture and the Perfect Man.* Inner Traditions International: Vermont.
64. Quayle, S. and Horn, T. R. (2017). *Unearthing the lost world of the cloudeaters.* Crane, MO: Defender Publishing.
65. Mason, P. (2010). *Quantum Glory.* Maricopa, AZ: XP Publishing.
66. Ibid.
67. Abbott, E. ([1884], 1994). *Flatland.* New York, NY: HarperCollins.
68. Otis, G. (1997). *The Twilight Labryinth.* Grand Rapids, MI: Chosen Books.
69. Ball, P. (August 11, 2016). The tyranny of simple explanations. *The Atlantic.* Retrieved from https://www.theatlantic.com/science/archive/2016/08/occams-razor/495332/
70. Otis, G. (1997). *The Twilight Labryinth.* Grand Rapids, MI: Chosen Books.
71. Hancock, G. (1995). *Fingerprints of the Gods.* New York, NY: Three Rivers Press.
72. Ibid.
73. Ibid.
74. Ibid.
75. Connecting pyramids with geographic mapping. (n.d.). *Mystery Pile.* Retrieved from https://www.mysterypile.com/connecting-pyramids.php
76. Blue Letter Bible. "Dictionary and Word Search for *radah (Strong's H7287).*" (1996-2020).
77. Wagner, C. Peter (2008). *Dominion Theology.* Chosen Books: Grand Rapids, MI.
78. Ibid.
79. Otis, G. (1997). *The Twilight Labryinth.* Grand Rapids, MI: Chosen Books.
80. Heiser, Michael S. (2015). *The Unseen Realm: Recovering the supernatural worldview of the Bible.* Bellingham, WA: Lexham Press.
81. Blue Letter Bible. "Dictionary and Word Search for *mal'ak (Strong's H4397)."* (1996-2020).
82. Blue Letter Bible. "Dictionary and Word Search for *nĕphiyl (Strong's H5303)."* (1996-2020).
83. Blue Letter Bible. "Dictionary and Word Search for *naphal' (Strong's H5307)."* (1996-2020).
84. Heiser, M. S. (2017). *Reversing Hermon: Enoch, The Watchers & The Forgotten Mission of Jesus Christ.* Crane, MO: Defender Publishing.
85. Heiser, M. S. (2015). *The Unseen Realm: Recovering the supernatural worldview of the Bible.* Bellingham, WA: Lexham Press.
86. Ibid.
87. Hancock, G. (2015). *Magicians of the Gods.* New York, NY: Thomas Dune Boods St. Marten's Press.
88. Annus, A. (2010). On the Origin of the Watchers: A Comparison Study of the Antediluvian Wisdom of Mesopotamian and Jewish Traditions. *Journal for the Study of Pseudepigrapha, 19,*(4), 277-320.
89. Ibid.
90. Pongratz-Leisten, B. (2008). Sacred Marriage and the Transfer of Divine Knowledge: Alliances between the Gods and the King in Ancient Mesopotamia. In M. Nissinen & R. Uro (Eds.) *Sacred Marriages* (pp. 43-73). Winona Lake, IN: Eisenbrauns.
91. Heiser, M. S. (2017). *Reversing Hermon: Enoch, The Watchers & The Forgotten Mission of Jesus Christ.* Crane, MO: Defender Publishing.
92. Blue Letter Bible. "Dictionary and Word Search for *'asher (Strong's H834)."* (1996-2020).
93. Martin, T. W. (2004). Paul's argument from nature for the veil in I Corinthians 11:13-15: A testicle instead of a head covering. *Journal of Biblical Literature, 123* (1), 75-84.
94. Ibid.
95. Heiser, M. S. (2017). *Reversing Hermon: Enoch, The Watchers & The Forgotten Mission of Jesus Christ.* Crane, MO: Defender Publishing.

96. Otis, G. (1997). *The Twilight Labryinth*. Grand Rapids, MI: Chosen Books.
97. Annus, A. (2010). On the Origin of the Watchers: A Comparison Study of the Antediluvian Wisdom of Mesopotamian and Jewish Traditions. *Journal for the Study of Pseudepigrapha, 19,*(4), 277-320.
98. Skiba, R. [cptmang]. (2014, January 28). *Archon invasion part 1- the origin of the Nephilim* [Video File]. Retrieved from https://www.youtube.com/watch?v=E8dUQOaSmSE
99. Kosior, Wojciech (2018-05-22), The Fallen (Or) Giants? The Gigantic Qualities of the Nefilim in the Hebrew Bible. *Jewish Translation—Translating Jewishness*, De Gruyter, 17–38.
100. Atsma, A.J. (2017). *Gigantes*. Retrieved from https://www.theoi.com/Gigante/Gigantes.html
101. Blue Letter Bible. "Dictionary and Word Search for *gê (Strong's #G1093)."* (1996-2020).
102. Blue Letter Bible. "Dictionary and Word Search for *genetê (Strong's #G1079)."* (1996-2020).
103. Blue Letter Bible. "Dictionary and Word Search for *genea (Strong's #G1074)."* (1996-2020).
104. Blue Letter Bible. "Dictionary and Word Search for *charam (#H2763)."* (1996-2020).
105. Schuelke, M. et al. (2004). Mysostatin Mutation Associated with Gross Muscle Hypertrophy in a Child. *The New England Journal of Medicine, 350,* pp. 2682-2688. doi: 10.1056/NEJMoa040933
106. Ibid.
107. Čatipović, B. (2004, September 4). Myostatin Mutation Associated with Gross Muscle Hypertrophy in a Child [Letter to the editor]. *The New England Journal of Medicine, 351.* pp. 1030-1031. doi: 10.1056/NEJM200409023511018
108. Morgan, H.D., Sutherland, H.G., Martin, D.I., & Whitelaw, E. (1999). Epigenetic Inheritance at the Agouti Locus in the Mouse. *Nature Genetics*, *23*(3), 314-318.
109. Waterland, R.A. and Jirtle, R.L. (2003). Transposable Elements: Targets for Early Nutritional Effects on Epigenetic Gene Regulation. *Molecular and Cellular Biology.* 23(15), 5293-5300.
110. Pembrey, M.E., Bygren, L.O., Kaati, G., Edvinsson, S., Northstone, K., Sjöström, M. & Golding, J. (2006). Sex-specific, Male-line Transgenerational Responses in Humans. *European Journal of Human Genetics (14)*, 159-166.
111. Weaver, I.C.G, Cervoni, N., Champagne, F.A., D'Alessio, A.C., Sharma, S. Seckl, J., Dymov, S., Szyf, M., & Meaney, M.J. (2004). Epigenetic Programming by Maternal Behavior. *Nature Neuroscience, 7,* 847-854.
112. Cao-Lei, L., Laplante, D., & King, S. (2016). Prenatal Maternal Stress and Epigenetics: Review of the Human Research. Current Molecular Biology Reports, 2, 16-25.
113. Leaf, Caroline. (2013). *Switch on Your Brain*. Grand Rapids, Michigan: Baker Books.
114. Blue Letter Bible. "Dictionary and Word Search for *tamiym (Strong's #H8549)."* (1996-2020).
115. Blue Letter Bible. "Dictionary and Word Search for *ra'ah (Strong's #H7200)."* (1996-2020).
116. Blue Letter Bible. "Dictionary and Word Search for *nagad (Strong's #H5046)."* (1996-2020).
117. Blue Letter Bible. "Dictionary and Word Search for *chuwts (Strong's #H2351)."* (1996-2020).
118. What are Dominant and Recessive? (n.d.). Retrieved from https://learn.genetics.utah.edu/content/basics/patterns/
119. Leaf, Caroline. (2013). *Switch on Your Brain*. Grand Rapids, Michigan: Baker Books.
120. Ibid.
121. Barron, J. (2012, June 4). Everything You Need to Know About Epigenetics. *Baseline of Health Foundation.* Retrieved from https://jonbarron.org/article/everything-you-need-know-about-epigenetics on February 13, 2019.
122. Strong, J. (1890). "Nimrod," *Strong's Exhaustive Concordance of the Bible.* Blue Letter Bible.
123. Blue Letter Bible. "Dictionary and Word Search for *chalal (Strong's #H2490)."* (1996-2020).
124. Blue Letter Bible. "Dictionary and Word Search for *gibbowr (Strong's #H1368)."* (1996-2020).
125. Blue Letter Bible. "Dictionary and Word Search for *gabar (Strong's #H1396)."* (1996-2020).
126. Dizdar, R. [Josh Tolley]. (2016, September, 29). *We are tracking Satanic super soldiers in ALL U.S. cities.* [Video File]. Retrieved from https://www.youtube.com/watch?v=zbeREVAxHuE
127. Blue Letter Bible. "Dictionary and Word Search for *nachash (Strong's #H5175)."* (1996-2020).
128. Blue Letter Bible. "Dictionary and Word Search for *nachash (Strong's #H5172)."* (1996-2020).
129. Blue Letter Bible. "Dictionary and Word Search for *nasha (Strong's #H5378)."* (1996-2020).

130. Nasha. (2018). *BibleHub.com.* Retrieved from https://www.biblehub.com/hebrew/5378.htm
131. Quayle, S. and Horn, T. R. (2017). *Unearthing the lost world of the cloudeaters.* Crane, MO: Defender Publishing.
132. Blue Letter Bible. "Dictionary and Word Search for *rĕkullah' (Strong's #H7404)."* (1996-2020).
133. Blue Letter Bible. "Dictionary and Word Search for *ra'ah (Strong's #H7200)."* (1996-2020).
134. Blue Letter Bible. "Dictionary and Word Search for *laqach (Strong's #H3947)."* (1996-2020).
135. Schultz, D. R. (1978). "The origin of sin in Irenaeus and Jewish Pseudepi- graphical literature." *Vigiliae Christianae 32*, 161-190.
136. Blue Letter Bible. "Dictionary and Word Search for *'akal (Strong's #H398)."* (1996-2020).
137. Quayle, S. and Horn, T. R. (2017). *Unearthing the lost world of the cloudeaters.* Crane, MO: Defender Publishing.
138. Blue Letter Bible. "Dictionary and Word Search for *owlam (Strong's #H5769)."* (1996-2020).
139. Blue Letter Bible. "Dictionary and Word Search for *alam (Strong's #H5956)."* (1996-2020).
140. Blue Letter Bible. "Dictionary and Word Search for *zaqen (Strong's #H2205)."* (1996-2020).
141. Blue Letter Bible. "Dictionary and Word Search for *shem (Strong's #H8034)."* (1996-2020).
142. Blue Letter Bible. "Dictionary and Word Search for *tsayid (Strong's #H6718)."* (1996-2020).
143. Blue Letter Bible. "Dictionary and Word Search for *pariym (Strong's #H6440)."* (1996-2020).
144. Blue Letter Bible. "Dictionary and Word Search for *enantion (Strong's #G1726)."* (1996-2020).
145. Genesis 10 (2019). *John Gill's Exposition of the Bible.* Retrieved from https://www.biblestudytools.com/commentaries/gills-exposition-of-the-bible/genesis-10-9.html
146. Commentary on Genesis 10 (2019). *Matthew Henry's Commentary.* Retrieved from http://www.blbclassic.org/commentaries/comm_view.cfm?AuthorID=4&contentID=13019&commInfo=5&topic=Genesis&ar=Gen_10_9 >
147. Genesis 10 (2019). *John Gill's Exposition of the Bible.* Retrieved from https://www.biblestudytools.com/commentaries/gills-exposition-of-the-bible/genesis-10-9.html
148. Josephus, Flavius (1773-1775). *The Works of Josephus. Complete and Unabridged. New Updated Edition.* Translated into English by William Whiston. *I. The Life of Joshephus. Written by himself. II. The antiquities of the Jews. In twenty books. III. The wars of the Jews or the history of the destruction of Jerusalem. IV. Flavius Josephus against Apion or antiquity of the Jews.*
149. Nimrod (n.d.). *Appendixes to the Companion Bible.* Retrieved from http://www.therain.org/appendixes/app28.html
150. Strong, J. (1890). *Strong's Exhaustive Concordance of the Bible.* Blue Letter Bible.
151. Armstrong, H. W. (1974). *The plain truth about Christmas.* Retrieved from https://www.bibletools.org/index.cfm/fuseaction/Library.sr/CT/HWA/k/464/Plain-Truth-About-Christmas.htm
152. Birthday. (2008). In *Encyclopedia Judaica.* Retrieved from https://www.jewishvirtuallibrary.org/birthday
153. Daniel-Rops, H. (1981). *Daily life in the time of Jesus.* Ann Arbor, MI: Servant Publications.
154. Clarke, A. (2015). *Adam Clarke's Bible Commentary in 8 Volumes: Volume 5, The Gospel According to St. Mark, Vol 5,* p. 370. CreateSpace Independent Publishing Platform.
155. Heiser, M. S. (2017). *Reversing Hermon: Enoch, The Watchers & The Forgotten Mission of Jesus Christ.* Crane, MO: Defender Publishing.
156. Ibid.
157. Blue Letter Bible. "Dictionary and Word Search for *shem (Strong's #H8034)."* (1996-2020).
158. Horn, T. and Putnam, C. (2015). *On the Path of the Immortals.* Crane, MO: Defender Publishing.
159. Heiser, M. S. (2015). *The Unseen Realm: Recovering the supernatural worldview of the Bible.* Bellingham, WA: Lexham Press.
160. Blue Letter Bible. "Dictionary and Word Search for *tartaroō' (Strong's #G5020)."* (1996-2020).
161. Horn, T. and Putnam, C. (2015). *On the Path of the Immortals.* Crane, MO: Defender Publishing.
162. Mark, J. J. (2014). The Queen of the Night. In *Ancient History Encyclopedia.* Retrieved from https://www.ancient.eu/article/658/the-queen-of-the-night/.
163. Blue Letter Bible. "Dictionary and Word Search for *liyliyth (Strong's #H3917)."* (1996-2020).

164. Harvey, J. C. (2015). *Red: A History of the Redhead.* New York NY: Black Dog & Leventhal Publishers.
165. Blue Letter Bible. "Dictionary and Word Search for `am (Strong's #H5791)." (1996-2020).
166. Blue Letter Bible. "Dictionary and Word Search for tow`ebah (Strong's #H8441)." (1996-2020).
167. Blue Letter Bible. "Dictionary and Word Search for heteros' (Strong's #G2087)." (1996-2020).
168. Blue Letter Bible. "Dictionary and Word Search for galah (Strong's #H1540)." (1996-2020).
169. Gigantism (2003). *Miller-Keane Encyclopedia and Dictionary of Medicine, Nursing, and Allied Health, 7th Edition.* Retrieved from https://medical-dictionary.thefreedictionary.com/gigantism.
170. Blue Letter Bible. "Dictionary and Word Search for acaph (Strong's H#622)." (1996-2020).
171. Blue Letter Bible. "Dictionary and Word Search for 'Agag (Strong's #H90)." (1996-2020).
172. Blue Letter Bible. "Dictionary and Word Search for ruwm (Strong's #H7311)." (1996-2020).
173. Hitchcock, R. D. (1869). *Hitchcock's Bible Names Dictionary.* Retrieved from https://www.blueletterbible.org/search/Dictionary/viewTopic.cfm?topic=HT0000175.
174. Josephus, Flavius (1773-1775). *The Works of Josephus. Complete and Unabridged. New Updated Edition.* Translated into English by William Whiston. *I. The Life of Joshephus. Written by himself. II. The antiquities of the Jews. In twenty books. III. The wars of the Jews or the history of the destruction of Jerusalem. IV. Flavius Josephus against Apion or antiquity of the Jews.*
175. Blue Letter Bible. "Dictionary and Word Search for rapha' (Strong's #H7495)." (1996-2020).
176. Josephus, Flavius (1773-1775). *The Works of Josephus. Complete and Unabridged. New Updated Edition.* Translated into English by William Whiston. *I. The Life of Joshephus. Written by himself. II. The antiquities of the Jews. In twenty books. III. The wars of the Jews or the history of the destruction of Jerusalem. IV. Flavius Josephus against Apion or antiquity of the Jews.*
177. Porter, J. L. (1877). *Giant cities of Bashan and Syria's holy places.* T. Nelson and Sons: London.
178. Billington, C. E. (2007). Goliath and the Exodus giants: How tall were they? *Journal of the Evangelical Theological Society, 50*(3), 489-508.
179. Quayle, S. (n.d.) *Sihon's and Og's Overthrow.* Retrieved from https://www.scribd.com/document/2579230/The-Giants-After-the-flood
180. Heiser, M. S. (2015). *The Unseen Realm: Recovering the supernatural worldview of the Bible.* Bellingham, WA: Lexham Press.
181. Gilbert, D. P. (2017). *The great inception: Satan's PSYOPS from Eden to Armageddon.* Crane, MO: Defender Publishing.
182. Heiser, M. S. (2017). *Reversing Hermon: Enoch, The Watchers & The Forgotten Mission of Jesus Christ.* Crane, MO: Defender Publishing.
183. Heiser, M. S. (2015). *The unseen realm: recovering the supernatural worldview of the Bible.* Bellingham, WA: Lexham Press.
184. Sheets, T. (2016). *Angel Armies.* Shippensburg, PA: Destiny Image Publishers.
185. Quayle, S. (2015). *Genesis 6 Giants.* Bozeman: MT, End Times Thunder Publishers.
186. Blue Letter Bible. "Dictionary and Word Search for gadowl (Strong's #H1419)." (1996-2020).
187. Blue Letter Bible. "Dictionary and Word Search for anaq (Strong's #H6060)." (1996-2020).
188. Heiser, M. S. (2015). *The Unseen Realm: Recovering the supernatural worldview of the Bible.* Bellingham, WA: Lexham Press.
189. Heiser, M. S. (2017). *Reversing Hermon: Enoch, The Watchers & The Forgotten Mission of Jesus Christ.* Crane, MO: Defender Publishing.
190. Gilbert, D. P. (2017). *The great inception: Satan's PSYOPS from Eden to Armageddon.* Crane, MO: Defender Publishing.
191. Livingston, D. (2003). *The fall of the moon city.* Retrieved from http://www.davelivingston.com/mooncity.htm
192. Levy, T. (2008). *Ethnic identity in Biblical Edom, Israel and Midian: some insights from mortuary contexts in the lowlands of Edom.* Retrieved from https://www.researchgate.net/publication/240638882
193. Levy, T., Adams, R. B., and Muniz, A. (2019). *Archaeology and the Shasu Nomads: Recent Excavations in the Jabal Hamrat Fidan, Jordan.* Retrieved from https://pdfs.semanticscholar.org/ea5d/ea1e690e522dbda8996e53cf77d61dc7d8d9.pdf.

431

194. Text: A. H. Gardiner, Late-Egyptian Miscellanies, Vol. 7 (Bibliotheca Aegyptiaca; Brussels: Édition de la Fondation égyptologique Reine Élisabeth, 1937). Translations: e.g., ANET, 259 with notes; R. A. Caminos, Late-Egyptian Miscellanies (London: Oxford University Press, 1954).

195. Billington, C. E. (2007). Goliath and the Exodus giants: How tall were they? *Journal of the Evangelical Theological Society, 50*(3), 489-508.

196. Josephus, Flavius (1773-1775). *The Works of Josephus. Complete and Unabridged. New Updated Edition.* Translated into English by William Whiston. *I. The Life of Josephus. Written by himself. II. The antiquities of the Jews. In twenty books. III. The wars of the Jews or the history of the destruction of Jerusalem. IV. Flavius Josephus against Apion or antiquity of the Jews.*

197. Weisman, C. A. (1996). *Who is Esau-Edom?* Apple Valley, MN: Weisman Publications.

198. Josephus, Flavius (1773-1775). *The Works of Josephus. Complete and Unabridged. New Updated Edition.* Translated into English by William Whiston. *I. The Life of Josephus. Written by himself. II. The antiquities of the Jews. In twenty books. III. The wars of the Jews or the history of the destruction of Jerusalem. IV. Flavius Josephus against Apion or antiquity of the Jews.*

199. Ibid.

200. Ibid.

201. Billington, C. E. (2007). Goliath and the Exodus giants: How tall were they? *Journal of the Evangelical Theological Society, 50*(3), 489-508.

202. Blue Letter Bible. "Dictionary and Word Search for *middah (Strong's H#4060)."* (1996-2020).

203. Weaving. (n.d.). In *International Standard Bible Encyclopedia* online. Retrieved from https://www.bible-history.com/isbe/W/WEAVING/.

204. Cedar. (n.d.). *In International Standard Bible Encyclopedia.* Retrieved from https://www.blueletterbible.org/search/Dictionary/viewTopic.cfm?topic=IT0001912.

205. Richter, C.K., Skulas-Ray, A.C., Champagne, C.M., & Kris-Etherton, P.M. (2015). Plant Proteins and Animal Proteins: Do They Differentially Affect Cardiovascular Disease Risk? *Advances in Nutrition, 6*(6), 712-728.

206. Gundry, Steven R. (2017). *The Plant Paradox: The Hidden Dangers in "Healthy" Foods That Cause Disease and Weight Gain.* New York, New York: Harper Wave.

207. McEvoy, B.P. and Visscher, P.M. (2009). Genetics of human height. *Economics and Human Biology, 7*(3), 294-306.

208. Olson, R. (2014). *Why the Dutch are so tall.* Retrieved from http://www.randalolson.com/2014/06/23/why-the-dutch-are-so-tall/.

209. Chopra, D. and Tanzi, R.E. (2015). *Super Genes.* New York, NY: Crown Publishing Group.

210. Ramos, J. (January 3, 2018). Redheads: They have genetic superpowers. *Science Trends.* Retrieved from https://sciencetrends.com/science-says-redheads-genetic-superpowers/.

211. 21 Great Polydactyly Statistics. (2019). HealthResearchFunding.org. Retrieved from https://healthresearchfunding.org/21-great-polydactyly-statistics/.

212. Kapoor, R. and Johnson, R. (December 1, 2011). Polydactyly. *New England Journal of Medicine, 365*, pg. 2122.

213. Wrobel, G. D., Helm, C., Nash, L., & Awe, J. J. (2012). *Ancient Mesoamerica, 23*, 131-142.

214. Sidder, A. (July 25, 2016). Extra fingers and toes were revered in ancient cultures. *National Geographic.* Retrieved from https://news.nationalgeographic.com/2016/07/chaco-canyon-pueblo-bonito-social-implications-polydactyly-extra-toes/.

215. Kolb, C.C. (1999). Man Corn: Cannibalism and Violence in the Prehistoric American Southwest. Christy G. Turner and Jacqueline A. Turner. University of Utah Press, Salt Lake City, 1999. *Bulletin of the History of Archaeology*, 9(2), pp.12–19.

216. Quayle, S. and Horn, T. R. (2017). *Unearthing the Lost World of the Cloudeaters.* Crane, MO: Defender Publishing.

217. Horn, T. and Putnam, C. (2015). *On the Path of the Immortals.* Crane, MO: Defender Publishing.

218. Willis, C. (December, 1998). The Story of the Strand. *The Strand Magazine.* Retrieved from https://strandmag.com/the-magazine/history/.

219. Fitzgerald, W. G. (December, 1895). The Property Office. *The Strand Magazine, 10,* 646-647. Retrieved from
https://archive.org/stream/TheStrandMagazineAnIllustratedMonthly/TheStrandMagazine1895bVol.XJul-dec#page/n657/mode/2up/search/giant.

220. Sasitorn, D. (personal communication, June 23, 2020).

221. Warren, A. (2002). *Waorani The Saga of Ecuador's Secret People: A Historical Perspecive.* Retrieved from
http://www.lastrefuge.co.uk/data/articles/waorani/waorani_page7.htm

222. Koestler, A. (1976). *The Thirteenth Tribe: the Khazar Empire and Its Heritage.* New York, NY: Random House.

223. Blue Letter Bible. "Dictionary and Word Search for *mĕcillah (Strong's #H4546)."* (1996-2020).

224. Blue Letter Bible. "Dictionary and Word Search for *shachah (Strong's #H7812)."* (1996-2020).

225. Wagner, C. P. (1996). *Confronting the Powers.* Ventura, CA: Regal Books.

226. Ibid.

227. Apocrypha: Acts of John (n.d.). Retrieved from https://www.interfaith.org/christianity/apocrypha-acts-of-john/.

228. Foerster, B. (2015). *Elongated Skulls of Peru and Bolivia.* Digital book published by Booknook.biz.

229. Ibid.

230. Foramina of the Skull (December 7, 2011). Anatomy Zone. Retrieved from
http://anatomyzone.com/tutorials/musculoskeletal/foramina-of-the-skull/

231. Yoshioka, N., Rhoton, A. L. Jr., Abe, H. (2006). Scalp to meningeal arterial anastomosis in the parietal foramen. *Neurosurgery, 58* (1 Suppl), 123-126.

232. Boyd, G. I. (1930). The Emissary Foramina of the Cranium in Man and the Anthropoids. *Journal of Anatomy, 65* (Pt 1), 108-121.

233. Holloway, A. (January 13, 2017). Mummified Head of Newborn Baby with Extremely Elongated Skull Found in Peru. Ancient Origins. Retrieved from https://www.ancient-origins.net/news-mysterious-phenomena/mummified-head-newborn-baby-extremely-elongated-skull-found-peru-007359

234. Bronfin, D. R. (2001). Misshapen Heads in Babies: Position or Pathology? *The Ocshner Journal, 3*(4), 191-199.

235. Holloway, A. (July 23, 2016). New DNA Testing on 2,000-Year-Old Elongated Paracas Skull Changes Known History. Ancient Origins. Retrieved from https://www.ancient-origins.net/news-history-archaeology/breaking-new-dna-testing-2000-year-old-elongated-paracas-skulls-changes-020914

236. Foerster, B. (2015). *Elongated Skulls of Peru and Bolivia.* Digital book published by Booknook.biz.

237. Pigafetta, A. (1534). *Magellan's Voyage* (R. A. Skelton, Trans., 1969). New Haven, Conn: Yale University Press.

238. Fletcher, F. (1652). *The World Encompassed by Sir Francis Drake.* London: Nicholas Bourne.

239. Kerr, R. (1824). *Voyages and Travels, Arranged in Systematic Order.* Edinburg, Scotland: William Blackwood and London, England: T. Cadell.

240. Winnemucca, S. H. (1883). *Life Among the Piutes.* Boston, MA: Cupples, Upham & Co.

241. Loud, L. L. and Harrington, M. R. (1929). *Lovelock Cave.* Berkeley, CA: University of California Press.

242. Ibid.

243. Dansie, P. D. (1975). John T. Reid's Case for the Redheaded Giants. *Nevada Historical Society Quarterly, Fall,* 153-167.

244. Ibid.

245. Georgia's Sand-Dunes Yield Startling Proof of a Prehistoric Race of Giants (August 2, 1936). *The Salt Lake Tribune.* Retrieved from https://www.newspapers.com/image/598594082

246. Kiernan, K. (November, 2011). Preston Holder on the Georgia Coast, 1936-1938. *The SAA Archeological Record, 11*(5), 30-33.

247. Powell, J.W. (1887). *Fifth Annual Report of the Bureau of Ethnology to the Secretary of the Smithsonian Institute, 1883-1884.* Washington, D.C.: Government Printing Office, Smithsonian Institute, p. 98.

248. Monster Skulls and Bones (April 5,1886). *The New York Times.*

249. Gunther, J. (1955). *Inside Africa.* London: Hamish Hamilton Ltd.

250. Xu, D., Pavlidis, P., Taskent, R. O., Alachiotis, N., Flanagan, C., DeGiorgio, M., Blekhman, R., Ruhl, S., and Gokcumen, O. (2017). Archaic Hominin Introgression in Africa Contributes to Functional Salivary *MUC7* Genetic Variation. *Molecular Biology and Evolution, 34* (10), 2704-2715.
251. University at Buffalo. (2017, July 21). In saliva, clues to a 'ghost' species of ancient human: The evolutionary history of a salivary protein may point to interbreeding between humans and an enigmatic ancient relative. *ScienceDaily*. Retrieved November 26, 2019 from www.sciencedaily.com/releases/2017/07/170721113415.htm
252. Lovari, L. P. (2018). *Manetho: History of Egypt*. Montevarchi, Italy: Harmakis Edizioni.
253. Knox, A. (January 11, 2015). After Flub, BYU Professor Restores Egyptian Ties. *The Salt Lake Tribune*. Retrieved from https://archive.sltrib.com/article.php?id=2035510&itype=CMSID
254. Petrie, W. H. F. and Quibell, J. E. (1897). *Naqada and Ballas*. London, England: Bernard Quaritch.
255. Ibid.
256. Ibid.
257. Diodorus, S. (1814). *The Historical Library of Diodorus the Sicilian in Fifteen Books* (G. Booth Esq., Trans). London, England: W. M'Dowall.
258. Ibid.
259. Quayle, S. (2015). *Genesis 6 Giants*. Bozeman, MT: End Times Thunder Publishers.
260. Herodotus (440 B.C.). *The History of Herodotus, Book V*. (G. Rawlinson, Trans.) Retrieved from http://classics.mit.edu/Herodotus/history.5.v.html
261. Clement, T. F. (n.d.). *Stromata, Book VII, 4*. Retrieved from http://www.earlychristianwritings.com/text/clement-stromata-book7.html
262. Webber, C. (2001). *The Thracians 700 BC to AD 46*. Oxford, England: Osprey Publishing Ltd.
263. The Two Maximini. *Historia Augusta*. Retrieved from http://penelope.uchicago.edu/Thayer/E/Roman/Texts/Historia_Augusta/Maximini_duo*.html
264. Stannard, J. (November 1, 2019). Pliny the Elder. *Encyclopaedia Britannica*. Retrieved from https://www.britannica.com/biography/Pliny-the-Elder
265. Pliny (77 A.D.) *Pliny's Natural History* (P. Holland, Trans., 1601). London, England: Printed for the Club by G. Barclay. Retrieved from https://archive.org/details/plinysnaturalhis00plinrich/page/n7
266. Ibid.
267. Mair, V. H. (2016). Ancient Mummies of the Tarim Basin. *University of Pennsylvania Museum of Archaeology and Anthropology, 58*(2), 25-29.
268. Haze, X. (2018). *Ancient Giants*. Rochester, VT: Bear & Company.
269. Boirayon, M. (2015). *Solomon Islands Mysteries*. Kempton, Ill: Adventures Unlimited Press.
270. Ibid.
271. Who were the Nabataeans? (2002). Nabataean History. Retrieved from http://nabataea.net/who.html
272. Freedman, B. H. (October 10, 1954). *The Truth About Khazars*, a letter written to Dr. David Goldstein, 960 Park Avenue, New Yok City.
273. Parker, C.F. (1949). *A Short Study of Esau Edom in Jewry*. London, England: The Covenant Publishing Co.
274. Elhaik, E. (2012). The missing link of Jewish European ancestry: Contrasting the Rhineland and Khazarian hypotheses. *Genome Biology and Evolution, 5*(1), 61-74.
275. Sand, S. (2009). *The Invention of the Jewish People*. Brooklyn NY: Verso Books.
276. Spingola, D. (2012). *The Ruling Elite*. Trafford Publishing. www.trafford.com.
277. Rosenthal, Herman (1906). *Chazars*. Jewish Encyclopedia. Retrieved from http://jewishencyclopedia.com/articles/4279-chazars.
278. Sand, S. (2009). *The Invention of the Jewish People*. Brooklyn NY: Verso Books.
279. Strom, K.A. (October 18, 2010). *A Jewish Defector Warns America*. Retrieved from https://nationalvanguard.org/2010/10/a-jewish-defector-warns-america/
280. Freedman, B. (1954). *The Truth About the Khazars*. Letter written to Dr. David Goldstein. Retrieved from http://www.hugequestions.com/Eric/TFC/FreedmanFactsAreFacts.html
281. Eisen, Y. (n.d.). *The Babylonian Talmud*. Retrieved from https://www.chabad.org/library/article_cdo/aid/2652565/jewish/The-Babylonian-Talmud.htm

282. Schiffman, L. H. and Pattengale, J. (2017). *The World's Greatest Book.* Franklin, TN: Worthy Publishing

283. Mann, D. (2017). The Jewish Talmud and its use for Christian apologetics. *Christian Research Journal (40)*, 4.

284. Johnson, M. R. (n.d.) *Defending the Khazar Thesis of the Origin of Modern Jewry.* https://www.rusjournal.org/wp-content/uploads/2019/03/Khazaria.pdf

285. Finklestein, L. (1938). *The Pharisees.* Philadelphia, PA: The Jewish Publication Society of America.

286. Johnson, M. R. (n.d.) *Defending the Khazar Thesis of the Origin of Modern Jewry.* https://www.rusjournal.org/wp-content/uploads/2019/03/Khazaria.pdf

287. Johnson, M. R. (n.d.). *The Regime: Usury, Khazaria and the American Mass.* Retrieved from https://www.rusjournal.org/wp-content/uploads/2016/08/Usury-2.pdf

288. Blue Letter Bible. "Dictionary and Word Search for *nasha (Strong's #H5378)."* (1996-2020).

289. Johnson, M. R. (n.d.). *The Regime: Usury, Khazaria and the American Mass.* Retrieved from https://www.rusjournal.org/wp-content/uploads/2016/08/Usury-2.pdf

290. Weisman, C. A. (1996). *Who is Esau-Edom?* Apple Valley, MN: Weisman Publications.

291. Sand, S. (2009). *The Invention of the Jewish People.* Brooklyn NY: Verso Books.

292. Cox, W. (2007). *Sons of Japheth: Part I.* Christian Churches of God retrieved from http://ccg.org/english/s/p046a.html

293. Parker, C.F. (1949). *A Short Study of Esau Edom in Jewry.* London, England: The Covenant Publishing Co.

294. Johnson, M. R. (n.d.) *Defending the Khazar Thesis of the Origin of Modern Jewry.* https://www.rusjournal.org/wp-content/uploads/2019/03/Khazaria.pdf

295. Ibid.

296. Josephus, Flavius (1773-1775). *The Works of Josephus. Complete and Unabridged. New Updated Edition.* Translated into English by William Whiston. *I. The Life of Joshephus. Written by himself. II. The antiquities of the Jews. In twenty books. III. The wars of the Jews or the history of the destruction of Jerusalem. IV. Flavius Josephus against Apion or antiquity of the Jews.*

297. Sand, S. (2009). *The Invention of the Jewish People.* Brooklyn NY: Verso Books.

298. Elhaik, E. (2012). The missing link of Jewish European ancestry: Contrasting the Rhineland and Khazarian hypotheses. *Genome Biology and Evolution, 5*(1), 61-74.

299. Belief Systems Along the Silk Road. (2019). Asia Society. Retrieved from https://asiasociety.org/education/belief-systems-along-silk-road

300. Das, R., Wexler, P., Pirooznia, M., and Elhaik, E. (2013). Localizing Ashkenazic Jews to primeval villages in the ancient Iranian lands of Ashkenaz. *Genome Biology and Evolution, 8*(4), 1132-1149.

301. Sand, S. (2009). *The Invention of the Jewish People.* Brooklyn NY: Verso Books.

302. Ibid.

303. Parker, C.F. (1949). *A Short Study of Esau Edom in Jewry.* London, England: The Covenant Publishing Co.

304. Blue Letter Bible. "Dictionary and Word Search for *'admoniy (#Strong's H132)."* (1996-2020).

305. Blue Letter Bible. "Dictionary and Word Search for *adam (Strong's #H119)."* (1996-2020).

306. Candle Color Meanings. (n.d.) *Spiritual Magickal.* Retrieved from https://www.spiritualmagickal.com/candle-colors-meanings.htm

307. Blue Letter Bible. "Dictionary and Word Search for *yada` (Strong's #H3045)."* (1996-2020).

308. Blue Letter Bible. "Dictionary and Word Search for *tsayid (Strong's #H6718)."* (1996-2020).

309. Blue Letter Bible. "Dictionary and Word Search for *tsuwd (Strong's #H6679)."* (1996-2020).

310. Rogers, K. (n.d.) *The Esau Effect.* Retrieved from http://themessianicmessage.com/esau_effect.htm

311. Sand, S. (2009). *The Invention of the Jewish People.* Brooklyn NY: Verso Books.

312. Ibid.

313. Johnson, M. R. (n.d.) *Defending the Khazar Thesis of the Origin of Modern Jewry.* https://www.rusjournal.org/wp-content/uploads/2019/03/Khazaria.pdf

314. Elhaik, E. (2012). The missing link of Jewish European ancestry: Contrasting the Rhineland and Khazarian hypotheses. *Genome Biology and Evolution, 5*(1), 61-74.

315. Blue Letter Bible. "Dictionary and Word Search for *Skythēs (Strong's G#4658)."* (1996-2020).

316. Harvey, J. C. (2015). *Red: A History of the Redhead.* New York NY: Black Dog & Leventhal Publishers.

317. Brook, K. A. (2006). *The Jews of Khazaria.* Lanham, MD: Rowman & Littlefield Publishers.
318. Harvey, J. C. (2015). *Red: A History of the Redhead.* New York NY: Black Dog & Leventhal Publishers.
319. Clark, A. (1831). Isaiah 34. In *Commentary on the Bible.* Retrieved from https://biblehub.com/commentaries/clarke/isaiah/34.htm
320. Orwell, G. (1949). *1984.* New York, New York: New American Library.
321. Beeston, W. (1858). *The Roman Empire the Empire of the Edomite.* London: George Cox.
322. Bacher, W. (1906). Targum. *Jewish Encyclopedia.* Retrieved from http://jewishencyclopedia.com/articles/14248-targum
323. Beeston, W. (1858). *The Roman Empire the Empire of the Edomite.* London: George Cox.
324. Brady, C.M.M. (n.d.) *Targum Lamentations.* Retrieved from http://targum.info/meg/tglam.htm
325. Rogers, K. (n.d.) *The Esau Effect.* Retrieved from http://themessianicmessage.com/esau_effect.htm
326. Mulligan, G. (January 27, 2013). Genocide in the Ancient World. *Ancient History Encyclopedia.* Retrieved from https://www.ancient.eu/article/485/genocide-in-the-ancient-world/
327. Dmitry, B. (August 30, 2016). Complete List of Rothschild Owned and Controlled Banks. *News Punch.* Retrieved from https://newspunch.com/complete-list-of-rothschild-owned-and-controlled-banks/
328. Graham. O. J. (1984). *The Six-Pointed Star.* Fletcher, North Carolina: New Puritan Library.
329. Red Shield and Green Shield (n.d.). The Rothschild Archive. Retrieved from https://www.rothschildarchive.org/family/the_rothschild_name_and_arms/any_questions
330. Morton, F. (1961). *The Rothschilds.* New York, NY: Diversion Books.
331. Saussy, F. T. (1999). *Rulers of Evil.* Reno, NV: Ospray Bookmakers.
332. Weishaupt, A. (2011). *The Illuminati.* Hyperreality Books at Smashwords. (Original publication in 1776).
333. Morton, F. (1961). *The Rothschilds.* New York, NY: Diversion Books.
334. Jacobs, J., Singer, I., Haneman F. T., Kahn, J., Lipkind, G., de Haas, J., and Bril, I. L. (1906). Rothschild. *Jewish Encyclopedia.* Retrieved from http://jewishencyclopedia.com/articles/12909-rothschild
335. Niles Register (1835, September 19). Interesting Articles. *Weekly Register,* 49, p. 41 (N.Y. Herald reprint).
336. Howard-Browne, R. and Williams, P. L. (2018). *The Killing of Uncle Sam.* Tampa, FL: River Publishing.
337. Hitchcock, A. (2010). The History of the House of Rothschild. Retrieved from https://rense.com/general88/hist.htm
338. Ibid.
339. Chernow, R. (1993). *The Warburgs.* New York, NY: Vintage Books.
340. Hitchcock, A. (2010). The History of the House of Rothschild. Retrieved from https://rense.com/general88/hist.htm
341. Chernow, R. (1993). *The Warburgs.* New York, NY: Vintage Books.
342. Yuz, T. (November 8, 2018). Jacob Schiff: The Right Hand of American Expansionism. *Sigma Iota Rho (SIR) Journal of International Relations.* Retrieved from https://www.sirjournal.org/research/2018/11/8/jacob-schiff-the-right-hand-of-american-expansionism
343. Griffin, Edward G. (2010). *The Creature from Jekyll Island.* 5th edition. Westlake Village: American Media.
344. Liao, J. (January 25, 2017). *Communism: The Leading Ideological Cause of Death in the 20th Century.* The Epoch Times. Retrieved from https://www.theepochtimes.com/communism-the-leading-ideological-cause-of-death-in-the-20th-century_2212529.html
345. Chernow, R. (1993). *The Warburgs.* New York, NY: Vintage Books.
346. Ibid.
347. Griffin, Edward G. (2010). *The Creature from Jekyll Island.* 5th edition. Westlake Village: American Media.
348. Ibid.
349. Chernow, R. (2004). *Alexander Hamilton.* New York, NY: Penguin Press.
350. U.S. Constitution Signed (September 17, 2019). History. Retrieved from https://www.history.com/this-day-in-history/u-s-constitution-signed
351. Chernow, R. (2004). *Alexander Hamilton.* New York, NY: Penguin Press.
352. Griffin, G. E. (2010). *The Creature from Jekyll Island.* 5th edition. Westlake Village: American Media.
353. Ibid.
354. Chernow, R. (2004). *Alexander Hamilton.* New York, NY: Penguin Press.

355. Myers. G. (1910). *History of the Great American Fortunes, Vol III*. Retrieved from https://archive.org/details/historygreatame01myergoog/page/n202

356. Goodson, S. M. (2017). *A History of the Central Banking and the Enslavement of Mankind*. London, England: Black House Publishing, Ltd.

357. Ibid.

358. Griffin, G. E. (2010). *The Creature from Jekyll Island*. 5th edition. Westlake Village: American Media.

359. Howard-Browne, R. and Williams, P. L. (2018). *The Killing of Uncle Sam*. Tampa, FL: River Publishing.

360. Henderson, D. (June 8, 2011). Federal Reserve Cartel: Freemasons and the House of Rothschild. *Global Research*. Retrieved from https://www.globalresearch.ca/the-federal-reserve-cartel-freemasons-and-the-house-of-rothschild/25179

361. Ibid.

362. Remini, R. V. (1988). *The Life of Andrew Jackson*. New York, NY: Harper & Row.

363. Howard-Browne, R. and Williams, P. L. (2018). *The Killing of Uncle Sam*. Tampa, FL: River Publishing.

364. Sand, S. (2009). *The Invention of the Jewish People*. Brooklyn NY: Verso Books.

365. Singer, S. J. (June 13, 2018). *Nathan Birnhaum, Founder of 'Zionism.'* Retrieved from https://www.jewishpress.com/sections/features/features-on-jewish-world/nathan-birnbaum-founder-of-zionism/2018/06/13/

366. Herzl, T. (1946). *The Jewish State*. New York: American Zionist Emergency Council. (Original work published 1896)

367. Sand, S. (2009). *The Invention of the Jewish People*. Brooklyn NY: Verso Books.

368. Katibah, H. I. (1920). *The Case Against Zionism*. New York, New York: Palestine National League.

369. What is Christian Zionism? (n.d.). Retrieved from https://www.christianzionism.org/

370. Hedding, M. (n.d.). *Christian Zionism 101*. Retrieved from https://int.icej.org/media/christian-zionism-101

371. Hex. (2020). *Merriam-Webster*. Retrieved from https://www.merriam-webster.com/dictionary/hex

372. Kiel, Y. (2019). The Usurpation of Solomon's Throne by Ashmedai (b.Giṭ. 68a-b). In Rubanovich, J. and Herman, G. (Ed), *Irano-Judaica VII: Studies Relating to Jewish Contacts with Persian Culture Throughout the Ages.* (pp. 439-472). USA: The Amnon Netzer Center for Iranian Jewish History and Heritage.

373. Scholem, G. (September, 1949). *The Curious History of the Six-Pointed Star*. Commentary Magazine. Retrieved from https://www.commentarymagazine.com/articles/the-curious-history-of-the-six-pointed-starhow-the-magen-david-became-the-jewish-symbol/

374. Henry, M. (1960). *Commentary on the Whole Bible: New One Volume Edition*. Grand Rapids, MI: Zondervan Publishing House.

375. Hislop, A. (1857). *The Two Babylons*. London, England: Houlston and Wright.

376. Graham. O. J. (1984). *The Six-Pointed Star*. Fletcher, North Carolina: New Puritan Library.

377. Seal of Solomon (n.d.). Mackey's Encyclopedia of Freemasonry. Retrieved from http://masonicdictionary.com/sealsolomon.html

378. Edmond James de Rothschild (n.d.). *The Rothschild Archive*. Retrieved from https://family.rothschildarchive.org/people/50-edmond-james-de-rothschild-1845-1934

379. Ferguson, N. (1998). *The House of Rothschild: The World Bankers 1849-1999*. New York, NY: Penguin Books.

380. Syrmopoulos, J. (June 21, 2017). Lord Rothschild Explains How His Family Embraced Zionism, Created Israel. *Renegade Tribune* Retrieved from http://www.renegadetribune.com/lord-rothschild-explains-family-embraced-zionism-created-israel/

381. [GBPPR2]. (2011, April 16). *Benjamin Freedman's 1961 Speech at Willard Hotel (Complete)* [Video File]. Retrieved from https://www.youtube.com/watch?v=HhFRGDyX48c

382. Pre-State Israel: Zionist Organization Statement on Palestine at the Paris Peace Conference (n.d.). *Jewish Virtual Library*. Retrieved from https://www.jewishvirtuallibrary.org/zionist-organization-statement-on-palestine-at-the-paris-peace-conference

383. Rothschild Land Purchases and Early Israel (n.d.). *Sursock House*. https://sursockhouse.com/rothschild-land-purchases-and-early-israel/

384. Our Mission (n.d.). *Torah Jews*. Retrieved from https://www.truetorahjews.org/mission

385. Bacher, W. (1906). Talmud. *Jewish Encyclopedia.* Retrieved from http://www.jewishencyclopedia.com/articles/14213-talmud
386. Frankfurt's Judengasse (n.d.). Museum Judengasse. Retrieved from http://www.judengasse.de/ehtml/page812.htm
387. Baba Bathra 54b (n.d.). Babylonian Talmud: Tractate Baba Bathra. Retrieved from http://www.come-and-hear.com/bababathra/bababathra_54.html#T274
388. Baba Kamma 113b (n.d.). Babylonian Talmud: Tractate Baba Kamma. Retrieved from http://www.come-and-hear.com/babakamma/babakamma_113.html#E41
389. Pranaitis, I. B. (1892). *The Talmud Unmasked.* St. Petersburg, Russia: St. Petersburg Printing Office of the Imperial Academy of Sciences.
390. Freedman, B. (1954). *The Truth About the Khazars.* Letter written to Dr. David Goldstein. Retrieved from http://www.hugequestions.com/Eric/TFC/FreedmanFactsAreFacts.html
391. Pranaitis, I. B. (1892). *The Talmud Unmasked.* St. Petersburg, Russia: St. Petersburg Printing Office of the Imperial Academy of Sciences.
392. Ibid.
393. Our Approach to Zionism (n.d.). *Jewish Voice for Peace.* Retrieved from https://jewishvoiceforpeace.org/zionism/
394. Brown, M. L. (November 18, 2012). *Who is a Jew? Questions of ethnicity, religion and identity.* Retrieved from https://askdrbrown.org/library/who-jew
395. North, G. (2012). *Priorities and Dominion.* Dallas, GA: Point Five Press.
396. Daniel-Rops, H. (1961). *Daily Life in the Time of Jesus.* Ann Arbor, MI: Servant Books.
397. North, G. (2012). *Priorities and Dominion.* Dallas, GA: Point Five Press.
398. Pranaitis, I. B. (1892). *The Talmud Unmasked.* St. Petersburg, Russia: St. Petersburg Printing Office of the Imperial Academy of Sciences.
399. Ibid.
400. Ibid.
401. Ibid.
402. McCash, June H. (2014). *Jekyll Island's Early Years: From Prehistory Through Reconstruction.* University of Georgia Press.
403. Swanton, John R. (1922). *Early History of the Creek Indians and Their Neighbors.* Smithsonian Institution Bureau of American Ethnology, Bulletin 73. Government Printing Offices: Washington, D.C.
404. Florida History Blurred by Myth on State's 500 Anniversary. *Miami Huffington Post.* April, 6, 2013
405. Theodore de Bry Engravings of the Timucua (n.d.). *Florida Memory: State Archives and Library of Florida.* www.floridamemory.com/items/show/294774.
406. Onofrio, Jan (1995). *Dictionary of Indian Tribes of the Americas, Volume 1.* American Indian Publishers, Inc. pg. 433
407. McCash, June H. (2014). *Jekyll Island's Early Years: From Prehistory Through Reconstruction.* University of Georgia Press.
408. Melanich, Jerald T. (1996). *The Timucua.* Blackwell publishers: Cambridge, Massachusetts.
409. Ibid.
410. McCash, June H. (2014). *Jekyll Island's Early Years: From Prehistory Through Reconstruction.* University of Georgia Press.
411. Swanton, John R. (1922). *Early History of the Creek Indians and Their Neighbors.* Smithsonian Institution Bureau of American Ethnology, Bulletin 73. Government Printing Offices: Washington, D.C.
412. Alexander, Michael (Ed.) (1976). *Discovering the New World, Based on the Works of Theodore de Bry (1591).* Harper & Row: New York.
413. Swanton, John R. (1922). *Early History of the Creek Indians and Their Neighbors.* Smithsonian Institution Bureau of American Ethnology, Bulletin 73. Government Printing Offices: Washington, D.C.
414. Ibid.
415. Ibid.
416. Ibid.

417. Beckett, John (2017). *The Path of Paganism: An Experience Based Guide to Modern Pagan Practice.* Llewellyn Worldwide: Woodbury, MN.
418. Swanton, John R. (1922). *Early History of the Creek Indians and Their Neighbors.* Smithsonian Institution Bureau of American Ethnology, Bulletin 73. Government Printing Offices: Washington, D.C.
419. Mac Leod, William Christie (1931). "Child Sacrifice in North America, with a note on suttee." *Journal de la Societe des Americanistes.* Tome 23 n 1, pg 127-138.
420. Hastings, J., Selbie J. A., Gray, L. H. (Eds.) (1914). *Encyclopaedia of Religion and Ethics: Volume VI Fiction-Hyksos.* Charles Scribner's Sons: New York.
421. Blue Letter Bible. "Dictionary and Word Search for *taphaph (Strong's #H8612)."* (1996-2020).
422. Blue Letter Bible. "Dictionary and Word Search for *malak (Strong's #H4427)."* (1996-2020).
423. Alexander, Michael (Ed.) (1976). *Discovering the New World, Based on the Works of Theodore de Bry.* New York: Harper & Row.
424. Swanton, John R. (1922). *Early History of the Creek Indians and Their Neighbors.* Smithsonian Institution Bureau of American Ethnology, Bulletin 73. Government Printing Offices: Washington, D.C.
425. Mathisen, David W. (November 18, 2014). Chiasm and the Spirit World [Blog Post]. Retrieved from http://.mathisencorollary.blogspot.com.
426. Bence, Timothy. "Canaanite Altars and The Federal Reserve." Interview by Rob Skiba. June 9, 2014. Retrieved from http://smgolden.com/documents/gen6/Canaanite%20Altars%20and%20The%20Federal%20Reserve.pdf
427. Petrie, Alistair (2000). *Releasing Heaven on Earth.* Chosen: Grand Rapids, MI.
428. Mason, P. (2010). *Quantum Glory.* Maricopa, AZ: XP Publishing.
429. Emoto, M. (2005). *The Hidden Messages in Water.* (D. A. Thayne, Trans.). New York, NY: Atria Books.
430. Petrie, Alistair (2000). *Releasing Heaven on Earth.* Chosen: Grand Rapids, MI.
431. "Huguenot History." *The Huguenot Society of America,* www.huguenotsocietyofamerica.org.
432. McCash, June H. (2014). *Jekyll Island's Early Years: From Prehistory Through Reconstruction.* University of Georgia Press.
433. "Jekyll Island." *Wikipedia.* Wikimedia Foundation, 15 October 2014. Web. 23 October 2014.
434. Ibid.
435. Ibid.
436. Griffin, Edward G. (2010). *The Creature from Jekyll Island.* 5th edition. Westlake Village: American Media.
437. Nevins, A. (1940). *John D. Rockefeller: The Heroic Age of American Enterprise.* New York, NY: Charles Scribner's Sons.
438. Garten, J. E. (2016). *From Silk to Silicon.* New York, NY: Harper Collins.
439. Ibid.
440. Chernow, R. (1990). *The House of Morgan.* New York, NY: Grove Press.
441. Ibid.
442. Lowenstein, R. (2015). *America's Bank: The Epic Struggle to Create the Federal Reserve.* New York, NY: Penguin Press.
443. Ibid.
444. Chernow, R. (1993). *The Warburgs.* New York, NY: Vintage Books.
445. Wolraich, M. (2014). *Unreasonable Men: Theodore Roosevelt and the Republican Rebels Who Created Progressivism.* New York, NY: Palgrave MacMillan.
446. Lowenstein, R. (2015). *America's Bank: The Epic Struggle to Create the Federal Reserve.* New York, NY: Penguin Press.
447. Ibid.
448. Chernow, R. (1990). *The House of Morgan.* New York, NY: Grove Press.
449. Chernow, R. (1993). *The Warburgs.* New York, NY: Vintage Books.
450. Lowenstein, R. (2015). *America's Bank: The Epic Struggle to Create the Federal Reserve.* New York, NY: Penguin Press.
451. Naclerio, R. A. (2013). Paul M. Warburg: Founder of the United States Federal Reseve. *History Faculty Publications,* Paper 99. http://digitalcommons.sacredheart.edu/his_fac/99

452. Vanderlip, Frank A. (1935, February 9). "From Farm Boy to Financier," Saturday Evening Post Archives.
453. Forbes, B.C. (1916, October 9) "Men Who Are Making America," B. C. Forbes Publishing Company, pg. 398. Universal Digital Library Collections.
454. Kellock, H. (1915, May). Warburg, the Revolutionist. *The Century Magazine, 79-86.*
455. Naclerio, R. A. (2013). Paul M. Warburg: Founder of the United States Federal Reseve. *History Faculty Publications*, Paper 99.
456. Kellock, H. (1915, May). Warburg, the Revolutionist. *The Century Magazine, 79-86.*
457. "cartel." *Investopedia.com.* Investopedia, LLC. November 6, 2014. <Dictionary.com http://www.investopedia.com/terms/c/cartel.asp>.
458. Griffin, Edward G. (2010). *The Creature from Jekyll Island.* 5th edition. Westlake Village: American Media.
459. Mullins, E. (2014). *A Study of the Federal Reserve and Its Secrets.* Blacksburg, VA: Wilder Publications.
460. The week. (1914, January 1). *The Nation, 98* (2531). Retrieved from https://www.scribd.com/document/293816330/December-23-1913
461. The United States Constitution Article 1 Section 8 – Enumerated Powers (2013). Retrieved from http://www.americanusconstitution.com/article1section8.html
462. Maloney, Michael (2008). *Guide to Investing in Gold and Silver.* New York: Business Plus.
463. Owen, R. L. (1939). National Economy and the Banking System of the United States. *76th Congress, 1st Session, Document No.23.* Retrieved from https://ia800300.us.archive.org/27/items/NationalEconomyAndTheBankingSystemOfTheUnitedStates/NationalEconomyAndTheBankingSystem.pdf
464. Kershaw, A. P. (1997). *Economic Solutions.* Boulder, CO: Heal Our Land.
465. FAQs (March 1, 2017). Who Owns the Federal Reserve? Retrieved from https://www.federalreserve.gov/faqs/about_14986.htm
466. [The Corbet Report] (July 6, 2014). *Century of Enslavement: The History of the Federal Reserve* [Video File]. Retrieved from https://www.youtube.com/watch?v=5IJeemTQ7Vk&t=3509s
467. Ibid.
468. Lindbergh, C. A. (1923). *The Economic Pinch.* Costa Mesa, CA: The Noontide Press.
469. FAQs (December 11, 2019). What are the Federal Reserve's Objectives in Conducting Monetary Policy? Retrieved from https://www.federalreserve.gov/faqs/money_12848.htm
470. Maloney, Michael (2008). *Guide to Investing in Gold and Silver.* New York: Business Plus.
471. [The Corbet Report] (July 6, 2014). *Century of Enslavement: The History of the Federal Reserve* [Video File]. Retrieved from https://www.youtube.com/watch?v=5IJeemTQ7Vk&t=3509s
472. Kershaw, A. P. (1997). *Economic Solutions.* Bolder, CO: Heal Our Land.
473. [The Corbet Report] (July 6, 2014). *Century of Enslavement: The History of the Federal Reserve* [Video File]. Retrieved from https://www.youtube.com/watch?v=5IJeemTQ7Vk&t=3509s
474. Crozier, A. O. (1912). *U.S. Money vs Corporate Currency: "Aldrich Plan,"* Cincinnati, OH: The Magnate Company. Retrieved from https://archive.org/details/usmoneyvscorpor00crozgoog/page/n361/mode/2up/search/Octopus
475. The Great Depression (2013, November 22). *Federal Reserve History.* https://www.federalreservehistory.org/essays/great_depression
476. Ibid.
477. Romer, C.D. and Pellis, R.H. (1998) Great Depression. *Encyclopaedia Brittanica.* Retrieved from https://www.britannica.com/event/Great-Depression
478. 1932 Congressional Record 12595 (1932, June 10) (statement of Rep, Louis T. McFadden).
479. Ibid.
480. Crozier, A. O. (1912). *U.S. Money vs Corporate Currency: "Aldrich Plan,"* Cincinnati, OH: The Magnate Company. Retrieved from https://archive.org/details/usmoneyvscorpor00crozgoog/page/n361/mode/2up/search/Octopus
481. Blue Letter Bible. "Dictionary and Word Search for *nasha (Strong's #H5378)."* (1996-2020).
482. Nasha. (2018). *BibleHub.com.* Retrieved from https://www.biblehub.com/hebrew/5378.htm
483. Maloney, Michael (2008). *Guide to Investing in Gold and Silver.* New York: Business Plus.

484. Richardson, G., Komai, A. and Gou, M. (2013, November 22). Roosevelt's Gold Program. *Federal Reserve History*. Retrieved from https://www.federalreservehistory.org/essays/roosevelts_gold_program
485. Ghizoni, S. K. (2013, November 22). Nixon Ends Convertibility of US Dollars to Gold and Announces Wage/Price Controls. *Federal Reserve History*. Retrieved from https://www.federalreservehistory.org/essays/gold_convertibility_ends
486. Maloney, Michael (2008). *Guide to Investing in Gold and Silver*. New York: Business Plus.
487. Ibid.
488. Booth, D. D. (2017). *Fed Up: An Insider's Take on Why the Federal Reserve is Bad for America*. New York, NY: Portfolio Penguin.
489. Office of the Comptroller of the Currency (April 2008). *Quarterly Report on Bank Trading and Derivatives Activities* (Fourth Quarter 2007). Retrieved from https://www.occ.gov/publications-and-resources/publications/quarterly-report-on-bank-trading-and-derivatives-activities/files/q4-2007-derivatives-quarterly.html
490. Office of the Comptroller of the Currency (December 2019). *Quarterly Report on Bank Trading and Derivatives Activities* (Third Quarter 2019). Retrieved from https://www.occ.gov/publications-and-resources/publications/quarterly-report-on-bank-trading-and-derivatives-activities/files/q4-2007-derivatives-quarterly.html
491. Powell, J. H. (2015, February 9). *"Audit the Fed" and Other Proposals*. Remarks given at Catholic University of America, Columbus School of Law, Washington, D. C.
492. Amadeo, KI. (2020, February 7). *Who Really Owns the Federal Reserve?* Retrieved from https://www.thebalance.com/who-owns-the-federal-reserve-3305974
493. Subcommittee on Domestic Monetary Policy and Technology before the Committee on Financial Services, U.S. House of Representatives (2011, October 4) (Testimony of Robert D. Auerbach).
494. United States Government Accountability Office Report to Congressional Addresses (2011, July). The Federal Reserve System: Opportunities Exist to Strengthen Policies and Processes for Managing Emergency Assistance.
495. Ibid.
496. Ibid.
497. Jacobs, S. (2010, February 5). JPMorgan CEO Dimon Gets $16M Stock Bonus for 2009. *The Seattle Times*. Retrieved from https://www.seattletimes.com/business/jpmorgan-ceo-dimon-gets-16m-stock-bonus-for-2009/
498. The Fed Audit (2011, July 21). Bernie Sanders U.S. Senator for Vermont Press Release. Retrieved from https://www.sanders.senate.gov/newsroom/press-releases/the-fed-audit
499. Ibid.
500. Grim, R. (2009). Bernanke: 'I Don't Know' Which Foreign Banks Got Half Trillion U.S. Dollars. *HuffPost*. Retrieved from https://www.huffpost.com/entry/bernanke-i-dont-know-whic_n_244302
501. Eisenhower, D. D. (1961). *President Eisenhower's Farewell Address*. Retrieved from https://www.militaryindustrialcomplex.com/military-industrial-complex-speech.asp
502. Kennedy, J. F. (1961). *The President and the Press*. Address before the American Newspaper Publishers Association. Retrieved from https://www.jfklibrary.org/archives/other-resources/john-f-kennedy-speeches/american-newspaper-publishers-association-19610427
503. Reagan, R. (1964). *A Time for Choosing*. Retrieved from https://www.reaganlibrary.gov/timechoosing
504. Bush, G. H. W. (1991). *Address Before the Joint Session of the Congress on the State of the Union*. Retrieved from https://bush41library.tamu.edu/archives/public-papers/2656
505. Meged, M. (1960). Sabbatai Zevi by Gershom Scholem. *Commentary Magazine*. Retrieved from https://www.commentarymagazine.com/articles/mati-meged/sabbatai-zevi-by-gershom-scholem/
506. Plen, M. (n.d.). Who Was Shabbetai Zevi? *My Jewish Learning*. Retrieved from https://www.myjewishlearning.com/article/shabbetai-zevi/
507. Ibid.

508. Frank, Jacob, and the Frankists. (2020). *Encyclopedia.com.* Retrieved from https://www.encyclopedia.com/religion/encyclopedias-almanacs-transcripts-and-maps/frank-jacob-and-frankists
509. Ibid.
510. Gershom, S. (1965). *On the Kabbalah and Its Symbolism.* (R. Manheim, Trans). New York, NY: Schocken Books.
511. Chamish, B. (2012). *Deutsch Devils.* Rense.com. Retrieved from https://rense.com/general47/deut.htm
512. Chamish, B. (2005). *Shabtai Tzvi: Labor Zionism and the Holocaust.* Tel Aviv, Israel: Modi'in House.
513. Barruel, A. A. (1995). *Memoirs Illustrating the History of Jacobinism.* Fraser, MI: American Council on Economics and Society (Original work published 1799).
514. Ibid.
515. Ibid.
516. Ibid.
517. Kershaw, A. P. (1997). *Economic Solutions.* Bolder, CO: Heal Our Land.
518. Payson, S. (1802). *Proofs of the Real Existence, and Dangerous Tendency of Illuminism.* Charleston, SC: Samuel Etheridge.
519. Hitchcock, A. (2010). *The History of the House of Rothschild.* Retrieved from https://rense.com/general88/hist.htm
520. Ibid.
521. History: The Origins of Freemasonry (n.d.). *Masons of California.* Retrieved from https://www.freemason.org/discoverMasonry/history.htm
522. Robison, J. (1798). *Proofs of a Conspiracy Against All Religions and Governments of Europe, Carried on in the Secret Meetings of Free Masons, Illuminati, and Reading Societies.* Philadelphia, PA: T. Dobson.
523. Hall, M. P. (1929). *Lectures on Ancient Philosophies.* New York, NY: Jeremy P. Tarcher/Penguin.
524. Fagan, M. (1967). *Illuminati: Book 1.* Compiled and Edited by David Major. Bendigo, Australia: A Distant Mirror Publisher
525. Ben-Gurion, David (January 16, 1962). Next 25 Years. *Look Magazine.* Retrieved from http://christianobserver.net/jerusalem-will-be-the-seat-of-the-supreme-court-of-mankind-david-ben-gurion/
526. McCabe, J. (1913). *A Candid History of the Jesuits.* London, England: Eveleigh Nash.
527. Saussy, F. T. (1999). *Rulers of Evil.* Reno, NV: Ospray Bookmakers
528. Ibid.
529. Ibid.
530. Marsden, V. E. (1934). *The Protocols of the Meetings of the Learned Elders of Zion.* London, England: Britons Publishing Society.
531. Ibid.
532. Ibid.
533. Ibid.
534. Ibid.
535. Ibid.
536. Spencer, L. and Krauze, A. (2012). *Introducing Hegel: A Graphic Guide.* London, England: Icon Books, Ltd.
537. Ibid.
538. Bollinger, T. and Bollinger, C. (March 9, 2020). Coronavirus: Detention, the Demise of Freedom, the Perils of 5G & Personal Protection. *The Truth About Cancer.* Retrieved from https://thetruthaboutcancer.com/coronavirus-detention-freedom-5g/
539. Kissinger's Infamous 1992 Bilderberg Quote in Evian, France. (2006, January 23). Retrieved from https://rense.com/general11/ksss.htm
540. Hieronimus, R. (2006). *Founding Father, Secret Societies.* Rochestor, VT: Destiny Books.
541. Heiser, M. S. (2015). *The Unseen Realm.* Bellingham, WA: Lexham Press.
542. Benefiel, J. (2012). *Binding the Strongman over America.* Oklahoma City, OK: Benefiel Ministries, Inc.

543.   Blue Letter Bible. "Dictionary and Word Search for *Ba`al Hamown' (Strong's H#1174)."* (1996-2020).

544.   Shrestha, S. S. et al. (2011). Estimating the Burden of 2009 Pandemic Influenza A (H1N1) in the United States, April 2009 – April 2010. *Clinical Infectious Disease, 52,* Suppl 1, 75-82.

545.   Robb, G. (April 6, 2020). St. Louis Fed's Bullard pitches universal daily COVID-19 testing to help restore economy's health. *Market Watch.* Retrieved from https://www.marketwatch.com/story/feds-bullard-says-there-is-good-news-for-those-worried-about-the-economys-future-that-universal-covid-19-testing-will-help-restore-economic-health-2020-04-05

546.   Gates, B. [u/thisisbillgates] (2020, March 18). I'm Bill Gates, co-chair of the Bill & Melinda Gates Foundation. AMA about COVID-19. [Online forum post]. Retrieved from https://www.reddit.com/r/Coronavirus/comments/fksnbf/im_bill_gates_cochair_of_the_bill_melinda_gates/f kupg49/

547.   Reagan, T., Cort, G. (October 23, 2009). Sealed Cases in Federal Courts. *Federal Judicial Center.* Retrieved from https://www.uscourts.gov/sites/default/files/sealed-cases.pdf

548.   Johnson, K. (March 11, 2020). DOJ Takes New Aim at Violent Aim at Mexican Drug Cartel CJNG; 250 Arrests in the U.S. *USA Today, Politics.* Retrieved from https://www.usatoday.com/story/news/politics/2020/03/11/doj-takes-aim-violent-mexican-drug-cartel-announces-250-arrests/5023376002/

549.   Exec. Order No 13818, 3 C. F. R. 60839-60843 (2017).

550.   Strum, B. (February 2, 2018). *Rothschild Family Sells Large Austrian Hunting Estate.* Retrieved from https://www.mansionglobal.com/articles/rothschild-family-sells-large-austrian-hunting-estate-87753

551.   Kennedy, J. F. (1961). *Inaugural Address, January 20, 1961.* Retrieved from https://www.jfklibrary.org/archives/other-resources/john-f-kennedy-speeches/inaugural-address-19610120

552.   Sheets, D. (September 26, 2019). Head of the Year 5780. *Glory of Zion International TV.* Retrieved from https://tv.gloryofzion.org/head-of-the-year-5780

553.   Otis, G. (1997). *The Twilight Labryinth.* Grand Rapids, MI: Chosen Books.

Index

Made in the USA
Columbia, SC
06 June 2022

61415203R00248